When Beckham Went to Spain

Praise for Jimmy Burns's *Hand of God: The Life of Diego Maradona*

'It's a corker. The roller-coaster of Maradona's extraordinary life is here in all its painful glory. Burns has written a compassionate, informative and, in these days of spiralling wages and fallen idols, instructive biography, aided by a magnificent lead character. Stunning' *Total Sport*

'Like the Gallagher brothers, Maradona's life has had its fair share of sex, drugs, and rock 'n' roll. Only more so. For with Diego you can add poverty, corruption, conspiracy, adultery and sainthood . . . What Burns does so superbly is explain why Maradona is like he is and why he is loved, without being an apology for him . . . Love or hate the man, his is one of football's greatest stories and so this is the best football book in ages' *Goal*

'Jimmy Burns's elegantly written and painstakingly researched account of one of the all-time great players steers the reader through all the twists and turns of Maradona's career' *When Saturday Comes*

'Diego Maradona stopped being the world's finest soccer player and started being a tragic, tormented figure because he was deluded, manipulated and exploited' *Inside Sport*, Australia

'More than just a biography, Burns has managed to write a portrait and to embed it into a comprehensive description of sports and society over the last three decades. Simply good stuff and interesting reading' Andrea Herren, FIFA

'The life and crimes of Diego Maradona are chronicled in a revealing biography. This well-researched book shows his life has been a violent mix of sporting brilliance and personal disgrace. The hand of God weighed down by feet of clay' Mike Walters, *Daily Mirror*

'This is a praiseworthy attempt to unravel this brilliantly talented but weak-willed man, who lived to fulfil his football dream but could not resist the temptation to abuse his body with drugs. A compelling cocktail of celebration and cheating' *Daily Mail*

'This is an absorbing account of an often unappealing subject' *Observer*

'A drug-taking prima donna is the subject of this excellent and well-researched book. Shame about the subject. *Hand of God* would have been more accurately titled "Hand of the Devil" or "Hand of the Cheat" . . . This first biography of a sporting idol who turned out to have feet of clay will be difficult to surpass' Greg Struthers, *Sunday Times*

'Burns tells the story of Maradona with much skill and verve. He expertly untangles the various networks of manipulation . . . Our memories of the book will be less to do with Maradona's personality than with those who have so brutally exploited its clear weaknesses. The seamy backstairs politics of international soccer have never been more tellingly exposed. One day, perhaps, Maradona will read this incisive study and learn what happened to his "magical" career' Ian Hamilton, *Financial Times*

'Burns is the perfect man to put the Maradona saga into context. He is not just a knowledgeable football fan. He is also an expert on Argentina and a skilled investigative journalist. As a result his book combines a compelling personal story with intelligent analysis of the role played by football in general – and Mr Maradona in particular – in Argentinian politics and society . . . Those who have an interest in the sociology of football, in modern Argentina and in the "story behind the headlines" will admire Burns's disturbing book, which easily transcends the normal confines of sports journalism' *Economist*

'Jimmy Burns is incapable of writing boringly. He has done as good and as honest a book as could be written about the poor boy from the wrong end of Buenos Aires, who went high and has fallen far . . . *Hand of God* is illuminating and atmospheric as it cuts through the web of myth, mystery and full-blooded hypocrisy that surrounds one of the world's most adored and detested sportsmen' Hugh O'Shaughnessy, *Irish Times*

'This book is exhaustively researched and splendidly written. It includes a fascinating chapter "Harry goes to Buenos Aires" which tells of the events surrounding the amazing attempts of Sheffield United manager Harry Haslam to bring Maradona, then virtually unknown, to England in 1978. I can vouch for the accuracy of this particular chapter' Tony Pritchett, *Sheffield Star*

'Jimmy Burns has written a jaw-on-the-floor fascinating book. Informed by a deep understanding of Argentine and English and a love of football, Burns is ideally placed to tackle the complex development of Maradona from shanty-town prodigy to five-drug-cocktailed footballer of USA

'94. Burns exposes the sycophants around Maradona and is not shy to point out his pomposity . . . His style is straightforward storytelling; the result could prove to be a modern footballing classic' John Naughton, *FHM*

'Burns's forensic skills are to the fore in this deft, perceptive study of politics, corruption, exploitation and the occasional dash of genuine sporting genius' *Time Out*

'Jimmy Burns casts a cold eye on the rearing of a money-making machine . . . This is a solid and penetrative piece of reporting on the resurrection of a footballing God who simply will not die . . . Burns's style is unemotive but *Hand of God* is an affecting tale' Hugh MacDonald, *Glasgow Herald*

'Maradona's life, diligently chronicled in this perceptive and fair-minded book, is one of grotesque farce, a bilious sequence of operative catastrophes. Gazza's career compared with this looks like *Emmerdale* sat next to the Borgias . . . this is not, however, mere sensationalist sleaze. Burns knows Argentina well and his charting of the shanty boy's trajectory towards moral and pharmaceutical meltdown is detailed in this scrupulously perceptive and fair-minded book' Pete Davies, *Independent*

'An excellent biography. In the detail you would expect from an award-winning investigative financial writer, Burns traces the tendrils of ownership which controlled Maradona's career from the start' James Lawton, *Daily Express*

'A piece of master craftsmanship' Hen Span, *Het Parool*, Holland

'Reads like a passionate novel of investigation . . . much more than just a biography, it's about a world of corruption, intrigue and exploitation' *As*, Spain

'A great achievement by one of Europe's most daring journalists' *El País*, Spain

'Few people emerge innocent in this book' *La Nación*, Buenos Aires

'The story of a poor kid whose dreams become true and then turn into his worst nightmare' *Regina 12*, Buenos Aires

By the Same Author

Beyond the Silver River
Spain: A Literary Companion
Hand of God: The Life of Diego Maradona
Barça: A People's Passion

When Beckham Went to Spain

Power, Stardom and Real Madrid

JIMMY BURNS

MICHAEL JOSEPH
an imprint of
PENGUIN BOOKS

MICHAEL JOSEPH

Published by the Penguin Group

Penguin Books Ltd, 80 Strand, London WC2R 0RL, England

Penguin Group (USA) Inc., 375 Hudson Street, New York, New York 10014, USA

Penguin Books Australia Ltd, 250 Camberwell Road, Camberwell, Victoria 3124, Australia

Penguin Books Canada Ltd, 10 Alcorn Avenue, Toronto, Ontario, Canada M4V 3B2

Penguin Books India (P) Ltd, 11 Community Centre, Panchsheel Park, New Delhi – 110 017, India

Penguin Group (NZ), cnr Airborne and Rosedale Roads, Albany, Auckland 1310, New Zealand

Penguin Books (South Africa) (Pty) Ltd, 24 Sturdee Avenue, Rosebank 2196, South Africa

Penguin Books Ltd, Registered Offices: 80 Strand, London WC2R 0RL, England

www.penguin.com

First published 2004

1

Set in 13.5/16 pt PostScript Monotype Garamond
Typeset by Rowland Phototypesetting Ltd, Bury St Edmunds, Suffolk
Printed in Great Britain by Clays Ltd, St Ives plc

A CIP catalogue record for this book is available from the British Library

ISBN 0-718-14747-2

To Tom, David, and Maria-Belen

For Hugh who taught
me much
On his 70's
Birthday
Many happy
memories
Vincenzo Jenny

Love — Rod
January 2005

'Trophies tell the whole story. The result of wise presidential administrations, the talent of great players, the fascinating power of an impressive stadium and the unswerving support of Spain's most loyal and numerous fans. Trophies are equivalents of victories, triumph won through the ages, on a variety of pitches and competitions. Trophies are tangible details, concrete facts that define the holder without need for clichés. Each trophy won closes a period of time in which Real Madrid was better than its rivals. The end result is the sum of these trophies, and the well deserved title of the Best Club of All Time – the Best Club in History.'

Posted at the entrance to the Real Madrid museum

Contents

List of Illustrations		xi
Acknowledgements		xiii
Foreword		xv
1.	Star Chasing	1
2.	To the Market	25
3.	White Dreams	52
4.	The Ballad of David Beckham	86
5.	Tilting at Windmills	124
6.	Spain Divided	149
7.	Divine Intervention	186
8.	The Good Dictator	224
9.	Changing Times	263
10.	The Passion of Being Boss	301
11.	The Ballad of David Beckham Continued . . .	338
12.	Bombing Madrid	379
	Bibliography	403
	Index	406

List of Illustrations

1 Beckham celebrates a goal against Real Betis with Ronaldo.
2 Alfredo Di Stefano relishes victory over FC Barcelona in the 1958–59 season.
3 Gento, Olsen, Di Stefano, Molowny and Joseito in the 1953–54 season.
4 Franco honours Santiago Bernabéu in 1967.
5 Bernabéu boosts the morale of the players in 1973.
6 Maradona playing for FC Barcelona (1983).
7 Emilio Butragueño showing his skills (1995).
8 Emilio Butragueño in the 1987–88 season.
9 Real Madrid fans celebrate a *Primera Liga* victory over Celta Vigo in 1998.
10 *Ultra Surs* during a Real Madrid clash with Bayern Munich in 2001.
11 Real Madrid players celebrate winning the 2001 Spanish league championship.
12 Matador Raúl brandishes the Spanish flag after Real Madrid win their ninth European Cup trophy in 2002.
13 Florentino Perez with José Maria Aznar and other Spanish politicians in 2003.
14 King Juan Carlos and Florentino Perez at the Santiago Bernabéu stadium in 2001.
15 David and Victoria Beckham in Madrid in 2003.

All photographs copyright Marcamedia, Barcelona, Recoletos Grupo de Comunicación S.A.

Acknowledgements

This book could not have been written without the co-operation of Real Madrid, past and present. While the various people at the club who helped in one way or another are too numerous to mention, I would like to extend a special thanks to the following: Marta, Mabel, Paco and the rest of the press office; Xavier García Coll; Emilio Butragueño, Manolo Redondo, José Angel Sanchez, Jorge Valdano, and their staff coordinated by the inexhaustible Julia. The club is fortunate in counting on the loyalty of those who were there when I most needed them. They include Chencho Arias, Vicente Del Bosque, Manolo Sanchis, Zoco, and the Lopez Quilez family. Along the way numerous supporters, fans, and fanatics made this project not only worthwhile but also fun. They include Marcelino Alonso, Ignacio de Barrio, Diego Cavero, Borja Fernandez-Galiano, Juan Milagro, Alfonso del Moral, Ricardo Rodriguez, Gerardo, Alberto, and José Emilio. Spain's leading sports daily *Marca* offered invaluable logistical back-up: thanks to Paz Aparicio, Rocío Balson, Hugo Brassey, Ulises Sanchez Flor, Manolo Saucedo, Patricia, Beatriz, Luis Fernando Rojo and all the team in the library.

Of the other journalists and historians from whose support and insights I benefited, again the list is too long to do it proper justice. But my special thanks go to both Sid Lowe and Thilo Schäfer who provided advice with patience and generosity, along with Julian García Candau, David Sharrock, Santiago Segurola, Orfeo Suarez, Juan Pablo Fusi, Amando de Miguel, Patrick Buckley, Henk Spaan, Simon Kuper, Regino Carlos, Fernando Perez Ollo, Anthony Luke, Patrick Harverson; at the *Financial Times*, David Owen, Tom O'Sullivan, Charles Morris, and Peter Cheek and all the library staff, and particularly Leslie Crawford, Joshua Levitt, and Isa Gutiérrez de la Camara in the Madrid office. My assistant June Uppal was a bastion of good humour, steady nerves, and general loveliness. Across Spain, old friends once again delivered, not least Arancha Arielza, Alberto Aza, Jordi Badia, Alfons Godall, Marjoryn van de Meer, Peter Nicholson, Carlos Oppe, Frank Porral, Toni Ruíz, José Maria Telles, Carlos Tusquets and Xavier Zarzalejos. My agent Caroline Dawnay was there for the idea and the faith as was Rowland White at Michael Joseph/Penguin and John English who edited the final manuscript. My brothers Tom and David, and my sister Maria-Belen along with their respective families provided warmth and hospitality. Finally the biggest thanks of all to Kidge, Julia and Miriam, who helped see it through.

Foreword

This is a book that maybe David Beckham might come round to reading one day. Beckham has had enough written about him that simply to add another profile to the already lengthy list of instant portraits of the player, the man, or the phenomenon would I think have been a wasted exercise. Instead I have put his story in the broader context of the history and culture of Spain and Real Madrid as a way of explaining the challenge Beckham – the player, the man, the celebrity – took on when he decided to leave Manchester United in the summer of 2003.

Football and David Beckham have come a long way since he joined Manchester United in 1990 – a teenager brought up in Chingford, Essex, who as a schoolboy had visited Barcelona's Nou Camp on a schoolboy talent prize. After the Premier League was founded in 1992, and Sky TV sold the TV rights to more than 160 countries, Beckham was gradually transformed into a celebrity sportsman who could transcend local loyalties and bring in millions.

Beckham's move to Real Madrid in the summer of 2003 represented the biggest challenge of his career. Real Madrid had created a team with the best players in the world. He had to prove that he was more than just a portable marketing brand to the club's members and fans, the most exacting and critical in football, and to others who harboured doubts that he was really worth it. Beckham's survival in Madrid depended on much more than his ability to sell shirts in Tokyo. Spaniards wanted Beckham to prove himself as good a player, if not better, than the cohort of brilliant Spaniards, Latin Americans and Frenchmen who had helped Real Madrid conquer the world.

Elsewhere in Spain the fans of other Spanish clubs, most notably that of Real Madrid's arch rivals FC Barcelona, looked and prayed that the Beckham experience would turn into a humiliating disaster. Beckham's first year in Spain in fact turned into a season of two halves, with Real Madrid starting it hoping to win the Spanish League and King's Cup and the UEFA Champions League, and ending it without a single piece of silverware.

And yet this did not take away from the weight of history that the club still carries with it, its continuing powerful presence in the world of football, and the certainty that the Beckham phenomenon will be with us for a while yet. Some Real Madrid officials who granted me interviews for this book, namely Carlos Quieroz and Jorge Valdano, lost their jobs at the end of the season. Another interviewee, Spain's ambassador to the UN Chencho Arias, changed posting this summer, bidding farewell to the Chinese ambassador by giving him a Ronaldo Real Madrid shirt. Their comments, insights and general presence inform a narrative that attempts to weave together the history of Spain, Real Madrid and Beckham.

Spain had never been just another foreign country. South of the Pyrenees and next to North Africa, it was both part of and separate from the rest of Europe. Over the centuries it had attracted an odd assortment of visitors and travellers – mad knights, Protestant spies, pilgrims, Bible-punchers, eccentric aristocrats, philosophers, poets, soldiers, brilliant footballers. To all of them Spain proved a discovery, a strange idiosyncratic land open to the lessons of the outside world, and yet deeply rooted in its traditions; a nation made up of different cultures, not easily understood.

Spain's backwardness and sense of isolation lingered well into the twentieth century – through the chaos and ravages of the Spanish Civil War and then under the authoritarian rule of its victor General Franco. In a society where democratic rights were denied, football assumed a new invigorated popularity, both as a distraction and as a cause, with two teams in particular, Real Madrid and FC Barcelona, following divergent political paths.

While FC Barcelona became a symbol of Catalan nationalist and democratic aspirations, Real Madrid laid claim to the soul of Spain, the nation's shop window and star export, winning more European Cups than any football team in history and securing international recognition as the world's most successful and powerful club. During the 1950s and early 1960s, thanks to its charismatic president Santiago Bernabéu, Real Madrid laid claim to providing the world with the best Spain could offer – a melting pot of multicultural talent, led by the legendary Argentine-born Alfredo Di Stefano, that anticipated the globalization of football as mass entertainment.

But it was also a club that was bitterly resented by its enemies for its arrogance and close involvement in the politics of power as exercised and manipulated from the nation's capital. The Bernabéu era was destined to become a key point of reference for the ambitions and tensions that drove Spanish football as the country moved from dictatorship to democracy. Real Madrid celebrated its centenary pledging itself to becoming the biggest, richest and most successful sporting institution of the twenty-first century, hugely raising the expectation of triumph when Beckham came to Spain.

Readers of my previous books know that my interest in the myths, vested interests and political intrigues surrounding major football stars began when I lived and worked in Argentina during the 1980s and subsequently researched a biography of Diego Maradona. But there is another reason why I came to write about Beckham and Real Madrid. As occurred with my history of FC Barcelona, this book would never have been written had I not been born in Madrid to a Spanish mother in 1953, the year when Di Stefano came to Spain. Although my maternal grandfather was among the first *Madrileños* to kick a ball around, and my Spanish family home was in the same avenue as the Santiago Bernabéu stadium, I was never a Real Madrid fan – because of its identification with the Franco regime.

And yes, I admit that in recent years I have become a product of globalization. I have done what I once vowed I would never do – paid to watch *La Primera Liga* on TV as well as in the stadiums. I enjoy football played at its best. I find big players and big clubs and their capacity to extend themselves around the world fascinating sociologically and politically – and arguably you can't get bigger than Real Madrid and Beckham. Researching the club's history, and following it in modern times, turned into a personal journey for me, and I have drawn on the memories of friends and my own experiences of Spain to try and shed fresh light on one of the most extraordinary cultural and social encounters of our times – when the world's most famous footballer went to live and play in Madrid.

Thus the story of Beckham and Real Madrid is my vehicle for explaining the changes in Spain, in football, and in Beckham's life. These changes run through this book sometimes in parallel, sometimes meeting and crossing paths, before drawing together in a chronicle of a year of hope, passion and tragedy. This is a story not just for football fanatics, but also for readers with a broader interest in Spain. Although he never authorized it, I hope David Beckham enjoys it.

Jimmy Burns
Madrid and London, June 2004

1. Star Chasing

In the summer of 2003 Real Madrid's Santiago Bernabéu stadium was undergoing some major renovation work befitting the ambitions of the world's self-proclaimed greatest football club, and in line with UEFA regulations. Late on the last sultry night of August, David Beckham emerged from the dressing room and into a building site and there among the dust, like a proverbial phoenix rising from the ashes, calmly ran the gauntlet of the world's media, smiling like he hadn't done for a while.

Packs of Englishmen and Spaniards combined with Frenchmen and Japanese, squeezing tight and struggling with cameras and microphones to pick up Beckham's every utterance, however bland and inconsequential. If there was a story yesterday and today and tomorrow, he was it, no question. Near by, the large room set aside for the official press conference with the manager Carlos Queiroz, remained empty. Other players walked past and out, ignoring without difficulty the half-hearted pleas for a comment. Beckham by contrast seemed not only the focus of attention but to be almost glowing in the white light.

'If there are doubts about me, it's up to me to silence them,' said Beckham, walking slowly along the metal fence, which barely separated him from the frenzied media scrum. He wanted to leave no one in any doubt about his mood of elation, as he continued, 'I am the happiest I've been in a year and a half.' Or his sense of diplomacy and place. Yes, he had started learning Spanish because he was looking forward to a 'long time in Madrid'. And no, he wasn't about to declare himself politically, still less show disrespect for the Spaniards and their football by claiming to be the best.

'There are no easy games in Spain, there are so many great players and teams,' he said, before confiding that Queiroz – the quiet unassuming Portuguese former assistant manager to Sir Alex Ferguson at Manchester United – had advised him to go out and express himself as well as play for the team. It was the kind of responsibility Beckham believed himself capable of giving to any team, whether it was Real Madrid or his country – an Englishman abroad who was still a patriot. But there were words of wisdom still to come. 'The difference in Spain is, if you give the ball way, it's more difficult to get it back,' he said.

Outside, along the ramp that leads up to the adjoining street from the club's private garage, hundreds of young, mostly female, Real Madrid fans waited for their newly discovered idol. They screamed *'guapo'* – 'good-looking' – several times over, and jumped excitedly as Beckham later emerged, driving his car, accompanied by his wife Victoria.

Barely two months had passed since the English captain had signed his transfer from Manchester United to Real Madrid for £25m. In mid-June the formal announcement of the deal, ending a seemingly endless cycle of speculation and denial, had coincided neatly with the start of a promotional tour for his sponsors in Japan, Malaysia, Thailand and Vietnam. The trip, on which he was accompanied by Victoria, served as a reminder of the bankability of his brand in that part of the world. The tour respected a celebrity status that the Beckhams still enjoyed as a couple in Asia, she as much as him basking in the glow of popular adulation verging on hysteria. In Spain pictures of the couple were splashed over the front pages of the local press. Reports focused on Beckham's glittering pop-star lifestyle and marketing power. British journalists laid siege to Real Madrid's training sessions to try and gauge the mood of the players. The bulk of the team struggled to maintain concentration ahead of a decisive final game of the Spanish season which would decide the championship in the club's favour. Among some of the Spanish players there was disquiet with the timing of the high-profile signing, and for giving the impression that somehow Real Madrid had become Beckham, before he had even played a game with the team. Real Madrid's sporting director Jorge Valdano was on hand to calm frayed nerves. He stressed that Beckham had not asked for any special treatment from the club and had not insisted on keeping the number 7 shirt number which he had inherited from Eric Cantona and made him famous at Manchester United. At Real Madrid the number 7 shirt was worn by a Spaniard – Raul, the team captain who was still hugely popular among the local fans. Beckham's new number was destined to be '23' – the same as Michael Jordan's. 'You can never have too many stars. Beckham is very versatile and we're building a squad, not just a team,' Valdano said, before adding, 'It's a perfect signing because it keeps both the marketing and sporting departments at Real Madrid very happy.'

Real Madrid already had three of the world's finest players – Ronaldo, Luis Figo and Zinedine Zidane – who between them had helped the club extend its popularity in Europe,

South America, Africa and the Middle East. Real Madrid now sought to exploit Beckham's iconic status in the US and among the Far East's merchandise-hungry fans just as Manchester United had done. Articles on Beckham in the US media in newspapers like the *New York Times*, and the box-office success of *Bend it Like Beckham* served as reminders that the player managed to fuel some interest within an American nation which, at least among its non-Hispanic white population, remained still relatively unstirred emotionally by football as a sport and as mass entertainment despite all the involvement of big US brands in sponsoring the game. Real Madrid had always regarded the US as a tough market to crack, but changing demographics meant a growing Hispanic or Latino population which it believed was working in its favour. The extraordinary enthusiasm Beckham generated among the young in the Far East had been demonstrated during the 2002 World Cup in Japan and South Korea, where local fans wore England shirts emblazoned with his name and obsessively followed his every move.

After his personal promotional tour of Asia in June 2003, Beckham returned to Madrid for his formal signing ceremony as a Real Madrid player on 2 July. From the moment he stepped down onto the tarmac at the military airbase of Torrejon, his visit was surrounded by the glitz and glamour befitting his transformation into an icon of popular culture. The fact that almost every move he made was filmed by his agency SFX for a promotional video underlined the overall impression of a choreographed piece of marketing. Beckham had his long blond hair gelled back and tied in a knot – his latest hairstyle eschewing defined sexuality. From his white jacket to his boots, via ripped jeans, he was dressed courtesy of Dolce & Gabbana. He was accompanied by his wife Victoria and their elder child Brooklyn. Victoria looked thin and tense, less at ease than her husband. Beckham was filmed having his medical check-up, and arriving at a hotel, before engaging in the rituals that were supposed to remind people that he had signed up to a football club called Real Madrid. He signed his contract with the club president Florentino Perez, and held up his new Madrid shirt with Alfredo Di Stefano, the player who fifty years earlier had helped transform Real Madrid into the most successful football club in the world. 'I've always loved football. Of course, I love my family. Football is everything to me and joining Real Madrid is a dream come true,' Beckham told his world-wide audience. His first words in Spanish were '*gracias*' and the club's rallying cry '*Hala Madrid*' – 'Let's go, Madrid' – first uttered many decades previously, so legend has it, by a young member of the Spanish royal household.

Later a perfect photo-opportunity designed to promote further the image of a family man in harmony with Spain's biggest sporting institution was staged at Real Madrid's old training ground. Dressed in Real Madrid strip for the first time, Beckham was juggling the ball with his feet – the kind of trick most professional players could do with their eyes closed. A young boy ran across the turf, apparently breaching security and made as if to embrace the world's most venerated athlete. He was greeted by Beckham with a smile and open arms, before the boy called Alfonso, the son of a Madrid fan, found himself draped in a team shirt to the cheers and screams of the crowd, and the instant registration by photographers and film crews.

*

By coming to Madrid, Beckham seemed to have drawn a line in his life and that of others. The adulation that had followed him around the globe was moving into uncharted territory. Much of Beckham's life, from childhood through to adulthood, had been defined largely by his relationship with his father Ted, an ardent Manchester United fan and Sir Alex Ferguson, his club manager for fourteen years. To some extent Beckham's promotion to England captain and the confidence invested in him by Sven-Goran Eriksson had mitigated the fall-out from his broken relationship with Ferguson. Victoria had also played a crucial role in breaking Ferguson's monopoly on Beckham after the couple met in 1997. It was thanks to her that Beckham developed a celebrity status outside football, her fame growing proportionately with his, the two combining to create a brand in its own right.

And yet the tension that lay beneath the surface of the slick marketing machine surrounding Beckham's presentation in Madrid surfaced during those frenzied twenty-four hours. The Spanish media already showed themselves rather more interested in Beckham than in Posh & Becks, and Victoria herself seemed rather less at ease in the new Spanish setting than say Tokyo. While David was undergoing his medical, Victoria was taken on an early private tour of the Spanish capital recommended by the club in the hope that she would quickly get used to the idea of living there. She returned looking visibly drawn and tense. Jostled by the media scrum as she got out of a car, she tripped and nearly fell to the ground – an incident that nearly brought one of her bodyguards to blows with a photographer from *Marca*, one of the world's biggest selling sports newspapers. That morning the editor of *Marca* Elias Israel had written that in all his years as a sports journalist he could not remember handling a media circus like the one surrounding David Beckham's first hours in Madrid. 'The media earthquake that the Englishman provokes with each step he takes, the fascination he awakens in football fans (and among those who do not like football) shows that we are in the midst of a sociological phenomenon . . .'

Victoria seemed to leave Spaniards less awestruck. Local journalists reported she looked too thin and ill-tempered. 'The ex-Spice Girl walks around as if she is about to break up,' wrote one of them in his notebook. It was clear that once the initial euphoria surrounding his signing had subsided, Beckham himself had much to prove as a footballer, playing with and against some of the top stars in the game. Beyond the fascination with his hairstyle, his wardrobe and his wife, Beckham was stepping into a club immersed in the politics and history of Spain and self-consciously obsessed with its status as one of the biggest and most successful sporting institutions in the world.

After the crowd-pulling signing ceremony at the beginning of July, Beckham had ended his first appearance playing for Real Madrid – in a pre-season friendly against Valencia – on a damp note. He was substituted after an hour during which he had struggled to get into the game and been booed by the Valencia fans who during the 1990s had got used to witnessing some high-quality European and Latin American football in their Mestalla stadium. Spanish commentators dismissed it as a dud performance, giving Beckham an early taste of what he could expect if he didn't live up to expectations.

By the time, a week later, Real Madrid travelled to Mallorca for the first leg of the Spanish SuperCup, Beckham faced further criticism. Those voicing their doubts about him in public included the former Spanish national coach Javier Clemente, a tough-talking Basque who had a reputation for offering the kind of truths others would prefer to leave unstated. In a controversial interview earlier that summer, Clemente had declared his firm belief that Real Madrid had made a mistake in signing Beckham, because he was 'very expensive' and the club already had star players like Figo who played potentially better in a similar position. Clemente was also not convinced that Beckham had put the troubles of his life behind him. 'Beckham is a very good player, but he has a lot of other things going on in his life and these could cause problems,' Clemente warned.

King Juan Carlos of Spain had once entertained Diana, Princess of Wales, at his holiday home in Mallorca. Now he was there to watch the latest English celebrity struggle to improve his reputation in the San Moix stadium. Beckham helped set up Real Madrid's first goal, his corner followed by a Figo volley into the net on nineteen minutes. For the rest of the game, Roberto Carlos took all Real Madrid's free-kicks, and Figo all the corners even though the Englishman's reputation as a footballer rested in large measure in his skilled use of the dead ball. Beckham's influence was restricted as he played in central midfield, a position he had yet to grow into. Substituted nine minutes into the second half by the Frenchman Claude Makelele (at the time on the verge of being transferred to Chelsea), Beckham showed his frustration by kicking at the bench before sitting down to watch his new team go down to a 1–2 defeat without him.

The thousands of British tourists in Manchester United shirts and England shirts watched the game that day with a large dose of nostalgia for the time when Beckham belonged to them only. And there were Spaniards there because they wanted to see if Beckham was really as big as *los ingleses* made him out to be. As for the Mallorca fans, they were there to see Real Madrid beaten.

The Spanish media coverage the next morning showed that for all the hype surrounding his transfer, Beckham would be judged in Spain entirely on his ability to guarantee Real Madrid's success during his first season at the club, facing a tougher judgement than most ordinary mortals. The Spanish sports daily *As* awarded him the '*Vaya Dia*' ('What a dreadful day') award, the leading broadsheet *El País* claimed that Beckham not only 'lacked class but also lacked spark', while the conservative *ABC* bemoaned the player's 'invisibility'. British journalists watching the game were less critical, noting Beckham's thirty-four completed passes of which just five were misplaced, and his generally workmanlike attitude, something that did not surprise them. In contrast to the Spanish media, there were English journalists who had been following Beckham for years. What Spanish and English seemed to agree on was that the match exposed some weaknesses in Real Madrid as a team – notably a vulnerability in defence, and what one British observer, Sid Lowe, noted in his diary as a 'lack of organization, the superstar overload and the side's anarchic nature', aspects which had been made painfully clear when Figo decided to take the rest of the corners after Beckham had created the opening goal and Roberto Carlos fluffed the only free-kick in Beckham range.

Before the month of August was over the *Sun* newspaper

published an interview with Beckham, in which the player detailed his depressive encounters with Victoria, when things were at their worst at Manchester United, his feuds with Ferguson, his agony over his parents' divorce, and his expectations of his new life in Spain. Asked how different his life would become now he had moved to Madrid, Beckham replied that he would miss some of his friends and those members of his family who would not be able to be there all the time, like his nan and granddad. He'd also miss pie and mash and jellied eels. Apart from that he was looking forward to life in the Spanish capital. His son Brooklyn was already enjoying the sun and the swimming pool. Beckham declared himself '110 per cent committed' to his new club, a challenge that was both 'exciting and a hard one' but he felt he was up to going 'all the way'. The interview formed part of a carefully staged publicity campaign surrounding the publication of the player's autobiography – Murdoch papers doing their plug for a book published by a Murdoch-owned publishing house.

Both interview and book reflected a dual devotion to his family and his fame. The book was dedicated to 'Victoria, Brooklyn and Romeo the Three People who always make me smile. My babies forever. Love David.' It was signed 'Daddy' in Beckham's own hand. The interview underlined the picture of David and Victoria Beckham as a perfect couple – mutually supportive, very much in love, and capable of overcoming crises. 'Victoria was the only one I could talk to . . .' headlined the *Sun*, as Beckham related his moments of self-doubt at Manchester United and in the aftermath of his red card in the 1998 World Cup game against Argentina. Asked whether Victoria would be happy to be based in Spain,

Beckham replied, 'That's what we have to do. We have to fully commit ourselves to Spain and to Real Madrid and that's what we're doing.'

To the *Madridistas* such comments and revelations still seemed to matter little as they gathered late that summer for Real Madrid's opening matches of the 2003–04 season. What they wanted to see was whether there was substance to Beckham as a player behind the hype of his celebrity status.

That August, Beckham silenced his doubters and put on a brilliant display where it mattered most – in the Bernabéu stadium, before one of the most exacting and critical crowds in football. As the *Sun*'s Steven Howard wrote in a glowing dispatch, 'They had been writing the obituaries long before David Beckham even set foot on the Bernabéu turf . . . well, to adapt a line from Mark Twain, reports of Beckham's death have been vastly exaggerated.'

It was the *SuperCopa* second-leg encounter against Mallorca, and Beckham scored his first goal for Real Madrid on Spanish soil, striking home a rare header from a cross by Ronaldo in the 72nd minute. 'What nobody expected,' commented José Samaño of *El País*, 'was that Beckham would score with his head, something that helps him stand out off the pitch but never on it.' The stadium erupted in a collective celebration. Beckham had been recognized not just as a goalscorer but as someone who had reacted under pressure and thrown himself into the game from the outset. No longer did he seem the odd man out in a team that had grown used to playing without him. His free-kicks and crossfield passes helped him play a pivotal role in Real Madrid's 3–0 victory (4–2 on aggregate) and allowing him a lap of honour with his new team mates and his first piece of

Spanish silverware. 'Beckham delight' typified the headlines. 'It was incredible,' said Beckham later. 'I dreamed of making my debut at the Bernabéu and scoring. I couldn't ask for more.' Beckham was not alone in believing that things were looking up.

Later that week I caught a lift to the Bernabéu with Ulises Sanchez Flor, a journalist with the Spanish sports daily *Marca*. Ulises's job was exclusively focused on following Real Madrid day in day out, living and breathing with the club, listening, observing every move and gesture of its players and club management, as if they were the blood flowing through his veins. A man of few words but considerable insight and instinct, Ulises became a necessary companion during my research for this book. In that first meeting I was anxious to test the hype behind the headlines, to assess the mood in the Real Madrid dressing room, to get a sense of how Beckham was beginning to be judged locally, now that he had arrived in Spain.

Ulises shared few doubts that Beckham was in the process of proving his worth to Real Madrid on the field as much as off it. 'He is very motivated . . . works very hard . . . really wants to win through,' he told me as we made our way in the heat and through the crowds along the Castellana avenue where I had been born half a century before. I remarked that both in Valencia and Mallorca, the media had come away with the impression that some of the Real Madrid players had appeared to be ignoring their new colleague. Ulises suggested that the opposite was the case and that, as Beckham would himself later insist, several of the Real stars, led by Roberto Carlos and Ronaldo, had gone out of their way to make the new boy feel at home. Beckham's virtually zero knowledge of the Spanish language put him at a slight disadvantage but there were players on hand – Figo among them – who used their mastery of English to facilitate communication. 'There is a surprising atmosphere of solidarity in the dressing room,' Ulises insisted.

It seemed important that Figo was helping out, Ulises suggested, because Figo was a good friend of Raul, the Spanish captain, who in turn was widely seen as the favourite son of Jorge Valdano, Real Madrid's sporting director and one of the club's key figures. And yet there was a note of warning about the life that awaited Beckham outside the Bernabéu and how it might be exploited by the British tabloids and Spain's *prensa rosa* or gossip media. From the moment Beckham had set foot in the country, paparazzi and reporters had declared open season on anything and everybody who claimed to have some connection to the English star. The mood and character of a very Spanish soap had already been set in motion by a notorious TV 'model' called Nuria. As dusky and outspoken as the legendary operatic Carmen, this Beckham-baiter claimed to have already bedded half the Real Madrid side and was marking her time before adding the Englishman to her list.

That night in August, thoughts of Nuria temporarily dissipated as Ulises and I approached the huge mass of concrete that was the Bernabéu, glowing in the dark, bulging with fans from around the world, but mostly from Spain. For in that moment it was Ulises who volunteered an image that he believed tied Beckham not to the tawdry machinations of the gutter press but to the special nature of football as watched by *Madridistas*. 'This is a crowd that likes a player that sweats his shirt, and has *cojones*.'

In the match that followed against Real Betis, Real Madrid's first home game of the league championship, Beckham did indeed play his rocks off, settling effortlessly on Real Madrid's glittering stage and writing a personal script made for dreamers. In just the third minute of the match he scored the first goal of the Spanish season when he met a Ronaldo pass with a relaxed side-footed shot into net. After Real Betis had equalized, he was instrumental in setting up the second-half winner with a trademark long pass to Zinedine Zidane who then crossed for Ronaldo to smash it in on the half-volley – a true constellation of stars hard to beat in footballing astronomy.

Over the highest tiers of the Bernabéu the cranes stood like resting giants, a fitting backdrop to the work in progress – transforming the stadium into all that is best and most entertaining in world football. Florentino Perez, the Real Madrid president, the man responsible for combining the likes of Raul, Figo, Zidane, Ronaldo and Beckham in one project of excellence, was watching his players line up at the start of the second half of the game against Betis, when across the turf ran a naked man in an attempt to get a touch of the ball. One after another the players looked at the man and chuckled. Perez, looked on and smiled. In his live coverage, a Spanish television commentator remarked, 'This is very British; let us hope this doesn't catch on in Spain.'

In fact the rare Spanish sighting of Mark Roberts, the world's most notorious professional streaker, was at that very moment being displayed on local TV with none of the prurience usually accorded to such occasions in Britain. Roberts could be seen in all his full comical glory, surrendering himself to a no-less comic ejection by a couple of overweight security staff. Since first running across a rugby pitch in Hong Kong back in the early 1990s, Roberts had earned a place in the *Guinness Book of Records* with over one hundred appearances around the world, but this one would take some beating for sheer audience participation. 'It's been an incredible experience, with all those people shouting and laughing like mad,' Roberts said later that evening as he demolished a hamburger.

Roberts had put the Bernabéu of Florentino Perez to the test and had not found it wanting in its modernity. This was a stadium that the enemies of Real Madrid like to caricature as a relic of Francoism and yet there were its players and its president sharing a light-hearted moment with the fans as a naked man temporarily interrupted play. Watching the incident I could not help but think back to my childhood in Spain during the 1950s and early 1960s and the sight on a beach of nude tourists being arrested by paramilitary civil guards as if they had committed a heinous crime. That all now seemed to belong not just to another time in history, but to another country.

Even without Roberts's presence, Perez could afford a smile or two. From being one of the most successful businessmen in Spain, Perez had become one of its most powerful men, personifying the scope and scale of modern football at its most ruthlessly ambitious. Under him the presidential box and the expanded executive sections had become a symbol of contemporary Spain – its heads of state, local politicians, celebrities and thrusting entrepreneurs gathered there like bees to honey. Few foreign investors could afford not to use their Madrid season ticket as the vehicle for building their client base. The Japanese and others from Asia were among those willing to pay well over the odds for a chance to watch Beckham at the Bernabéu alongside his fellow stars. When things go as well as this, wrote the Spanish author and journalist Antonio Burgos, you can hear birds singing in the ticket offices, clouds lift thanks to the increase in TV revenue, and the president of the club becomes the undisputed Sun King. 'There are those who say that in Madrid there is no such thing as a royal court any more. Surely we can talk of the Court of King Florentino in the presidential box of the Bernabéu every Sunday?'

Among the lower serfs of this dominion were those more radical elements of Real Madrid's fan club who somehow have mixed up their football loyalties with a nostalgic obsession with a nation most Spaniards have chosen to relegate to the dustbin of history – united, great, intolerant, as totalitarian and self-deluded as Franco once willed his country to be. Before the match they appeared in a side-street, taking the territory that adjoined the stadium. I had seen these people some years back while researching a previous book on Spanish football. They were still there, the *Ultra Surs*, moustachioed or shaven headed, with their war paint and ritualistic fires, their litany of abuse and their invocations of Spain and Hitler, chanting '*Que Viva España*' and '*Sieg Heil*' and the enduring legacy of domination – '*La Dictadura del Real Madrid*', a hotchpotch of ideological lunacy.

While it was hard to ignore its potential for destabilization in a country whose government struggled to treat new immigrants with decency, their impact within the Bernabéu was relegated to a restricted area. Those used to tougher football fan environments like Argentina and England complained that the Bernabéu was subdued by comparison. What they meant was that it is too civilized, too family-oriented, too functional. Perez thought this was the kind of atmosphere that made his club less alienating and more global – you could put it on show anywhere in the world and not risk a pitched battle.

While a few hundred *Ultra Surs* kept their end up, with their pulp songs and chants, thousands of other supporters took their cue from the more universal themes of the club's newly crafted official hymn as delivered by Placido Domingo. They smoked cigars, digested their brandies, ate large sandwiches; they brought their wives and daughters, sons, and in-laws; they rose to their feet and applauded good moves, and whistled at their team whenever it looked like losing the supremacy most of them regarded as God-given. For if there was a defining trait of Real Madrid fans it is their unbending belief that there was no other club in the world as great as theirs, indeed no other club so deserving of greatness. What Real Madrid fans considered a collective self-belief, their enemies saw only as arrogance. Beyond the Bernabéu it bred resentment and hatred. *Madridistas* put it all down to envy. Among their more populist totem banners was that of a fighting bull astride the Spanish colours, with a pair of huge testicles – a symbol of Spain, not just Madrid.

In the summer Beckham came to Spain, bullfighting still filled arenas around the country, not least in Madrid's famous 'cathedral' of bullrings Las Ventas. It was there, just over a month before Beckham signed his contract with Real Madrid, that the young bullfighter turned pop celebrity *El Juli* fought alone and killed six bulls in one afternoon. (Normally a bullfight is shared by three matadors, each killing two bulls.

But *El Juli* wanted to prove he had the strength and courage to carry out the task singlehandedly.) *El Juli* made a name for himself at the end of a millennium because of his youth – he was only ten when he first fought a bull and fifteen when he turned fully professional. In 2003 a tourist promotion for Andalusia, the region from where most of the best bull-fighters in history are reputed to come, toasted the Madrid-born *El Juli* for his exceptionally brave and agile style. It recommended seeing him to those interested in attending their first bullfight.

And yet the jury was out on *El Juli* even as he killed his six bulls. There were aficionados who considered him a bit of a charlatan, not quite risking it as much as he made out he did. They accused him of taking short cuts to win over less knowing crowds, of using his looks of a young Adonis to distract from his absence of real artistry at the moment of truth. There were others who thought he was simply either tired or had lost something of his nerve after killing hundreds of bulls over several seasons and being gored on too many occasions.

The ease with which a Spanish crowd can turn from adulation to fanatical condemnation was pointed out by Ernest Hemingway in his seminal treatise on bullfighting, *Death in the Afternoon*, written many years before *El Juli* was born. A Spanish writer who hated bullfighting, Eugenio Noel, has separately written, again decades ago, that the national spectacle was both a symptom and a cause of all that was wrong with Spain. From the bullring, according to Noel, we got the following characteristics of the Spanish race: a majority of crimes committed with a knife, the *chulo* (a *Madrileño* working-class spiv), and its ridiculous machismo.

What is certainly true is that bullfighting has never been considered a sport by those who participate in it even if certain images and stereotypes have transferred to football. A *Madridista* can move seamlessly from Las Ventas to the Bernabéu knowing that what he may witness in both rings plays out on the volatile terrain of passion while subject to the blind workings of fate.

Beckham was as beautiful as *El Juli*, his claim to fame on a somewhat larger scale, one that defied national boundaries, tradition, culture while teasingly projected in a tone and attitude modern Spaniards could mould for themselves in an image they could understand. When he scored his first goals for Real Madrid, fans coined the term *matador* in praise of his ability as a skilful fighter for the ball and his delivery of it. Not since Gary Lineker was called that while playing for FC Barcelona during the 1980s had an Englishman stirred such emotions in Spanish football. The day after the Betis match, *Marca* headlined with the phrase '*El Club de la Coleta*' – the club of the ponytail. It showed Ronaldo jokingly celebrating Beckham's first goal of *La Liga* by clutching the Englishman's alice band while delving again into the language of the bullfight. Bullfighters cut off their *coletas* when they have been disgraced or decided to retire. Thus Beckham managed to turn what older *Madridistas* had considered a sign of dubious sexuality into a mark of Spanishness.

As the man responsible for bringing David Beckham to Spain, Florentino Perez had every reason to feel satisfied. The gods appeared to be smiling on the latest stage in his ambitious project to enhance Real Madrid's record as the most successful football club in history, but also to make it the most popular worldwide. Perez wanted to deliver 'dream

teams' led by superstars, *galácticos* that cut across tribal prejudice and spread out across the globe, attracting a universal
fan base.

Three years before Beckham's arrival, Perez had based a
flamboyant campaign for the job of president of Real Madrid
on a pledge to acquire the talents of Luis Figo, the Portuguese
midfield star of FC Barcelona, the club's historic rivals. He
backed it up with a pledge to use $8.5m of his own money
to buy season tickets for the club's members if he failed to
land the player. He won the election and secured Figo. The
Portuguese was bought for a then record £37.4m. Over the
next two seasons came Zinedine Zidane, for an extraordinary
£46m and then Ronaldo for £29.8m. In his handling of the
transfers, Perez showed himself a skilful negotiator. With his
three star signings, the world's three best players at the time
– 'three golden balls born to play for Real Madrid', as Perez
put it prior to Beckham's appearance – Real Madrid added
the following cups to its unrivalled silverware: two league
championships, one Champions League, a European Super
Cup, and the World Club Championship.

By the summer of 2003, Perez believed he had already
hit on a magic formula. Having inherited a club that was
deeply in debt he presided over a marked improvement in
the club's finances, initially thanks to a controversial property deal exploiting the enviable location of Real Madrid's
training ground. In a series of interviews with Spanish and
foreign media, he boasted that ticket sales had more than
doubled, with 200,000 requests over and above the Santiago
Bernabéu's capacity for each game. Far from acting as a
source of strain on the club's finances, Perez argued that it
was the big stars he had acquired who had sparked the

commercial turnaround. Beyond sporting success, they provided an economic yield in more merchandising sales, bigger sponsorship deals, more money for promotional tours in the US and Asia. With the coming to Spain of the biggest of all English stars, Perez seemed moved almost to poetry. As he told the *Financial Times*, 'It is an association of interests. When Real Madrid signed Beckham what resulted was an explosion of two great brands whose raison d'être is universality.'

And yet the Beckham signing had also put the club's footballing priorities under the microscope. Before his arrival Real Madrid fans and commentators believed that the club's standards had slipped despite winning the Spanish league title for the twenty-ninth time. Such criticism reflected the weight of history that the team carried on their shoulders, the expectations generated by previous triumphs, and previous incarnations of stardom. It was also a product of the power of the Spanish sports media, which in the capital had two mass-circulation tabloids focused on the politics and football of Real Madrid, along with a posse of TV and radio journalists on permanent assignment to the world of the Santiago Bernabéu, on and off the pitch. Media and fans fed off each other to an extraordinary degree, a constant form of pressure that demanded success and spectacle.

The fact that Real Madrid had been defeated by Juventus in the semi-finals of the European Champions League was regarded as a blot on the club's record, while the subsequent clinching of the Spanish league title was linked to the late-season collapse of the underrated Real Sociedad, the dark horse of the season. The subsequent rumblings of discontent emerging from within the Real Madrid dressing room, when some players showed themselves reluctant to celebrate the title win, were regarded in some quarters as conduct unbecoming a club whose self-image was not just of greatness but also of chivalry. From the highest levels of the Florentino Perez regime, a story was spun that the coach Vicente Del Bosque had lost control of his players, and that the dressing room had become dominated by the machinations of Fernando Hierro, the brash and outspoken captain.

Perez told anyone who was listening that with Beckham's arrival Real Madrid was entering a new stage that required a different coach and a restructured squad. The choice of Carlos Queiroz as Del Bosque's replacement sprung in part from Perez's ambition to consolidate Real Madrid as a leading global brand. Queiroz had coaching experience in the US and South Africa, whose national team he had guided to the 2002 World Cup finals. In Portugal he had managed Sporting Lisbon and the Portuguese national team, helping the development of emerging stars like Figo. And he had been recruited in the summer of 2002 by Manchester United – a signing, according to Michael Crick, that reflected Sir Alex Ferguson's stance that his club was no longer an English or British club but a 'European operation which should acquire players, tactics and techniques from all over the globe'. It was a philosophy long ago adopted by Real Madrid but which had not always produced the required results.

Advised by Jorge Valdano, his sporting director, Perez believed that, with his background, Queiroz might act as a stabilizing influence in the dressing room, and help smooth Beckham's transition from Manchester to Madrid, integrating him with the rest of the team in a way that would raise its quality and ability to win. 'Queiroz puts a lot of emphasis on the physical and tactical side. That is the profile we are looking for,' said Perez in an interview in July 2003.

At United Queiroz had been credited with bringing about some improvements in the team's defence. He was moving to Real Madrid, one of the most attack-minded teams in the world. The club's traditional belief was that such attacking boldness should translate not just into hugely entertaining football but also more goals than the opponent. The problem came when the opposition exploited the team's vulnerable defence. Queiroz, it was said, had been brought in to bring more balance to Real Madrid in a way that did not make it stultify their attacking instincts.

And yet the shake-out was not to everyone's liking. When he sacked Del Bosque, Perez sacrificed a loyal and widely respected *Madridista*, who had devoted his professional life to the club since first playing for its youth team as a teenager. There was a feeling among the club's traditionalists, shared by the coach himself, that Del Bosque had been dispensed with as part of a business plan that brought with it huge risks in footballing terms.

One of the most insightful football writers in Europe, Gabriele Marcotti, was among those who argued that Perez had built his house on foundations of sand. For the summer that Beckham came to Spain was also the summer that Real Madrid reduced its strength in depth by releasing – either on permanent transfer or loan – a coterie of players including those who could not easily be dismissed as simply overpaid, such as Claude Makelele, Flavio Conceiçao, Savio, Fernando Morientes and Pedro Munitis.

As would later emerge, Queiroz either seriously miscalculated or misunderstood the nature of his new appointment when he came to Real Madrid. Maybe because he had worked alongside Alex Ferguson, the biggest boss in English football, Queiroz believed that Perez would heed his plea for a transfer policy that would not leave the team potentially so exposed in defence, and more generally in all positions, given the shortage on the bench of players of sufficient quality or experience. On top of their pre-season promotional tours and other commercial commitments, the team of the *galácticos* had a gruelling fixture list ahead of them straddling *La Liga*, the King's Cup, and the Champions League. That Perez convinced himself Real Madrid could win them all with the squad that he had fashioned was based on the illusion that the *galácticos*, not least Beckham, were superhuman.

2. To the Market

I am sure that I was alone among the Madrid-born occupants of the Bernabéu that night at the start of Beckham's first season in Spain to spare a private note of sympathy for FC Barcelona, that other Spanish club – it preferred to consider itself Catalan – that over the years had developed its rivalry with Real Madrid into one of Spain's great political and cultural dramas. In researching and writing a history of Barça I had come to know the club and its supporters, not least a young, ambitious lawyer called Joán Laporta. As president-elect of FC Barcelona, Laporta had made a much-publicized bid for Beckham earlier that summer only to see his efforts disappear like grains of sand through open fingers.

It was in March 1998 that I had first got to know Laporta. Then in his late thirties, he was engaged in an audacious attempt to unseat one of the most powerful men in Catalonia, the then president of Barça, Josep Lluís Nuñez. A vote of no confidence in the Nuñez presidency had been forced by a coalition of opposing factions, put together by Laporta, called the Blue Elephant, the opening salvo of a war of attrition that within five years would see the disappearance of Nuñez and all his cohorts from the Nou Camp – including his deputy Joán Gaspart who briefly succeeded him – and their replacement by a new regime headed by Laporta. In my book, *Barça: A People's Passion*, I exposed Nuñez as a ruthless bully, a construction magnate who had made a fortune destroying old buildings and speculating on new property. His opponents denounced what they alleged was Barça's transformation into a personal fiefdom under a despot. Laporta and his allies had chosen as their emblem a mammal that stood for virtue and responsible leadership, which didn't abused its enormous size, retaining essential nobility amid nature's barbarous instinct for survival of the fittest and the materialism of the modern world.

Nuñez seemed to make a habit of mishandling great stars. They came and went at frequent intervals leaving most Barça fans with the frustration of knowing what might have been had they been allowed to stay just a little longer. Maradona, Romario, Rivaldo, Cruyff, Ronaldo, Figo – each had made his mark at the Nou Camp only to leave in a cloud of controversy. In their campaign strategy the Blue Elephant of Joán Laporta made much in particular of Nuñez's acrimonious relationship with Johan Cruyff. The sacking of Cruyff as manager by Nuñez in 1996 was portrayed as a mistake of monumental proportions – the loss of a figure who for Barça's followers had iconic status.

Cruyff was sold to FC Barcelona by the Dutch champions Ajax in 1973 for a then record transfer fee of £922,000. He had an immediate impact on Barça, demonstrating his extraordinary technique and pace on and off the ball. The fans believed they had the best footballer in the world in their midst, and Cruyff did not disappoint them, inspiring the team to play with confidence and style. In his first season Cruyff led FC Barcelona to a memorable 5–0 victory over Real Madrid at the Beranabéu on the way to Barça's first championship title in fourteen years. Barcelona and many parts of Spain bubbled with 'Cruyffmania'. After that, Barça won only one title with Cruyff as player – the Spanish Cup, during his final season in 1978. And yet Cruyff remained hugely popular, and enhanced his reputation still further during his period as manager. Over seven seasons under Cruyff's inspiration, in addition to the European Cup, Barça won four consecutive league championships.

Laporta had the Cruyff era very much in mind when in his bid for the presidency in the early summer of 2003 he homed in on David Beckham as the international star he believed could restore FC Barcelona to its former greatness. A financial strategy paper drawn up by his advisers focused on the extent to which a global star like Beckham would boost the strength of Barça's global marketing, and raise the revenue from its TV and sponsorship contracts.

Laporta privately approached Manchester United towards the end of May, a few days before the official launch of the two-week presidential campaign. He had watched the English club reclaim the Premiership crown and Beckham's part in it. Before that Laporta had seen confirmation of Beckham's own global status when during the 2002 World Cup in the Far East the Englishman had thrown local crowds of Japanese and Koreans into frenzy while capturing the attention of a worldwide TV audience. Asia was a market that remained relatively unexploited by FC Barcelona and Real Madrid.

From informal contacts with Manchester United, and a close reading of the British media, Laporta had convinced himself that the club and Sir Alex Ferguson had decided not to resist a serious bid whether it came from Spain or Italy. But the reality fell well short of the kind of certainties that Laporta seemed to convey during his campaign in which he boosted his popularity ratings by declaring publicly that he was negotiating Beckham's transfer to FC Barcelona.

On 5 June 2003, ten days away from the FC Barcelona presidential elections, Laporta was happy to confirm publicly that he had started negotiations 'some time ago' for the signing of Beckham. By then it had emerged that Laporta had appointed his running mate Sandro Rosell to act as his representative in his meetings with Manchester United's chief executive Peter Kenyon, and in any other business involving foreign players. While he made clear that the talks on the future of Beckham were continuing, Laporta announced that he had finalized a deal to bring the Turkish international goalkeeper Rustu Recber to FC Barcelona under his presidency. Rustu had become available that summer on a free transfer from Fenerbahce. Voted the second-best goalkeeper in the 2002 World Cup finals, after Oliver Kahn of Germany, Rustu had fuelled the interest of several European clubs, including Manchester United and Arsenal.

Far less trumpeted at the time were the secret talks Rosell was engaged in to secure the Brazilian midfielder Ronaldinho – another of the stars of the World Cup – whose days at the French club Paris St Germain (PSG) were drawing to a close. Rosell, a member of one of Catalonia's richest families and whose father Jaume had served as secretary of FC Barcelona during the last years of the Franco regime, had close ties with Ronaldinho and his agent brother Roberto de Assis dating back to the late 1990s. Rosell was based in Brazil as an executive for Nike. Ronaldinho, then playing for Gremio in his home town of Porto Alegre, signed a long-term marketing contract with Nike in 1999 covering his club and international appearances. The contract envisaged improved terms if he were ever transferred to one of the five clubs then considered the biggest in the world – Juventus, Milan, Manchester United, Real Madrid and FC Barcelona. Still young and untested at club level in Europe, Ronaldinho was advised by his brother to go for a less ambitious transfer to PSG initially, signing with the French club in January 2001.

European interest in the player increased in the aftermath of the World Cup the following year. Rosell relocated to Barcelona and approached Ronaldinho in March 2003 when world champions Brazil played a friendly in Mexico. At the time FC Barcelona was immersed in one of the worst crises of its history. In the midst of a disastrous run in the Spanish league the club's Dutch coach Louis van Gaal had been sacked, and its president Joán Gaspart had been forced to resign. Radomir Antic was appointed interim manager under a caretaker president, while the club prepared for new elections at the end of the season. By then the candidacy of Joan Laporta was being prepared by a group of close friends, among them Rosell. It was Rosell who told Ronaldinho that Laporta was serious in his aim to restore FC Barcelona to its former greatness, and that he saw the Brazilian playing a key role in such a future.

Rosell continued to work as an executive for a Barcelona-based marketing company wholly owned by Nike until November 2002 before setting up his own sports consultancy and later emerging as Laporta's electoral running mate. He continued to maintain informal links with Nike. In the final stages of the FC Barcelona election campaign, Rosell's Nike connections were denounced by the rival candidate, the advertising executive Luis Bassat, in an attempt to embarrass Laporta who claimed he was independent of any multinational interests. Nike for its part issued a denial that it had ever played a part in brokering transfer deals between clubs. The sportswear company had lucrative deals with Manchester United and FC Barcelona as well as individual players who straddled the commercial interests of global football, among them Ronaldinho. (Beckham had signed a contract with Adidas, as had Real Madrid.)

Amid the commercial interests lurking in the background of European football in the early summer of 2003, the election campaign for the presidency of FC Barcelona between the handsome young lawyer Laporta and the elderly overweight businessman Bassat was played out with the razzmatazz of a US presidential primary and the dubious tactics of a banana republic.

Laporta formally announced his candidacy on 14 May 2003. A week earlier Rosell had secretly contacted Francis Graille, the president of PSG, and reiterated his interest in Ronaldinho. The formal reply was that the player was not for sale. Undeterred, Rosell met with Ronaldinho's agent brother Roberto. He was told that Real Madrid and Manchester United were showing an interest in the player that could not be ignored. Rosell found out that Real Madrid's Florentino Perez was offering to buy Ronaldinho for around 30 million euros on the condition that he would remain on loan to PSG for one more season – a financial arrangement which Perez believed fitted in with his plans to buy Beckham sooner rather than later. Meanwhile reports in the British media in early June suggested that Kenyon had all but tied up a deal to bring Ronaldinho to Manchester United, without waiting a year.

On 10 June 2003, four days before voting in the FC

Barcelona presidential elections, Manchester United issued a statement confirming that its club official had met Laporta, resulting in an undisclosed offer being made for the transfer of Beckham to the Catalan club. But the agreement made clear that it was conditional on Laporta actually being elected president, and more crucially on Manchester United reaching agreement with Beckham on his contract. Laporta had by this stage had a preliminary contact with Tony Stephens of the SFX sports agency, who represented Beckham, but had not met the player himself. Stephens had told Laporta to pursue his negotiations on Beckham's transfer directly with Manchester United.

Ignoring the ambiguity and qualifying small print issued by the Manchester United statement, Laporta seized on it to support his campaign pledge that Beckham would be his once he was elected. Opinion polls suddenly showed him pushing ahead as a clear favourite to win the election. Despite privately knowing that he had no agreement with Beckham himself, Laporta went on selling the idea that the English player could be there for Barça's taking, once Bassat had been defeated of course. 'I want him to be the leader of a new Barcelona ... I think Beckham could be like Johan Cruyff when he first came here in 1973. Beckham could be the Cruyff of 2003,' Laporta said as voting approached. When Cruyff signed up for FC Barcelona in 1973, he unwittingly became a political emblem at a time when the club when the spirit of Catalan resistance was being fuelled just as the last bastions of the Franco regime were digging in. The ageing *Caudillo* had appointed the hard-line admiral Luis Carrero Blanco as his president. There was growing opposition from those calling for autonomous political rights in Spain's regions. That December Carrero Blanco was blown to pieces by a bomb placed by the Basque terrorist group ETA as he was on his way to Mass in a church in Madrid.

Much as he had striven to eschew any involvement in politics in his native Holland, Cruyff found the birth of his son within weeks of his arrival in the Catalan capital being transformed into a political act. Local nationalists made much of the fact that Cruyff insisted on registering his son as Jordi – the Catalan for George and the local patron saint, despite a Franco ruling that only Spanish names could be used on official documentation. A few days later, in February 1974, Cruyff led Barça to that historic 5–0 win over Real Madrid in the Bernabéu. The *New York Times* correspondent at the time remarked that Cruyff had done more for the spirit of the Catalan nation in ninety minutes than many politicians had achieved in years of stifled struggle.

Thirty years on Laporta's nationalist politics were looked on somewhat wearily by SFX, not least because they were being expounded at a time when Barça themselves had much ground to recover in terms of sporting achievement.

It took Florentino Perez just a matter of days to puncture Laporta's dream of having Catalan Cruyff reincarnated in the figure of Catalan Beckham. The Real Madrid president seized an opportunity that had in effect been handed to him on a plate by others, not least Manchester United's Peter Kenyon, and Laporta himself. It was while sunning himself on holiday in California in June that Beckham, to his chagrin, heard that Manchester United had issued a statement confirming that they were in negotiations with Laporta about his future. The news conveyed to him over a transatlantic phone call by his agent Tony Stephens came to Beckham as a total and unwelcome surprise, according to the player. This was despite the fact that both Kenyon and Stephens had separately reached the conclusion the previous month that Beckham's days at Ferguson's Manchester United were coming to an end. Kenyon had contacted Stephens in the middle of May 2003 and offered to initiate talks on a new contract with Beckham. The last contracts had been finalized in March 2002, after eighteen months of tortuous negotiations, with Beckham delaying agreement until the uncertainty surrounding Ferguson's permanence at Manchester United had been cleared up, and he'd been assured of greater control over his image rights. While the contract was not due to expire until 2005, the club had no wish to wait until its star player had been placed on the free transfer list before tying down a deal from which the club could profit. According to Patrick Harverson, Manchester United's head of communications at the time, the offer of a new contract at the club, which included a pay rise, was a test of Beckham's resolve to stay at the club but Stephens's response was 'lukewarm to indifferent'. SFX's version is that Kenyon had made it pretty clear to Stephens that he was prepared to let Beckham go, and it was on the basis of this information that the player's agent had entered into initial contacts with Italian and Spanish clubs to sound out which among them might be prepared to come up with a decent offer. Beckham's own version is that even at this stage, he felt that signing a new deal with Manchester United was still possible although such a prospect was becoming increasingly remote. In his autobiography he says that he told his father that the only reason he'd ever leave United was if the club wanted him to and at that moment it felt as if 'they're not bothered either way'.

At FC Barcelona Laporta discovered belatedly that Stephens and Beckham were interested in Real Madrid, the one club the player would consider going to if and when he left Manchester United. In the final days of the FC Barcelona election campaign Laporta tried to contact Stephens and had left messages, but none of his calls had been returned. The wall of silence fuelled Laporta's worst suspicion – that whatever Manchester United had agreed to state in public, Stephens was deliberately paving the way for a deal with Real Madrid. At the same time it would appear that Laporta's running mate Rosell had invested more time in trying to secure a deal with his old friend Ronaldinho, clearly allowing Real Madrid to outmanoeuvre FC Barcelona on Beckham.

Recalling his own feelings at the time, Beckham did not hide the anger he felt with both Kenyon and Laporta. As he put it in his autobiography, *My Side*: 'I was angry all right. I didn't like the news, and how I'd found out about it, some time after the rest of the world, was humiliating.'

In his account of the saga Beckham makes some allowances for the fact that as a publicly quoted company, Manchester United had been under pressure to release its statement about its contacts with FC Barcelona, particularly once they had begun to leak in the press. That Stephens was not forewarned of the statement may have been the result of the absence on holiday at the time of Patrick Harverson, Manchester United's affable communications director with whom Beckham's agent had always maintained cordial relations.

In fact, by then directors at Manchester United had reconciled themselves to the idea that Beckham's time at the club was over and were more than happy to use Laporta's presidential ambitions to set a benchmark for negotiations with Real Madrid. Manchester United's senior executives were only too aware of the long history of bitter rivalry between Barca and Real Madrid, not least when it came to capturing star players. They knew too how both Spanish clubs had entered the twenty-first century envious of Manchester United's penetration of the US and Asian markets. And yet despite his global projection and the popularity Beckham still enjoyed among Manchester United fans, the club's directors thought they could justify selling Beckham in business terms. From Manchester United's point of view Beckham that summer arguably represented a significant risk. His market value was depreciating because, under the European law which governs the movement of footballers between clubs, players can leave without a fee when their contracts expire. Beckham's contract with Manchester United was due to expire in 2005 by which time his value to the club would have fallen from £30m to zero. Then there was the Ferguson issue. With the Scotsman's contract as manager renewed, Beckham was facing the prospect of becoming an increasingly frustrated player at Old Trafford. By contrast Florentino Perez saw things differently. He believed that Beckham would help Real Madrid penetrate new markets, namely in Asia. He also had no doubt that Real Madrid was big enough to cope with his celebrity status, while exploiting to the full his potential as a player. Attitude had always mattered at Real Madrid, and Perez saw in Beckham the kind of determination on the field that would excite fans and galvanize a team of foreign superstars and home-grown talent into a formidable team that would inspire fear in Spain and abroad.

Rumours had circulated in April that Real Madrid might be interested in Beckham, but Florentino Perez said at the time, 'Never, never, never' to such a notion. The Spanish club had also issued an unprecedented statement saying it had 'no intention' of negotiating such a deal. Later Perez would insist that both statements were true at the time. Although as he told my colleagues at the *Financial Times*, David Owen and Thilo Schäfer, 'In football, as in life or politics, you should never say never.' Curiously the phrase echoed one made by Beckham himself on 22 April 2003, a day before Manchester United played Real Madrid in the second leg of the quarter-finals of the Champions League.

Beckham was by then already registering in the future transfer plans of Florentino Perez, the Real president. Jorge Valdano, the club's sporting director, had hinted as much on 26 March when he publicly declared: 'Beckham looks like the next big project for us.' Perez was impressed by Beckham's popularity in Asia, a market where Real Madrid, like FC Barcelona, still lagged well behind Manchester United. He also admired Beckham as a player although he was prepared to wait for the moment where he could negotiate from strength and drive a hard bargain. He believed that that moment could not be far off, mainly because of what he preceived as the deteriorating relationship between Beckham and Ferguson. As Valdano put it to me, 'Beckham comes into our plans about three months before the end of the 2002–03 season. [That] was when we began to realize that Manchester United was in a selling position because of the stories that were circulating in the British press . . . but it was only when Manchester United made clear to us that it wanted to sell, that we decided seriously to negotiate.' According to Valdano, it was during conversations held between Perez and Kenyon of Manchester United at the G-14 meeting (the group of Europe's fourteen most powerful clubs) at the end of April 2003, that the Real Madrid president made clear his interest in negotiating the transfer of Beckham if and when the player was formally put on the market.

When Manchester United issued its statement confirming it had been in talks with Laporta, Perez formally threw his hat into the ring just as Kenyon had expected him to do. It took only one call from the Perez camp to the offices of the Manchester United boss to realize what a fundamentally different situation Beckham was now in compared to earlier in the spring. In the intervening months the relations between Beckham and Ferguson had deteriorated. The tension between the two men surfaced with a vengeance thanks to the huge media coverage given to the cut Beckham ostentatiously displayed after having a boot kicked at him by an irate Ferguson. Then came Ferguson's decision to leave Beckham on the substitutes' bench for the second leg of the Champions League quarter-final against Real Madrid. After that Beckham tried to placate the Manchester United fans by insisting that he wanted to stay at the club but the damage to his sense of self-esteem and worth within the club proved irreparable.

Manchester United directors themselves believed that the breakdown of trust and respect between the player and Ferguson had reached such a point that to have Beckham staying at the club could potentially provoke more trouble than he was worth. Beckham's decision to continue to invest time in personal marketing exercises arranged by his agent, outside his club's control, only added to Ferguson's deeply held conviction that his one-time protégé had let his stardom get in the way of his football. But as Beckham himself realized by the time of his return from California, it was not just the relationship with his manager, which had been tense all season, that was the issue. Now for the first time since he had joined Manchester United as a young teenager, Beckham realized that his relationship with his club was slipping away. When Perez contacted Kenyon after the Manchester United/ Laporta statement, he was left with no doubt that the club was prepared to let him go; moreover it had no objection to Real Madrid pursuing a deal by talking directly to the player and his agent.

As Manolo Redondo, Perez's right-hand man at Real Madrid, put it to me: 'We had developed good relations with Manchester United at senior level . . . We had an agreement that one club would not try and poach the other's player unless he was up for sale . . . It was now clear to us that Manchester United wanted to sell Beckham, so we moved in.'

Secret negotiations on Beckham's transfer to Real Madrid subsequently took place in Sardinia between Manchester United executives and José Angel Sanchez, the club's head of marketing. Sanchez was a fluent English speaker who was used by Perez not just as a translator but as an informal negotiator throughout the Beckham transfer saga. However, he was forced to adopt a low profile so as not to fuel resentments among those members of Perez's staff who prided themselves in their knowledge of football as a sport. When the meeting was leaked to the *Sun*, Real Madrid's Jorge Valdano issued a statement admitting that Real Madrid and Manchester United officials had met on the island, but only to discuss marketing strategies of mutual interests! 'Beckham is not a subject that falls in the remit of those responsible for marketing,' Valdano said.

The full details of the tortuous, diversionary and occasionally Machiavellian steps that led to Beckham's transfer to Real Madrid, the extent to which players such as Ronaldinho and Rustu may have been used as part of the negotiations or as simple decoys, and the exact form and value of payments that changed hands, may take years to emerge. But it is clear that the story is rather more complex than the fairy godmother role assigned to Florentino Perez by the player himself in his latest autobiography.

Beckham relates how it was on 15 June 2003, in the midst of a family barbecue at his house in Sawbridgeworth, that he rang first Kenyon and then, for the first time, Perez. It became clear to Beckham that he had reached the end of the road with Manchester United, and that Perez wanted him. According to the player's own account, Beckham played by the book in insisting that until he had settled the terms of his buy-out from Manchester United with Kenyon, he could not express a preference in public for going to Real Madrid. Perez, speaking through an interpreter, replied that if Beckham did come to Madrid he would never regret it. 'We don't want you here for the publicity or to sell shirts,' Beckham reported Perez as saying. 'I think you are one of the best players in the world and we believe you can make our team a better team.'

The conversation took place on a Sunday, a day in Spain, as in much of the Latin world, for Mass and for football. Later that evening Real Madrid, watched by its coach Vicente Del Bosque, would beat their old city rivals Atlético 4–0 away in the Vicente Calderón stadium, taking them within one game, the following Sunday, of the league championship. Del Bosque, a former Real player who had trained the club's youth team, would be replaced within days by Carlos Quieroz, Manchester United's assistant manager. In Barcelona that same Sunday the membership of FC Barcelona was turning up in record numbers to cast their votes in the presidential campaign. Latest opinion polls predicted that Laporta, still holding out the possibility of securing Beckham, would edge ahead of his main rival, Luis Bassat. That night the results showed that Laporta had won with 52 per cent of the votes, the biggest election victory in the history of FC Barcelona. With the evidence of hindsight, one can only speculate what might have been the final vote had Beckham's barbecue exchanges and the negotiations leading up to it been leaked to the media.

However, the parties involved in them apparently saw no advantage in being drawn even more than they had been already into the politics of Catalonia, even though Beckham had made his mind up that in the choice between FC Barcelona or Real Madrid there was no contest. Days before the FC Barcelona election, Laporta's opponents sought the advice of Steve Archibald, the retired Scottish international who had retained business and consultancy interests in Catalonia since playing for Barça during the 1980s. Archibald informed Bassat that Beckham was on his way to Madrid, and there was no hope of him coming to Barcelona. Bassat rang Florentino Perez and asked that he make an announcement making this clear. Perez refused.

As a result Bassat was left floundering as Laporta pushed ahead. Laporta campaigned on a promise to honour the mystique surrounding Barça – its history of political struggle against the Franco regime, its deep-rooted and loyal local following, and the sympathy it generated beyond Catalonia both in Spain and around the world. But the trump card he played to win the election was Beckham. At times he seemed to have convinced himself that he would get him.

Yet the reality at Barça was that whoever emerged victorious as its new president would have his room to manoeuvre limited by the disastrous legacy resulting from years of poor administration. Whatever claims were being made by Laporta about Beckham coming to FC Barcelona were undermined by the club's balance sheet which was bleeding to death due to a combination of administrative and sporting failure. The club was running an estimated loss of 60 million euros a year, with its debt, built up over years of lavish spending on under-performing footballers like Overmars and Kluivert, estimated at 200 million euros. The club's failure to win a Champions League place in the coming season, and the way it was struggling at the time in the Spanish league to qualify even for the less prestigious UEFA Cup after one of the worst seasons in its 104-year history, contrasted with Real Madrid's continuing achievements at national and league level under Florentino Perez. It meant that Barça could look forward only to devalued revenues from TV and merchandising deals in the short term, with limited spare cash to build up the team.

By contrast, Real Madrid had undergone one of the most extraordinary transformations of any football club in history since Florentino Perez had been elected as president in 2000. In terms of silverware alone, Real Madrid's success on the field was already unrivalled anywhere in the world. But Perez, a leading European construction magnate who had gained a reputation as one of modern Spain's most successful businessmen, set the precedent, emerging as one of the foremost star-catchers in the history of sport.

On one of his first visits to the Bernabéu as a young boy during the 1950s, Perez had experienced the extraordinary international projection Real Madrid had built for itself during that decade with its cup-winning line-up – a mixture of international stars and home-grown talent and led by the great Argentine Alfredo Di Stefano. It was in 1953, fifty years before Beckham came to Spain, that Di Stefano signed his memorable first contract with Real Madrid after FC Barcelona had failed in its attempt to secure him. That era had not only carved out a huge reputation for Real Madrid in the football history books. It had helped put the isolated and ostracized post-war Spain of General Franco on the international map. At the start of a new millennium, Perez had a vision that adapted the lessons of the past and tried to give them a new relevance in the context of a world without frontiers. He had promised and delivered on an electoral pledge to pinch the Portuguese international Figo from FC Barcelona. He had then brought to Madrid the Frenchman Zinedine Zidane and the Brazilian Ronaldo, the best players of the last two World Cups. Together with Raul, the young striker regarded by Real fans as the best Spanish footballer, and the Brazilian Roberto Carlos, one of the most impressive and versatile full-backs to be found anywhere, Perez had put together the matrix of a truly global team with the potential for limitless football success and the development of a massive international following with the pot of gold that that entailed in marketing and sponsorship terms. As Perez was to boast, when interviewed by the *Financial Times*, after his

Beckham deal, one of the more eye-popping aspects of his stewardship, given the broader financial problems affecting the football industry, was his apparent ability to load up with stars while simultaneously presiding over a marked improvement in the club's finances. His forecast in July 2003 was that the following season Real Madrid would make a surplus of 25 to 30 million euros based on costs of 215 million and revenues of 240 million euros. When he won the presidency, Real Madrid was losing about 50 million euros, on a turnover of 120 million.

Perez had a high regard for Beckham both as a footballer and a business proposition. Indeed he considered both elements inseparable from each other – a view that had informed his purchase of Real's other superstars. One of his foremost advisers on player quality, the Argentine-born Jorge Valdano, had singled out Beckham as probably the only English player who could genuinely lay claim to being of world-class quality, capable of competing with the best that the rest of Europe and South America could throw onto the field. Valdano had played alongside Maradona in the Argentine team that famously dispatched England in the World Cup in Mexico in 1986. Ten years later, during Euro '96, he had shared his low opinion of the mediocrity of English football during a quiet supper he and I had with Santiago Segurola of *El País*, in a dingy pasta den off London's Edgware Road. Valdano was between jobs at the time, working part-time as a radio commentator. 'These English players, they play with the imagination of factory workers,' Valdano told me. It was the ebbing tide of the Gascoigne era, and Beckham's star had yet to enter the constellation of international football.

Valdano subsequently watched Beckham grow as a player during Manchester United's European performances and England's World Cup games. A prolific writer and arguably one of the most literate football players ever, the university-educated Valdano came to describe Beckham thus in a book published before his transfer to Madrid:

He is a central midfielder exiled to the wing. A player with vision, competitive courage and a striker of the ball so clean that the fans, following the ball's trajectory, can read on it the name of the manufacturers. Beckham's defining characteristic is that he hits the ball like no one else, filling the ball with privileged information.

Off the field at the highest level of Real Madrid, meanwhile, there had grown, under the presidency of Florentino Perez, a keen interest in finding a formula that would help the club increase its presence in areas of the world where in football marketing terms the Manchester United brand had taken a commanding position. Surveys compiled by Real's head of marketing José Angel Sanchez confirmed the extent to which the club lagged behind Manchester United among non-Latino North Americans and in Japan, China and south-east Asia. Behind the Perez business strategy was a perception – made manifest during the World Cup in Asia and Korea in 2000 – of the extent to which football had become the genuine people's game of the modern age, crossing national boundaries, overturning traditional regional hegemonies, and turning into a universal entertainment business.

A new promiscuity had entered the business of football, with fans – thanks to the instant access provided by TV –

following individual players as they moved from club to club. As the writer Simon Kuper has pointed out, the death throes of the one-club local fan had been accelerated by the Beckham phenomenon. Kuper has described Beckham's global iconic status thus:

Beckham's speech – inarticulate, clichéd, and in a high-pitched monotone – alienated many English people, who could locate him precisely on the national class ladder. (He is Essex man, a sub-section of the southern lower-middle-class.) However these verbal nuances escaped foreigners. Like Marilyn Monroe or Charlie Chaplin, Beckham had a visual appeal that transcended language barriers.

Soon after Beckham had been secured by Real Madrid, I flew with a group of English state-school kids from Heathrow to Madrid's Barajas airport. As we taxied before take-off, our plane was already alive with adolescent chatter and giggles. It was hard to make out what excited the kids most – the sight of Concorde alongside us, as delicate and purposeful as a mosquito, preparing itself for its last flight, or the days ahead, where they were down for a week of football training and sightseeing care of Real Madrid. If the retirement of the supersonic jet was where humanity had stepped back from the future, Real Madrid was taking a big jump forward in the business of football, where the only limit appeared to be that which money could not buy. At that moment, for those kids, the thoughts of Concorde and Real Madrid seemed merged as one, both adulated for the power and wealth they represented, the sheer blitz of media coverage they had generated, the status symbols they had become.

When the FIFA-sponsored training programme had first
been discussed the year before, parents at a north London
school had been given the choice of the kids visiting one of
the following clubs: FC Barcelona, Lazio of Rome, Boca
Juniors of Buenos Aires, or Real Madrid. They'd voted
unanimously to go to Madrid. Why such an assertive vote? I
asked their PE teacher Gary Denstone, as we flew over
Southampton and down towards the Bay of Biscay. 'It's to
do with Real Madrid's status as a club that has won more
European Cups that anyone else, it's from watching them
play in the Champions League on TV, it's to do with their
star players. For them Real Madrid equates with success,' he
told me. While the English club allegiances of these north
Londoners were shared among Arsenal, Manchester United
and Liverpool, they saw no contradiction in following Real
Madrid too. 'They are really into developing their skills and
feel motivated by the Real Madrid stars,' said Denstone.

Of course neither parents nor kids, nor Denstone for
that matter, could have predicted twelve months earlier that
Beckham would also be in Madrid, but now that he was there
the whole trip had become even more special. Having Becks
there, as Gary put it, was a Real bonus. It had always been a
once in a lifetime tour. With Beckham joining Real Madrid
the kids had entered Neverland. These English subjects
were no hooligans on their way to the Costa, but universal
explorers on their way to check out the galaxy. In that hot
European summer of 2003 – when British gardens turned to
desert and France's elderly died when abandoned by their
sons and daughters – Beckham was twenty-eight years old
with at least three years left in him to excel in top-flight
international football at its most intense. While he was not

born with the natural talent of say a Maradona, he had improved his skills through practice and sheer hard work. He believed that only with Real Madrid could he match – and even exceed – the success he had enjoyed at Manchester United. While he had made more millions off the pitch than on it, Beckham claimed that his two priorities at that stage in his life were football and his family. Once the extended honeymoon with Manchester United was over, it became clear that the offer of joining the star-studded global tapestry that was Real Madrid while serving as England's captain was a hugely attractive proposition. As Real Madrid's marketing director José Angel Sanchez later recalled: 'David struck us as someone for whom football was more important than anything else and we saw that what he wanted was to play in a team with several of the best players in the world. We offered him a unique incentive, more important than money, and he saw that to go anywhere else but Real Madrid after Manchester United would have been a setback for his career.'

It was his telephone conversation with Perez, which Sanchez helped interpret, which convinced Beckham that Real Madrid really wanted him as a player, not simply as a vehicle for selling more shirts. In the negotiations that followed Real Madrid paid rather less for Beckham than Ferguson had wanted, and secured 50 per cent of the player's personal sponsorship deals. But Beckham had had enough of being treated like an ordinary squad player in his last months under Ferguson, and was convinced that Real Madrid would help underline his credentials as a world-class player – while doing no harm to his celebrity status. Beckham had a much greater belief in himself as a celebrity and as a player than Ferguson had shown in him.

Such self-confidence was not shared by Beckham's wife Victoria whose own career as a pop singer and occasional model had struggled to keep afloat on its own terms since the break-up of the Spice Girls. To the extent that 'Posh' believed that her career had any future in the summer of 2003, it must be in London and New York, and the fashion houses of Milan, not Madrid. From a personal perspective, both Italy and Spain brought back some bad memories. The Beckhams had spent a fraught attempted patch-up holiday in a hotel near Lake Como when she was pregnant with Brooklyn and they were escaping from mischievous tabloid gossip about his past relationships with other women. It was a harrowing time that left Victoria with little wish ever to go back to Italy for family reasons. As she put it in her autobiography *Learning to Fly*: 'So now all you football fans that think I want David to move to Milan, with its Gucci and its Prada, you know the truth. As much as that part of Italy is a beautiful place, with its mountains and scenery and everything, I could never live there, because I could never go back to Lake Como again.'

When her husband signed for Real Madrid, Posh already carried similarly mixed memories of Spain. She remembered happy beachside holidays with her family as a young girl like millions of other tourists and a wild time she later spent dancing and singing in Mallorca's Magaluf on a girls' night out with Sarah Bosnich, whose marriage to the Chelsea goalkeeper Mark was then on the rocks. There was also the time soon after Como when she and David found that their conciliatory dinner at Puerto Banus's exclusive Marbella Club had been caught on camera. The subsequently published photographs displayed them as lustful lovers, tongues entwined. Victoria later recounted how embarrassed her brother was when he saw the scene splashed across the tabloids.

She had grown used to publicity and openly courted it in her time with the Spice Girls, but Barcelona was one major city where all five of them suffered a major PR reverse which Catalans would not easily forget. They were booed off the stage after they had issued instructions that no pictures could be taken of them during their performance. A city that had historically valued the eccentricity of artists as much as the success of its football team felt insulted. 'After Barcelona, we were really quite scared,' Victoria later recalled. How different from the experience of Spain's literary hero Don Quixote for whom Barcelona was the 'seat of courtesy, the haven of strangers, the refuge of the distressed, the mother of the valiant, the champion of the wronged, the abode of true friendship, unique both in beauty and situation'.

I have pointed out in an earlier book, *Spain: A Literary Companion*, that Spain was never part of the European Grand Tour that in the days before mass travel took Englishmen and women to places like Italy and Greece. Travel and accommodation were too uncomfortable, the food too unplatable, the threat of bandits too real to attract the kind of visitor who from the seventeenth century onwards went in search of nothing more than his own peers in a novel, mildly exotic setting. Spain attracted a different kind of traveller – mad knights, Protestant spies, pilgrims, Bible pedlars, eccentric aristocrats, philosophers, poets, soldiers. To all of them Spain proved a discovery, a strange idiosyncratic land, not easily understood.

The pros and cons of moving to Spain in the twenty-first

century were discussed by the Beckhams late into the night of 15 July 2003. According to David's own account, their minds were made up by two o'clock the next morning. Beckham was so enthusiastic about the prospect of playing for Real Madrid that it was easy for him to look forward to living in Madrid with some excitement too. By contrast Victoria had nothing drawing her to the Spanish capital but her husband.

Two days later, young Japanese female pilgrims who for months had been worshipping at a three-metre-high chocolate shrine of David Beckham in Tokyo's fashionable Shibuya district got to see the real thing. David accompanied by Victoria arrived at Narita airport at the start of a promotional tour that allowed her to bask in the glow of their shared celebrity status. Beckham had boarded his flight in Manchester but was already effectively a Real Madrid player. Later that summer he returned to Asia with his new club on a tour that left some of his new team mates exhausted but confirmed that Beckham, an integral part of Florentino Perez's business strategy, had a lot to prove, not least on Spanish soil.

To many Catalans the fact that Beckham had seemed to be FC Barcelona's, only to be in the end 'robbed' by Real Madrid, had a certain historic inevitability about it. They could remember how the great Di Stefano had slipped through their fingers in the early 1950s. More recently they had lost Luis Figo, bought by Perez as part of his presidential campaign. When Beckham had rejected Laporta's approaches and signed his contract with Real Madrid, the long-serving president of Catalonia's regional government Jordi Pujol rang Rosell and begged him to salvage what was left of Barça's pride: 'Sandro, for the sake of every Catalan's morale, you've got to get Ronaldinho now.' By then Manchester United's attempts to get the Brazilian were in crisis. The player's agent and manager Roberto Assis would later claim that Manchester United's Kenyon lost his trust when he offered a price, only subsequently to reduce it after the Beckham deal with Real Madrid had been signed. Kenyon for his part had all along suspected Roberto Assis's motives in dealing with Manchester United, believing, as his communications director Paddy Harverson put it to me, that, 'Assis was stringing us along', using the English club to secure a deal with Barça – arguably a better fit for Ronaldinho than United.

Despite its financial woes and failure to win a place in the Champions League, the Catalan club had in the past raised the profile of some of Brazil's best players led by Romario, Rivaldo and Ronaldo. As a city Barcelona was a place that suited Latin Americans. Finally FC Barcelona had a much less star-studded team than Real Madrid but one which potentially allowed Ronaldinho to flourish as a saviour.

On 17 July, the day after Beckham decided to accept Real Madrid's offer, Ronaldinho took up FC Barcelona's. Only Manchester United lost both players. The politics of Spain had prevailed.

3. White Dreams

Gerardo Perez – no relation to Florentino – was born in 1959, the year Di Stefano's legendary Real Madrid side won the fourth of five consecutive European Cups. He was seven years old when, in 1966, the club next became European champions. Two years later Real Madrid reached the semifinal, only to lose to Manchester United – a defeat *Madridistas* blamed on an own goal by Zoco, a defensive faux pas, a mere blip in its unrivalled supremacy. The legend persisted: Real Madrid was destined to be the greatest football club of the twentieth century.

We met in November 2003, three months into Beckham's first season in Spain, in the cafeteria of the shopping mall adjacent to the Bernabéu stadium, where some of the more dedicated aficionados gathered before matches. When this stadium was built in the late 1940s, it was on the outskirts of the city. Madrid had since grown up around it with its apartment blocks and office towers. Gerardo, at the age of forty-four, was a physical education teacher and president of one of the club's main supporters' groups, the *Gran Familia*. The name lent itself more than anything else, like the stadium named in his honour, to the enduring memory of Real Madrid's longest-serving president Santiago Bernabéu – father figure, benevolent dictator, visionary, who for better or worse stamped his personality on the club's collective identity.

'Real Madrid hadn't won the league for years, it didn't

have a proper stadium, it didn't have decent players . . . then Bernabéu came along and said let's build a stadium, let's invest in players, let's win titles. Thanks to him the club became great,' Gerardo recalled. He did so with a huge dose of nostalgia for a time when the club – its star players included – seemed more intimate and accessible to ordinary people like himself.

'I went to school with the Salesian brothers not far from the Bernabéu. At break time we'd jump the school gates and run down the street to get the autograph of any player we wanted. They all knew us by our first names. I was still just a small boy then. Gento asked me to go the local pharmacy and pick up some medicine he had ordered. I did that on several occasions. One day, out of curiosity to see what medicine the great Gento was taking, I unwrapped the neat package the pharmacist always gave me. Inside was a packet of condoms . . .'

In contrast to the myth of the Great Father was the reality of the wayward offspring, as human as Spain itself. Within three years of Bernabéu's death in 1978, the first officially sponsored supporter's group Gerardo had helped form, the *Peña Las Banderas*, found itself infiltrated and effectively taken over by more radical and violent group of fans bent on imitating the hooligan culture of England and Italy. They came to be known as the *Ultra Surs*.

'One day I was with a group of friends, when these guys came in and ran their hands through the bar, breaking all the bottles. Then they went outside and started jumping on the roofs of the cars . . . Later they began travelling with the team, looking out for a fight with whoever supported the opposing team,' Gerardo told me.

It wasn't that Spaniards had suddenly turned violent, but that football had become a focus for those of a violent disposition. Some of these initially fitted the stereotype of the uneducated dispossessed working-class thug, taking advantage of the new civil liberties after Franco's death. But from their inception the *Ultra Surs* included the student sons of well-off Madrid families, a baby-boom generation bent on having a wild time. Twenty years on, the *Ultra Surs* were still sustained as an organization thanks to the help of lawyers and IT experts who helped them dodge prosecution and set up websites, but they were smaller and less active, their presence inside the Bernabéu controlled rather than suppressed by a club that now claimed to extend its popularity across class, race, and nations.

Gerardo found the business strategy driving such global ambition an unsetting one. Supporters' groups like his, along with the shackled survivors among the *Ultra Surs*, were there to provide the atmosphere. But they knew that in common with supporters of, say, Manchester United, they were, as Simon Freeman has put it in *Own Goal*, his book on English football, only the 'tip of the consumer iceberg'. They felt expendable, an endangered species. And yet their loyalty remained undiminished – and that had something to do with the players they remembered.

Di Stefano, Gento, Juanito, Butragueño, Sanchis, Raúl . . . these were among the names that Gerardo felt had defined the archetypal Real Madrid player, a mixture of skill and determination and the will and ability to triumph. I wanted to know Gerardo's thoughts on Beckham. He had not singled out a foreign player for praise, other than Di Stefano, and he ended up a naturalized Spaniard, choosing to see out his retirement in Spain rather than in his native Argentina. There was no hiding the enthusiasm this Spaniard Gerardo felt for the boy from Chingford.

'Tell you the truth, before Beckham came here we knew he was good from the dead ball, but I thought he was a bit of a softy, and not all that skilful – couldn't dribble round a chair you put in front of him. But since he's come here, he's been really tough, a real fighter for the ball. He's proved himself a brilliant passer. OK, he's still not a great dribbler but he knows how get round an opponent. In football terms we've got more than our money's worth. Maybe if Bernabéu was alive he might have tried to get him to take his earring off and cut his hair. But then Spain is not what it was when Bernabéu was alive. These things don't trouble people any more.'

What troubled people outside Madrid was the enduring arrogance of a club that had the audacity to believe that it was marked out for special status by the hand of God, one that had some of the best players simply because it had bought them, like mercenaries. 'There are players who are born to play for Real Madrid,' Florentino Perez had grown accustomed to saying in justification of the players he bought. A mixture of fear and loathing accompanied the team on its travels round Spain. And yet if Real Madrid was Spain's most hated club, it was also its most loved. To that extent few institutions still contributed as much to the perpetuation of a country's divisions – the two Spains. During the season Beckham came to Spain, market research carried out for the club suggested that it had the support of half of Spanish football fans. The boos, whistles and occasional outbreaks of physical aggression that greeted the men in white during away games in stadiums packed with fans loyal to their local club belied the network of supporters' associations or *peñas* Real Madrid boasted across the country. In some of the more politicized regions of Spain, where Real Madrid was seen as the central authority's Trojan horse, just as in the days of Franco, the *peñas* survived like besieged outposts of an empire, defiant in the face of local hostility – Spanish football's civil guards.

On the evening before Real Madrid played away in the autonomous region of Navarre against the Pamplona club Osasuna, I drove to the nearby small town of Peralta where I had been told one such *peña* had its unofficial headquarters in a small bar. I drove through a patchwork of fields irrigated by the river Ebro, crossing a stone bridge to where Peralta had settled and grown behind a medieval fortress. To my initial surprise the bar, far from tucked away in an obscure backstreet, was on the main square, along with the church and the mayor's office – and it was called the Bar Madrid.

It served as a reminder of the complexity of local politics. Navarre was considered by Basques as the cradle of their stateless nation dating back before Roman times. Radical separatist supporters of ETA believed that the old kingdom should be part of an independent Basque state along with the Spanish and French frontier districts that straddle the Pyrenees. And yet sympathy for such a project was focused in the mountainous northern area of Navarre. Peralta lay in the southern lowlands, a region that has traditionally enjoyed good communications with the rest of Spain, including Madrid. Throw into the political and cultural melting pot the presence throughout Navarre of a strong strand of staunchly traditional Catholicism which sided with Franco during the Spanish Civil War, and was subsequently rewarded with special privileges, and it was easier to understand why the Bar Madrid existed. It saw no reason to hide its posters of Real Madrid teams and photographs of players who had visited the area, or make excuses for the fact that the town's local football club played also in white.

A collective stare faced me as I walked in, only to break into a warm welcome when I spoke in a Castilian accent, nonetheless serving as a reminder that Spain has its divisions, even in Peralta. Some locals seemed to have suspected I was a supporter of ETA.

The *peña* secretary José Manuel Jiménez was working behind a bar his grandfather established after the Civil War. Framed behind him was a photograph of Raul, famously silencing Barcelona's Nou Camp stadium after scoring a goal. 'My father was sixteen during the war. He served as a bugler with one of Franco's generals. He didn't have to fire a shot,' José Manuel told me.

I asked him whether loyalty to Real Madrid had run through three generations. 'My father only started supporting Real Madrid after the war – before that he was an Athletic Bilbao fan . . . It wasn't politics – well, not entirely – you see there came a point when Real Madrid began to win everything and Bilbao didn't any more.'

For José Manuel, born in 1949, there was no doubt how Real Madrid had become the undisputed giants of his culture. Thanks to the Di Stefano era, football had become as popular with the Naverrese as running bulls and boxing. There was little else worth watching in Spain then. 'How can I forget Di Stefano – picking up the ball from in front of his own goal, and running with it to the other end before scoring . . . his enthusiasm was contagious . . .'

José Manuel was in full flow when the local member of Herri Batasuna, ETA's political wing, who had been responsible for my earlier mistaken identity, appeared at the entrance to the bar, shouted 'Real Madrid sons of bitches' and ran off again – a token reminder of the very contemporary politics of resistance.

The more radical of Osasuna's fans – vociferous and potentially violent – were supporters of a Basque homeland. During the Pamplona bullfighting festival – immortalized by Ernest Hemingway – they ran the bulls and mocked the conservative families who occupied the best seats in the bullring, those in shadow. The radicals took their seats in the blazing sun of the bullring just as they occupied the most explosive stands at the Osasuna stadium.

Like a bullfighter who has lost his nerve, José Manuel confessed to being none too keen to brave it at the stadium when Real Madrid played there the following day. 'If some of us go, it will be without scarves or banners so no one can identify us, and we'll keep quiet. The stadium's full of separatists who think we're fascists, and Pamplona is more Basque than Peralta – that's why we haven't got a *peña* there.'

The next day several members of the *Peña Peralta* did go to Pamplona, initially to a hotel reception offered in honour of the club president Florentino Perez. Among the party faithful, Florentino Perez was relaxed. While he had a reputation of getting on with most people, this was very much the general with his troops, the senior executive with his employees, pumping flesh, sharing jokes, boosting morale. Perez had not got where he had got to in the world of business and in the world of Real Madrid without carefully cultivating his public persona. Occasions like this were designed to portray him not as a cold calculating businessman but as a genuine *Madridista* who loved football with a passion and respected the fans. Here on the Navarre front no one was made to feel expendable, although he carefully avoided giving away any details about his plans for the future.

When a fan approached him and asked when Real Madrid was going to buy a decent defender, Perez deftly ignored it, turned to his wider audience and smiled: 'You see the kind of questions I'm asked? I guess we're all getting spoilt . . . but let's not complain – we've had three consecutive wins after Seville.' Real Madrid had lost 1–4 away to Seville, their defence cut apart by Jose Antonio Reyes in one of his final matches before his move to Arsenal. The *galácticos'* first humiliation of the season had curiously coincided with an eclipse of the moon.

At the Pamplona reception the Real Madrid faithful were treated to an impressive selection of local *tapas*, red wine and photographs with *Florentino*, as everyone called the president. The fans included Raúl Martínez, who said that his business, when not following Real Madrid, was selling locally tinned red peppers, the sharp-nosed ones which were a speciality of the region. Of everything he had seen so far that season, Beckham had impressed him the most. 'Right from the first game he's shown total commitment. What's more, he claps the fans. We hadn't seen a Real Madrid player do that for a long time – that's noble stuff,' Martínez said raising his glass of wine.

That night, as the Real Madrid players emerged from their hotel rooms to make their way to the match, Beckham was surrounded by a group of hysterical teenagers, begging for his autograph, blowing him kisses, screaming '*Guapo, guapo, guapo*' as he boarded the team coach. It had been like this in almost every Spanish city visited during the season – the celebrity adulation before politics and football took over. Real Madrid supporters were neither seen nor heard at Pamplona's El Sadar stadium and Beckham along with his team mates were jeered for most of the game. At one point a young ballboy threw a missile at the Englishman while he was taking a corner. Beckham looked back and gestured like a teacher admonishing an unruly pupil. Such defiance was winning over the Real Madrid fans but here in enemy territory it only fuelled the general air of animosity. Osasuna held Real Madrid to a 1–1 draw which the home fans celebrated as a major victory.

The local team played with a passion and determination that most of the *galácticos* seemed unable to match. Beckham's own contribution to the game was undermined by the recurrence of an injury which left him limping towards the end. Nevertheless, of a game that Real Madrid traditionally lose, *Marca* had this to say: 'With Beckham, Madrid no longer lie down.'

It wasn't the first time an Englishman had had a taste of Navarrese bravado in battle. It brought to my mind an English officer who had fought in this region of Spain during the Carlist wars of the nineteenth century. 'Many would caper and dance Fandango on the tops of the breastworks with balls and shells flying on all sides . . . They would clap their buttocks in derision as the guns fired, waving their caps and black flags and shouting, "Down with the Queen! Carlos for ever!"' wrote the officer.

Outside the dressing rooms it was another world as Beckham engaged in complicit post-match chatter with a group of Spanish-based English tabloid sports journalists, each of whom owed his living to writing about matters other than the politics of Spain.

– David, congratulations on your OBE.
– Thank you.
– Any mention from your team mates . . .?
– Yeah, they've obviously got it mixed up and they've all been calling me Sir and err a few have been saying Your Highness and bowing to me so it's been quite funny. (Collective giggles)
– Now Victoria's got her new album coming out quite soon; have you heard any of it . . .?
– I've heard it all.
– What do you think?
– I love it.
– And what does Brooklyn think of it all?
– He loves it and one particular song he loves but err you have to wait . . . but err she's worked hard she deserves err a lot of credit for the way she works and sometimes she doesn't get that err but she deserves it . . .
– Do you think it could be Christmas number one?
– Err you never know . . . Let's wait and see. I'd like to think that it will be but as I said, you never know . . .

Posh never did get to number one that Christmas.

Very early one morning, before the sun had risen over the Spanish capital, I met a group of Real Madrid fans at Barajas airport before flying to Germany for the first leg of Real Madrid's Champions League tie with Bayern Munich. The trip had been organized by another of Real Madrid's big supporters' associations, the *Peña Cinco Estrellas* (Five Stars Group) – the name deliberately chosen as a reminder of how stardom was an integral part of the club's identity. In the era of the *galácticos* this *peña* had become increasingly active in getting Real Madrid fans to travel abroad in greater numbers than they had ever done before. There were over 3,000 of us flying to Germany in several planes, a larger quota of visiting supporters than was even allowed in many Spanish stadiums. On the plane I sat next to Raul, a young fan who with his unsmiling dark looks resembled his namesake on the Real Madrid team. He was unshaven, tanned and looked fit thanks to working on a building site. While he tried to follow the team wherever it went, he had become increasingly dis-illusioned with the atmosphere in the Bernabéu – anaesthe-tized *Ultra Surs*, conservative ticket holders and a growing number of VIPs and tourists. 'People turn up ten minutes before the game, light their cigars and sit there like turkeys – it's a joke. They only clap if the team wins. Do you call that support?' He also believed that there was a new emerging generation quite happy to watch the team on TV, much like any other reality celebrity show.

Among the oldest passengers was Manolo, an eighty-four-year-old pensioner who recalled going to the old Chamartín stadium in 1928. 'I remember jumping over the wall or asking the gate keeper to let me through – I'd watch the matches for free ... I remember watching the Reguero brothers, Quincozes, Zamora ... what a great defence we had, what great players we had,' Manolo remembered.

During the Civil War Manolo fought for the Republican side, was interned by the Franco forces and subsequently condemned to forced labour. Not until 1945, six years after the Civil War had ended, was he allowed to return to normal citizenship. 'The authorities never admitted the castle where I was imprisoned existed – it's as if we hadn't existed – but I have not forgotten,' he told me.

From his bald head to his large waist, Manolo had several Real Madrid scarves wrapped around him. He may have looked eccentric but he was sober as a judge. I asked him how was it possible that he had gone on supporting Real Madrid.

'My wife was a fan of Atlético de Madrid – she said that it, not Real Madrid, was the club of the poor. But after the Civil War Atlético had more military people running it than Real Madrid did and if there is one thing I've never liked it is the military – it spent too many years thinking it ruled the country.'

Many of those who had opposed Franco in the Civil War later chose exile. Manolo had reinvented himself as a taxi driver and a Real Madrid fan. It was true that military officers had for a while run Atlético de Madrid, but the club was never the great Spanish export that Real Madrid became under Franco, and continued to be after his death. To support Real Madrid meant survival and a sense of belonging. As far as Manolo was concerned, football provided the continuity that politics interrupted.

One day I rang up New York to arrange a meeting with a man who by appointment and self-definition straddled football and politics – Inocencio Arias, Spain's ambassador to the United Nations and a Real Madrid fanatic.

I had first got to know the Alicante-born 'Chencho' Arias, as he is better known, back in the late 1970s. He was a young diplomat and I a young foreign correspondent, based in Lisbon. We struck up a friendship regularly commuting to Madrid to keep abreast of the political and social developments of the post-Franco era, when not playing games with the Soviet journalists based in Portugal. The *Tass* and *Novosti* correspondents were on the payroll of the KGB keeping tabs on the manoeuvrings of the American embassy and the local communist party.

Apart from his bow ties, and love of good food and wine, the most extrovert and accessible diplomat I have ever had the privilege to know had long developed the one real passion of his life. I had yet to develop it. His was called football.

Chencho was not born with it, not did he carry it in his genes. He had discovered it as a student, a sudden conversion, the nature of which he described in an article he wrote for *El Mundo*, in a special edition celebrating Real Madrid's centenary year.

There was no thunder, nor was I on horseback, nor was I on the way to Damascus . . . I was converted, when I was younger than St Paul was when he saw the light, in a football field in the town of Alicante. It was the spring of 1960 or 1961. The local team Hercules was playing Real Madrid in the *Copa del Generalísimo* . . . the radiance, the flash of beauty, must have been of the same calibre as that which struck the saint. Real Madrid dazzled with their technique and class. They won 5–1 . . . I walked away, thoughtful and in a state of levitation, and from then onwards, while the passage of years may have made me more sceptical and mistrustful in so many things, I live not within but in an infinity of Sunday afternoons and European nights – and that I owe to Saint Alfredo and his companions . . .

Our careers took us into different time zones and it was nearly twenty years after Lisbon, in the mid 1990s, that Chencho and I met again, near Almería during a summer school on football and politics organized by Madrid University. He gave a lecture on Real Madrid during the Franco years, arguing that the club's success had been due to the greatness of its players and the vision of its president Bernabéu, and that the regime had learnt how to exploit this to its advantage. This was why Real Madrid was Franco's club, not because it had referees on its side, as well as ministers, as the club's opponents claimed.

In a book published in 2003 Chencho showed that his faith in the club remained untarnished. Entitled *Real Madrid's Three Myths*, it was a personal tribute to the brilliance of three players who had left an enduring stamp on the club's sense of self-worth – Di Stefano, Butragueño and Raúl. Part interview, part personal odyssey, the book confirmed Chencho's total identity with the club, verging on an obsession. He told the story of how once during the 1980s, when he was under-secretary for foreign affairs, he smuggled a miniature TV into a banquet in the royal palace given by King Juan Carlos. That evening Real Madrid were playing Atlético de Madrid. Chencho could not bear to miss it, and watched the match with the TV hidden in a copy of the guest of honour's typewritten speech. He was still watching it when he was approached by one of the royal footmen, with a message from the king: 'His Majesty asks that you let him borrow the TV,' the footman said.

Chencho traced his discovery to his boss, the foreign minister Fernando Ordoñez who, sitting near the king, and knowing the monarch's love of sport, had raised the subject of football before pointing at his under-secretary and offering a live update of the Madrid derby. 'I think Ordoñez acted correctly, with very good diplomatic reflexes. Football can be a very useful subject to bring up in important meetings. What a pity that some people hate the game – what ignorance!' Chencho wrote.

I remembered this anecdote as I sat down with Chencho many years later to discuss Real Madrid and the world. He had stopped off in the Spanish capital on home leave, having flown in from the US via meetings in Brussels and Vienna. He had asked that we meet in a café off the Puerta del Sol. As every guide book on Spain will tell you, all roads lead to Madrid and kilometre zero can be found in the Puerta del Sol, known more by its square than any gateway, where Spaniards from every region gather, as do foreigners. Madrid regards itself as at once the least Spanish and the most Spanish town in the country – the least Spanish because it is the most modernized and international, and the most Spanish, perhaps because for four centuries it has imposed itself as the nation's capital, drawing in a mixed population from all regions of Spain and beyond. Of the Puerta del Sol the English travel writer H. V. Morton had once remarked: 'At first a confusion and then, when you have become familiar with the city, a fascination. It is a magnet. Somehow you always find yourself there; if you are lost, you go there and recover your bearings.'

The café was filled with *Madrileños* in no hurry to go anywhere and to discuss important matters of life. I began by asking Chencho how he had managed to combine his hectic life as a UN diplomat with keeping up with the passion of his life. 'Thanks to satellite TV I can see most games – it's only when there is a mid-week Champions League tie and I'm in the Security Council that I have a problem. But the day when there isn't a Council meeting I gather a dozen friends of mine together – journalists, local executives and ambassadors – and invite them over to watch the game at home.'

Ambassadors watching football? How could he explain that?

'It's Beckham, he's changed the course of Spanish history – we're on the map now in the US and in Asia. Thanks to him we Spaniards have achieved what we never achieved with Philip the Second. As long as Beckham is with Real Madrid, the sun won't set on the empire.'

I wondered whether he took a miniature TV to the Security Council. He told me that he didn't have to. Once during a meeting of the Council, Kofi Annan passed him a piece of paper. Chencho thought it might have something to do with the upcoming vote on Iraq. Instead the UN secretary-general had written a question: 'When are we going to see Real Madrid in Madrid?' A month later Annan was in Madrid for a donor's conference on Iraq and that evening joined Chencho in the presidential box of the Santiago Bernabéu.

'The match wasn't too good, but Kofi enjoyed the atmosphere. "Very impressive," he said leaning over at one point. During the interval we talked politics,' Chencho recalled.

So did he see Real Madrid opening frontiers, bringing peace to foreign lands?

He paused and sipped his coffee, his eyes drifting around

the crowded room. 'Let's not mythologize too much . . . Remember how two countries, Honduras and El Salvador, went to war because of football? But people know more about Spain thanks to its football, just as they know more about Africa because of its footballers. They warm to the evidence that foreigners who seemed to belong to another planet are capable of creating something beautiful.'

The history of Real Madrid has been punctuated with famous foreigners, and famous Spaniards who have shared trophies and generated the enthusiasm of supporters. The best among them inspired whole teams with their skill, application and intelligence. But only a few have possessed the necessary talent and personality to become real greats in the history of Real Madrid. What these players had in common with the myths of that other great club Manchester United was, to paraphrase the words of Jim White (for the Manchester United fan was referring to his own club), 'the strength of character and a mental resilience to sustain them through the critical core of their employment: being a Real Madrid player'.

In his book dedicated to Real Madrid's 'three myths', Chencho recalled how even in his busiest times as a government official based in Madrid during the 1980s he had tried to see every game in which Emilio Butragueño played: 'It was like following a famous matador – you had to hurry and see Butragueño for fear that an injury like a bull's goring might deprive you of relishing his art for ever.' He blamed mandatory diplomatic attendance at a reception given for the Queen of England – '*Oh, My God!*' he cried with typical Andalucian drama – for missing the game in which *El Buitre* scored Real Madrid's 3,500th goal.

To watch *El Buitre* was to experience his swerves and accelerations through defenders, his explosive speed inside the penalty box – an ability to be where you least expected him, and to create a goal out of nothing. But it was also to experience a whole new generation of *Madridistas*, warming to his magic and that of the other players with whom he forged the core of the team – Sanchis, Sanchez, Michel, Pardeza and Vasquez, part of the so-called *Quinta del Buitre* (see page 295) – in the honeymoon years of Spain's post-Franco democracy. 'It was on the football pitch that they came to represent society with their innovation even if in their private lives they were quite conservative – they weren't great party goers, nor did they take drugs,' Chencho recalled. 'They got to the heart of people because they were incredibly skilful but most of all because they had as their standard bearer a player with exceptional charisma called Butragueno.'

As we drank another coffee, I asked myself whether in the years I had worked as a foreign correspondent, I had ever come across a member of the British foreign office speaking so openly about football and politics or with such passion. The question drew a blank. By contrast, but for his trademark bow tie, Spain's ambassador to the United Nations that morning seemed indistinguishable from the other Spaniards, crouched over the match reports of *Marca* and *As*, submerged in caffeine and tobacco fumes, and the general lightness of living in a capital city well above sea-level.

Chencho had yet to have his fill of *El Buitre*. 'He was nice-looking, well-mannered, educated and kind – the kind of boy every Spanish mother wanted their daughter to marry . . . He played four and a half good years but he had something which few players in the world have – an ability to play with the ball in a very reduced area which electrified the fans. In my case, he'd make me cry.'

By way of illustration our coffee cups became goalposts and our respective spoons, players. 'You know what the son of a bitch would do? He'd play with the ball just by the goalpost, stop dead in his tracks. And I'd be saying to myself, how the hell is he going to get round the defender, when he's taken him from the inside, then scored – like a bullfighter killing the bull after drawing him in with his cape . . . it was incredible . . .'

After that it was difficult to imagine what else could possibly move Chencho as much. But I had read in his book that apart from the funeral of some Spanish Jesuit priests who had been murdered by a death squad in El Salvador, and the final scene of some movie he'd seen in New York, he could only recall really crying on a third occasion – the goal scored by Raúl in the 1998 World Club Championship in Japan. He had watched the goal on TV in another of those crowded, smoke-filled Madrid cafés where he had a tendency to find his true self. Clarence Seedorf had struck a long pass from midfield, from right to left. Raúl received the ball, controlled it perfectly with the left foot, beat one defender, then another, before pushing it to his right and striking it home.

'Proust's exquisite cake was cattle shit compared to what I relished in that moment – Real Madrid in all its glory,' recalled Chencho.

But there were other goals that he would deem worthy of mention as a 'piece of art' – like Raúl's goal against Valencia in the Champions League final of 2000 which secured Real Madrid's eighth European Cup win. After receiving a long pass from Savio well inside his own half, Raúl ran the length of the pitch before dribbling round the goalkeeper Cañizares – not just any goalkeeper but a Spanish international and among Europe's best – and stroking the ball into the net. Manchester United fans would no doubt prefer to forget the two goals inside three minutes Raúl scored against their team five weeks earlier at Old Trafford. (It was after another double strike in the 2003 quarter-final that Raúl earned the rare accolade from United boss Alex Ferguson as 'the best player in the world'.)

Raúl Gonzalez was born in Madrid in 1978, two years after David Beckham was born in Leytonstone. Having played as a junior with Atlético de Madrid, he moved to Real at the age of seventeen, just when Butragueño's individual star was fading, and FC Barcelona had superseded the *Quinta del Buitre* as the spectacle that Spanish football fans longed to see. It was Barça's 'dream team' of foreigners and home-grown talent, coached by Johan Cruyff, that had stirred people's imaginations in the early 1990s winning the European Cup and four consecutive league championships. During the second half of the decade Raúl contributed more than any other Real Madrid player individually to the club's resurgence. In June 2002 Raúl's record among the players attending the World Cup in Japan and Korea marked him out as a special case. Turning twenty-six years old, he had won three European Cups, two Spanish championships, and scored more goals than any other player in the Champions League and for the Spanish national side. A profile by Simon Kuper in the *Observer* asserted that at the highest level of the game there was no more proven match-winner than Raúl, who 'may confidently be expected to keep performing the way he is now, or better, for another five or six years'. Kuper had this to say about the dark-eyed Raúl:

If there is any love or loyalty behind those eyes it is only his inner circle of family and one or two friends who know about it. Otherwise he is humourless, pitiless, calculating, and ferociously single-minded. Think Al Pacino in *The Godfather.* The one who systematically annihilates his enemies as his child is being baptized. That's Raúl.

I asked Chencho what – apart from the success – had marked Raúl out not just as one of Real Madrid's greatest players, but one of the most loyally followed by the fans. 'He had balls, he played his heart out, and surprised people with his devil's trick. The fact that he was born in Madrid, in a working-class neighbourhood, helps too.' One of ours, in other words.

Alfredo Di Stefano, the third legend to whom Chencho had devoted his book, was born in Argentina but had long been mythologized as an inseparable part of Real Madrid's identity as a club. Chencho had dreamed as a young student during the Franco regime of becoming Di Stefano and play-ing in the Bernabéu. He settled instead for a short period as a Real Madrid director when he tried and failed to put some order into the club's chaotic financial affairs prior to the arrival of Florentino Perez. On Di Stefano's qualities as a player, Chencho liked to quote Matias Prats, the Spanish TV and radio commentator who helped turn Spanish football into a mass sport during the Franco years: 'An air of wonder invaded the stands whenever Di Stefano defended his own goal, and then seconds later went on the offensive, leading behind him a whole team. That way of playing transformed all imaginable systems.'

But Di Stefano contributed more than any other player to creating the myth of Real Madrid's invincibility after which players could neither be poor nor average – they simply had to be the best and winners too. As Chencho put it, 'Real Madrid loves the beauty of those who triumph.'

Between us we had consumed enough coffee to lift a few trophies and run several times round the Bernabéu. Sadly as two o'clock approached we each had to go to separate 'working' lunches. We were a few days away from Christmas, a date *Madrileños* consider less important than the festival of the Three Kings on 6 January. Real Madrid was halfway through its first season with Beckham. I had begun to suspect that to place Beckham among Chencho's pantheon of gods might be premature but I asked him where he stood all the same. We were back to where we started, at the United Nations of global football. 'We had more silverware than Manchester United. Now thanks to Beckham we're better known worldwide. Even Kofi Annan rings me up and asks – how is Beckham doing?'

When setting out to research the history of Real Madrid, I was struck by how few books had been written about the club in Spanish compared to the huge bibliography I had had to grapple with in Spanish and Catalan when looking at its rival FC Barcelona. It was not just a difference in quantity, but a striking contrast in depth. Much of what had been written about FC Barcelona focused not just on the club but the whole cultural and political context in which it had developed. By its own definition Barça was more than a club – it was the expression of Catalonia's national identity, distinct from the rest of Spain, and resistant to the centralized power exercised from Madrid. The fact that Catalanism was repressed while FC Barcelona was allowed to go on playing during the Franco years meant that in Catalonia football became a vehicle with which to evade censorship. Thus football in that part of Spain attracted the musings of journalists and writers, becoming transformed into a political statement, an exercise in democracy.

The empathy that Spanish intellectuals led by the Catalan Left felt for FC Barcelona was distinctly lacking when it came to Real Madrid. From the perspective of the anti-Francoists, the club all too often seemed to mirror the regime in its arrogant appropriation of what it meant to be Spanish. As for the unquestioning popular support the club generated by its triumphs, this turned football into the culture of evasion, the 'opium of the masses' – so its critics believed.

In the aftermath of Francoism it fell to Jorge Valdano, a former player and coach of Real Madrid – and during the presidency of Florentino Perez director of sport – to articulate a different intellectual perspective on the club, one that aimed to justify its claim to being the greatest in the world in a language that its enemies could understand and even sympathize with even if it was mistrusted by the more conservative *Madridistas*. It was perhaps just as well that Valdano was neither Spanish nor born in Madrid. He was able to come to the club pure, without prejudice.

Valdano was born in Las Parejas, a small town in the middle of the Argentine prairie known as the *pampas*. The year of his birth, 1955, was also when the first government of General Juan Perón, Argentina's populist leader, was overthrown in a military coup, one of several that made the country's politics increasingly violent and divisive. Valdano studied law for one year and became a professional footballer in turbulent times. He left Argentina for Spain towards the end of 1975, two months after Franco died, and in the midst of a breakdown of institutional order in his own country under the government of Perón's widow Isabelita, the outcome of which would be another coup, and the 'disappearance' of thousands of political dissidents. Valdano played for Alavés and then Zaragoza before joining Real Madrid in 1984. Three years later he retired as a player after being felled by hepatitis.

By then Valdano had played alongside Butragueño and, as a member of the Argentine national squad, Maradona. It was the talent of both men that influenced his appreciation of football as an art form. So did the thoughts of César Menotti, the Argentine coach who won the 1978 World Cup and who was at FC Barcelona when Valdano played for Zaragoza. Menotti's philosophical tract *Football Without Tricks* had sold well in post-Falklands Argentina during the early 1980s. In it he had contrasted his admiration for a free and creative style of football with the 'tyranny' of the defensive, destructive play favoured by authoritarian managers. Such tyranny, in Menotti's view, had its most brutal exponent in Javier Clemente, then manager of Athletic Bilbao, who would go on to become manager of Spain. Within days of his arrival in Spain Menotti engaged in a widely publicized verbal slanging match with Clemente, declaring that 'the day Spain [i.e. Clemente] decides to be a bullfighter rather than a bull on the pitch it will play better football.'

After playing at Real Madrid, Valdano spent five years

reporting on Spanish football as a radio and TV commen-
tator, as well as writing newspaper columns with a cultured,
philosophical style which earned him the nickname *El Filósofo*
(the philosopher). His first appointment as manager was at
Tenerife where he presided over an epic victory over Real
Madrid. It was 7 June 1992, the last weekend of that season's
Primera Liga, and Real Madrid were just one point ahead of
FC Barcelona, who were playing at home against Athletic
Bilbao. Less than four months earlier Valdano had reflected
on Real Madrid's vulnerability as a team at the time: 'Nowadays it's an insecure team that doesn't see the opposition as
a possibility but as a threat, and has therefore lost its most
important quality: its ability to inspire fear in its rival.' Many
years later the thought would once again become a reality in
the later stages of Beckham's first season with Real Madrid,
and would cost Valdano, among others, his job. But in
Tenerife in that summer of 1992, when Barcelona celebrated
the Olympics, and the Canary Islands the 500th anniversary
of Columbus's stop-over on his way to the Americas, Real
Madrid scored the first two goals only to end up losing the
game 2–3. In his pep talk before the match Valdano had told
the Tenerife players to take up the challenge of defeating a
team that had 'all the prestige of history on its side'. Tenerife's
victory later that evening secured Barça the championship
after they had beaten Athletic Bilbao. Some of the more
hard-nosed *Madridistas* would never forgive Valdano the
betrayal. Nevertheless the then president Ramón Mendoza
saw him as a potential saviour in the crisis of confidence that
had engulfed Real Madrid, offering him a job as coach.

In the memoirs he published before he died, Mendoza
writes that the long-serving president of the Argentine Foot-

ball Association Julio Grondona used to complain that Valdano talked too much about political and social issues and didn't spend enough time playing football. In his native Argentina Valdano was given another nickname – 'the radish', because he was red on the outside and white on the inside. Mendoza overcame his initial objection to Valdano – that he asked for too much money. He withdrew an offer, only to put it back on the table. Thanks to Mendoza, Valdano, the poet philosopher of Spanish football, returned to the 'White House' in the mid-1990s as coach. He promoted Raúl from the youth team and brought with him from Tenerife his fellow Argentine Fernando Redondo. They joined the brilliant Dane Michael Laudrup – transferred from FC Barcelona – and the Chilean international Ivan Zamorano in a team that also included Spanish defenders of the calibre of Manolo Sanchis and Fernando Hierro. It was a combination strong enough to challenge Cruyff's 'dream team' to which Valdano had handed the *La Liga* title when he was at Tenerife. Real Madrid beat Barça 5–0 in the Bernabéu, sweet revenge for the 0–5 they had suffered in an earlier encounter at the Nou Camp.

In Valdano's first season as coach Real Madrid won *La Liga* for the first time in four years. The following season he took Real Madrid into the quarter-finals of the Champions League where they lost on aggregate against Juventus. The club ended sixth in the league. Valdano was sacked in January 1996. 'I am leaving with a bitter aftertaste. It is a sad moment. But I leave honoured at having formed part of this club,' Valdano said at the time. There followed a further journalistic interlude leading up to his appointment by Florentino Perez, giving him overall responsibility for the team and the club's transfer policy.

Over the years Valdano and I had curiously lived in each other's company without always knowing it. The year he left for Spain I had helped organize a human rights campaign in England to expose the emergence of the same right-wing death squads from which he, as someone politically identified with the Left, had felt it necessary to escape.

Later we were drawn together by Diego Maradona, his idol and my biographical subject. Courtesy of a mutual friend Santiago Segurola of *El País*, Valdano agreed to meet me for lunch in an old Austrian restaurant called Edelweiss near the Spanish parliament. He was working as a journalist at the time. Valdano remembered Maradona's second goal against England in the World Cup of 1986, in which he dribbled his way through an entire defence, like a treasured dream. Valdano famously had remarked once that rarely had he slept through a night without dreaming of a goal that was both spectacular and beautiful – but that goal left all others trailing.

Valdano was playing on the wing and having picked up speed from inside his own half was the best positioned to run with Maradona, but he soon realized that there was no part for him to play in the creation of a goal that could never have been rehearsed. 'At first I went along with him out of a sense of responsibility, but then I realized I was just one more spectator,' he told me. 'I didn't feel that there was anything I could do. It was his goal and had nothing to do with the team. It was Diego's personal adventure, one that was totally spectacular.'

Diego seemed just that, a precious dream in our shared subconscious, when I caught up with Valdano several years later in his latest job as sporting director where he often doubled up as chief spokesman for Florentino Perez. We met in the administrative building of the Bernabéu stadium, a functional set of offices where well-dressed executive types rubbed shoulders with efficient young secretaries in a frenzy of activity. We sat in the wood-panelled boardroom, decorated with trophies and photographs captured during Perez's first term of office. The air of triumphalism was palpable. Valdano, tall, trim, and impeccably groomed and suited, looked the perfect executive even if he was nursing a cold.

I began by asking what he thought the essence of Real Madrid was, and whether he believed it was something that changed according to political and cultural circumstances. 'The club's myth draws its strength from issues that have exclusively to do with sport,' he said, 'and there are two individuals who played an essential role in the creation of a collective ideal: Di Stefano because of his talent, because he personified the will to win and the spirit of sacrifice and commitment, and Santiago Bernabéu because his presidency was characterized by discipline, authority, world leadership, victory and spectacle – all the things which a Real Madrid supporter demands from a team.'

There was thus no room for politics, just great football which defied any other ideological allegiance and which demanded that the game be played with skill and beauty and the ability to succeed. In case I was misinterpreting him, I quoted back something he had written in an intellectual magazine called *La Revista del Occidente* in 1986: 'A team is above all a state of mind and Real Madrid has managed to convert itself into a registered trademark which its supporters demand in every player over time – sacrifice, order, and a richly mixed team prepared to meet the greatest of challenges and at the same time capable of instilling in the opponent a sense of insecurity, and fear.'

Valdano said: 'Yes, I stick by that. Call it a battle hymn if you like – particularly to the effect that playing in the Bernabéu stadium has on Real Madrid and, adversely, on visiting teams. Real Madrid players have to assume their responsibility, their historic destiny to win . . . they have no other excuse when they are defeated. Real Madrid is a team that only thinks in football terms, not political or nationalistic ones . . . I think that's a huge advantage it has over FC Barcelona which thinks too much in political terms. The worst thing you can do to a football player is to give him an excuse to justify his frustration.'

I had come to Valdano wanting to talk about football and politics. Valdano, whose biographers once called a 'left-wing humanist', and some Real Madrid fans dubbed simply 'red', wanted only to talk football. There was now a slight tension between this somewhat wordy Argentine philosopher turned Real Madrid apologist and myself, a *Madrileño*, born and bred, who had lived the history of Spain, with and without football. The two subjects seemed as inseparable to me even from the perspective of a club that had historically been in denial. Valdano sensed it too. He offered me a drink. I accepted and talked football.

Valdano has never been short of words so I quoted back at him another judgement of the many he had issued over the years – a humorous dig at the English misuse of the long ball. It appears in a book of his thoughts called *Sueños de Fútbol* (Dreams of Football), published in 1995 just after he had moved from Tenerife to Real Madrid. It was his perspective on English football – a view I found unchanged when we met a year later in London during Euro '96. 'Just as humanity looks for the missing link between the ape and man,' he wrote, 'so do English teams look for it between rugby and football. These days they are kicking balls up into the sky. I'm warning you just in case you're thinking of flying.' Did he still feel that way about English footballers?

Valdano sipped his coffee and then answered without pause or further reflection. 'I think English football has had good footballers at various times in its history, beginning with Bobby Charlton and then with players that somehow defy the rule books, like Best. If there was one man who contributed to developing a sense of magic in modern football it was Cantona – a bohemian, a player of great imagination and personality, and huge technical resources. I think it was the arrival of foreign players that gave English football its diversity and enriched it . . . it's much more attractive these days. Now Beckham: what characterizes him is that he has a lot of the traditional English footballer in him – courage, commitment, solidarity with the team – but also other traits which I would call more universal – his touch, his ability to pass and strike . . . Real Madrid fans like players who fight, but they bless those who meet a high standard in terms of skill.'

I hadn't actually asked Valdano about Beckham. Later as I walked away from our meeting I caught sight of the commemorative tablet at the entrance to the members' office. 'In this factory, in this stadium, we turned our dreams into reality' – Alfredo Di Stefano.

I hadn't seen so many children dressed in white since my daughters' school Nativity play. Aged roughly seven to thirteen the kids spread out across an impressive campus of football training pitches, pop music blaring through loud-speakers, parents and teachers mingling in the general excitement. You could have mistaken the scene for a fairground fancy-dress parade were it not for the presence of a Real Madrid delegation led by Florentino Perez and Jorge Valdano, shaking hands and posing for group photographs in the manner of celebrities, or politicians seeking votes. What made the collective air of celebration and utter self-confidence so disarming was the time and the place – the day before a match between Real Madrid and FC Barcelona, not in Madrid but in Barcelona.

There were few better symbols of Real Madrid's ambition to break down boundaries in the twenty-first century than this blatant intrusion into what had once been considered unequivocally enemy country, in the city of the club's biggest football rival in a region of Spain that stubbornly hung on to its political and cultural identity as Catalonia. But this was not so much an invasion force as a calculated seduction from within, the forging of new loyalties in a global world.

The children were no angels. They were wearing club colours. We were in the *Escuela de Fútbol del Real Madrid* – the Real Madrid football school – inaugurated when Florentino Perez was elected president in 2000. 'The idea was to try and promote a more constructive, peaceful and educational way of supporting Real Madrid which could be applicable around the world, an example of social integration. And we began in Barcelona, a real challenge,' said Ignacio Marquez, the school's director – no bearded professor, but a slick young lawyer who was an avid reader of the *Financial Times*, when not supporting the cause of Real Madrid.

The school, extending over 25,000 square metres of prime real estate, was not short of funds. It was run according to administrative and financial agreements between Real Madrid and an educational foundation dedicated, according to its statutes, 'to the investigation and development of the teaching of football'. It was, so Marquez claimed, state-of-the-art stuff: 'the development of spectacular individual skills with tactics and strategies of play of an international standard.' Those who taught at the school were professional footballers from South America and Africa, and some of Real Madrid's own training staff. 'We like to see ourselves like a school of footballing excellence – we develop an individual's skills in a way that when he eventually joins a club it feels it has the best player,' Marquez continued.

Similar schools were being planned from Mexico to Shanghai – maybe someday even in Iraq. In his ambition to develop Real Madrid as a global brand, Florentinto Perez appeared to have put a new interpretation on the famous axiom of the Jesuit order: 'Give me a boy at seven, and he is mine for life.' It was not expected that each and every one of these boys would go on to become a Real Madrid player, but the calculation was of an increasingly worldwide connection with the club, with all the marketing spin-offs which that entailed.

You didn't have to look far to realize the racial and cultural mix of the school was partly determined by the sons of immigrants – Asians, South Americans, Africans, Arabs, Eastern Europeans, some of them indistinguishable from those of Spanish descent. All dressed in white, some of them seemed already to be halfway to playing like miniature versions of Real Madrid's stars on a good day, dribbling and passing with a disarming speed and vision and scoring some incredible goals, almost as if they'd been cloned. Training at the school was in addition to full-time education, but it was not just football that was taught. While in Catalonia's schools Catalan was taught as the first language, here Spanish was taught as a priority, along with English and French. Dressed in the colours of a club many Catalans despised, promoting a language – Spanish – that was officially frowned upon locally . . . Was this not a recipe for division and alienation? I asked Marquez.

He saw it differently. If Catalonia was as democratic as it claimed to be, it had to accept diversity – and this included respecting the views of those who did not see this region as a separate nation but as part of Spain. 'Take these immigrant children: they come to Barcelona, they come to Spain . . . for them to wear the Real Madrid colours is to fulfil the dream of their lives, to feel part of something which is probably more important than the government of the country. And what we are doing here is helping that process of belonging, by not only showing them how to play good football but to be good in human terms – values like sacrifice, generosity, companionship . . .'

Marquez had not only begun to sound like a missionary, he felt he had no need to apologize for being one. By now he had stopped to pose in a large group photograph with Florentino Perez, surrounded by mini-*galácticos* and watched by parents visibly glowing with a sense of collective pride. True converts, every one, although perhaps not quite ready for the football equivalent of martyrdom. The pupils were encouraged, for their own safety's sake, not to walk out into the streets of Barcelona dressed in the colours of Real Madrid. 'To be honest, it's not recommended to go round

Madrid sporting the colours of FC Barcelona either . . .'
Marquez added, 'There are extremes on both sides.'

Before I left, I asked Marquez how much he would encourage Beckham as a role model for the kids at his school. 'I think he is a difficult example . . . his image is not an easy one to replicate, you could say that to be like Beckham is impossible in reality and that can make kids here feel as if they're underachieving, depressed even.'

During my visit I had seen no blond kids with their hair tied in an alice band. But I thought I saw a scrawny *latino* with bandy legs – not unlike a young Raúl – who took a corner kick, bending it like Beckham.

4. The Ballad of David Beckham

It had been announced as the party of the year and those invited that weekend in May 2002 to the English country estate in Hertfordshire, popularly known as 'Beckingham Palace', were not disappointed. Beckham – Manchester United star, captain of the England team, and fashion icon – was already worth more as a celebrity than any other footballer had ever been in history. He was dressed as a Samurai warrior at this Japanese-themed party held a month before the start of the first World Cup ever to be held in Asia. His pop-star wife, ex-Spice Girl Victoria, otherwise known as 'Posh', was five months pregnant with her second child and was dressed as if she was about to clinch a Brit award. Guests – requested to wear white tie or diamonds – included an assortment of big names from media, music, sport, business and film, from Richard Branson and Mohammed Fayed to Sir Elton John, Mick Hucknall, Joan Collins and the cream of English football led by the national coach, the Swede Sven-Goran Eriksson and his Italian girl-friend Nancy. The Beckham mansion was decorated with sixty thousand imported orchids and bamboo trees, and hundreds of no-less exotic lanterns. Buddhist monks in orange robes were there along with the Japanese delicacies.

Richard Williams, a sports writer with the *Guardian*, had written not long before that the Beckhams represented 'everything that is most repellently excessive about pro-

86

fessional football in the age of satellite TV'. From a feminist perspective, another English writer Julie Burchill had a year earlier published a short book celebrating Beckham as the exemplar of the new man – dedicated to his wife, a proud father and a refreshing departure from the booze-ridden hooligan culture of too many English players and their fans. I had a particular point of reference by which to judge the Beckhams, that of the life of Diego Maradona, about whom I had written a book in the mid-1990s and whose progressive self-destruction I had been charting during a decade in which Beckham's celebrity and sporting star had steadily risen.

Maradona was not only a footballing genius, but was also the precursor of the business of football that Beckham made his own – the big transfers, the sponsorship and merchandising deals, the global projection brought by TV. It didn't really matter that Maradona played his best games before the Internet took off. He became a global superstar without it, and experienced the pressures of fame at a level that no football player before had done.

When I read the reports of the Beckham party, I recalled how some twelve years earlier Maradona had thrown a marriage party in Buenos Aires, a piece of conspicuous indulgence designed to tell the world that he was up there among the powerful and the great. It was Maradona's way of telling his fans, like Evita had told the 'shirtless ones', that anyone can make it as long as you use your talent and you have God on your side. Such was the media speculation surrounding the event that Marcos Franchi, one of its organizers and Maradona's accountant, was forced to clarify that alleged prostitutes were in fact interpreters and that the white powder laid out in bowls on guests' tables was sugar not cocaine. It was nevertheless all downhill after that – the boy, as the Italians put it, had fallen from the stars into the farmyard manure.

By contrast there was not even the faintest rumour to suggest that the Beckham party was an orgy of drugs and sex. Much of the £3,000 each guest paid went to a charity for the protection of children threatened with abuse. The waitresses, dressed like geisha girls, were pretty rather than provocative and large areas of Beckingham Palace had been set aside for David and Victoria's first-born son Brooklyn and other children to play in. Ever since he had been born, Brooklyn had been adored and protected by both his parents – not so a ten-year-old boy I met with his mother one damp December day near Naples in 1995. His name was Diegito, named after Maradona, the father who abandoned him at birth. Only when Diegito, the boy, became a teenager did he meet his father for the first time in Italy, before Maradona returned to Buenos Aires leaving him with his mother Christina Sinagra once again.

It was just over four years later, in the spring of 2000, that I found myself back in England, and preparing a profile on David Beckham in the run-up to the European Championships which I had been commissioned to write by the Dutch football journal *Hard Gras*. In order to get a sense of my subject I decided to pay a visit to Chingford, the London suburb where Beckham had spent most of his childhood. It was a short train journey from Liverpool Street station but, as train journeys often do, it drew my thoughts out beyond the time and the place, to the last time I had travelled to the outskirts of a big city in search of a footballer's roots.

'If you want to understand Diego, you've got to first

understand life in the *villa miseria*, the shantytown,' my friend Maria Laura had advised me. So I had taken a train from downtown Buenos Aires out to the southern suburb, beyond the bridge of Avellenada and the port where British sailors had first brought the game of football to South America. Having changed trains, I journeyed on to Villa Fiorito where the child Maradona had learnt to play football in the dust. Villa Fiorito was a backward and often dangerous neighbourhood, a hang-out for those without steady jobs or decent homes, for criminals and no-hopers. You lived by your wits and your instincts, and if and when you escaped the neighbourhood you took your neighbourhood codes with you.

There was no dust in Chingford. I found a polished piece of very English suburbia, with its little station, corner shops and tree-lined avenues filled with some upwardly mobile representatives of the English working class who had moved there following the end of the Second World War, leaving the immigrants to set up their markets and mosques amid the shoddy postwar debris of East London. Chingford was Conservative country (yes, with a big 'C'), memories of Churchill and safe seats for Tory heavyweights like Norman Tebbit.

The Beckham family home at number 43 Hampton Road was much like all the other houses in the airy residential zone up a hill. No palace certainly, but something more than a tin hut. It was made of pebble-dashed Victorian brick like countless bed and breakfasts along the English coast. It was just another cosy house in a cosy neighbourhood. My guide that day was a local kid called Daniel. No street beggar this one. He'd taken a lunchtime break from a local state school that boasted one of the highest educational standards in the region. He looked like a bit of a thug – older than his sixteen years – but Daniel wanted to look like David Beckham, and what's more, the latest version of David Beckham at the time: the one before he grew his hair long and put it in a ponytail. 'Look at my hair, mate, I've cut it all off, and my ear – it's got a ring,' said Daniel.

He then pointed to his trainers and Manchester United shirt with the name Beckham and number 7 stripped across the back. So why this enthusiasm for Beckham? I asked him.

'Why doyathink, mate? I wannabe famous and rich like 'im,' he told me. Sure, I insisted, but what did he think of him as a player. 'He's the best, I mean he can cross better than anybody, can't he?' said Daniel, before adding almost as an afterthought: 'Although maybe he can't dribble and shoot with his left foot like Madonna, I mean Maradona.' I reckoned that Daniel must have been about three years old when England played Argentina in that quarter-final in Mexico 1986, when Maradona scored his first goal with his hand, before delivering a second goal of such sublime mastery that it came to be seen as one of the crowning sporting achievements of the twentieth century. Daniel had watched a replay of the goal on TV with his dad a few weeks previously.

I had picked up a promotional video on Beckham that spring showing what was still portrayed as a stable family environment. It predated his parents' divorce. Joanna, one of David's two sisters, recalled how she used to kick a ball around with her brother on the neat little lawn at the back of the house. His father Ted, a kitchen fitter who taught his son the basics of football, insisted that success hadn't really changed the way he lived. Ted and his wife, a hairdresser, at the time still lived together in the house in Chingford, and he still did the occasional plumbing job. He talked about his son's success with the wonder-struck amazement of a first-time lottery winner. 'I sometimes drive around in my van, and I just drift away. I still can't believe how it all happened,' said Ted.

The way it happened was not a rags-to-riches tale, more like the uncluttered, self-disciplined, sheer aspirational and determined-to-make-it success story that once turned Margaret Thatcher, the daughter of a grocer, into a prime minister. Beckham was very much a Thatcherite child now grow up under New Labour. He made a success out of the one thing his dad, his mum, his sisters, his mates, his teachers and he himself thought he could be good at if he only worked at it: football. The fact that there was nothing remarkable about his family other than its utter ordinariness helped too. The fact that his parents held together while he was growing up, provided a necessary stability as David turned from child to youth.

When David moved up to Manchester, there was no traumatic displacement. He was simply moving from one family to another, from one protective unit to a much larger base-camp under the control of a paternalistic commander called Alex Ferguson. One can imagine Beckham's life turning out rather differently had he spent his adolescence in Chingford, getting drunk with his mates in the local pub, as the youth of Essex were prone to do at weekends, when not working as a tradesman like his father. That things turned out rather differently was largely due to Ted, a Manchester

United fan whose obsessive loyalty for the club had developed, as it had for so many others of his generation around the world, out of sympathy for the players killed in the Munich air crash of 1956. It was Ted who had instilled in his son a love for Manchester United from an early age, despite the fact that most men in Chingford, and David's two grandfathers, supported Arsenal or Spurs or Leyton Orient.

As a boy David was given a Manchester United kit as a Christmas present, and was taken by his father to see the club whenever they came down to London to play in away games. David's long-lasting hero dates from those times: Bryan Robson. When Beckham was a young teenager, Robson agreed without fuss to sign his autograph, a gesture David came to emulate many times once he had become the centre of popular adulation.

Manchester United fan and chronicler Michael Crick described Robson as an all-round player, 'a tackler, passer, runner, midfield engine, and inspirational team leader of great stamina and vision, superb with his timing and a regular scorer of goals – often vital ones'. While this would have been quite enough for any young footballer to aspire to, it is less easy to reconcile Beckham's clean-living image with Robson's legendary love of alcohol. If Robson became an early role model for Beckham it was because as captain of Manchester United and captain of England he showed a remarkable ability to conduct his own life in the way he chose to while playing good football. Beckham didn't follow Robson's hard-drinking habits but he did follow Posh and the cult of celebrity while dedicating himself to the one thing he knew he could do best – play football. He also, like

Robson, and George Best, came to inherit the number 7 shirt at Manchester United. Later in his career, after he had left Manchester United and was installed as manager at Middlesbrough, Robson paid Glasgow Rangers £3.45m for Paul Gascoigne in the belief that the player who had preceded Beckham as English football's greatest international star had stardom still left in him. But it was a hope which proved forlorn. Gascoigne's qualities as a footballer – his quickness of touch, dribbling skills, strength and balance – combined with his often outlandish behaviour on and off the field had once made him, to quote his lawyer, Mr Silverleaf, more famous than the Duke of Wellington – and more popular with hard-drinking male football fans. As mused by the poet Ian Hamilton, one of his biographers, Gascoigne seemed to suffer a form of Tourette's Syndrome, displaying 'an excess of nervous energy, and a great production of strange motions and notions: ticks, jerks, mannerisms, grimaces, noises, curses, involuntary imitations and compulsions of all sorts, with an odd elfin humour, and a tendency to antic and outlandish kinds of play'. Gascoigne, like George Best, like Maradona, succumbed to the pressures of fame – beer, women and his own inherent demons made mincemeat of whatever talent he had been born with.

By contrast Beckham may not have been born with such natural talent as Gazza's but managed, more successfully, to save his football from the demons within and without. An early teacher's report at his Chingford school showed the extent to which football made up for Beckham's lack of academic inclinations. He had a 'natural ability to succeed in sports', it said. Without the urgency that comes with hunger but resolute nonetheless, Beckham, as his teacher later put it, 'learnt the basics' and worked on them, with genuine enthusiasm for the game. He was football mad, and from an early age it was evident that the boy carried a drive within him that set him apart from the other kids who kicked the ball around in school games.

By the age of eight he was playing for a local team Ridgeway Rovers at weekends, his emerging skill as a footballer captured on a camcorder and noted for posterity by the amateur team's coach Stuart Underwood. What stood out was Beckham's touch and the way he struck the ball. The film captures the young Beckham – short, spindly framed and with his blond hair sticking out at sharp angles – looking up as he strikes a free-kick, over a wall of boys and over the young keeper's head, firmly into the back of the net. Underdeveloped physically he may have still been, but there was the kind of promise to his game that made him an irresistible catch for the talent spotter.

In 1986, at the age of eleven, and with £125 borrowed from his maternal grandfather Joseph Watts, a print worker who retired before the new technology made print workers like Joseph Watts redundant, Beckham entered Bobby Charlton's Soccer Skills Tournament, and was on the winning side at Old Trafford. The prize was a trip to Barcelona and the chance to meet the then coach of Barça Terry Venables, and two of the British players he had brought into the post-Maradona squad at the Catalan club: Gary Lineker and Steve Archibald. Appearing on a TV celebrity show, Beckham said he wasn't very interested in the royal family, as he was much too caught up in his football. To prove his point, he stood up, picked up a ball, and for about thirty seconds kicked it from one foot to the other. 'I was so impressed with the lad,' Venables later recalled, 'that I rang up my dad in London and told him to keep an eye on him.'

Venables had had rather less faith in Maradona. When he took over as Barça coach, Venables found Maradona heavily in debt and out of favour with the club president. It was in Barcelona that Maradona had also tried cocaine for the first time. Venables decided to build a new team without him and gave his blessing to Maradona's transfer to Naples.

Those who already had their eyes on the young Beckham were scouts working for Manchester United. At the age of sixteen he joined the club as an apprentice, leaving his school in Chingford with the blessing of his parents, who trusted in their son's ability to keep on the straight and narrow in an adult world. Such parental support was important in Beckham's development as a young player, as were his new colleagues in the youth team and Ferguson, the man he quickly came to know as 'the boss'.

Beckham was in the Manchester United team that won the English FA Youth Cup final in 1992. Three years later, and after a short period on loan to lowly Preston North End, he made his debut appearance in Manchester United's first team against Leeds United. He was nineteen years old.

By this time, April 1995, Manchester United were undergoing a revival under Ferguson. The Scottish-born 'boss' had moved there at the end of 1986 after a successful period as manager at Aberdeen. He had immediately set about strengthening a club that had not won the English league or the European Cup since the halcyon days of Bobby Charlton, George Best and Denis Law in the 1960s but which nonetheless had a huge tradition and history to live up to. Manchester United boasted bigger crowds than its northern rival

Liverpool, and more fans around the world. This was not just the result of the Munich air disaster when eight of the promising 'babes' of manager Matt Busby were killed on their way home from a European game in Belgrade. Manchester United's popularity among old and new generations was also linked to its reputation for entertaining, swashbuckling football, a reputation Ferguson was determined to enhance. Nevertheless it was Merseyside's dominance of English football and Manchester United's years of underachievement which Ferguson set out to reverse as a priority.

A trade unionist whose upbringing had been moulded in the Calvinist work ethic of the Glasgow shipyards, Ferguson took to arriving at his office at 7.30 each morning and got to work on moulding his team. As one of the club's most perceptive analysts Jim White has put it:

Players like Moran, McGrath, Whiteside and Strachan dominated the team he inherited. They were strong players, skilful players, great players, but were also men who approached their profession with a sense of humour, a degree of proportion. Proportion and humour are not really characteristics you would attribute to Alex Ferguson at the best of times. And in 1986 he found nothing to amuse or divert him about the nineteen years of underachievement he had inherited.

It took another four years for Manchester United's fortunes to begin to turn around. In 1990 they won the English FA Cup, beating Crystal Palace – in the final after a replay. In the following spring the club floated on the Stock Exchange, so as to raise new capital from the public and institutional investors. While many fans were opposed to the flotation, and Ferguson himself was less than enthusiastic about it, it laid the basis for the economic transformation of the club into a multinational business more than capable of ruthlessly exploiting the glory that now began to be relived on the pitch. The new chief executive and largest shareholder in the new Manchester United Public Limited Company Martin Edwards played a leading role in the development of the Premier League. Twenty-two clubs in the old first division of the Football League reorganized in a way that could allow them to negotiate bigger deals with the TV companies, beginning with the £304m contract with BSkyB, the satellite channel that was to have a key role to play in globalizing the business of football and its fan base.

Such deals meant that big fish got the biggest share of the monies. Once again Ferguson was initially critical, describing the new arrangements of the Premier League as a 'piece of nonsense'. But as his biographer Michael Crick points out, his remark came to seem somewhat ironic given that Manchester United under Ferguson's management went on to dominate the first decade of the new arrangements in a way that no club had ever done before in English football, winning seven of the first nine Premiership titles, with the club reaping the financial benefits of the TV deal he had initially denounced.

In the summer of 1995, after Manchester United had surprisingly failed to win either the Premiership or the FA Cup, Ferguson sold Paul Ince, Andrei Kanchelskis and Mark Hughes, defying the anger of some of the fans and putting his faith in his own ability to make plans for the future. Managing the transfers, Ferguson would later say, turned out to be as simple as a bus ride. 'I tell the players that the bus is moving. This club has to progress. And the bus wouldn't wait for them. I tell them to get on board. Or they'll miss out. At this club we won't stop, we don't take rests; the procedure goes on and on.'

Beckham was conscious from his early days at Manchester United of having joined one of the most famous and exciting clubs in the world, where all the players involved, whatever their age, were made to feel part of the family. He later revealed how personally upset he was with the departure of Hughes and Ince – the first was a 'great player' and, along with Bryan Robson, one of his heroes from teenage days, the second a big personality who 'drove the team on'. Nevertheless he spent his formative years at the club training with his generation of young Turks, players like Ryan Giggs, Gary and Phil Neville, Nicky Butt and Paul Scholes who rose with him from the ranks of the youth squad to the first team and later to international status. Promotion had to be earned in a hugely competitive environment, not least within the club itself. Players had to fight their way through to the first team and earn their right to remain there. A myth which Beckham would one day find himself confronting was that after leaving Old Trafford there was only one place any ex-Manchester United player could go and that was down.

In the year Ferguson's new bus got going, Beckham was loaned for a month to Preston North End, a third division club in one of northern England's dullest towns. There he played some raw football, and was made to take his kit home and get it washed after each game. At the time when he might have been tempted to think that the whole world was opening up to him, the experience reminded Beckham that he still had things to prove. Preston was an education in a key sense: it focused his mind on Manchester United, how much he missed it, how much he wanted it. Loaning him was a calculated ploy by a manager who wanted Beckham – together with the other emerging young players – to live and play in the way he demanded, or as Jim White puts it, 'with wholehearted devotion to the bus, and more particularly, to the driver'. Ferguson's own perception of Beckham was that he had with him a player that with careful nurturing, training and discipline would go from strength to strength. In fact the season in which Beckham firmly established himself in the first team – 1995–96 – got off to an inauspicious start. Beckham scored a goal, but a team which also included Butt, Scholes and the Neville brothers, Gary and Philip, crashed 1–3 to Aston Villa, fuelling a flurry of negative media comment. This began with the former Liverpool player turned TV pundit Alan Hansen telling millions of TV viewers: 'You can't win anything with kids.'

However, within a year such scepticism seemed a thing of the past. The expectation generated by Beckham was exemplified in a profile written by Karen Buchanan in *Four-FourTwo* magazine. 'His dream was always to play for the club he idolizes, with the players he's always admired. Now he's achieved that dream he's not about to screw it up,' wrote Buchanan, underestimating Beckham's ambition.

Ferguson kept the faith in his young Turks. 'I was reassured with Beckham's promise,' he later recalled. 'He was a late developer but was coming into the reckoning and although I wasn't sure whether he would be operating wide on the right or in central midfield, he was certain to be an increasingly important member of the squad.' Ferguson was confident that he had under his wing a young talent who would prove as distinctive to his generation as the Busby babes had been in theirs, only this time – fingers crossed – the promise would be fulfilled, with a little help from surviving older members of the team with experience and talent such as Eric Cantona, the current highly talented player to wear the coveted number 7 shirt.

The Frenchman had arrived at Manchester United half-way through the 1992–93 season, having fallen out with the management at Leeds United, and had been instrumental in helping his new club win their first championship for twenty-six years. Prior to his arrival in the UK, Cantona had played in his native France, drifting around half a dozen clubs. In 1989 Alfredo Di Stefano, who had long retired as a player but had returned to Real Madrid as an adviser, recommended Cantona to the club president Ramón Mendoza. At the time Cantona was playing for Olympique Marseille. 'I was asked, "Who is this Cantona?" I nearly died,' Di Stefano later recalled. 'How was it possible that no one had seen him? . . . He was an extraordinary player.' Di Stefano's advice was ignored.

It was a curious twist of fate. As Roy Keane, one of his new colleagues at Manchester United, later put it: 'Cantona was nothing if not controversial. He'd had numerous clubs but had never settled . . . he wouldn't conform, did things his own way, and appeared as if he didn't give a fuck.'

Cantona did indeed show a tendency to do his own thing in training, had a fierce temper, and sometimes showed a distinct lack of enthusiasm for winning the ball back. But he earned the respect of his team mates for his talent on the field – his deadly finishing, control of the ball and his creative passing which could turn a game round in an instant. With his leadership he helped polish the potential that lurked within Ferguson's bus, encouraging Beckham and the other young thoroughbreds to get used to the idea of being the best and winning. Beckham said of Cantona in his interview with Karen Buchanan: 'He doesn't always say much but he is always supportive. He will wink at me and that's all the encouragement I need. You must know you are doing it right when the great man does that.'

The flamboyant Frenchman was responsible for many things during his time at Manchester United. He broke the team's sense of insularity. He also taught it a thing or two about the power of the media and the sponsor and the way that marketing could be exploited. In commercial terms he set an example which Beckham, more than anybody, would follow. Cantona was rarely out of the marketing spotlight, and his own personal scrape with disaster showed the extent to which sheer self-belief and some moral support, not least from sectors of the media, could ensure redemption on earth. In January 1995 Cantona was sent off and performed his infamous kung-fu kick against a Crystal Palace fan who he alleged had insulted him. For his sins, Cantona was fined, suspended from playing for six months, and had his prison term commuted to 120 hours' 'community service' coaching some of Manchester's underprivileged children after a magistrate had found him guilty of common assault.

Ferguson had thought of sacking him, and then decided against it having considered an argument put to him by a personal friend and Manchester United fan Sir Richard Greenbury, the chairman of Marks & Spencer. As revealed in Crick's biography of Ferguson, Greenbury pointed out the parallels with the American tennis player John McEnroe who had a habit of throwing a wobbly on court. It was simply, Greenbury argued, a will to win that would on occasions boil over into rage. And in football winning often seemed to matter more than good behaviour. When Cantona returned the following season to Manchester United he did it with the professionalism his team mates venerated – scoring nineteen goals, and being honoured with the English football writers' Footballer of the Year award.

Beckham had not yet made his United debut on the night of Cantona's unfortunate kung-fu kick. But he watched it from the stands. What had always impressed Beckham about Cantona were his commitment and his passion. What happened that night did not alter his opinion of the man or the player, and Beckham would later remark that it was thanks to Cantona's return that Manchester United pulled off the double. As for Cantona's violence on that winter's night in Selhurst Park, Beckham couldn't bring himself to condemn it. On the contrary he was to come pretty close to justifying it. As he put it in his autobiography, 'I'm not saying what Eric did was right but you have to remember that in any other circumstances, if someone was screaming that stuff at another person, you'd be surprised if there wasn't trouble.'

At the start of the 1996–97 season Beckham scored one of the greatest goals ever scored in the Premiership: a shot from just inside his own half, which swerved and swooped like a Cruise missile into the net after beating the Wimbledon goalkeeper Neil Sullivan. British commentators were the first to point out that this was a shot that Pelé had tried once and failed. That Pelé may have had other qualities which Beckham had yet to prove he would ever have was not considered. The goal, captured on TV first and then by the written word, travelled the world electronically and made those sophisticates of football in southern Europe and South America take notice. It gave Beckham international status as well as recognition as a footballer of skill and vision. Only top-class players had the ability to play with such accuracy with their heads up. As Beckham's colleague at Manchester United Gary Neville described it later: 'Most players couldn't kick that far and make it look that sweet. They could probably leather it after a twenty-yard run-up, but David struck it after just one step.'

A month later Beckham was promoted to the national squad by Glenn Hoddle, the new England manager. The previous summer, Hoddle's predecessor Venables had left Beckham out of the European Championship finals held in England, having judged him not yet sufficiently matured. Hoddle appeared to have no similar doubts, judging that the inclusion of young bloods like Beckham and Michael Owen was a good bet for the future, an inspirational new departure for the England team's prospects now that Paul Gascoigne's star was fading. In his inaugural press conference, Hoddle lavished praise on Beckham, describing him as a player 'who sees the furthest pass first'.

By now Beckham had signed a contract to be represented by Tony Stephens, the agent who was to play an important role in transforming the Manchester United player into a celebrity athlete of global stature.

The encounter that was to spark off the world of football's most enduring celebrity relationship occurred on 15 March 1997. On that day Victoria Adams, better known as 'Posh' Spice, exchanged telephone numbers with David Beckham after watching Manchester United play Sheffield Wednesday.

The story is now legendary. Victoria had first seen David in photographs. David had first seen Victoria in a pop video, while relaxing with his friend Gary Neville in a hotel in Tbilisi, Georgia, during one of Manchester United's European excursions. 'Posh' was dressed from head to foot in a black PVC catsuit, and wearing a black wig (her natural hair was dark brown). She was singing and dancing to the Spice Girls' second number one hit 'Say You'll Be There!'

David remembered being hit by an arrow. 'I pointed to the TV screen and told Gary: "That is the girl for me and I am going to get her." I was sure, just from seeing her on the video, that she was the one I wanted, and I knew that if she wanted me we would be together for ever.' Thus were the seeds sown of the most star-studded love-match in the history of sport since baseball star Joe di Maggio married Marilyn Monroe.

Victoria and David had their first fleeting encounter in February of that year, when on the instigation of her then manager Simon Fuller, a Manchester United fan, she had gone to see Beckham play at Chelsea. Victoria subsequently related in her autobiography that Fuller's ambition at the time had been to have her dump her then boyfriend Stuart in favour of someone famous, like a footballer. 'When it came to footballers Simon was completely star struck and he was obviously determined to meet this Beckham and was using me as an excuse,' she recalled in *Learning to Fly*. By her own admission, footballers did not at the time enter her category of suitable men. As she put it, 'I'd seen footballers in the Epping Forest Country Club. I'd read about them in the press. Immoral, drunk, shagging everything that moves, hitting the women they keep at home. Ought to be locked up the lot of them. I want someone who isn't going to have affairs. Who is going to completely devote themselves to me. Anyway what's so clever about kicking a football?' Victoria said she felt attracted to a footballer who was shy despite being well known. David thought what won her heart was partly that he was good at his job, and also that they were both successful and could relate to each other as equals.

In his unauthorized biography of the Beckhams, Andrew Morton suggests that what Victoria and David found in each other was a mixture of trust and understanding along with the reassurance of mutual admiration – love-struck celebrities boosting each other's egos. And yet if she was more famous than he was when they met, they were also different. According to Morton, while to play football for Manchester United seemed at the time to be the horizon of David's ambition, the goal that Victoria was seeking was more intangible, that of celebrity and fame. Victoria resented the implication that there was something wrong in having her own ambition to do something with her life, while remaining supportive of her husband.

The year before Morton published his book after facing off a legal challenge from the Beckhams, Victoria had published her autobiography in 2002 detailing and justifying the journey she had taken from insecure teenager to international star, while restating her enduring love for David. And while she acknowledged that she would never be as committed to football as David's parents had been, and his place of work might not be entirely convenient for her, she insisted she was prepared to be supportive of her husband's happiness which she saw as inextricably linked with his ability to play football at the highest level.

As a couple the Beckhams came to be followed with increasing obsession by the paparazzi, the tabloid press, TV documentary makers, and supermarket and fashion magazines who saw the combination of a world-class footballer and a world-famous pop star as a media gift made in heaven. In the early days of the relationship, David's Manchester United colleague Ryan Giggs made a habit of calling him on the telephone and pretending to be Victoria in a high-pitched voice. Alex Ferguson, by contrast, had little time for such frivolities and from the outset of the Beckham union began to look on Victoria as a destabilizing influence on David's life. When Beckham had started off at Manchester he had impressed Ferguson with his single-minded commitment to training as well as his discipline before and after a game. But now Ferguson resented relinquishing control of Beckham's life as the player grew closer to Victoria. The couple played out their relationship in public: he gave her a much-photographed Christmas gift of a £13,000 diamond-studded cross and in January 1998, less than a year after they had first met, they announced their engagement. The announcement was, as far as the tabloid press was concerned, the most eagerly awaited marital pledge since that of Prince Charles and Diana – indeed those media pundits pontificating on the emerging Beckham phenomenon saw it as trying to fill the emotional and cultural void left among the British people by the collapse of the royal marriage and the death of Diana. Like a couple that really did look very much in love, David and Victoria showed off their gifts to each other: a diamond solitaire ring worth £40,000 for her, and an equally stunning diamond and gold band for him, bought from a Hollywood jeweller. 'I could not be happier right now,' a beaming David

Beckham told the world's media; 'I have my dream woman.'
As Ellis Cashmore has written in his analysis of Beckham
as a cultural phenomenon, the marriage turned the football star into an all-purpose celebrity. 'The synergy produced in the fusion of two performers, each drawn from
different spheres of entertainment, created new and perhaps
undreamed-of possibilities in marketing, merchandising
and promotions in sport, pop, fashion and, eventually,
patriotism . . .'

Beckham's engagement to Posh, while promoting the
image of the couple, did no harm to his personal elevation
to celebrity status in his own right, promoting a range of
carefully selected products, from hair lotion and fashion
eye-wear to mobile phones and sports shoes. He was, as a
glowing profile of him in *The Times* put it in March 1998,
an 'ad-man's dream'. The profile was built around a TV
commercial Beckham was shooting at the Adidas UK headquarters in Stockport. Watching Beckham arrive in his mauve
Porsche, the *Times* man seemed overwhelmed by the mere
sight of him.

Beckham steps out of the car and peels off his track suit to reveal
a body sculptured purely for the purpose of playing ball. His legs
are chunkier than the thighs of a racehorse; his torso, stripped of
any excess fat, is lean to the point of anorexia. His 6ft frame is a
footballer's body – like a boxer's turned on its head, with all the
muscle below the belt. He runs a hand through his well-cut
blondish hair, carefully flicking the strands that fall asymmetrically
over the corner of each eyebrow, strikes a model pose and waits
patiently, smiling shyly at the wonder of it all.

Beckham was only twenty-two and with a great deal of celebrity as well as football still left in his body.

During the 1996–97 season Beckham's match-winning performances helped Manchester United win their fourth Premier League title and reach the semi-finals of the UEFA Champions League before losing to Germany's Borussia Dortmund, the eventual winners of the competition that year with a victory over Juventus. As a result he was voted England's Young Player of the Year.

The following season was disappointing for Beckham, with Manchester United humiliated by Barnsley in the FA Cup, and eliminated in the quarter-finals of the Champions League by Monaco, a side widely seen by commentators as much weaker than Manchester United. Alex Ferguson's customary outburst of anger after the defeat was even more outspoken than usual. Luckily for Beckham, it was not him but Nicky Butt who on this occasion was on the receiving end of the boss's wrath. 'I'm out of the fucking European Cup now, Butty, and it's your fucking fault! What are you fucking doing?' Ferguson screamed.

Meanwhile in the Premier League, Manchester United's reputation as the unchallenged masters of English football found itself temporarily usurped by a reborn Arsenal under its intelligent new manager Arsène Wenger. The Frenchman, whose quiet reflective mannerisms in interviews belied a fierce determination to win, brought a new sophisticated style of management to English football, radically changing diets off the pitch and tactics on it, with an assortment of exciting Dutch and French players who put many of their English counterparts in the shade. In the last stretch of their bid for the Premiership that season, Arsenal beat Manchester United at Old Trafford during a run of ten straight victories, playing some of the best football produced by an English club in recent times. Beckham obtained some personal consolation by being selected for the England squad in that summer's World Cup in France, although he could not have predicted the impact playing in it was to have on his career.

English football at the time appeared to be caught up in the atmosphere of general political, social and cultural revival that followed from the 1997 election victory of Tony Blair at the head of a rejuvenated and ambitious New Labour party. Blair made much of his love of football, and the Beckhams were among the bright young couples openly courted by what the US magazine *Newsweek*, in a famous special issue on British society under New Labour, called 'Kool Britannia'. And yet the attempt by Blair's first sports minister Tony Banks to secure the staging of a future World Cup in England ended in failure partly due to the enduring blight of English hooliganism on foreign territory. Then England came to the tournament in France managed by Glenn Hoddle whose past fame as a gifted footballer in the 1970s and 80s had clearly not prepared him for the job of getting the best out of English football in the last World Cup of the twentieth century. He was under the influence of a strange spiritual healer who knew nothing about football but offered advice about players anyway. The brilliant but wayward Gascoigne was dropped from the team, while the man many English fans now saw as their saviour-in-waiting, David Beckham, was left on the bench for the first two games, playing for an hour in the 1–2 defeat by Romania.

Beckham played from the start in England's third game of the competition, against Colombia. He scored the second goal in a 2–0 win with a typically clever right-footed free-kick. He also showed an ability to fill a more central, influential position in midfield rather than out on the flank.

Then came the game against Argentina in the second-round, knock-out stage of the tournament. The encounter between the countries had a history of controversy behind it. It was caught up in politics, war and the primitive instinct of xenophobia. Who among the older generations could forget the 1966 World Cup Anglo-Argentine quarter-final at Wembley when the Argentina captain Antonio Rattin circled the ground exchanging insults with queen and country after being expelled by the German referee? Or Maradona's Hand of God in Mexico 1986? And in between there was the Falklands War in 1982, in which over 1,000 Argentine and British soldiers were killed fighting for a group of islands in the South Atlantic over which each of their countries claimed sovereignty.

Hoddle had told his players to forget the war, but the *Daily Mirror* on the morning of the match in Saint-Étienne had not forgotten Maradona: '8pm Tonight: Payback Time', it declared across its front page, with a picture of the Argentine star handling the ball past goalkeeper Peter Shilton. The first forty-five minutes were played with pace and determination from the outset, the 2–2 scoreline at half-time reflecting how evenly balanced the teams were. While Argentina had greater possession, England were quick in exploiting the chances that came their way. Then two minutes into the second half disaster struck. Beckham was lying on the ground after being brought down by Simeone when he suddenly kicked out at the Argentine – a gesture of impetuous folly which earned Beckham a red card.

England went on to lose the game after a penalty shoot-out. It was the end of another World Cup dream. Beckham became the convenient whipping boy for the tabloid press, his one apparent foul overshadowing all the good work he had contributed, not least setting up Michael Owen's run and beautifully executed goal, England's second. 'That was rock bottom because the whole experience hit me. I am quite an emotional person . . . But I had not cried like I did then since I was a child. For ten minutes, I just lost it,' Beckham later recalled.

He flew to New York and sought solace for eleven days in the company of Victoria. The Spice Girls were just setting out around the US to promote their latest album. She recollects it as one of the high points in her career as a pop artist, conquering the American market in a way that had only been done before by the Beatles and hard rock bands like Led Zeppelin and the Rolling Stones. She believed then that the Spice Girls had also reached out to an untapped new generation of American kids who 'just wanted to have fun'. 'It was only after our success that pop music began to take off in America, with people like Britney Spears and 'N Sync. We opened up the door for acts like this,' she later claimed.

In the weeks that followed, effigies of Beckham were burnt by angry zealots; his family home in Chingford was besieged by the media as if the building contained a serial killer. At the start of a new season and amid anonymous threats against his life and that of Victoria, the couple were offered police protection, and took on extra private security staff. Victoria's own trust in David was put to the test as a series of tabloid articles focused on alleged past and present girlfriends. Pregnant with their first child, Victoria felt vulnerable, insecure. She suspected the worst. But in her autobiography she details what she claims was the healing process that came with his emphatic denials and their decision to steer through the crisis together, on the evidence that the enemy they both faced was not within their home but outside, and that they had more to gain by sticking together than falling apart.

Against their better instincts West Ham fans were persuaded by their club management to call off a mass anti-Beckham protest they had planned one Saturday, showing 10,000 red cards from the terraces. But at other Manchester United away games, fans of some clubs booed every move made by Beckham, alluded to his alleged infidelities and chanted obscenities about Victoria. Questions about Beckham's future in English football became daily commentary in the British press with many sports journalists predicting that the player would leave for Italy permanently to escape all the bad feelings.

The Beckhams did take a weekend break near Milan in an attempt to lay to rest the gossip about infidelities but the rumours that Beckham would seek exile from Britain by transferring to a foreign club proved premature. Sectors of the media had underestimated the staying power of the Beckhams as a celebrity couple, and David's own commitment to developing his talent as a footballer at Manchester United.

Soon after the World Cup the Beckhams featured in a BBC TV documentary called *The Football Millionaires.* 'I think a majority of people dislike me for jealousy reasons,' David said before adding, 'I think there are more people who dislike me than like me. I'd like to be really popular but I don't think that's going to be.' It would prove to be false modesty. As the 1998 World Cup faded into history – it took about six weeks for the Beckham taunting to fall off the tabloid agenda – Beckham re-emerged with his image not only intact but seemingly strengthened as celebrity and player. In this he was helped by the way he and his wife continued to promote themselves as a couple, and his own ability to prove himself on the field.

Before a year had passed, the magazine *Vogue* published an interview with the Beckhams under the headline 'Life is Sweet' and subtitled with the following text: 'She's a member of the biggest girl band ever, he plays football for England's most successful team, together they're worth £18m, and they're still in their early twenties.' In a colour photo spread, a pregnant Victoria and equally fashion-conscious David – with Calvin Klein pants peeping above his jeans – lay on the floor, modelling a loving pose in the corridor of a Manchester hotel. The writer of the cover story Christa Souza described the couple turning up for the photo shoot dressed in matching white Polo Sport jackets and matching Stussy baseball caps. 'Overgrown kids are *exactly* what Victoria Adams and David Beckham are and as such it's difficult not to feel a wave of affection at the thought of them carefully laying out all the tabloids every morning to see which ones their pictures are in and discussing who is more famous.'

Within ten months of the debacle in France, Beckham had been completely vindicated as a player, producing some of the best football of his career and being recognized by United fans as their Player of the Year.

With Manchester United playing some excellent football at home and abroad, Victoria gave birth to baby Brooklyn at the Portland Hospital in central London. It was a grey day on 4 March 1999 but the event was treated in some quarters with the fanfare of a royal event. As Andrew Morton described it, it was not just the birth of a child, but the creation of a dynasty, made to measure for an aspiring new century. The firstborn was destined to play football like Dad – bookmakers offered odds of 10,000 to 1 that Brooklyn would be sent off while playing against Argentina. He was also destined to become the most photographed baby at the end of a millennium and the beginning of another, a symbol of the enduring strength of the celebrity cult that the Beckhams had turned into an art form and a social phenomenon. With a perfect sense of timing, Victoria declared that the boy had been conceived in New York following Beckham's World Cup dismissal.

The day before his first son's birth, Beckham had covered himself in glory during Manchester United's quarter-final Champions League 2–0 conquest of Inter Milan. Johan Cruyff was so impressed by Beckham's performance that he described him as one of the elite players in Europe. 'He is truly gifted . . . if you want to win a major European trophy and show class along the way, you must play attacking football and he is ideal for an attacking formation . . . He is a fabulous crosser of the ball and possesses terrific skills,' commented Cruyff at the time.

The TV screens around the world were endlessly repeating memorable action replays of Beckham's portfolio of crosses – deep ones, short ones, curlers, chips, thunderbolts. There was no end of skilful passes, as well as goals, the player's unusual arrangement of bones and hinges bending the ball in ways others couldn't even imagine.

In May of that year Beckham found himself a central figure at the Nou Camp in one of the most thrilling final moments ever seen in a European match. Manchester United were 0–1 down to Bayern Munich in the final of the Champions League and with the fourth official indicating that there were three minutes of injury time left. Manchester United won a corner on the left and Beckham took it. With United's Danish goalkeeper Peter Schmeichel out of his own area and rushing forward to provoke confusion among the defending Germans, the ball was mishit by Giggs, but struck home by Teddy Sheringham. The stadium, half packed with United fans, seemed to erupt with the level of noise normally only experienced whenever Barça scored a goal against Real Madrid. Then with the final minute ticking away, Beckham took another corner. He curled it to the near post, Sheringham flicked it on, and Ole Gunnar Solskjaer volleyed into the roof of the net. Fifteen seconds into the restart the referee blew the final whistle. German players collapsed on the turf. Some of them seemed to eat it. Manchester United players and fans felt like taking the whole stadium with them there are then and holding it for ever in glorious memory. The victory was the crowning achievement of an extraordinary season for Beckham and his club. Manchester United were European champions for the first time since 1968. The club had also won the Premier League and the FA Cup, making it a famous treble. Only three sides in Europe had ever achieved the feat before – Celtic in 1967, Ajax in 1972 and PSV Eindhoven in 1988.

That summer, on 4 July 1999, the Beckhams married. With

exclusive rights of media coverage of the occasion sold to *OK* magazine (picked by Victoria in preference to *Hello!*, another glossy magazine that had earned a reputation for featuring relationships that were doomed to be short-lived), the event took place in an elegant eighteenth-century castle outside Dublin. Among the invited guests were the Manchester United players and Alex Ferguson. None of them had ever been to a wedding quite like it. As for David Beckham, the disaster of the sending-off at Saint-Étienne seemed a distant memory after living through one of the most rewarding six months of his life both in emotional and professional terms. But no sooner had the wedding ended, than a new potential storm cloud began to loom over Beckham's personal and professional horizon. This was the prospect of deterioration in the relations between him and Ferguson that would eventually contribute to Beckham's departure from Manchester United to a country unimagined in his childhood dreams.

The first major and widely publicized row between Beckham and Ferguson blew up in February 2000 when the player missed a training session and claimed that it was because Brooklyn was ill with gastroenteritis. Despite the alleged illness, Victoria attended a fashion gala in London. Ferguson was furious that Beckham had apparently agreed to baby-sit ahead of a potentially crucial Premiership match with Leeds United, their nearest rivals at the time in the race for the championship. Ferguson fined Beckham £50,000 (the equivalent of two weeks' wages) and left him out of the team against Leeds. Two months later Ferguson was in secret contact with Luis Figo's agent José Veiga to explore the possibility of transferring the Portuguese from FC Barcelona to United. According to evidence unearthed by Michael Crick, Ferguson was secretly developing the idea of swapping Figo for Beckham. But then Ferguson changed his mind, calculating at the time that he would face a huge backlash from United fans and the media if he allowed Beckham to go to Spain. Ferguson also felt that despite the problems of his celebrity life Beckham still was respected by the other United players of his generation – a camaraderie that continued to produce results. That season United ended their Premiership campaign with eleven successive wins and a record eighteen-point winning margin over runners-up Arsenal.

During the European Championships in Holland and Belgium that summer, Beckham's occasional flashes of brilliance struck one of the few positive notes in a generally mediocre campaign by England. 'He has no ego. He is prepared to be a general if that is needed, and also a soldier if that is needed,' commented the national team manager Kevin Keegan. During England's game with Germany, Beckham's trademark free-kick evaded a crowded penalty box and set up a winning goal by Shearer after fifty-two minutes. The victory over one of England's historic rivals for the first time in competitive fixtures since 1966 elevated Beckham once again to national hero status. Within weeks he was made captain of the England squad by Keegan's successor Sven-Goran Eriksson. With a formidable record in European club football, the Swede recognized in Beckham a talent capable of lifting England's game and making it more competitive internationally.

The Eriksson–Beckham axis seemed set to take the world by storm in September 2001 when England, needing a positive result in the World Cup qualifier in Munich, were inspired by the captain to an astonishing 5–1 win over the Germans. Then, five weeks later, Beckham's 25-yard free-kick against Greece three minutes into added time secured England's qualification for the World Cup finals in Japan and South Korea. 'Beckham has done it,' screamed the BBC's Alan Green, as English fans got up and danced. Eriksson called it the most important goal of his life.

The contrast with Ferguson could not have been more marked. Asked for his comment on Beckham's goal of salvation, the United boss darkened and scowled before telling journalists: 'The media has gone over the top as usual. You do not care a damn about us. It is about selling newspapers for you people. You do not have to pick up the pieces, pick a team and bring your players back to earth.' The comment was followed by a decision to drop Beckham from the next United game and to continue dropping him, off and on, in subsequent weeks, which may have resulted from a dip in the player's form, but it made Beckham feel unfairly treated. It was the definitive beginning of the end of his time at United.

Beckham's career was approaching a critical juncture that not only trailed memories in its wake but was preceded by pointers and foreshadowings. Perhaps at the time these intimations were not fully recognized as such but eventually were seen as part of a pattern. Before Beckham's transfer talks got under way, the player had two Spanish prologues in the form of United's two Champions League encounters with Real Madrid. The two clubs shared a history of mutual respect dating back to the 1950s when United became the first English club to challenge Real Madrid's emerging international prowess. In 1957 the pre-Munich crash Busby babes lost to Real Madrid in the semi-finals of the European Cup. The patched-up post-crash United side went down to Milan in the tournament the following year.

Two years later, in 1960, a nineteen-year-old Alex Ferguson was among the 135,000 packed into Hampden Park to watch Real Madrid win their fifth consecutive European Cup, a feat which has never been matched in the modern game. Real Madrid beat Eintracht Frankfurt 7–3, with Puskas the 'galloping major' scoring four goals and Di Stefano a hat-trick, in one of the most thrilling international club encounters ever. Another eight years passed before Busby's third great team achieved their European Cup triumph, beating the Portuguese champions led by the legendary Eusébio 4–1 at Wembley.

In April 2000 Real Madrid and United faced each other in the quarter-finals of the Champions League. It was the pre-Perez era before the word *galáctico* had entered the Real Madrid lexicon. Without the hype, the men in white were still a formidable team. Tough, quality players of the calibre of Redondo, Roberto Carlos and Morientes, with the twenty-three-year-old Raúl already established in the pantheon of home-grown gods. Raúl's reputation had grown as a proven match-winner; he had the ability to turn a game round thanks to his rock-hard single-mindedness and what Valdano called his 'insolent self-belief', qualities he deployed with the sole purpose of winning.

To his fans Raúl was untouchable. After the 0–0 first leg result in a vibrant Bernabéu, Raúl and Real Madrid showed what they were capable of at Old Trafford. With a brace of brilliant goals, Raúl lit up the Manchester night as the Spanish side withstood a late United recovery to win 3–2. For all Beckham's creativity and competitiveness – and a smartly taken goal – coming back from a three-goal deficit was just beyond them.

As far as Spanish journalists were concerned it was Beckham who, as Real Madrid's historian Luis Miguel González put it, 'shone when his team most needed it'. It was a generous comment, not shared by all United fans, some of whom later resented the way Beckham chose to recollect his team's defeat in his autobiography: 'It didn't make up for being beaten but I was pleased about my goal that night.' From the Reds' perspective it seemed a somewhat crass comment to make on a match that despite United's sense of invincibility in the Premier League had left them outclassed and unable to defend the Champions League. As Keane later described Real Madrid: 'they were so technically adroit we were chasing shadows.'

Three years later Manchester United faced Real Madrid again in a quarter-final of the Champions League, this time against an imperious team which boasted the most dazzling group of superstars since the Di Stefano era. Beckham would later admit to feeling overawed like never before when he arrived to play the first leg at the Bernabéu – the scale of the place, its sense of tradition, and the history of great games, great players and success that hung in the atmosphere. His mother, who watched the game that evening in the first tier reserved for United fans, had a premonition there and then that Beckham would end up one day playing in a white shirt. United were beaten 3–1 in front of 75,000 Real Madrid fans who expected nothing less than the very best of their team. The football played that night by the team led by Zidane,

Figo and Raúl was mesmerizing. So many players were involved every time Real Madrid came forward that United seemed unable to know how to react for most of the game, standing off their illustrious opponents, instead of trying to play them one to one.

Raúl, identified by Ferguson as the genius of Real Madrid, was unable to play in the second leg because of an appendix operation. Beckham began on the bench because Ferguson had chosen to play Juan Sebastian Verón instead despite the fact that the Argentine had not played for seven weeks through injury. Twelve minutes into the game Ferguson's face visibly fell when Real Madrid produced their football version of pinball wizardry, first-touch passes of impeccable fluidity and accuracy involving four players – McManaman (a rare game for him), Figo, Zidane, back to Guti – ending with a right-footed shot by Ronaldo, so powerful and fast that it beat Barthez at his near post. Moments later Verón performed a shocking two-footed foul on the shins of Makelele. Real Madrid seemed to lose their rhythm for a while, apparently inviting United to probe their vulnerability in defence. Solskjaer broke through between Helguera and keeper Casillas, and then chipped the ball for Van Nistelrooy to tap in the equalizer. Within ten minutes Real Madrid had delivered another display of genius, Zidane, Figo and Roberto Carlos combining in another spellbinding passing movement, before Ronaldo effortlessly rolled in his second goal. On a night you couldn't afford to blink, it took just a further two minutes for United to draw level again, this time through an own-goal as Helguera deflected Verón's cross past Casillas. Ronaldo completed his hat-trick six minutes later, pounding his shot from outside the penalty box. It was a performance that earned the Brazilian a standing ovation from the 67,000 fans at Old Trafford, when he was substituted seven minutes later, a moment that the Brazilian said afterwards would remain with him for the rest of his life. Others, including Real Madrid president Perez and coach Del Bosque, wouldn't forget it either, as an example of football at its most noble.

But the match was not over. Beckham had been brooding on the bench for an hour. As one seasoned United observer Rob Hughes put it, 'He was aware that Ferguson was cooling on him, and that Real Madrid might see him as a marketing gadget.' Beckham was brought on as a substitute for Verón. While the Argentine departed to applause from the United fans, Beckham's arrival was greeted with an eerie silence. Beckham scored from a free-kick, in his view the best he had ever managed in a United shirt. He then grabbed a second after Casillas had deflected a shot from Van Nistelrooy. Before the game was over, Beckham took another free-kick from the edge of the box, but the shot went over the bar. The game ended with Real the winners 6–5 on aggregate, and United out of the Champions League, once again outclassed by Real Madrid.

'It was a great advertisement for the game,' Del Bosque told me afterwards, 'a good sporting spirit, a magnificent spectacle. As for Madrid, it's a club that not only has to win but has to do it with a certain style – it showed that on that night in Old Trafford.'

As for Beckham, the sight of him fraternizing with the Real Madrid players then turning to the crowd and returning their applause, before abruptly changing and leaving Old Trafford, came to be seen by fans of Real and United alike as symbolic of a future foretold. Beckham himself claimed that he wasn't conscious of saying goodbye that night, and that all he was doing was savouring the end of a game in which he believed he had proved his commitment and worth to United.

I asked Del Bosque what he thought. 'I don't know whether or not at that very moment Beckham had consciously decided he wanted to go to Real Madrid. But what I do know is that if Beckham had already been a Real Madrid player and the coach had chosen to start that game with him on the bench, the coach wouldn't have survived the evening without getting sacked.'

5. Tilting at Windmills

The year David Beckham was born, 1975, was also the year that Francisco Franco died. The Beckhams were a modest family with as yet no dynastic pretensions. The old general, also known as the *Caudillo* (Leader), had ruled for four decades, for better or worse, influencing every aspect of Spanish life, including football. He had spent years trying to ensure that his death would not mean a dramatic break with the past but rather an orderly continuity into the future.

Franco's death was officially announced by his tearful and loyal prime minister Carlos Arias Navarro on the morning of 20 November. As his biographer Paul Preston later recorded, 'Outfitters and haberdashers ran out of black ties and black cloth for armbands, yet it is said that some people danced in the streets of some Basque towns.' Franco was loved as much as he was hated although few Spaniards could claim not to have owed him part of themselves. The duality of emotions of a people that felt either liberated or repressed by Franco was nowhere more apparent than in Catalonia, that region of Spain that had defined its own nationhood in terms of its relative autonomy from Madrid. The president of FC Barcelona Agustín Montal sent two letters of condolence, one to Franco's private office, the other to his widow Carmen Polo. Two other directors of the club celebrated by playing with a bust of Franco before letting it shatter on the ground.

In Madrid half a million people filed past Franco's body

– 'and not just to reassure themselves that he was dead,' adds Preston. The sense of mourning extended to many of the fans who over the years had packed the Santiago Bernabéu stadium, and the senior management of Real Madrid, which had earned worldwide recognition as the most successful football club in Europe during the Franco years. Few were as saddened by the news as Bernabéu himself. He had served Real Madrid as a player, trainer, secretary and director. He had gone on to become one of the most powerful figures in post-war sport, remaining as unchallenged president of Real Madrid since 1943, four years after Franco had emerged victorious from the Spanish Civil War. At the outset of the conflict Bernabéu was denounced as a fascist by a fellow member of the Real Madrid board, and took refuge in the French embassy. He later volunteered to fight on Franco's side, first in the conquest of Cuenca under the command of Camilo Alonso Vega and then in a division commanded by General Agustín Muñoz Grandes on the Catalan front. 'I was in the reconquest of Catalonia, the reconquest of an independent Catalonia for the greater glory of Spain,' he later recalled, adding that in his view the problems of the Catalans had no other solution than domination by Madrid.

Born in Almansa, near a huge medieval castle that stands to this day as testimony to the final battle in which King Philip V defeated the armies of Catalonia and Valencia and submitted them to the reign of Castile, Bernabéu always saw Madrid and its surrounding region as the very soul of Spain to which all parts of the country should show due reverence.

Castilians are the Spaniards with the biggest and most rounded *cojones* [testicles]. Those who live on the Castilian *meseta* [plateau], moulded by the cold and the heat, have been sufficiently tough to prevail in every sense over those of other regions. Castile imposed its language on the whole world and gave fruition to all the enterprises and ideas that in their days made Spain great. I am sorry for the Catalans, the Galicians, and the Basques, but the Castilians were always cleverer than they were and on the battle ground, in hand to hand fighting, they gave them a right ear-bashing through every stage in history. Me a separatist? No. What happens is that I hear a lot of stupid things said which no one stands up to.

Three days after Franco's death, and two hours after his body was laid to rest in the Valley of the Fallen, a league match between Real Madrid and Zaragoza was marked with a minute's silence in honour of his memory. Real Madrid won the game and went on to win the championship. Within weeks Bernabéu was re-elected for a fresh four-year term while telling the club membership that they should start thinking of a successor. There was a sense that the club was reaching the end of an era. In the 1976–77 season, the 75th anniversary, Real fell to ninth place in the league and fared even worse in the Spanish Cup.

Mid-way through the following season, Bernabéu accepted the resignation of his manager the Yugoslav Miljan Miljanic from his hospital bed, while being treated for terminal cancer. He was replaced by Luis Molowny, under whose stewardship Real Madrid won the league championship again. But soon after sunrise on 2 June 1978 Bernabéu died, aged eighty-three.

In researching this book I had no doubt that of the many potential interviewees I had drawn up few could provide a better insight into the curious paradoxes that have affected the history of Real Madrid than Vicente Del Bosque. In recent years this man had become familiar to a worldwide TV football audience of millions – those who were not Real Madrid fans were somewhat puzzled by the sight of the overweight, balding and moustachioed Del Bosque, often silently observing his team from the Real Madrid bench, and rarely showing any signs of emotion.

Del Bosque was replaced by Carlos Queiroz at the start of David Beckham's first season with Real Madrid. But he continued to cast a long shadow over the history of the club. Unlike Beckham or Queiroz, he had lived and breathed Real Madrid most of his professional life, first as a player straddling Franco's and post-Franco Spain and belatedly as manager when Real Madrid won two European Cups in the first three years of the twenty-first century and were proclaimed the best team in the world.

I visited Del Bosque at his spacious apartment in a quiet, smart residential block, removed from the bustle of the city centre, but within a five-minute drive from the Bernabéu stadium. The main sitting room had the predictable totems of success – silverware and plaques, among them one naming him the best football manager in the world. But it was also taken up with more simple pursuits like his young son's computer course in Basic English, and surprising touches of humour such as a caricature effigy of Joán Gaspart, seen by fans as one of the most disastrous presidents in the history of FC Barcelona, looking slightly grotesque and smiling, like a Goya witch.

Del Bosque was born in Salamanca near the river Tormes. This old university city had historically considered itself the heart and soul of Spanish history. To this day foreign students from all over the world take special summer courses, their presence a reminder of the late Middle Ages when as a university town it belonged to that select group whose other members were Oxford, Paris and Bologna. Salamanca was immortalized by several of Spain's leading writers including the great dramatist and poet Lope de Vega. In the run-up to the Spanish Civil War it became the adopted place of learning for one of the great thinkers of the twentieth century, the Spanish philosopher Miguel de Unamuno, one of Del Bosque's great idols.

Unamuno had very little time for football which he considered a semi-barbarous activity. He felt it distracted Spaniards from thinking about what really mattered, like love and death, God and above all the nature of Spain. 'The football public is in Spain not much different from the bullfighting public and no more educated,' wrote Unamuno in 1924; 'a sportsman is usually a frivolous person, who doesn't feel passion, the noble passion of life.'

According to Del Bosque's biographer, Unamuno was one of his intellectual gurus. So I asked arguably Real Madrid's most successful manager whether he felt his own character defined by being born in Salamanca. 'I think the climate, the society in which you're born into, defines much of your life – in that sense I've considered myself a classic Castilian all my life,' Del Bosque answered.

Quite what did he mean? I thought of what Bernabéu had once said about what made Castilians better – that they had bigger and more rounded *cojones* than other Spaniards. But Del Bosque put it slightly differently. 'I would say we are people with a sense of responsibility, somewhat august, cold, quite serene, without great eccentricities.'

If I'd failed so far to begin to grasp what a different world this football club was taking me into compared to the last one I'd entered, I did now. When researching FC Barcelona I had heard repeated reference to the 'essence' of what it meant to be a Catalan – what identified him as an individual and as part of his own nation. Catalans believe there is a part of themselves that is *seny* – roughly translated as common sense although not much different from what Doctor Johnson called 'bottom': that is, 'an instinctive and reliable sense of order, a refusal to go whoring after novelties'. But then the Catalans also claim to have within them *rauxa* – an uncontrollable emotion, an outburst, any kind of irrational activity.

But to talk to Del Bosque was to be reminded of the strange unity that many *Madrileños* passionately believed underlined Spain despite its regional diversity. He asserted that being from Salamanca gave him a special understanding of the rest of Spain for the simple reason that many of its inhabitants had over the years emigrated to other regions such as the Basque country and Catalonia, just as they emigrated to Madrid. He now saw Spain as an undivided member of the European community, and Real Madrid as an example of the changes that had taken place in European football culture. 'I think that with every day that passes Spain is integrating more and more with the rest of Europe – it's no longer the north of Africa ... I think that with every day that passes there should be less need to believe in frontiers – and fortunately frontiers are disappearing. I think that thirty years of democracy have made this country more tolerant, less radical ... a lot of those who lived the drama of the Civil War have died – that has helped cure the wounds.'

Del Bosque recalled how Franco had tried to 'protect' Spanish football by banning foreign players from the Spanish competition that bore his name, the *Copa del Generalísimo*, even if Real Madrid, like other Spanish teams, became more cosmopolitan well before English clubs did. 'Thankfully there was another tendency in our football culture that looked outwards, beyond more open borders, and that brought in foreign players, foreign styles which enriched us.' The more traditionalists among the Real Madrid supporters say a turning point came in 1974 when Miguel Muñoz, the club's Spanish coach for over a decade, was replaced by the Yugoslav Miljan Miljanic. However, Del Bosque, who carries Spanishness deep within his soul, witnessed the impact of foreigners both as a player and later as a coach, and judged it only in positive terms. Having players like Ronaldo, Roberto Carlos, Makelele, Figo, Zidane and Raúl in his dressing room he had experienced at first hand the benefits of a multicultural melting pot.

And yet by the time Real Madrid decided to boost its united nations with David Beckham, club president Florentino Perez had judged Del Bosque surplus to requirements. 'I wasn't involved in any way when the club decided to buy Beckham but nor was I involved when the club bought Figo, Zidane and Ronaldo – they were all strategic decisions made directly by the president.' The nearest the club came to consulting Del Bosque was when Valdano rang him two weeks before the formal signing and told him that it looked as if Beckham was coming to the club. 'I'm telling you this so you don't find out about it through the press,' Valdano told him. I asked Del Bosque what he thought about Beckham. It was long after the decision had been taken without him and Beckham was already approaching the midpoint of his first season with Real Madrid.

'If they had consulted me, I would have said bringing Beckham to Real Madrid is fine by me, although we were losing out defensively in the midfield once we lost Makelele and didn't replace him. But let me speak here as a simple football fan. I think that Beckham was formed by a great club [United]. He has great qualities – a team player, a great touch, good vision of play, good creative play. I wasn't surprised by the way he began playing at Madrid. *Madridistas* have always liked a player who works, who shows commitment. He is a very complete player who plays actively in defence and midfield. He is both generous with and fights for the ball,' Del Bosque said.

I wanted to draw him back to the country that once was. He had been born in Spain in 1950. I was born in Spain three years later. We belonged to the first post-war generation of Spanish children who while still in childhood had begun to glimpse the beginning of a better future while destined to remain forever conscious of the memories of the Civil War of our elders and the hardships that they had to put up with for our sakes. Did he remember how isolated from the rest of the world Spain still seemed when we were growing up?

Del Bosque hesitated before answering. For the first time since we'd started talking, I felt as if he was trying to struggle with himself, honestly coming to terms with the direction he intuitively realized the conversation was going – into the politics of Spain, touching the politics of Real Madrid. 'Of course one felt it. I don't like to talk about this because it seems to identify one politically but I remember my parents feeling very insecure about everything that was going on, speaking in whispers about certain subjects such as that there was no more precious gift that a human being could have but his freedom . . .'

Del Bosque paused, looked at me as if for reassurance, and then began to tell me about his father. He was struggling with his ghost, explaining in his way why it was that he had come to think as he did about Spain and Real Madrid, and how football shouldn't get mixed up in politics. 'He was radical, he had progressive ideas – we've become more moderate fortunately – but he was caught up in the war, he was taken prisoner by the Franco forces, near Mingilla, in the Basque country. He had a really bad time of it – two, three really hard years. You see he was a pure-blooded Republican. He worked as a clerk for RENFE [the national railways], but they arrested him in Salamanca serving out his military service. He used to talk to me so as to convince me that nothing of what he lived through should ever be repeated . . . I think we Spaniards of today are not sufficiently thankful to his generation.'

I asked Del Bosque what he, his father's son, had felt the day Franco had died. 'Inside the club we all took it pretty calmly. We were after all politically independent. Where was I when he died? I can't remember . . . oh hang on – yes, I think we were playing a game in Corunna and we played that night . . . I remember that in those days everyone in Spain was talking about whether there was going to be *ruptura* or *reforma* [a total break from the past or just an orderly reform]; fortunately we took a path that allowed us to live our lives normally.'

Politics was something that stood awkwardly between him and the club that had sacked him under Florentino Perez.

Del Bosque added, almost as an afterthought, 'I also don't want to be too precise about this, but there were a lot of Spaniards who had fought Franco and wanted change, and there were others who were saddened.'

I remembered what the writer Manolo Vazquez Montalban had said once about certain Spaniards coming to terms with the Franco years – they seemed to move 'between amnesia and memory' – but decided to keep that to myself. Del Bosque already seemed slightly irritated when I had asked him whether it was fair to have once considered Real Madrid Franco's team. 'Not especially. Anyway Real Madrid was a football team . . . it was outside politics . . . it's a simplification to call it pro-Franco. Real Madrid is pluralist, it's got a huge number of followers of all tendencies . . .' he answered, moving seamlessly from the past to the present. When Santiago Bernabéu died in June 1978, Del Bosque was one of the Real Madrid players that honoured him by carrying his coffin.

Bernabéu was born in 1895, the year that José Martí led a rebellion in Cuba, one of the remaining outposts of the Spanish empire. Within three years and following a humiliating naval defeat by the United States, Spain had been forced to sign over the independence not just of Cuba, but also of the Philippines and Puerto Rico, leaving only the small North African enclaves of Ceuta and Melilla. In Spain the loss of imperial status, the public destruction of its image as a great power, was viewed as a national disaster. Spaniards entered the twentieth century trying to come to terms with what had gone wrong to produce such a decline, such a divergence in progress and ambition from the rest of Europe.

Spain had undeniably run counter to the mainstream of European history. Alone among European nations, it had had three-quarters of its territory overrun by Arabs in an occupation that lasted more than seven hundred years. Although Spain subsequently became the first country in Europe to aspire to a unified state, its cultural and geographical diversity threw up challenges to centralized power, with demands for greater autonomy spearheaded by the regions of the north. The nineteenth century had seen Spain struggling to develop an agreed strategy of economic and political development amid foreign occupation, civil war, military coups and royal dynastic divisions. And of all Spain's major towns, it was the imperial capital Madrid which seemed to disappoint foreigners and inhabitants alike mostly because of its apparent failure to achieve the ambitions invested in it. To visitors accustomed to London and Paris, Madrid seemed lacking in charm and grandeur, an artificial creation, living an unreal life. Lacking the industry and commerce of ports like Bilbao and Barcelona, or the romanticism of towns like Seville, Madrid seemed a nominal capital which received its life and impulse from beyond its boundaries, instead of communicating it from within. Its innate vanity came to be wonderfully described by Benito Perez Galdós, in his novel *Fortunata y Jacinta*. He described Madrid as a 'metropolis in name only – a bumpkin in a gentleman's coat buttoned over a torn, dirty shirt'.

The novel was published in 1876 but survives as a lasting testimony to the *Madrileños'* ambivalent attitude to foreign influences. The shawl shop run by Gumersindo and Isabel Arnaiz is Madrid in microcosm, both open to change and resistant to it. Their daughter grows up in an atmosphere 'redolent of sandalwood and Oriental fragrances'. Gumers-indo, struggling with bankruptcy, curses the foreigner who had made his life hell and changed irrevocably the Madrid he once knew. His wife however takes a more pragmatic approach to things foreign as she observes the obsession with fashion of the *Madrileños* and their desire to be taken seriously.

It was foreigners who brought football to Spain. As in Latin America, what would in time come to be known as the 'people's game' followed the imperial flag of Victorian England. Spain's first football club Recreativo de Huelva was founded in 1878 by the English management of the nearby Rio Tinto copper mines. The mineral deposits – one of Spain's major assets at the time – had been sold to a group of European businessmen with trading interests in the Anda-lusian port of Huelva, headed by the London banker Hugh Matheson, in exchange for the equivalent of £3.5m in gold coins. The British of Rio Tinto brought football with them as a way of 'civilizing' the locals and easing the tense industrial relations which overshadowed the history of the mines. As Rio Tinto's historian David Amery admitted, 'It is a sad fact that most Spaniards who know something of the history of Rio Tinto seem to remember first the strikes, the violence and the bloodshed, and normally lay the blame for these at the door of the British company.'

Two decades would elapse before the English helped create another historic sporting institution – Athletic Bilbao – in a town also known for its trade links with the British Empire. Two years later it was Catalonia's turn to see the light, with the foundation, by a Swiss businessman and a group of English enthusiasts on Christmas Eve 1900, of FC Barcelona.

The Spanish capital would have its first football club named after it registered in 1902. Madrid FC, as it was first called, had its roots in the dreams of a group of Spanish intellectuals who believed that football held the key to modernity. The first enthusiasts of the game in Madrid were middle-class admirers of northern European ways, with a distinctive philosophical spring in their step. They were the students who adhered to the Free Institute of Education, a movement dedicated to the creation of non-dogmatic learning in schools and universities as the precondition of a liberal democracy. Pupils were encouraged to play games and take walks in the countryside as part of a more rounded learning process than the regimented upbringing favoured by traditional sectors of the Catholic Church and the military.

Football's belated journey from the arid south-west to the north of Spain and to Madrid, and its later translation into a mass national sport, reflected the shapelessness of Spanish society and in part its differentiation from the rest of Europe for much of the nineteenth and part of the twentieth centuries. The Spain of small towns with their local fiestas linked to religious icons and localized economic activity would persist alongside the Spain of the cities and bullfighting, the national fiesta with its roots in the *Iberia* of Roman times which had become a business enterprise in the nineteenth century with the railways being exploited for the regular transport of both fighting bulls and spectators. In spite of the attempts of Spanish reformers to introduce football, its spread to the lower classes was much slower than in England.

· In *Red Faces*, his history of Manchester United, Stephen F. Kelly has no doubt where 'this going to football matches' all began. As he puts it:

In Manchester it started long before Manchester United had ever been dreamt of. By 1878, when Newton Heath were formed, there were already leagues in and around the Manchester area with small groups of supporters, mainly friends and family, going along to support their team, though usually to home matches rather than away. The roots of football go back to churches (Protestant and mainly of the more liberal variety such as the Methodists), working men's associations, even public houses.

By 1909 football in England had grown sufficiently for an FA Cup final at the Crystal Palace in London to attract 70,000, its expansion only interrupted in 1915 by the pre-dations of the First World War. That the first games of football in Madrid were played in a field near the old bullring, with participants using a room in a local bullfighting *taverna* as one of their meeting places, was perhaps not entirely coincidental. Football, far from seeking to take the place of bullfighting, came to co-exist with it quite easily as a cultural and social phenomenon, generating similar passion and language, with the great players joining the great matadors in the pantheon of popular mythology.

And yet in its early beginnings football in Madrid had a foreign touch to it, which went beyond the philosophy of students and was apparent at a practical level. Madrid FC's first book of rules was imported from Manchester. The white colours which have distinguished the club to this day were copied from those of the Corinthians, a London amateur club. An Englishman is remembered as among the early personalities who helped shape the club's character. His name was Arthur Johnson, a businessman who spent much of his free time both training and playing with some of the first enthusiasts of the game in Madrid, while helping to translate the book of rules.

Of Johnson, Julian Palacios has left a sympathetic written portrait. It is kept in the club's archives and quoted in one of its early official histories, the *Libro de Oro*. Palacios found a striking contrast between Johnson's dedication and knowledge of the game and the chaotic play which characterized some of the Spaniards, not least that of the goalkeeper. While the latter spent his time sipping a soft drink in front of his goal, Johnson, in the words of Palacios, 'not only knew more about the game than anybody else', but equally important he was *un inglés muy simpático* (a very likeable Englishman). Johnson took his football so seriously that according to Palacios he was married one day and back playing the next, with no time set aside for a honeymoon, not even in Spain!

The weekly *El Cardo* newspaper in March 1903 published a thumbnail sketch of one of Madrid FC's first teams. At twenty-three Johnson was the veteran in a team whose average age was nineteen and whose youngest, sixteen-year-old Pedro Parages, was one of those enlightened youths who had learnt the game in England. 'Johnson is the captain of the team – he distinguishes himself with his tackling, agility and elegance of body. He plays in various positions, centre-half, centre-forward and goalkeeper. He also plays others sports, namely lawn-tennis and rugby.' The rest of the team was made up of a former player from Bilbao, seven other Spaniards – two of them born in Cuba and one in Guatemala – and a Frenchman who had also learnt to play in England. His name was Chalmandrier. 'He plays as right-half and distinguishes himself by the great security and elegance with which he plays.'

One wonders how a player like Johnson would have

managed with his football had he faced the kind of pressures which surrounded David Beckham when he came to Spain almost exactly one hundred years later. And yet this early history of Real Madrid shows the extent to which the initial roots of Spanish football owed much not just to England but to an openness to a variety of models of play and experience, that broke free from the corset of tradition and regional or national prejudice. Turning the pages of *El Cardo*, one finds none of the celebrity hype and commercialism that surrounds the modern game, but Beckham came to play with the commitment of Johnson on a good day, and Zidane at his best showed the commanding presence once shown by Chalmandrier.

The first administrators of Madrid FC were two brothers, Juan and Carlos Padros. They were born in Catalonia, the region that perhaps more than any other has come to see Madrid as enemy country in football terms and which in turn has fuelled bitter animosity among the more fanatical *Madridistas*. It is a curious paradox which serves as a reminder that beneath the myths created by the warring factions, or their apologists, the history of Spain was a complex affair. Partisanship has inevitably meant that the Padros brothers have been used by some Catalans to embarrass *Madridistas*, as when the Barcelona paper *Mundo Deportivo* in December 1992 boldly headlined an article: 'A Catalan Founded [Real] Madrid.'

The fact that the newspaper could claim an exposé nine decades after the event seemed to reflect the unwillingness of Real Madrid's official historians to come to terms with the fact that Catalans were among the club's founding fathers. Whatever the myths and obfuscations, the Padros brothers were never anything other than a product of their times and circumstances. They were young children when their parents migrated to Madrid from Barcelona in 1876. Their father was a cloth merchant who ran a small shop in Barcelona's old Jewish quarter near the Plaza de San Jaume. He spoke French as his second language and made frequent visits to the north of England to look at textiles. Catalonia's own early industrial revolution had gone through a period of boom and bust. By contrast Madrid in 1876 looked poised on the edge of political reform that promised to make civil war and military coups a thing of the past. The Bourbon dynasty had been restored under King Alfonso XII and one of Spain's greatest statesmen Antonio Canovas de Castillo helped draw up a liberal constitution that he hoped would better the shortcomings of English parliamentarism and make Madrid a respected capital of a country united under a constitutional monarchy. It was to this Madrid that the Padros family moved in the second half of the nineteenth century.

It was only in the first decade of the twentieth century following Spain's imperial collapse, that the forces of Catalan nationalism were revived, marking out FC Barcelona's destiny as a political vehicle for which Real Madrid was not just another club, but another country. By then the Padros family shop on the Calle Alcalá had become somewhat more successful than the Gumersindos immortalized by the novelist Galdós. Even before work began on the Gran Vía in 1910, linking the old city with the new neighbourhoods which now make up central Madrid, the Calle Alcalá was one of Madrid's most important streets. It was then a bustle of coffee shops and small traders. At the beginning of the twenty-first century the headquarters of one of Spain's leading banks stands near to where the Padros family's shop used to be. Not that the average tourist or *Madrileño* would necessarily know that for there is no plaque marking the spot.

Between the official foundation of Madrid FC in 1902 and the outbreak of the Spanish Civil War in 1936, the club had seven presidents, including two terms of two years each involving the Padros brothers. During these thirty-four years football grew from being the pastime of a small group of foreigners and well-heeled nationals to a sport with a broader following across the social divide. The 1920s saw a significant demographic shift in Spain. With South America cut off during the First World War as a destination for Spanish emigrants escaping from rural poverty, there was a major population move from the countryside to the big towns. Madrid like Barcelona was forced to absorb an influx of low-income families, many of whom turned to football as a form of entertainment and social integration.

While FC Barcelona became identified with Catalan nationalism, Madrid FC enjoyed political patronage from the centre of power. Under the presidency of Juan Padros, Madrid FC engaged the sympathies of the new King Alfonso XIII by suggesting that his accession to the throne be marked by the staging in Madrid of Spain's first football championship. It was a suggestion quickly taken up with the capital's hippodrome the venue for an event that drew 5,000 spectators. Despite his stuffy upbringing, the latest Bourbon to assume the Spanish throne considered himself an open-minded modern king whose interest in leisure activities from cars to clay-pigeon shooting was on a level with his talent for political intrigue. His unqualified embrace of football sprang from his desire to be seen as a go-ahead monarch even if he came to put too much political faith in reactionary army officers. It was one of these military men, General Miguel Primo de Rivera, captain-general of Catalonia, who took over the running of the country in 1923, with the acquiescence of the king, ushering in a period of dictatorship that was to prove rather more benign to some Spaniards than to others.

By that year the king had already conferred the title of *Real* or Royal on Madrid FC, as he had done with other emerging football clubs that he considered loyal and worthy of his patronage such as Espanyol, Sociedad and Betis. The club moved its stadium from the small site in O'Donnell Street, near Madrid's Retiro park, to the 15,000 capacity Chamartín stadium, constructed where the Santiago Bernabéu stands today, but which at that time was on the outskirts of the city. The development of modern urban Madrid in that neighbourhood would come much later in the century.

Chamartín was still more country than city at the time but it was just 700 metres along the Castellana from the hippodrome, and proved as popular with the fans. Two years into the Primo de Rivera dictatorship the stadium was inaugurated amid much celebration in the Spanish capital. The young prince Don Gonzalo kicked the ball 'of honour' with the phrase '*Hala Madrid*' – 'Let's go, Madrid' – which would become the club's official rallying cry. Real Madrid beat their guests the English champions Newcastle United by 3–0, one of them an own-goal. A local newspaper account of the match reported: 'Although the English showed some excellent passing and dribbling skills, they seem to lack the necessary speed, in which we Spaniards are notoriously superior.'

In fact the less than brilliant quality of Real Madrid's

football before and after the inauguration of Chamartín belied the apparent political patronage that the club enjoyed under both the king and the dictator. Since 1908 Real had won only one Spanish Cup (in 1917) and did not win another until 1934. The big prize, the league championship, eluded Real until 1932. This contrasts with the fortunes of the club that was emerging as one of its main rivals, FC Barcelona, which remembers the 1920s as a golden period in football terms as well as a period of political victimization. The decade saw five Cup triumphs and one league title, in 1929.

The fourteenth of June 1925 is a date forever remembered in the collective memory of Catalan nationalism as a day of infamy for it was then that the FC Barcelona stadium of Les Corts was closed down for six months by order of Catalonia's newly appointed captain-general Joaquin Milans del Bosch. The crime? The decision of some of Barça's supporters to whistle, and of the directors to stay sitting, during a rendering of the royal national anthem.

A very different anthem was played not just once but twice at Madrid's Atocha station on 6 May 1934 – the '*Himno de Riego*' of the Spanish Republic, brought in by the new civilian government which had rid the country of Primo de Rivera and exiled the king. There were no protests that day, just the celebration of thousands of fans. They were there to honour the Madrid FC team (the '*Real*' or Royal had been dropped in keeping with the political sympathies of the new government) that had just returned from winning the Spanish Cup in Barcelona. They had beaten Valencia 2–1, ending the four years of uninterrupted success of Athletic Bilbao in the competition and achieving Real Madrid's first Cup for seventeen years.

Real Madrid had by then bought Ricardo Zamora, the

legendary goalkeeper from the Barcelona club Espanyol, the first major transfer in Spanish football history. Zamora had started off his career at Espanyol in 1917, at the age of sixteen, before moving across the city to join FC Barcelona. Back then he was still a schoolboy wearing short trousers, but he soon adopted a dress code that marked him out as one of the great eccentrics on the field as much as off it. Maturing physically, he would later put on a polo-neck jumper and broad cloth cap before going to play a match. He said he wanted to protect himself from the sun and the blows of his opponents. In fact Zamora was fearless, throwing himself at the feet of his attackers, or venturing out with the ball, often leading a counter-attack well into the other half of the pitch. As the Uruguayan writer Eduardo Galeano remembered him,

the image of Zamora in those clothes became famous. He sowed panic among strikers. If they looked his way they were lost. With Zamora in the goal, the net would shrink and the posts would lose themselves in the distance. For twenty years he was the best goalkeeper in the world. He liked cognac and smoked three packs a day, plus the occasional cigar.

At Barça he came to be known as *El Divino* although his decision to return to Espanyol before moving to Real Madrid was viewed as something of a betrayal by some of the more obsessive Catalan nationalists. By contrast Real Madrid had little difficulty adopting Zamora as one of its heroes.

In 1933 Real Madrid secured from FC Barcelona another hugely talented and popular figure in Pepe Samitier, further strengthening a team that already boasted the pick of the crop from each of its competitors. *El Sami* had been a key figure in the Catalan club's first glory period. He now helped Real Madrid's resurgence. Samitier was an early exponent of what many years later came to be known as 'total football'. There were no positions off-limits to him, as he feinted and dribbled his way from one end of the field to the other, baffling his opponents, and often reducing his team mates to playing a purely supporting role. Although the invigorated Real Madrid in the mid-1930s included other players of talent like Quincoces and Pedro Reguiero, none – with the exception of Zamora – could equal *El Sami*'s personality. Samitier died in 1972 after serving for a while as manager at FC Barcelona before returning to Madrid. After a further spell with FC Barcelona he was buried with full honours in the Catalan capital, his coffin carried by past and present players from the club, and with many old friends from Madrid in attendance, including Bernabéu.

Although I never met Samitier personally, I was provided with a unique insight into the man in the late 1990s during a long conversation with his widow Tina. Her words now straddle the separate histories of Spanish football's two biggest rivals in ways I have come to appreciate even more with the passing of time, another testimony to the real history of Spain beyond that imagined by the partisans.

As we sat in her flat in Barcelona, Tina shared what she had come to learn about her husband with disarming frankness. 'They threw him out of Barcelona [football club] because of envy. The same thing happened when he was a player thirty years earlier. It had nothing to do with his ability. It hurt him a lot. He felt very down, betrayed, the worst that any person can feel. He never forgave the people who did it.

Pepe had a good memory. When they threw him out, Berna-béu said to him, "Why don't you come home?" Bernabéu treated him like a brother.'

Later in our conversation I asked Tina what her husband had thought of Franco. She answered: 'We never spoke about politics because Pepe was completely apolitical. He left Spain during the Civil War because everyone was leaving and because he was half famous and because he was afraid of being caught up in the repression. I remember once when we'd been married for a while Pepe came back from a trip abroad and said, "You'll never guess who I bumped into in the airport. I think it was Santiago Carrillo [head of the Spanish Communist Party who was then living in exile from the Franco regime]. He wasn't shocked, just interested in a purely human way. He didn't really worry about who he met. He was by nature open and down to earth. To Franco he used to say things like, "My General, you've put on a bit of weight," and he'd tap him on the tummy.'

Tina was very young when she married a much older Samitier in Nice in 1966. He had clearly enjoyed life as a bachelor, usually in the company of men. One of Samitier's great friends during his playing days was Carlos Gardel, the most famous of Argentina's tango artists. They were both rebels without a cause other than life itself. One expressed this with his football, the other with his songs. Gardel was killed in a plane crash in 1935 taking many of his secrets with him, although not the fact that it was Samitier whom he had always thanked for introducing him to the joys of football.

One of Real Madrid's most assiduous chroniclers, the jour-nalist and writer Julian García Candau, noted in a seminal work published in 1996 that 'it is a club that has always aspired to be where power is'. That players dropped the crown from the emblem on their shirts, and the club itself the title Real from its name soon after the proclamation of the Spanish Republic in 1931 and flight to exile of King Alfonso XIII, shows at the very least a certain element of political expediency. Within Madrid FC – as it was now officially known again – signs of tension surfaced in May 1935 as the Civil War loomed with the resignation of the president of the club Usera Bugallal, and two of his most senior advisers – one of them Santiago Bernabéu, the former player and trainer turned club secretary.

Usera Bugallal had struggled with limited success to get the president of the Republican government Manuel Azaña to drop an ambitious urban development plan which involved building along the Castellana and expropriating the Chamartín stadium. Azaña was an intellectual who before coming to power had struggled to make a living from writing, and was never much interested in football. Despite being born in the nearby university town of Alcalá de Henares and spending most of his life in Madrid, Azaña was critical of the political and social life of the Spanish capital he hoped to reform. Before the proclamation of the Republic, Azaña had declared that 'the entire history of Madrid consists of hand kissing and private or royal intrigues.' As for the lower classes, he added, they had always been absent from the history of the city 'except to cry hunger' and the 'unique occasion' when they had risen up against the invading troops of Napoleon in the Peninsular War. The philosopher Unamuno suggested that such comments sprang from Azaña's frustration as a writer. 'Beware of Azaña,' the old scribe wrote. 'He would be capable of starting a revolution in order to be read.'

To those in the high echelons of Real Madrid, Azana's plans for the Castellana smacked of revolution. Usera Bugallal approached the journalist and politician Rafael Sanchez Guerra, a member of the club who was one of the more moderate supporters of the Republican government, and asked him to intercede on the club's behalf. But uncertainty over the future of the Chamartín stadium did not abate. Bugallal resigned, and Sanchez Guerra replaced him as president of the club in a move enemies of both men put down to a cynical political calculation. By then Bernabéu, the man destined to have such a key influence on the history of Real Madrid, was an armed member of CEDA (Spanish confederation of autonomous movements of the Right), a political movement that grouped together monarchists, Christian democrats and a youth wing that inclined towards fascism, of which he was sports secretary.

6. Spain Divided

It was an occasion that David Beckham would later come to remember as marking a watershed of his time in Spain. On the night of 10 March 2004 the Santiago Bernabéu stadium erupted in a collective roar as Beckham and his team mates ran out to play the second leg of their Champions League clash with Bayern Munich, their bitterest European rivals.

The German champions had had a habit of spoiling Real Madrid's European ambitions. Add to this the repressed memory of Franco's flirtation with Nazism during the Second World War, and post-war Germany's exploitation of Spanish immigrant labour for its economic regeneration, which was a possible explanation as to why Bayern's captain Oliver Khan was taunted with dog-barking noises as part of the abuse dished out by Real fans to the visitors. Travelling with some of the more fanatical Real Madrid supporters to Munich for the first leg a few days earlier, I had been struck how some of them wanted to do just two things before watching the game in the Olympic stadium – sleep with a German girl and get drunk in the beer cellar where Hitler had launched his National Socialist movement. Whatever the reasons that lay behind the *Madridista* passion that night, the wall of noise it generated must have made Beckham feel as if he were leading England out to face Germany.

Watched by King Juan Carlos – a modern monarch who genuinely enjoyed the people's game – and millions of fans around the world, Beckham created the decisive goal that night, his cross clipping Zé Roberto, curving into the penalty area and finding Michel Salgado who passed for Zidane to finish from four yards. And then the Englishman went close himself, bringing half the stadium to its feet, before the ball drifted just wide of Kahn's left-hand post. Yet the real hero that night, as he was to prove in several other games of that season, was Real Madrid's young goalkeeper Iker Casillas, who saved a thundering volley from Zé Roberto, before later turning away a cross-shot from Roy Makaay.

The excitement of that game, and the elation that followed the final whistle as Real Madrid booked a place in the quarter-finals of a tournament the club hoped to win, proved cruelly deceptive. Not because Real Madrid were destined to be eliminated by rank outsiders Monaco, but because on that very night a group of Islamic fanatics were putting in place the final preparations for Spain's worst terrorist outrage the next day. Among the first suspects later arrested was a young North African immigrant who was found to have a Beckham number 23 shirt among his personal belongings. Football had been played against the wrong enemy, and not for the first time in Spanish history the sheer pleasure of the game was overshadowed by the brutal interference of violence on a horrific scale.

Minutes from the end of the first ever Spanish Cup final clash between the leading teams of Madrid and Barcelona, Ricardo Zamora, the man they had nicknamed 'The Divine One', threw himself full stretch towards the left-hand goal-post and blocked a last-ditch attempt at an equalizer by the Catalan striker Escola. Madrid FC (the 'Royal' had been ditched for political reasons) thus secured a 2–1 victory over the team that in time would come to be its biggest rival, FC Barcelona. That save was destined to be cherished as one of the most brilliant ever made by a Spanish goalkeeper.

The game was played in Valencia's Mestalla stadium. It was the 22 June 1936. Like a *torero* who had bravely fought and killed the fiercest bull in the land, Zamora was raised up on the shoulders of his ecstatic fans and paraded triumphantly. Within hours he and his colleagues had returned to Madrid by train to be greeted, as they had been after their previous Cup victory two years previously, by thousands at the Spanish capital's central railway station at Atocha. By then however no amount of celebration could hide the fact that Republican Spain was on the verge of disintegration, the incompatible politics of left and right lurching out of control towards civil war. As the British writer Jan Morris would later describe it, Spain was 'a mess of a country . . . tortured by conflicting ideologies . . . dogmas of monarchy, theocracy, despotism, democracy, socialism, anarchism, Communism, her rural poverty and urban squalor erupting into violence'. A day after the Madrid–Barcelona match, General Francisco Franco, the captain-general of the Canary Islands, wrote to the Spanish prime minister Casares Quiroga warning of growing military unrest.

Franco had yet fully to throw his hat into the ring with the plotters but it was now just a matter of time before he did. Elsewhere, right-wing officers and their civilian allies were already planning an uprising to put an end to what they regarded as the country's descent into Soviet-led anarchy. On 11 July the growing conspiracy took on a touch of Anglo-Saxon adventurism when a light aircraft took off from

Croydon airfield near London and flew towards the Canaries. Ever since the days of Francis Drake through to the Peninsular Wars of the Duke of Wellington and the later Carlist Wars, the English had shown a tendency – not always welcomed by the locals – to get involved in Spanish political affairs.

On board the small Dragon Rapide aircraft was Luis Bolin, a London-based right-wing Spanish journalist and committed anti-communist and two glamorous nineteen-year-old English girls of good upbringing, Diana Pollard and Dorothy Watson, both of whom were posing as tourists.

To ensure that Franco joined the military coup against Spain's Popular Front government, the main conspirators had arranged for the plane to pick him up in the Canaries and fly him, as part of a covert operation, to Spanish Morocco from where the first rebellious army units were to make their move. Money for the flight had been put up by Juan March, a Spanish businessman who had made his early fortune in his native Mallorca. Payment was transferred via an account in Kleinwort Benson Bank in the heart of the City of London and the plane secured thanks to the help of a retired British army officer, Captain Hugh Pollard. It was Pollard's daughter Diana who together with her friend Dorothy agreed to act as decoys, carrying secret documents between the covers of a *Vogue* magazine.

The uprising was set in motion on 18 July, with Franco's commitment to the event later recorded by his friend and confidant Bolin in terms that sought to transform him into the Great Crusader of Spanish mythology:

A lump rose in my throat when I saw him [Franco] wind around his waist the scarlet, gold-tasselled sash which in the Spanish

Army constitutes the most distinctive symbol of a General's rank. This was it. In his usual quiet and unassuming manner he had attired himself to take command of the forces that awaited his arrival. Years were to elapse before he donned civilian clothes again.

To write simply that the outbreak of civil war coincided with Spanish football's close season would be to trivialize the extent to which clubs, players and fans had their lives transformed. The fate of many Spaniards was sealed as much by where he or she happened to be as by ideological preference, with conflicting loyalties resolved by death or the threat of it. Violence of a most shocking kind would now spread across Spain, leading to the death of over half a million people and the geographical dislocation or exile of many thousands more by the time Franco secured his victory in 1939.

The plotters behind the nationalist uprising in Madrid included General Adolfo Meléndez, a man whose devotion to military duties – and right-wing politics – came to predominate over his love of sport. A keen cyclist and equestrian, Meléndez was among the first Spanish footballers in the early years of the twentieth century, helping set up the Spanish Football Federation, under the patronage of King Alfonso XIII, and serving as one of the first players and presidents of Madrid FC. So closely involved was Meléndez with the Franco uprising, that in the early summer of 1936 he decided to postpone his holidays in the town of Avila and instead stayed behind in the Spanish capital to help plan the overthrow of the left-wing Popular Front government. Meléndez was lucky to escape with his life.

In contrast to some other towns of Spain, where the

Franco forces succeeded in establishing early control, Madrid, like Barcelona and the main Basque cities, held firm amid the confusion of the plotters. Officers loyal to Franco belatedly gathered at the Montana barracks on the west side of Madrid, overlooking the river Manzanares. They were joined by civilian sympathizers. But those loyal to the government had already set in motion a pre-emptive counter-strike, with Dolores Ibárurri, the fiery communist who achieved mythical status as *La Pasionaria*, making the first of a series of radio broadcasts urging 'workers, peasants, anti-fascists, and patriotic Spaniards' not to allow the plotters to prevail.

The order *No pasarán* – 'they shall not pass' – eventually screamed over the airwaves. A crowd of thousands organized and armed by the socialist and anarchist trade unions surrounded the barracks, while loyal members of the air force and artillery units mounted a bombardment. On the second day of the siege an even larger crowd gathered in the capital's main square, the Plaza de España, with its statue of Don Quixote, the legendary literary figure whom Spanish intellectuals felt personified an unshakeable set of national traits.

As the author and journalist Robert Graham noted in his book *Spain: Change of a Nation*, 'The Castilian knight incarnated the spirit of non-compromise, so inflexible as to tilt against his own self-interest and against reality; his hopelessness and failure are forgotten beside his nobility of purpose.' The quintessential virtues of the Spanish male had long come to be seen as encompassing bravery, honour and pride in the conquest of love, or arms. In that hot sultry July of 1936, Don Quixote meant all things to all men. The left-wing militias saw his lance pointing towards the Montana barracks, encouraging them to take it. Those loyal to Franco had no doubt that Don Quixote's arm was outstretched in a fascist salute, and not bent like a revolutionary clenched fist.

In the hours, days, weeks and months that followed, scenes of heroism and brutality would be played out on the streets of Madrid. My own Spanish family, on my mother's side, would be among those deeply affected. Scarcely out of her teens, my mother and her sister were drafted as nurses to work among the war wounded in one of the capital's main hospitals. My grandfather was a writer and a doctor who was politically a liberal. Born in 1887, as a teenager he had been among the first *Madrileños* to play football at the beginning of the century, for a small amateur club called Vitoria. At the outbreak of the Spanish Civil War he volunteered, along with his daughters, to help the injured and the dying in one of the capital's main hospitals. Because my grandfather's friends included individuals fighting for the Franco side, he was deeply mistrusted by the communists and was brought in for questioning on two occasions by armed militias. Warned by close friends that he risked being executed if he remained in Madrid, he chose eventually to take himself and his family into temporary exile in France.

My family was still in Madrid when the Montana barracks fell, with many of its occupants massacred in an orgy of bloodshed. Those army officers who survived were taken off, tried and shot. They included several close allies of General Meléndez, who had chosen to stay clear of the barracks and await developments. He was at home when a group of armed militia, prompted by an anti-Franco neighbour, opened fire on the outside of his house, shattering the windows and damaging the shutters. To this day it has been impossible to establish a reason why Meléndez wasn't arrested there and then. But the apparent hesitancy of his enemies allowed him to escape into hiding, together with his family. Living in safe houses owned by those sympathetic to the military uprising across Madrid, Meléndez was eventually smuggled out of the Spanish capital and made his way to Burgos, where Franco had set up his headquarters. Meléndez survived the Civil War, serving under Franco as a quarter-master general. Fate had ensured that Meléndez would return to the world of Spanish football to play, along with others, a role in the post-war reorganization of Real Madrid.

Santiago Bernabéu, the man whose giant reputation was to loom over the fortunes of Real Madrid during the years of the Franco regime, also became embroiled in the Civil War. While Bernabéu was to describe himself as a 'liberal with education', he was denounced as a fascist to the marauding militias by an employee of the football club. He was saved from the firing squad thanks to the intercession of another Madrid FC supporter, and friend, the socialist Spanish ambassador in Paris Alvaro de Albornoz. Albornoz helped secure Bernabéu's safe passage across the border after he had been granted asylum in the French embassy in Madrid.

Bernabéu came back across the frontier, into northern Spain, in 1937 and enlisted with the Franco forces which had by then taken control of Irún. It was perhaps only appropriate that it was here in Irún that Bernabéu signed up for Franco's Great National Crusade against the forces of evil and the enemies of Spain. After all it was in this Basque border town that, back in the early 1920s, the young Real Madrid player Bernabéu had famously suggested to his team mates prior to their match with Real Unión de Irún that they should celebrate each goal they scored with the cry, '*Viva España*'. Real Madrid on that occasion lost 0–2 although the cry was destined to be resurrected on countless occasions by the club's fans once Franco had won the Civil War.

Bernabéu became a corporal in the Franco army and earned a military medal after participating in the rout of the Republican units in the Pyrenean town of Bielsa on 6 June 1938. Contemporary photographs show Bernabéu in his early forties, smoking a pipe and dressed in military cloak and fatigues, taking a stroll along the streets of 'liberated' San Sebastián. Basque nationalists surrendered their summer capital of Irún to Franco's chief military strategist General Mola on 3 September 1936 without a fight rather than risk the destruction of its impressive architecture and generous promenades.

The great and the good of Spanish society had kept a low profile since memorably forcing Coco Chanel to eat in her room at San Sebastián's Hotel Cristina because the conservative society ladies objected to the presence of the innovative dress designer in the same dining room as themselves. But they would soon emerge from the woodwork, mixing it with Franco crusaders in a self-conscious 'normalization' process that involved *Marca*, the first 'national' sports newspaper to be published under Franco's rule. Printed for the first time just before Christmas 1938 under the management of individuals closely allied to the Franco cause, the tabloid newspaper served two interrelated purposes: to act as the official organ on sports matters, and to turn the mass following of football that had been developing since the 1920s from the left towards the right of the political spectrum. Its first front page had a photograph of a blonde girl making the fascist salute in tribute 'to all the Spanish sportsmen and women'.

Marca was put to good use as a propaganda tool, focusing on those sports personalities who could be portrayed as victimized by anti-Franco forces and celebrated as examples of the New Spain that was being promised once the Great Crusade had prevailed. That Bernabéu had already been identified as a man with a future by Franco was suggested by a full-page profile the newspaper published of him in those days when he walked the streets of San Sebastián dressed as a corporal. The article honours a man who after giving 'some great days of glory' to Real Madrid as a player had gone on to serve as a director, before resigning out of political principle and devoting himself exclusively to supporting 'The Cause' for which Franco's generals rose on 18 July 1936. The newspaper profile elaborates on Bernabéu's escape from 'the ferocious persecution of the red hordes', noting that he had sought asylum 'in an embassy' (there is no mention of the helping hand apparently provided by a socialist ambassador), had pretended to be a patient in a general hospital before hiding in a chicken run and escaping through a trap door. Based on a loose interview, the article notes that while Bernabéu spent two years of the Civil War without engaging in active service, he had enthusiastically volunteered once he had entered the Franco-controlled zone and was now 'proudly' displaying the medal he had militarily 'conquered'.

Asked about the future, Bernabéu insisted that sport should be an essential part of the New Spain. 'The spectacle of a few sweaty youths must disappear and give way to a youth that is healthy in body and spirit under the direction of specialist trainers,' he commented. From Hitler's Germany to Mussolini's Italy the image of a uniformed and blemish-free youth was being extolled as an essential element of racial superiority. The Great Crusaders born in Castile were fast developing their own version of the essence of the Spanish race. The profile finally comments that Real Madrid would in the future need to draw on some of its veteran supporters for its transformation. 'If we can count among them people like our interviewee, the club's resurgence will be rapid,' it concludes.

The writer was none other than *El Divino* himself, Ricardo Zamora, the one-time goalkeeper of Barcelona who had transferred to Real Madrid before making that save against the Catalan club in the Cup final of June 1936. To this day Zamora remains one of a handful of players fought over as 'one of us' by the official historians of both rival clubs, largely because he refused to allow himself to be pigeon-holed politically. He happily accepted a medal from the Spanish Republican government before the outbreak of the Civil War. Before it was over, he had declared his sympathies for Franco, retired from football and worked as commentator for the conservative Catholic newspaper *Ya*.

There is a story that Zamora liked to tell as evidence that his popularity as a sportsman was more important than the prejudices fuelled by Spain's political passions. At the outbreak of the Civil War, Zamora found himself confronted one day by an anarchist militiaman, who, brandishing a knife, denounced him as an employee of a right-wing newspaper. Zamora had little doubt that the man appeared to be bent on killing him. Then suddenly the potential assailant dropped the knife and identified himself as an Madrid FC supporter.

The militiaman thanked Zamora for all the great saves he'd made and for helping the club clinch the last pre-war Cup in Valencia. Zamora there and then entered into a lengthy dialogue about Spanish football generally. The two men parted company, the best of friends.

Zamora was later imprisoned without trial in Madrid's Modelo jail. From the Andalusian capital of Seville, taken within hours of the military rising by forces loyal to Franco, General Queipo de Llano used a radio broadcast to claim that the 'nation's goalkeeper' was among dozens of well-known personalities who had been executed by the 'reds'. The rumour was initially taken seriously enough for Masses to be organized in his memory in traditional clerical towns like Valladolid. But it was pure invention, part of the propaganda war.

In the Modelo prison Zamora was periodically paraded by his captors in front of visiting officials as if he were a prize possession. To be called out of your detention because your name was on some list somewhere meant in those days the likelihood of being sent to your death. In Zamora's case the unexpected call-outs, the so-called *sacas*, were a form of psychological torture. He later recalled how his legs would physically tremble every time that happened. However, his spirits were kept alive thanks to the occasional football match prisoners and their jailers organized in the prison's main yard.

Zamora was eventually released after an international campaign on his behalf, particularly in France, and took refuge in the Argentine embassy where arrangements were made to transport him, his wife and young son, out of Spain. By then Zamora had had enough of being recognized, at least until he was safely out of Madrid. He emerged from the embassy wearing dark glasses and having grown a beard. The disguise did not fool another militiaman who came up behind him, tapped him on the shoulder, and said, 'Hey Zamora, *hombre*, what you doing with the beard?'

He too turned out to be a football fan. This time *El Divino* and his family were allowed to make their way to freedom via the ports of Valencia and Marseille, to Paris. Once safely in the French capital, he was interviewed by the newspaper *Paris Soir*. Zamora described himself as a 'one hundred per cent Spaniard' who after a long and successful career as a goalkeeper believed he deserved to be better treated by some of his compatriots than to fear for his life. 'What are my plans for the future? I haven't been executed, I'm happy, I feel young and strong, I love football more than ever and have no plans to give it up,' Zamora said.

He journeyed on to Nice where he played for the local team, along with Pepe Samitier, *El Sami*, the other star footballer who had transferred from Barcelona to Madrid before the Civil War. *El Sami*'s escape from the 'reds' also entered the mythology of the conflict, with Franco's sports mouthpiece *Marca* giving full coverage to his narrow escape from arrest, his days in hiding, and his eventual arrival on French territory 'with two suits, a lot of hunger, and exhausted'. Both Zamora and Samitier later returned to Spain, and eventually settled without difficulty under Franco's rule.

The coverage given to Zamora and Samitier's experiences both during and after the Civil War is far greater than that given to Gonzalo Aguirre and Valero Rivera, former vice-president and treasurer respectively of Real Madrid, partly because the players survived to tell their tale, while the administrators were taken away and shot in mysterious circumstances. Undoubtedly both Zamora and Samitier allowed themselves to be used as tools of propaganda by the Francoist side even if their role as political actors was unwittingly played, as Alfredo Relaño, the author and sports journalist has suggested. 'Of Zamora much was said during the Civil War. The outbreak of the conflict takes him by surprise in Madrid, and he is detained and imprisoned by militiamen. Why? For nothing. An arbitrary act like so many others in those days. Because he was a rich kid, one supposes. Zamora has in no sense distinguished himself politically,' writes Relano in his book *Football, told simply*.

With the passing of the years, Real Madrid tended to reduce its memories of the Civil War, while FC Barcelona rediscovered and exploited them, a contrast which can be explained by the changing nature of Spain as the country moved from dictatorship to democracy, and Catalan nationalism revived with the declining years of Francoism. The celebration of Real Madrid's centenary in 2002 had newspapers returning to forgotten archives and digging up old stories ignored for years that recorded Real Madrid's history as part of the history of Spain. And yet the club's own commemorative official history *One Hundred Years of Legend* distilled the three years of the Spanish Civil War in one paragraph: 'These were three years which muffled the clamour of the stadiums and fuelled hatred among Spaniards. The life of the Club was paralysed. The old Chamartín stadium suffered the consequences of war. Late in the spring of 1939, amidst the desolate landscape of the war, Real Madrid emerged from the ashes thanks to a group of fervent and enthusiastic supporters.' Nor did the club, under the presidency of Florentino Perez, seek to inform the new generations any better. A *History of Real Madrid for Young People*, an illustrated text book for school kids, makes no mention at all of the Civil War years.

Very different was my experience of researching the history of FC Barcelona in the run-up to its centenary in 2000, during which I discovered the extent to which the resurgence of Catalan nationalism within democracy has helped resurrect the figure of Josep Sunyol as a cultural and political hero. Sunyol was elected as a parliamentary deputy in 1931 for the left-wing Catalan nationalist group Esquerra Republicana. He became president of FC Barcelona in July 1935. Just thirteen months later, following the outbreak of the Civil War, Sunyol made his way to Madrid in a chauffeur-driven car and then up into the nearby Sierra de Guadarrama. The peaks of the mountain range and the low-lying hills had become one of the key battlegrounds for the control of Madrid which had resisted the military uprising. The Francoist forces had taken several major towns, including Burgos, Valladolid, Salamanca, Segovia and Zaragoza. Under a plan drawn up by General Mola, the forces had launched a two-pronged offensive on the Spanish capital, with the aim of capturing the two main approaches – the pass of Somosierra and a second pass known as the Alto de Los Leones. Here they had dug in with bunkers, trenches and machine-gun posts to continue fighting a war of attrition with militia groups loyal to the Republican government sent out from Madrid. A complex patchwork of military units spread out across the hills on either side of the pass. The situation was made all the more confusing by a relentless campaign of propaganda waged by the contenders which often distorted news from the front.

In setting off from Madrid that day in August, Sunyol appears to have been following other politicians and journalists who, out of a mixture of curiosity as to what was really going on and solidarity with the troops, had engaged in a somewhat dangerous form of 'war tourism'. It was dangerous because the nature of the military situation made it uncertain exactly which part of the mountains belonged to which side at any given time. Whether Sunyol's car subsequently drove into enemy territory by accident or design has to this day never been proved beyond doubt although it is not implausible that the Catalan politician may have been the victim of a betrayal. The fact is that Sunyol was detained on a stretch of road controlled by Francoist troops and subsequently shot.

In 1997, more than sixty years after his disappearance, I retraced Sunyol's final journey with the aid of a map and information put together by Antoni Strubell, an Oxford graduate. He had recently investigated Sunyol's death drawing on eyewitness accounts and newspaper archive material which had been silenced or buried over many years. On the outskirts of the town of Guadarrama, in a small clearing among pines, I found a discreet monolith with the simple inscription, 'José Suñol Garriga: Barcelona 21-VII-1898; Guadarrama 6-VIII-1936'. It had been unveiled on 4 June 1996 by Sunyol's Catalan supporters, with the blessing of the local mayor – a member of the ruling centre-right Partido Popular – and the local civil guard presenting arms as the Catalans sang their national anthem.

Those who built it had agreed to use the Castilian version of the names Josep and Sunyol, and to avoid any mention of his role either as a Catalan politician or as president of FC Barcelona, for fear that it might draw the attention of adverse fanatics bent on its destruction. As I subsequently discovered the location did not accurately mark the spot where Sunyol was executed but had been picked as part of a political compromise. The owner of the land where the death is believed to have occurred refused to have any memorial placed there, insisting that any monument to the Civil War dead should include one to his son, who was killed by Republican militias in the same area.

Clearly the huge cross and basilica built by Franco just a few kilometres away in the Valley of the Fallen was not adequate compensation. The spot identified by Strubell as the place of Sunyol's arrest and possible execution was a kilometre or so beyond the town, on the N-VI road, after a bend in the road. During the Civil War there was a mountain hut there, but that landmark had long since been removed when I visited the site. On the other side of the road stood a large military sanatorium. There were two conscripts on duty on my visit that day in the spring of 1997. When I asked them if they knew what had happened there during the Civil War, they simply replied that there had been 'a lot of fighting'. Then I asked them what football team they supported. Atlético de Madrid, they told me. They were playing cards and listening to the radio. No one had ever told them about Sunyol.

And yet for Catalan nationalists Sunyol has achieved the iconic status of a martyr, and helped perpetuate the myth of FC Barcelona as a persecuted club, at the expense of a more balanced dissection of the Civil War memory.

*

In Madrid the euphoria generated by the storming of the Montana barracks and the initial thwarting of the military uprising fuelled a revolutionary atmosphere that touched every aspect of life in the capital. In the words of the Republican president Manuel Azaña, 'the population showed off a new uniform of negligence, dirt, and rags . . . the race seemed darker, because the young warriors let their beards grow, almost always a black beard, and the faces became dark in the sun.' The rich and middle classes dressed down, restaurants were collectivized, the Ritz hotel became a military hospital, the Palace hotel a hostel for destitute children.

During the day loudspeakers placed in squares and main avenues spewed out an endless dose of propaganda. At night came the sinister sound of machine-gun and rifle fire as the first executions got under way. The novelist Ramon Sender described his own experience of the capital in those days of political ferment as a moment when 'passion infects the air, and no one can breathe, and when the most extraordinary events happen independently of any of the preparations which have been made.'

About 2,000 British volunteers joined the International Brigades against Franco, their bravery in the battles that were fought in defending Madrid helping to fire the population with a feeling that they were not alone. Some of the fiercest fighting involving the brigades took place in the winter of 1937 around the village of Las Rozas, on the road to Corunna, the setting many years later for one of Madrid's many satellite towns and a new football training ground used by the Real Madrid of Florentino Perez.

*

When Beckham began playing at Real Madrid, the world's media, many of whose representatives had turned up just for the initial occasion, complained about the poor facilities they had to deal with at Real Madrid's old training ground *Ciudad Deportiva*. The press room was a Portakabin built to hold thirty or so local journalists, a fraction of those who now followed Real Madrid regularly. To accommodate the invasion of Beckham enthusiasts, they removed the seats one day to fit everyone in. It was still an impossible squeeze. When the team temporarily moved out to the Spanish Football Federation's training ground in Las Rozas, while Perez got on with his latest urban development and the construction of new facilities, the media and the fans complained about the distance that separated them from the players and the heightened security arrangements that surrounded everything that moved in white. The players arrived and left in their fleet of luxury cars. After just a few days in Spain Beckham claimed that one of the things that most concerned him about his new life were the six or seven paparazzi cars that regularly chased him round town.

In London, near Westminster Bridge, on the south side of the river Thames, there was a monument to the British volunteers who had died fighting for Spain. If there was a plaque marking the site of their selfless heroism near where Beckham and his team mates limbered up, it was not easily identifiable. And yet much as Real Madrid had contributed to erasing the memory of the Spanish Civil War, the club had been severely affected by it.

Since its foundation in 1902 Real Madrid had survived the various changes of government, falling into step with political developments and maintaining its identity as a growing sporting institution. Now it faced a much more traumatic challenge to its organization than the forced ditching of the 'Royal' from its club name. The club, dreamed up by liberal intellectuals, and developed by businessmen, bankers and generals, was thrown to the revolutionary wolves, to be picked at according to their whim.

The moderate Republican president of the club Rafael Sanchez-Guerra was pushed out by a newly created workers' committee headed by two political commissars. Later there would be further political intervention by a communist army officer Lieutenant Colonel Antonio Ortega who took his orders from the Soviet secret police and was behind the arrest and subsequent execution of the alleged Spanish Trotskyite leader Andres Nin. Madrid FC, which over the years had increased its popularity across class lines, was declared the exclusive property of a left-wing Republic and the working masses it claimed to serve. The monthly membership dues were reduced although the appeal for existing members to keep up to date with the payments suggested a sinister motive. Those who didn't pay risked being identified as enemies of the Republic.

Sport in the capital became politicized consciously and overtly, with Chamartín, the Madrid FC stadium, playing host to military tattoos and exhibits by the newly created 'Spanish Battalion of Sport' which aimed to give off a collective air of revolutionary loyalty as well as Soviet-style vigour. The capital's population was encouraged to use the stadium's swimming pool. Once strictly members only, it was now open to the general public.

Madrid was gradually encircled by the Francoist forces, its

attempts at establishing a sense of new political and social order undermined by the forced conscription of the population – football players included – and the lack of decent communication with the rest of the country. The outbreak of the Civil War dispersed and effectively disintegrated the Madrid FC team that only weeks earlier had won the Cup in Valencia. Football continued to be played but mainly by soldiers enlisted on one or other of the warring sides. Spain became a patchwork of irreconcilable political territories so that an attempt by Madrid FC to play against Barcelona in the Catalan league was rejected by Barça officials on the grounds that such an encounter would undermine the regional identity of the competition. As a result Chamartín saw more Soviet-influenced sports demonstrations before falling into disuse and abandonment as the Franco troops drew nearer to the capital. Somewhat more fortunate, for a while at least, were FC Barcelona and a Basque national squad. For a while they maintained their cohesion playing in local competitions and touring abroad, raising funds for the cause of regional nationalism under a Republican flag. But in late 1937 world football's governing body FIFA gave official recognition to the new National Football Federation of Spain which had the support of Franco's generals. Less than two years later Franco proclaimed victory over the forces of evil and the enemies of Spain.

Franco's troops entered Madrid on 27 March 1939. Among the thousands of Republicans summarily executed after the surrender was Lieutenant Colonel Ortega, the former head of security who had for a while taken over the running of Madrid FC as a Soviet-style workers' federation. In Rome

Mussolini's foreign minister Count Galeazo Ciano noted gleefully in his diary: 'Madrid has fallen and with the capital all the other cities of Red Spain. The war is over. It is a new, formidable victory for Fascism, perhaps the greatest so far.'

Members of Real Madrid who had fought on Franco's side were shocked by the general scene of disrepair they found at the Chamartín stadium. Benches and fences had been torn up and burnt for fuel, and other materials such as bricks plundered for more urgent uses such as temporary accommodation. Part of the grounds had been used as a rough vegetable plot. The task of restoration was put in the hands of a group of army officers and civilians who had been members of the club before the outbreak of the Civil War and whose political sympathies had remained on the side of Franco throughout the conflict. The 'reborn' Real Madrid built up its membership with the active encouragement of the uncompromising state machinery which now took control of sport as it did of every aspect of Spanish life.

Spain during the 1940s was a country occupied by the army of Franco and largely administered by the Falange party. Unconditional loyalty to Franco was the predominant characteristic of the all-embracing 'Movement' which also contained within its ranks right-wing monarchists. The Movement sought to consolidate Franco's military victory, linking it to the contemporary fascism or National Socialism which Hitler and Mussolini were poised to unleash on a continental scale. Any possibility that sport of any kind could maintain a degree of independence from the political order that emerged in the aftermath of the Civil War was effectively destroyed by the February 1941 decree that established the new governing sports body, the Delegación Nacional de Deportes de Falange Tradicionalista Española y de las JONS (DND) with overarching power over the Spanish Football Federation (RFEF).

The DND was a Falangist institution staffed largely but not exclusively by Falangists. Its first head was the army general José Moscardo, venerated by the Falangists as the hero of the 1936 siege of Toledo's Alcazár, who knew little about football but was sufficiently loyal to the Movement to insist personally that before every sporting event competitors make the Falangist outstretched salute and chant the old war-cries of '*Arriba España*', and '*Viva Franco*'. Although not compulsory, the Falangist anthem '*Cara al sol*' was also sung at various sporting events.

Of over twenty players who played for the club in the run-up to the military uprising in 1936, only four rejoined Real Madrid – as it was renamed by Franco – at the end of the Civil War. They included Jacinto Quincoces, who during the early 1930s had become something of a legend in Spain as a great defender forming with Zamora an almost impossible barrier for any opposing team to breach. Quincoces drove a Red Cross ambulance during the Civil War. He played his final match as a professional footballer in 1942, then toyed with the idea of becoming an actor (a propagandist and heavily censored film industry was greatly encouraged by the new regime as a form of popular entertainment) before rejoining Real Madrid as a trainer.

Another pre-war Madrid star Luis Regueiro chose exile in Mexico, as did some of the players of the pre-war Barcelona and Bilbao teams, after spending part of the Civil War on foreign tours helping raise funds for the Republican forces.

Nevertheless the Franco regime found no shortage of politically trustworthy club presidents and players to fill the void left by the Civil War and exploit the need that many Spaniards felt to bring some entertainment back into their lives without the risk of being shot.

The resurgence of football as a popular sport in Spain during the 1940s stemmed from a widespread wish to find a distraction from the trauma of the Civil War and its aftermath. Football became part of a culture of evasion along with cinema, flamenco and bullfighting, which the regime was happy to encourage so as to anaesthetize intellectual dissent and impose social cohesion. The extent to which certain ideologues viewed football as a key vehicle for ensuring Spain's 'rebirth' as a nation – both united and great – was first made manifest in mass form not in Madrid but in Barcelona, on 29 June 1939, in the FC Barcelona stadium of Les Corts. It was on that day that General Moscardo gave his blessing to a ceremony designed to exorcize the football club and all its followers of all malevolent political spirits – specifically those that had Catalans pressing for most of their history for greater self-government than that allowed by Madrid. The main speaker was a fascist intellectual Ernest Giménez Caballero, who had helped draft Franco's 'decree of unity' after the Civil War, outlawing all movement towards greater political autonomy by regions such as Catalonia and the Basque country. In his speech Giménez Caballero spoke like a man possessed. He paid tribute to the glorious army that had 'liberated' Catalonia from those who wanted to break up Spain, and urged his audience to feel with him a new spirit sweeping through the stadium, and the land – a spirit smelling of 'flowers and Empire'.

Within three years Franco himself would come to the Catalan capital to celebrate the third anniversary of his victory. He was greeted by officers, bishops and local authorities. Three thousand doves were released in his honour before a triumphant march-past by the military and 24,000 Falangists. Most of Europe at the time was immersed in the Second World War. Franco wished to be seen as Spain's beloved leader who had not only won his nation's war but also secured its peace. The rhetoric belied a more complex reality. For all Franco's public self-confidence, Spain was a country divided within itself, with political executions of thousands of prisoners. It was also poor, its economic situation made worse by the trade restrictions imposed by the Allies who resented its clear sympathy for the Axis cause and tried their best to ensure that Franco did not become militarily more actively involved on the side of the Nazis.

My father, who served in the British embassy in Madrid, was among several foreign residents who reported on the poverty of Spain at the time, having found none of the romance about it that so many tourists have before and since. 'The long road to Madrid passed through villages shattered by the violence of war,' he later recalled in his memoirs; '. . . the centre of the city had escaped the sort of devastation that was so later to become commonplace all over Europe, but the discernible decay of a long siege, the crumbling outskirts, the scarce traffic and the empty shops all conveyed the sense of a sick city.'

Later that year of 1940 he travelled south towards Seville and sent a dispatch to the Foreign Office which I came across buried in British government archives years after he died. 'Whole villages have been without bread for weeks, large peasant families are living for days on less than one British woman's supper,' he reported.

By his own admission the British expatriates in Madrid were never short of bread, even in the lean war years. The embassy obtained all the items it wanted via Gibraltar and Mrs Taylor, another member of the British community who ran a tea-room near the fountain of Cibeles. My father, like Mrs Taylor, struggled to offset the influence of Nazi Germany on Spain. But perhaps because he subsequently met my Spanish mother, my father never lost his faith in the ability of the Spaniards themselves to resist surrendering entirely to Nazism. The more he penetrated Spanish life, the more he came to realize that it had a code, customs and a charisma exclusively its own. 'A foreigner could love or hate it: he could not be indifferent,' my father would say. He not only loved Spain. He married into it.

Nevertheless pressure on British interests in Spain increased with the collapse of France in 1940 and the arrival of the Germans on the Spanish border. 'The Germans made the most of it by sending in massed bands of their regiments who stamped their way down Madrid's main avenue (The Castellana) playing national music,' recalled my father in his memoirs. 'Himmler came too – to strengthen the ties of the Gestapo with the Spanish secret service.'

My father diplomatically kept his distance from the 'reborn' football stadium of Chamartín, but he couldn't resist going to see a bullfight one day (the British embassy counted one of Spain's top bullfighters Juan Belmonte as one of its 'friends'). His subsequent experience would leave him with a taste of what might have befallen him had he taken a similar interest in local football at that time. At the bullfight the guest of honour was none other than Himmler himself. My father calculated that the German national anthem would be played at the end of the *corrida* and thus planned to leave before the last bull. Instead the band struck up with '*Deutschland über Alles*' halfway through and the crowd (mostly Spanish) rose almost as one to make the fascist salute. My father decided to continue sitting. He was pushed and shouted at but he explained being an *inglés* he could do no other. In no time two plain-clothes members of the Gestapo took him by the arms and began leading him out. My father was eventually saved thanks to the timely intervention of an officer of the Spanish Civil Guard near the yard where the bull, once killed, was unceremoniously ripped apart by butchers. The Spanish officer told the Gestapo it was encroaching on Spanish sovereignty and freed my father on the basis of his diplomatic status.

Despite Spain's official neutrality on that occasion, Franco allowed the Germans to use Spain for intelligence activities and as a clandestine logistical base for some of its ships and aircraft. Franco's initial embarrassment at being supportive of a Germany that initially courted an alliance with Stalin ended with Hitler's invasion of Soviet Russia in June 1941. Britain by contrast was now seen as an ally of the communism against which Franco claimed to have fought his Holy Crusade during the Civil War. Sectors of the Spanish government helped orchestrate violent demonstrations against the British embassy. Football mirrored diplomacy. The few international encounters of Spanish clubs or the Spanish national team during this period were with the Germans or the Italians – celebrations of shared ideology rather than genuine competitive events.

One of the ways in which fascism tried to exert its

influence on Spanish football was by fuelling the myth that certain players were imbued with a style and attitude that defined their race. In a statement published in *Marca* in April 1942, the Spanish National Sports Delegation (DND) held up as an example of best practice football that was played by 'real men, like real Spaniards, which is to say in an aggressive but sporting way, with courage, passion, impetuosity, determination and virility'.

During the 1920s it was the direct, aggressive style of Athletic Bilbao that had been widely admired but with the recognition that such play had its roots in Britain, not Spain. In the early years of Francoism the '*furia española*' or Spanish fury was resurrected by the state's propaganda and redefined as the leading virtue of the New Spain. As the Falangist newspaper *Arriba* put it in an editorial a few months after the end of the Civil War: 'The *furia española* is present in all aspects of Spanish life, to a greater extent than ever since the "War of Liberation" . . . In a sport, the *furia* best manifests itself in football, a game in which the virility of the Spanish race can find full expression, usually imposing itself, in international contests, over the more technical but less aggressive foreign teams.' In 1941 all Spanish clubs were expected to emulate the example of the renamed Atlético de Bilbao. Franco not only ordered all English names to be dropped from the titles of Spanish clubs but also encouraged the political purge of 'regionalist' teams as was carried out at Bilbao by its Falangist director Eduardo Lastaragay. Basque-born players were encouraged to play so long as they were not separatists. So influential was Lastaragay that during the 1940s his club was once again held up as an example of the authentic *furia*.

In *Marca*'s preview of Bilbao's Spanish Cup final tie against

Valencia in 1945 in Madrid, Spaniards were encouraged to flock in their thousands to Madrid's Chamartín stadium to watch an exhibition of 'physical power, controlled aggression and combative approach, virtues which are again making us Spaniards highly respected and even feared in the world'.

Two years earlier the regime had struggled to keep a lid on the political fury that simmered during the semi-finals of the Spanish Cup between FC Barcelona and Real Madrid. The first leg was played in Barcelona's Les Corts. When not celebrating the three goals scored by their team, the home crowd spent most of the match booing and whistling at the Real Madrid players and the referee. Among those reporting on the match was Eduardo Teus, a former Real goalkeeper. He later wrote a lengthy article for the Madrid-based paper *Ya*, denouncing the crowd behaviour as a deliberate conspiracy against the state. The allegation marked the beginning of a campaign against FC Barcelona that was to increase in intensity in the days before the second leg in Madrid. On the eve of the match free whistles were handed out to local fans together with their tickets. The Barcelona players were visited in their dressing room by the Director of State Security José Finat y Escriva de Romani, the Count of Mayalde, and told that they were only being allowed to play because of the regime's generosity in forgiving their lack of patriotism. The team included several players who had been against Franco during the Civil War but had chosen to stay in Spain once it was over.

Real Madrid won 11–1. Teus described the result euphorically as the most resounding victory in the club's history. A more objective analysis of the match that day was written by Juan Antonio Samaranch. The man who would one day become president of the International Olympic

Committee was a young sports journalist for *La Prensa*, a newspaper owned by the Falange. Samaranch, a Catalan who nonetheless supported Franco, concluded that the intimidation of the Barcelona players had been of such a bellicose and threatening nature that it had become impossible for them to play football. 'It was not a question of playing badly or well,' wrote Samaranch, 'Barça simply ended up not playing at all . . . individual players were fearful of making even the most innocent of tackles because of the crowd reaction and therefore hardly touched their opponents.'

The atmosphere surrounding the match was graphically conveyed to me many years later just before he died by Angel Mur, the FC Barcelona masseur. The account stands to this day as a lasting testimony to a prolonged rivalry, arguably one of the most politicized and passionate in the history of football.

'The night before the game we had to change our hotel, and even then we didn't leave it all evening because we were convinced we would be lynched. Then the game came, and our goalkeeper was so petrified of being hit by missiles that he spent most of the game as far forward from his goal as possible, allowing the Madrid players to strike at the net from all directions. Not so far from where we were sitting, there was a man dressed in military uniform who kept on screaming throughout the game, "Kill these red Catalans, and kill these Catalan dogs." At one point I interrupted him and said, "Look, I may not have been born in Catalonia, but I feel I belong to it, and I'll go on working there because it is separate from the rest of Spain." The officer shouted, "You separatist son of a bitch!" and told me I was under arrest for sedition. It was at this point that the Marquis of Mesa de Asta, the government-appointed president of Barça, intervened, telling the officer to leave me in peace. The marquis had been installed by the regime and was a personal friend of Moscardo's, but the officer didn't recognize him. "Who do you think you are?" the officer said to the marquis. "You're under arrest as well – come with me." Then the marquis took out his credentials, and told the officer, "I'm terribly sorry, officer, but it's you who have to come with me."'

A regime that had based its public image on the restoration of national unity, and saw sport as a vehicle for defusing antagonisms of a dangerously political ilk, could ill afford such controversy on or off the pitch so soon after the end of the Civil War. What followed was a carefully orchestrated damage limitation exercise. By orders of Moscardo, Real Madrid and Barça were each fined 25,000 pesetas for their alleged part in the disturbances at Chamartín, while Barça was given an additional fine of 2,500 pesetas for the lack of respect shown to the visitors during the first leg at Les Corts. In a statement the Spanish Football Federation declared that money taken from the clubs would be used for promoting the involvement of youth in sport, a symbolic gesture aimed at underlining its faith that a new generation of football fans would be marked by a healthy respect for order and self-discipline. But such self-professed generosity failed to contain the repercussions of the first major scandal in Spanish football.

The man the regime had appointed as a safe pair of hands as the president of FC Barcelona, the Marquis of Mesa de Asta, resigned in protest after the rejection by the authorities of a letter of appeal against the fines imposed on a club he had grown to have some sympathy for. Again the regime opted for a Solomonian solution as a way of containing the crisis. It pressured Real Madrid's president Antonio Santos

Pedralba into resigning, a move that was destined to alter the fortunes of the club in a way that few could have predicted at the time. For the man encouraged to replace Pedralba was Santiago Bernabéu whose presidency would last for thirty-five years, outliving even Franco.

Bernabéu was a former player and the director of the club. He had also fought on the winning side of the Civil War and worked as a state lawyer. In the aftermath of the conflict he had stuck close to the right-wing officers and civilians who had recovered the club from its brief control by socialists and communists. To the regime Bernabéu seemed a perfect appointment – someone who claimed to be in touch with the fans as a sportsman and who at the same time had impeccable political credentials as a committed anti-communist and war veteran of the National Cause. Initially, however, the role he was asked to perform was that of a conciliator. Days after taking up his new post, Bernabéu extended a much publicized hand of friendship to the new president of FC Barcelona Colonel José Vendrell Ferrer – another safe military pair of hands, of the many that sought to influence Spanish football in those days. The 1–11 defeat in Chamartín had already entered the collective psyche of many Catalans as an ever-present symbol of persecution but in the new president of FC Barcelona – a government appointee – Bernabéu found a willing partner in the farce of official solidarity. The media for its part was ordered by the official censors to be more careful with its reporting of crowd reactions and foul play by players and desist from making any commentary that risked 'exacerbating regional passions'.

Later that autumn of 1943 'friendlies' were arranged between a Castilian eleven and a Catalan eleven. The matches, like the similarly orchestrated 'matches for peace' played between Real Madrid and FC Barcelona later in the winter, took place without ostensible animosity and vigorous hand-shaking between officials and players which a compliant media made much of as an example of a Spain reborn and at one with itself. The choreography, directed from the higher echelons of power, had a strong element of opportunism, coinciding as it did with a period in Spanish history when Franco felt insecure about his position at home and internationally and could not afford to allow the country's football stadiums to become the powder kegs of a political explosion.

Politics was destined to be the main lubricant of a sporting rivalry that resumed within a season and continued unabated into the twenty-first century. A few months after declaring his pact of friendship, Bernabéu mischievously allowed a secret meeting between one of his players and a Barcelona official to take place in a Madrid café before having the player publicly reject an offer from the club. He then torpedoed negotiations between the Catalan club and Luis Molowny, a rising young star who played as a forward for El Marino of Las Palmas. As FC Barcelona officials were making their way to the Canaries by boat to clinch the deal, Bernabéu sent the retired Real Madrid star Jacinto Quincoces to the islands by plane, his suitcase stashed with one-peseta notes. Molowny was secured by Real Madrid for a fee of 250,000 pesetas in the first of several controversial transfers that over the years would breed distrust and envy.

The bad blood that would run through almost every encounter between the two clubs over more than half a century became a constant of Spanish football, the changing rhythm and scope of its spilling dictated by design as much as by circumstances. It was a rivalry that fed on itself, reflecting the growing popularity of football as a sport. From the 1950s through to the late 1990s the clubs came to provide *La Liga* with its main scene of action. They would have the biggest stadiums and the most extensive media coverage. Their commercial weight and political influence would far outstrip those of any other cultural or sporting institution in the country.

Given Bernabéu's social, political and military background, it was perhaps hardly surprising that good relations with FC Barcelona did not top his list of priorities on a more permanent basis. Bernabéu was a man of ambition and vision who was able to harness the change and development of post-war Spain in a way that could benefit his club and the capital of a Spain that he firmly believed had its heart and soul in Castile. Within days of taking over Real Madrid's presidency he was working on plans for a new stadium which in time would carry his name. He had no doubt that a stadium planned to be one of the largest in the world would quickly achieve symbolic status, and draw to it Spaniards of diverse social backgrounds united in a common desire to put behind them the horrors of the Civil War.

Once again football in Spain was echoing politics. Three years earlier, in 1940, Franco had chosen the valley of Cuelagamuros, in the Sierra de Guadarrama to the north-east of Madrid, with its huge granite outcrops, as the setting of a monument to his Cause on a scale that would defy posterity, the Valley of the Fallen. According to the decree announcing its foundation, the huge cross and basilica were designed to have the 'grandeur of the monuments of old, which defy time and forgetfulness'. The main construction of the monument involved penal detachments and labour battalions of thousands of Spaniards who had fought, against Franco, for the Republic. The project took nearly twenty years to complete and cost almost as much as the monastery of El Escorial which King Philip II commissioned when Spain was still awash with gold and silver from its South American colonies.

In later years the suggestion made by some apologists for the Franco regime that the Valley of the Fallen had become a de facto monument to all the Civil War dead proved unconvincing, not least after Franco became the only Spanish veteran of the conflict to be buried there alongside José Antonio Primo de Rivera, the founder of the Spanish Falange. By the beginning of this century the monument was one of Madrid's least popular tourist sites and of diminishing interest to foreigners. Spaniards annually paying tribute to the tombs of Franco and Primo de Rivera had got smaller too. On the twenty-fifth anniversary of Franco's death in 2000, a Guardia Civil officer denied an outraged crowd of old fascists, nostalgics and neo-Nazis access to the Valley of the Fallen, where they wanted to honour their past leaders. The policeman said that it was a Monday, a day when all national monuments are closed in Spain, and he was not going to make an exception for the anniversary of Franco's death. The neo-Nazis called the policeman a 'bloody communist'.

Spain may have changed but back in the early 1940s there was synergy to be found between Franco's project and Bernabéu's that went beyond mere symbolism. The panel drawn up to consider the bids for the scheme for the new stadium was headed by Pedro Muguraza, the architect of the Valley of the Fallen, and Javier Barroso, a former Franco officer who as head of the Spanish Football Federation after the Civil War had encouraged the appointment of his good friend Bernabéu to the presidency of Real Madrid. Muguraza and Barroso kept Spain's post-war rebuilding work among friends by awarding the design contracts to the architects Muñoz Monasterio and Alemany Soler. The main construction work on both the Valley of the Fallen and the Bernabéu was carried out by Huarte, one of a group of building companies that made its fortune from privileged participation in Spain's post-war reconstruction under Franco. The costs of building Chamartín were undoubtedly reduced thanks to the availability of a large pool of cheap unemployed labour. Some of these would have served the first month or years after the end of the Civil War in prison although Chamartín would not have been short of men who had fought for Franco and had been demobilized. There is also some circumstantial evidence – impossible to verify – to suggest that building materials were shared between the Valley of the Fallen, Chamartín, and the early development of Barajas, Madrid's airport – part of Real Madrid's unofficial 'black legend' which some of the club's unofficial historians such as Julian García Candau and Fernando Carreño do not dismiss out of hand.

What is certainly true is that by the time he drew up his plans for the new stadium in Chamartín Bernabéu knew of a government scheme to turn the site into one of the biggest urban development areas of the capital with the extension of the Castellana. The days when the Real Madrid stadium stood on the outskirts of Madrid, surrounded by grazing sheep, were numbered.

For all its links with the regime at this time, there is no evidence to suggest that Real Madrid counted on massive direct financial support from the Franco state for a stadium that in the eyes of rivals would come to symbolize a new centre of power within Spanish football. In fact one of the differences between the early years of Franco and the experience of Germany and Italy under Hitler and Mussolini is that in Spain the regime was simply too hard-pressed economically to channel investments of its own into the development of sport as a national enterprise. What the Franco regime did was to act as a facilitator, encouraging the development of football in two key roles – as a form of mass distraction and as informal diplomacy.

In the immediate post-Civil War years the only concession to football clubs that the government would admit was privileged access to petrol, a rare commodity in those days, for travel to away matches. In later years club presidents were able to draw on limited sums from a state support fund for private sporting facilities. But Bernabéu's approach in April 1944 to the DND, the National Sports Delegation, for substantially more help to build the 70,000 capacity Chamartín was rejected. Instead the Franco state agreed to fund less than 4 per cent of the cost of the new stadium. The shortfall was met largely by raising money among the membership through the issue of bonds, monies which were repaid in periods of between eight and twenty years to investors, big and small. For post-war Spain this was an exercise in popular capitalism of which Bernabéu would later make much use to counter those who questioned his independence from political influence.

As he said famously in one interview: 'They call us the club of the Regime when in fact Real Madrid has always conducted itself with an honest behaviour which no one, unless he is a son of a bitch, can deny.'

7. Divine Intervention

They cut an odd couple that June in 2003, posing in front of millions of viewers around the world, from Madrid to Beijing – the lean young blond with his flowing locks and engaging smile next to the paunchy septuagenarian, bloated and wrinkled like an overripe fig, struggling to contain a look of wishing to be somewhere else. But the twinning of David Beckham and Alfredo Di Stefano was as necessary as it was contrived, designed as an image that summarized Real Madrid's past, present and future in a seamless bridge across a history of glory and greatness which no other football club in the world could match. I don't know to what extent Beckham even then really saw his destiny in the predilections, inclinations, habits and beliefs of someone old enough to be his grandfather, who had lived in another country, another era. But Di Stefano had become immersed in the history of Real Madrid and Spain, and Beckham had come to that club and that country. I'd been chasing the shadows of both men through time and space in ways that brought back memories and helped me look beyond the razzmatazz. Half a century earlier, the arrival of Di Stefano as a Real Madrid player marked a new departure in the history of the club, ushering in a period that would see the conquest of five consecutive European Cups. It was a curious beginning for me too, 1953, the year I was born, in the capital of Spain.

*

Spain was struggling to put the 1940s behind it like a bad dream. The 'years of hunger' were also the 'blue years' – the blue of the Falangist shirts that emerged from the Spanish Civil War sweating their pseudo-fascist ideology and enthroning Franco as the leader of a country that was both united and great. The country of course was neither united nor great – families cowed or embittered by their memories of the Civil War, the precise circumstances of the thousands executed on Franco's post-war orders locked away in some secret government archive, the country ostracized diplomatically within Europe and at the nascent United Nations. My Spanish family had its fair share of disruption even if, unlike those of many close friends, it had been saved from the horror of the execution squads by escaping abroad. My mother had returned from exile in Paris with my grandfather Gregorio, the doctor and writer who might have gone on playing football longer than his teens had he not broken a leg.

Franco had agreed to let him get on with his medical and literary activities so long as he didn't openly criticize his regime. According to documents uncovered by the historian Paul Preston, however, a proposal by one of Franco's post-war ministers to disband the Falange and include my grandfather in a national government of reconciliation was quite literally laughed out of court by the dictator himself. Franco wrote 'No' along a memorandum making the suggestion, and 'Ha, Ha, Ha,' by my grandfather's name. Franco also vetoed another suggestion from one of the less fanatical members of his regime that he be made ambassador to London. According to Preston, Franco distrusted Gregorio Marañón 'as someone who would be loyal to higher ideals than the survival in power of Franco'.

So my grandfather resumed his medical practice – attending the poor rather more often than the rich – and lectured in the Academy of Fine Arts on El Greco and his paintings. 'El Greco painted madmen – of that I am sure,' my grandfather used to say of one of Spain's most imaginative artists, 'because he intuitively realized how close madness was to sainthood.' He never went to the Bernabéu during the Franco years, choosing instead to spend his weekends in an old convent near Toledo he had turned into a country retreat. There was in fact a greyness about life in Spain then, not the mystical promise of El Greco, but an aimless impoverished world of the hopeless and the defeated, the defiant shouts of *'no pasarán'* as the International Brigades stuck it out on the western outskirts of Madrid, silenced seemingly for ever. As Damaso Alonso, a poet friend of my family's wrote, 'It was the silence of over half a million dead, according to the statistics.'

My early memories of the Madrid I was born in were those of a large provincial town struggling to emerge from the terrible sadness of war and its aftermath. In later years my relatively safe status in the midst of improving surroundings was sharply brought back into focus for me when, as a student, I read *The Hive*, the post-war novel by José Camilo Cela. He wrote of the surviving café culture that acted as a refuge from the misery outside, the war widows struggling to survive, the plain-clothes policemen bullying suspects, the carts of the garbage men 'coming down from Fuencarral and Chamartín, coming up from Las Ventas and Las Injurias, emerging from the sad desolate, landscape of the cemetery and passing – after hours on the road, in the cold – at the slow dejected trot of a gaunt horse or a grey, worried looking donkey.' I remember that sound, and how much smaller Madrid seemed then. Real Madrid's new stadium was on the outskirts, bordering the open countryside, a symbol of ambition facing the desolate landscape of Castile.

In the winter of 1949 the English writer Gerard Brenan journeyed to Spain on a return visit, having spent part of his youth there in the 1920s and later experienced the early days of the Civil War. They had been calling Franco's Spain 'Fascist' in the British press and Parliament for several years, but unlike Brenan, few of its critics had felt what it was like to live in it. He wrote of a country caught in its past, but beginning to find a way forward. The hotel in the Gran Vía where he stayed for the equivalent of fifteen shillings a day had not much to offer in terms of imaginative cooking while being organized with the same lavishness of personnel and attention to hierarchy as an old palace. One of its employees, a veteran of the Francoist army, complained that the black market was the 'only business in the country that was flourishing' and how, after the migration from the country-side to the towns, everyone was looking at ways of emigrating beyond Spain. Despite having loved Spain enough to have lived there as an expatriate, Brenan confessed now to having serious misgivings about Madrid, a city of barely a million and a quarter inhabitants, 'built in a wilderness and manufacturing next to nothing'. Out on the streets there were beggars with no legs, others creeping along on all fours. Many claimed to be 'war mutilated'.

And yet there had been much building since the end of the Civil War, over the ruins, even if the Spanish capital seemed to have been designed as the observation-point in a centrally organized prison. Brenan saw new blocks of flats, new ministries and offices – Madrid was spreading outwards, slowly but surely. Another sight of that Madrid was the new American cars, most of them belonging to government officials or rich people with the contacts and the money to get import licences, for Spain was virtually a closed economy.

I spent part of my childhood between England and Spain, smuggling things from London to Madrid, never the other way round – clothes, gramophone records, books and magazines. While England seemed to be very much part of the world, Spain even to my young eyes struck me as something of a world of its own, where kids of my age all seemed to be taught by either priests or nuns, and where boys dressed up as Roman soldiers or dreamed of being bullfighters, while girls pretended to be nurses, believing that one day they might marry a doctor. In the poorer *barrios* kids played on concrete, having to suffer the repression even when kicking balls around. As a song by Joán Manuel Serrat, the protest minstrel of my generation, would later put it, 'Kid. Stop fucking around with the ball . . . you can't do this, you can't say that.'

In her biography of Serrat the writer Margarita Rivière recalled that post-war generation that grew up in the 1950s, dreaming of breaking through the barrier imposed by the Francoist state, and 'installing themselves in a world that was bigger and more open'. The Spain of those days was in many respects still 'unique and dwarf like'. To feel the heartbeat of that small world, Spaniards would tune in to the radio, and listen to a high dosage of suitably depoliticized folkloric music – from bullfight music to military marches – prayers and romantic novellas, seasoned with good clean advice to lonely hearts. Like the cinema, Rivière tells us, it was 'the friendly and daily face of the regime, in which there was no room for silence'.

On his visit to Madrid at the end of the 1940s, Brenan noticed the contrast between the censored reporting on Spain in the local media and the full rein given to a virulent anti-communism. 'Every paper gives the impression that war is imminent and that the whole of Europe down to the Pyrenees will be overrun by Russian armies,' wrote Brenan. The campaign played in part to an essentially domestic agenda – smoothing the cracks within the regime by conjuring up memories of the Civil War 'Reds' and securing the Right on the common ground that could sustain Franco indefinitely. But it also showed Franco's Spain moving seamlessly from the awkward identification with the Axis powers into the new geopolitical context of the Cold War. In 1953 Franco followed up an agreement with the Vatican by signing a politically far more important deal with the newly elected US Republican president Eisenhower.

Although Spain continued to be excluded from NATO until the advent of democracy over thirty years later, Franco permitted the establishment of several US bases on Spanish territory in return for Washington's military and diplomatic backing, together with the promise of financial assistance once the regime had opened up the economy. By becoming an ally, however subordinate, to the US, Franco was no longer so isolated. In Norman Lewis's novel set in late 1940s Spain, *The Day of the Fox*, a Spanish communist assessed the potential for radical change in Spain before concluding that 'where a generation of dedicated revolutionaries had failed, a few seasons of tourist invasions would succeed'. For from the character's perspective, Spain would be 'democratised, hurled forcibly into this century, by the need to put on a good face for the benefit of spenders of sought-after currencies'. The comment was to prove prophetic given the impact that mass tourism was to have on Spain from the late 1950s onwards. By then, however, Spain's engagement with the outside world was breaking new frontiers thanks to the diplomacy of the best football team the world had ever produced.

While there was no shortage of war-weary and entertainment-starved Spaniards wanting to see competitive football recommence in the aftermath of the Civil War, it was only in the late 1940s that the popularity of the game reflected the improvement in the quality of individual players like Thelma Zarra and Piru Gainza of Athletic Bilbao (by this time the club had reverted to its original name), Basora and Cesar of FC Barcelona and Luis Molowny of Real Madrid. The tall, powerful and aggressive Zarra in particular was held up by the Spanish media in the post-war years as a personification of *furia* ('fury'). However, Spanish football was punished by the international community for the matches it had played with German and Italian teams during the Second World War just as Spain as a country suffered a more general diplomatic and economic embargo. Between 1945 and 1950 only Portugal and Ireland maintained sporting links, while the Spanish Football Federation's olive-branch approaches to its English and French and post-war Italian counterparts were rejected following advice from their respective governments. As a result the 1950 World Cup finals tournament held in Brazil proved an important political opportunity which the Spanish government made every effort to exploit, with a helping hand from FIFA, world football's governing body. FIFA had carefully arranged the qualifying groups, facing Spain with Portugal and the Irish Republic, so as to avoid the possibility of boycotts by Spain's opponents.

The importance the Franco government attached to the inclusion of the Spanish team was underlined by one of its key players, Molowny of Real Madrid, in a revealing interview he gave many years later to the British historian Duncan Shaw. According to Molowny, during their training sessions before flying out to Brazil, the Spanish players were told countless times by officials that they should regard themselves as ambassadors for a Spain that had until then been shunned by the rest of the world for 'daring to be different'. Players were told to be on their best behaviour at all times: '. . . To wear the official suit, to say the right thing to foreign pressmen, and even to pick up the opponent off the floor with a smile if you had fouled him.'

The players stuck to their brief religiously, proving themselves not only disciplined but successful in a way that would be remembered for many years as a rare exception for the historically underachieving national side. Spain attained a creditable fourth place in a tournament that generated huge coverage in the Spanish media. The authorities in all the major Spanish towns erected giant screens on which to show the team's matches recorded on 8mm film to large audiences back home.

Of all the victories none was more celebrated than its 1–0 group win over England – 'perfidious Albion' as Franco called it because of the British government's refusal to hand over Gibraltar and to back Spain's membership of NATO. The England team had come to Brazil as one of the favourites after the World Cup holders Italy had had their chances virtually destroyed when eight internationals were killed in the Superga plane crash of 1949. Among the English was Stanley Matthews, the one player for whom every Spanish football enthusiast, whatever his political inclination, had enormous admiration. As the tournament's incisive chronicler Brian Glanville has written, 'Yes, Matthews . . . held in deep suspicion by the English selectors as too brilliant, too agelessly indestructible an outside-right to trust.' Matthews had been playing for England since 1934, enjoying the kind of political continuity denied to the Spanish stars of his period. He was, according to Granville's portrait, now at the age of thirty-five as 'embarrassingly effective as ever', with his marvellous swerve intact.

England prepared for a match with a Spanish team that had a reputation for playing its defence square and thus vulnerable to the through pass. Milburn, the English centreforward brought in to exploit this weakness, headed a pass from Finney past the FC Barcelona goalkeeper Ramallets, only to have the goal disallowed by the Italian referee. Newsreel footage would subsequently indicate that Milburn was onside not off, but all that mattered to Franco's Spain was that the great emblem of the *furia*, Zarra, was the player who headed in the winner, from a centre by Basora, five minutes after half-time.

That '*Goooo!*' became the catalyst for an aggressive nationalism as it was screamed by Matias Prats, one of the regime's most popular sports journalists, to fifteen million Spanish radio listeners. In the euphoria of the moment, Prats claimed Spain's victory over England was indeed just revenge for its continuing occupation of Gibraltar.

With that goal Franco's Spain had defied the world. As

the author Vazquez Montalban would later recall with his characteristic sense of irony: 'Thanks to Prats, Bread and Bulls became Bread and Football . . . That GOL of his is the origin of "We Count on You" [the slogan used by the Franco regime to unify Spanish youth through the practice of sport], of the development of tourism, of Massiel's triumph in the Eurovision song contest . . . of the VII Development Plan.'

Since the late 1940s certain fascist symbols had been discreetly withdrawn from Spanish football in an effort to win outside friends. There were no more compulsory outstretched Falange salutes, for example, and the national team were allowed to wear their traditional red rather than the Falangist blue. And yet *Marca* described the win over England as the greatest Spanish victory since Franco's in the Civil War – a 'splendid demonstration to the whole world that the traditional Hispanic virtues of passion, aggression, fury, virility and impetuosity have been completely recovered in the "New Spain" born out of that bloody conflict.'

Such rhetoric was to prove misplaced. The Spanish national team failed to qualify for four of the next six World Cups, and performed badly in the two that it did play. Nevertheless the good impression created in Brazil by the Spanish team did help transform Spain from being an outcast into a full member of the international sporting community, being voted for the first time on to the executive committee of FIFA with the support of South American countries. It also marked the beginning of a new era in which Spanish clubs would dominate the attention of fans and diplomats, at home and abroad.

*

For all the attempts by elements of the political Right in Spain to conjure up a racial definition of football, success on the field then as it always would be was down to a mixture of individual skills that crossed borders and combined as part of a curious chemistry called a team. The Spanish national team that did so well in the 1950 World Cup had no fewer than eight players picked from one club, FC Barcelona, a reflection not of any commanding national trait, but of where some of the better players in Spain were then to be found, not all of them Spaniards. FC Barcelona's own strengths as a team were reinforced with the arrival of Ladislao Kubala. It was the exiled Hungarian who helped FC Barcelona win the Generalissimo's Cup in 1951, and in the following year, the Spanish league and cup double, the Copa Latina (played by the Spanish, Italian, French and Portuguese champions) and two summer tournaments, the Martini Rosso and the Eva Duarte. The Season of the Five Cups, as it was to be remembered by the Barça fans, contrasted with the lacklustre performance of Real Madrid in the golden anniversary of its foundation, and focused Santiago Bernabéu's mind on trying to secure a star signing who would revive his team's fortunes.

Bernabéu spotted an opportunity when at the end of March 1952, as part of the fiftieth anniversary celebrations, the Colombian team Millonarios played against Real Madrid at the Spanish club's new stadium. Of the players Bernabéu saw that day, none impressed him more than the Millonarios forward, the Argentine-born Alfredo Di Stefano. 'This guy smells of good football,' Bernabéu famously remarked.

Di Stefano, the son of working-class Italian immigrants, was born in a country that had learnt to play football from the British but had developed a style of its own, fast and individualistic. Maybe because Di Stefano was to spend much of his professional life separated from the more extreme nationalism bred by certain Argentine generals – even if he did play under Franco – *la Saeta Rubia* (the 'blond arrow') claimed never to forget what he owed the British Empire. He wrote this in his memoirs published in 2000:

There is a lot we owe British industry. We should pay tribute to the English who went all over the world with their railways, but also with their football. They went to America, to Asia, to Africa . . . In Spain, in Huelva, with Rio Tinto, they were also the first to bring football here. Thanks to them we have all the *raules* and the *kempes*, the *maradonas* and the *alfredos*. Thanks to their industry we have become a family.

Di Stefano's first home was just a few yards from the Boca Juniors stadium, and from the port of Buenos Aires, where Argentine football's earliest teachers, the English sailors, had first made their mark. He learnt to play with the school kids of his *barrio* while his father earned enough money as a foreman in the market to buy some land. Di Stefano's was not a rags to riches story like Maradona's although both men were destined to enter the history books as the greatest players of their age.

Di Stefano first made his reputation playing for River Plate, the other big club in the Argentine capital, jointly responsible, with Boca Juniors, over the years for one of the most fanatical local rivalries in the world. In the early days of Argentine football River Plate played near Boca in the south of the city. The clubs were thus linked organically to the same neighbourhood. Even when River Plate headed to the new modern suburbs on the north side of Buenos Aires to set up their new stadium, they continued to compete for the loyalties of the local Italian immigrant community. Di Stefano's own father was a River Plate fan and one-time player whose own contacts with the club paved the way for Alfredo's first trial.

Alfredo's introduction to River Plate followed his family's move away from the port area to higher ground to avoid the flooding from the river. He was by then a teenager who had learnt to develop his skills with the ball in whatever free space happened to be available – a piece of derelict land strewn with dust and stones, an empty street, a covered courtyard, a factory wall. The child Di Stefano grew up amid the *potreros* – the small yards and fields of the sprawling Buenos Aires, where large groups of kids (the poor always seemed to have a lot of kids) would often find themselves fighting for the ball with adult men. It was in the *barrio* that he learnt to kick the ball with his left and his right foot, to combine in quick one-twos, to dribble, keeping the ball on the ground whenever possible. It was there too that he learnt to rough it, to fight whenever it was necessary, with his first improvised team. The gang of players was called *Unidos y Venceremos* (United and we will win). Long after he had started playing for a club, Di Stefano would continue going back to the *barrio*. He did not want to be seen to forget his roots, for the *barrio* was 'like a nation, like a country'.

Such surroundings, like the beaches in Brazil, were to prove the natural training grounds for the stars from the Third World who would in time populate European football.

By the time Di Stefano discovered a love for the game,

football in Argentina had come a long way since the days when the English had first mucked in with the locals – 'natives' as some of the more colonial Brits saw them – in the first competitive encounter. While football was first played in Argentina during the 1880s, it was only in 1904 – two years after Real Madrid's foundation – that Southampton FC became the first British team to visit the country on a summer tour.

Matches played against the local teams – *Alumni, Británicos, Belgrano, Argentinos* – were all won easily. The local English-language newspaper the Buenos Aires *Herald* gushed in its reporting of the visitors' mastery. An editorial was full of praise for the evident racial superiority of those who had created the British Empire, and the lessons that could be learnt by those it had helped colonize, if only they were prepared to learn. 'Argentina's sons,' wrote the *Herald*, 'are laying up for themselves and for their descendants the priceless treasure of vigorous health and sound physique, constituting one of the prime factors in the making of a nation.'

The editorial could scarcely have imagined the extent to which within a generation home-grown Argentines would not only learn from their football fathers, but also bring about a considerable improvement with a style they could claim as their own. As David Dowding writes in his history of the Anglo-Argentine football rivalry, 'as a new generation of players emerged in the "oven" of Argentina's predominantly Spanish-Italian working-class culture, so new attitudes to the game were born . . . new styles of play, new interpretations of the rules, new expectations of crowd behaviour.'

During the 1930s and 1940s British football remained

engaged in Europe but less so with South America. In Argentina this period saw the development of what many Argentine fans look upon as their first golden age, years during which *la nuestra* – 'ours': meaning our style of play – came into its own. It saw the birth of a professional league and the building of the first big stadiums, and the kind of magic that players like Di Stefano and Maradona, learning from their elders, would dazzle global fans with.

La nuestra had its roots not in the manicured lawns of Victorian public schools but in the improvisation that comes with the crude social existence of underdevelopment. Thus evolved a form of fantasy football in which anything was possible. In the words of Dowding,

the love of fantasy expressed itself in a love of fantastic stunts, bicycle kicks and scissor kicks, incredible flicks and saucy back-heels, individual juggling and the collective painting of discernible patterns with passes . . . [*La nuestra* was] elegant, skilful and cheeky, a source of wonder and humour, more suited in some respects to a circus ring than a football pitch . . . the ball passed from performer to performer, each given his chance to entertain the crowd and top what had gone before.

When Di Stefano was playing for River Plate during the Second World War, his trainer and inspiration was Carlos Peucelle, who in his days as a player was nicknamed *Barullo* (mayhem) because of his tendency to play all over the pitch in no defined role other than as a constant threat or bulwark. In an enduring portrait in *Football in Sun and Shadow* Eduardo Galeano writes of Di Stefano:

The entire playing field fitted inside his shoes. From his feet the pitch sprouted and grew . . . he ran and reran the field from net to net. He would change flanks and change rhythm with the ball from a lazy trot to an unstoppable cyclone; without the ball he'd evade his marker to gain open space, seeking air whenever a play got choked off . . . He never stood still. Holding his head high, he could see the entire pitch and cross it at a gallop to prise open the defence and launch the attack. He was there at the beginning, during, and at the end of every scoring play, and he scored goals of all colours . . .

Many years later Di Stefano would recall his days as a professional in Argentina as a period when football had yet to lose its innocence, when players played for no other reason than a love of the game, unhindered by the machinations of politicians, the ambitions of club presidents, and the greed of intermediaries. Di Stefano's time at River Plate coincided with the coming to power of General Juan Perón and his wife Evita. The Peróns ruthlessly suppressed their political opponents and stirred a crude form of nationalism in Argentina. They sustained themselves in power with the support of sectors of the military and the trade union movement in a latterday pseudo-fascist state. Perón refused to give his support to a footballers' strike largely because his minister of the economy was the president of a football club. And yet Di Stefano remembered Perón as a defender of the working classes and Evita as an extraordinary woman.

Such retrospectives were tinged with a large dose of romanticism, as was his alleged encounter with the Argentine-born Che Guevara, the Latin American revolutionary, years before he was executed in 1967 by the US-backed Bolivian military. The year was 1952. *El Che*, then a twenty-four-year-old medical student, was roughing it round South America with his friend Alberto Granado on a Norton 500 motorbike. The two 'rambling tramps', as they called themselves, had a chance meeting with Di Stefano in Colombia where he was playing football for Millonarios. According to Granado's account of their journey, many years later, he and *El Che* asked Di Stefano for tickets to a football match while in the Colombian capital Bogotá, a request which the player was only too happy to comply with. In later years Di Stefano would recall the incident although he claimed to have been astounded to discover that one of the tramps had turned out to be *El Che*, who in the late 1960s became a global pop culture icon.

In a letter to his mother published after his death *El Che* suggests that his curious meeting with Di Stefano came after he and Granado had travelled to the Colombian capital after staying in a leper colony and organizing a football match with some policemen in the Amazon jungle, in a place called Leticia. 'At first', he wrote,

we only intended to coach them to the point where they wouldn't make fools of themselves, but they were so bad we decided to play, too. The amazing result was that what was considered the weakest team entered the one-day championship utterly reorganized, made it to the final and lost only on penalties. Alberto looked vaguely like Pedernera [an Argentine footballer] with his spot-on passes, so he was nick-named *Pedernita*, in fact, and I saved a penalty, which will go down in the history of Leticia.

Once in Bogotá, they coincided with a game between the local team Millonarios and Real Madrid. They watched the game in the cheapest stand, 'since our compatriots are harder to tap than ministers'. *El Che* said nothing about the game, noting only the terrible political context in which football was being played. 'There is more repression here than in any country we've been to . . . the atmosphere is tense and a revolution may be brewing . . . If the Colombians want to put up with it, good luck to them, but we are getting out of here as soon as we can.' *El Che* would have his revolution, in Cuba in 1959. Colombians just went on, as they had done for most of their history, playing football and killing.

Di Stefano always managed to avoid being pigeon-holed politically and felt no need to excuse himself for playing in countries run by corrupt or authoritarian governments. The passion of his life was football. 'In those days one played for the fun of it. One knew who the professionals were in River or Boca, but it wasn't like it is now. It was a popular sport. Why was one going to worry, as people do now, about making football a profession? Nowadays players have just turned seventeen and already the parents are saying, "Let's see if this one turns out to be a millionaire,"' he told his biographers Enrique Ortego and Alfredo Relaño.

Di Stefano claimed that his own serenity in the face of wealth sprung from his days of working on the land his father bought from his own savings. Childhood also equipped him with the toughness and resolution to give it his all in every game he played; for as another of his chroniclers Paco Peña put it, 'Alfredo doesn't sweat on football pitches, he hoses them with blood.' Di Stefano played one of his early games with an infected knee and a high fever. Thus was the legend of a true warrior born. His reputation as a player of extraordinary diversity and skill would quickly follow. He was called *la Saeta Rubia*, blond unlike most of the *latino* players, some of whom came from mixed Indian race, and quick, sharp and accurate as the deadliest arrow. By 1949 journalists in South America regarded him as the best forward on the continent – hugely precise on the ball, powerful with both feet and amazingly versatile across the pitch.

It was in that year that Di Stefano decided to quit Argentina for Colombia. Di Stefano was among a handful of players at River Plate to have survived the protracted and acrimonious strikes in Argentine football over pay and union rights but at the cost of having his wages frozen in an increasingly volatile political environment. By contrast Colombia had turned into football's equivalent of El Dorado since its new rebel league, unauthorized by FIFA, had gone professional in 1948, with local business barons spending fortunes building up local teams with star imports from other South American countries and Europe. Di Stefano was made an offer by the Bogotá team, aptly called Millonarios, which he found difficult to refuse. No matter that Colombia, which had just had a military coup, had one of the most corrupt societies in Latin America. It was playing host to some of the best football in the world, and offering unprecedented lumps of money to those prepared to play the game. When Di Stefano returned to Buenos Aires that Christmas he brought back more money with him than he had handled in all his time playing in the Argentine league. With Di Stefano, Millonarios won four local championships in as many years, establishing itself as one of the best teams in the world. Local fans claimed that with the Argentine in their midst, they had elevated

1. The beautiful game: Beckham celebrates a goal against Real Betis with Ronaldo.

2. Alfredo Di Stefano relishes victory over eternal rivals FC Barcelona (1958-59).

3. (*Left to right*) Gento, Olsen, Di Stefano, Molowny and Joseito in the 1953–54 season.

4. Franco's greatest export: the Spanish dictator honours Real Madrid's longest-serving president Santiago Bernabéu in 1967.

5. Bernabéu boosts the morale of the players in 1973. Zoco, his 'favourite son', is second from the right, facing.

6. The big challenge: when Maradona played for FC Barcelona (1983).

7. Emilio Butragueño showing his skills (1995).

8. Butragueño wears the smile of the post-Franco
generation (1987-88).

9. *Madridistas* on fire: the fans celebrate a *Primera Liga* victory over Celta Vigo in 1998.

10. *Ultra Surs* show their fanaticism as Real Madrid clash with Bayern Munich in 2001, a game the Spanish champions go on to lose.

11. Real Madrid players astride the statue of Cibeles, central Madrid, as they celebrate winning the 2001 Spanish league championship.

12. Matador Raúl brandishes the Spanish flag after Real Madrid win their ninth European Cup trophy, beating Bayer Leverkusen in the 2002 Champions League final.

13. The power of the presidential box: Florentino Perez with José Maria Aznar and other Spanish politicians in 2003.

14. A Royal club: King Juan Carlos and Florentino Perez at the Santiago Bernabéu stadium in 2001.

15. David and Victoria hand-in-hand in Madrid in 2003.

football to an art form. They called their team's performances 'ballets in blue'.

The Real Madrid president Santiago Bernabéu may have been impressed by Di Stefano that day in March 1952 when Millonarios played in the Spanish capital, four months before *El Che* saw him in Bogotá, but he was not alone. Also watching the Argentine was Pepe Samitier, the former FC Barcelona and Real Madrid player, who was then acting as a scout for the Catalan club while maintaining a personal friendship with Bernabéu. Di Stefano at the time was neither on the market or showing any signs of wanting to leave Bogotá. The situation changed later in the year when the financial bubble of Colombian football burst and some local clubs began to delay payments to players, filling Di Stefano with an unsettling feeling of déjà vu. His wife and two Colombian-born young children were the first to return to Buenos Aires to a new house they had bought there. That Christmas Di Stefano followed his family, leaving Colombia just as Millonarios were preparing to play a local summer tournament in Chile.

While the Colombian press speculated wildly that Di Stefano had disappeared after being kidnapped by some anonymous men from Barcelona, the Millonarios management took a more pragmatic line. The club president Alfredo Senior met Di Stefano in Buenos Aires and urged him to comply with his contract and return to Bogotá. Di Stefano refused, prompting Senior to report him to FIFA for breach of contract and to tell the world that the Argentine player owed him money. FC Barcelona had already made an initial informal contact with Di Stefano while he was still in Bogotá, which the player had at first rejected. They now decided to make a formal bid for him, opening up negotiations both with Millonarios and River Plate, which technically still owned him – or at least was contractually pledged to take him back from October 1954.

On 17 May 1953 Di Stefano arrived in Barcelona on the understanding that the Catalan club had a done deal with both River Plate and Millonarios. In fact, while River Plate had given its consent to Di Stefano's transfer, no such agreement had been secured from Millonarios. The misunderstanding reflected the confused tactics the Catalan club had adopted, involving both official and unofficial negotiators who between them could not agree to read from the same script. The official talks were entrusted to the Catalan lawyer Ramón Trias Fargas, an expert in commercial law, whose father had lived as an exile from the Civil War in Colombia and had good local contacts. But Trias Fargas found that his plans to reach a deal with Millonarios were undermined by the involvement of the club scout Samitier and a Colombian friend of his Joán Busquets who had poor negotiating skills and was mistrusted by the Bogotá club. Trias Fargas's life was not made any easier by the hesitant and equivocal attitude to the Di Stefano negotiations adopted by Marti Carreto, the FC Barcelona president. Every time Trias Fargas thought he had agreed to a figure with Millonarios, he had it rejected by Marti Carreto.

By contrast, Real Madrid showed itself both resolute and ruthless when it decided to make a formal bid for Di Stefano, moving, within days of Di Stefano's arrival in Barcelona, to turn to its advantage the confusion still surrounding his alleged transfer. Bernabéu entrusted a close collaborator

Raimundo Saporta to initiate talks with Millonarios, and to sign up to whatever payment the Colombians wanted. Saporta then travelled to Barcelona and spoke directly to Di Stefano who had already trained with FC Barcelona and played in some friendlies with Ladislao Kubala, matches the Hungarian star the Catalan club had signed up two years previously would always remember with particular fondness. As Kubala told me, on the rare occasions when he played with Di Stefano there was real understanding between them as players.

I had met Kubala in the mid-1990s. He was playing in a veterans team near the Nou Camp. As he told me, 'The trick with Alfredo was that you had to give him complete freedom of movement and a colleague who knew how to back him up. We'd take turns going forward, but always supporting each other. We were constantly changing positions. This meant that we were always with the ball, and always creating problems for our adversaries, particularly when they tried to mark us. Alfredo and I were always two against one, and that made the game easy . . . Of course I usually had Alfredo playing against me, and he was always a dangerous adversary, and an extraordinary player, quite unlike any other. He had speed, technique and a great vision. He also knew how to sacrifice himself for the good of the team. He was always a great example to the young players.'

Di Stefano's own memories of his brief spell at Barcelona were less generous. Although he shared a mutual respect with Kubala, he recalled those days as a period of boredom mixed with uncertainty, not helped by the incompetence and prevarication of Barça's high command which, as he described in his memoirs, verged on the farcical:

I went to the senior management who told me that they couldn't fix things, that they needed a third man, like in the Orson Welles film. 'You need a third man? But I am the third man. What is going on here? I'm going to buy myself a ticket and I'm heading back to Argentina. What am I doing here?' They had rented me an apartment in Balmes street and were paying me some money. But I didn't want to sign any piece of paper that didn't fix everything. They told me that Real Madrid had fixed things with Millonarios. So who was going to fix things now? I always said it didn't matter to me whether I played for Barcelona or Real Madrid. What I wanted was to play football . . .

As things stood, FC Barcelona had signed a deal with River Plate, while Real Madrid had reached an agreement with Millonarios which effectively showed that they were prepared to outbid their rival, and put their money where their mouth was. Before clinching the deal with Millonarios, Real Madrid's chief negotiator Saporta rang Bernabéu to remind him that FC Barcelona was still officially in the frame as far as its dealing with River Plate was concerned. 'It doesn't matter,' replied Bernabéu, 'you go ahead and sign as Millonarios has as much rights on this as River Plate . . . you pay whatever price is necessary, and afterwards we'll fix it.'

The price was $26,000 ($182,000 at today's value). Barça's president Marti Carreto had offered the Colombians less than half that. Real Madrid still had, as Saporta would later recognize, only one side of a two-sided contract signed. It was at this point of apparent stalemate and with Di Stefano's own patience rapidly running out, that Bernabéu and Marti Carreto called on the Spanish Football Federation to mediate; it in turn pushed it upstairs to the National Sports Directorate headed by General Moscardo, a man committed to the Franco regime's ideal of a compliant and united Spain. Moscardo's answer was that FC Barcelona and Real Madrid should come to an interim agreement to share Di Stefano, alternating over the next four seasons. Under the proposed deal, at the end of the four-year period all the parties would try to reach an agreement as to what to do with the player in the medium to long term. Both Bernabéu and Marti Carreto signed the deal on 15 September 1953.

A week later the FC Barcelona president resigned amid a revolt from his own management and the club's membership who felt he had sold them short. FC Barcelona's new management rescinded their side of the deal and instead surrendered Di Stefano to Real Madrid for a compensation payment of 4.4 million pesetas (about £40,000).

One of those closely involved in the negotiations on behalf of FC Barcelona, the lawyer Trias Fargas, went on to blame the club's loss of Di Stefano not just on the incompetence of his own president but also on a conspiracy orchestrated by Real Madrid with the blessing of the government. It was alleged by a subsequent generation of Catalan writers that Marti Carreto, a man not noted as a militant defender of Catalan nationalism, negotiated under pressure from high levels of power. A Catalan TV documentary marking the centenary of FC Barcelona in 2000 suggested that Marti Carreto was the victim of government blackmail because at the time he was suspected of being involved in tax evasion, along with other Catalan businessmen of the textile industry. No firm evidence was ever produced in support of any of this.

The facts as I have tried to relate them suggest that FC Barcelona not only allowed themselves to be completely outmanoeuvred, but also in the end fell victim to their pride in voluntarily giving up Di Stefano rather than accept a deal that would have him playing alternate seasons for Barça and Real Madrid. Undoubtedly though, the whole saga helped fuel the collective sense of victimization that Catalan nationalists have always felt in their relations with Spain's central government and which has helped politicize FC Barcelona's rivalry with Real Madrid. The sense of humiliation and anger was made worse by the fact that Di Stefano played the key role in the transformation of Real Madrid into the most successful Spanish club in the history of football.

When Di Stefano was finally won by Real Madrid, the club president Santiago Bernabéu was desperate for a team that could live up to the ambition symbolized by the new Chamartín stadium. The club had not won a championship title since way back in 1933. The 1947–48 season, the first following the stadium's inauguration, was so disastrous that the club struggled to avoid relegation. Bernabéu himself offered his resignation although this was promptly rejected by the Spanish Football Federation. Recovery came in fits and starts, leaving the club, third behind the champions FC Barcelona in the following season, and fourth behind the champions Atlético de Madrid the season after that. Then it was back down to ninth in the league before finishing the season of its golden anniversary in third position behind FC Barcelona, the champions again.

The newly signed Di Stefano arrived at Madrid's Atocha station on Wednesday 23 September 1953, having taken an overnight train from Barcelona with his young family. He was twenty-six years old. 'I had to adapt myself to Madrid immediately,' Di Stefano later recalled. It was no understatement given the speed with which his new club moved to make use of his services. Having arrived mid-morning, he was playing that afternoon in his first (exhibition) match, after a short medical check, against Nancy of France. Despite weeks without playing, and being several kilos overweight, Di Stefano scored in the 60th minute. Real Madrid lost 2–4 but the encounter stimulated the start of a growing interest in Di Stefano among European football fans, led by the French. The result anyway became a footnote within weeks as the club beat FC Barcelona 5–0 and went on to win the league, their first championship for eleven years. Di Stefano emerged as the league's top scorer, with twenty-nine goals. Real Madrid's first Golden Age was under way.

Di Stefano modestly recalled his first season with Real Madrid as one in which the team got to know each other and learnt to play half decently. Language was no problem for him – all the team players were Latin American or Spanish, as was the Uruguayan coach Enrique Fernandez, who had previously been at FC Barcelona. When he first arrived, Di Stefano could not understand how it was, looking at talented home-grown players like the inside-forward Molowny and the goalkeeper Juanito Alonso, inherited from the previous season, that the club had so underachieved.

Three months before the Argentine's arrival, Bernabéu had secured the services of Paco Gento, a young winger from Santander, one of several players whose skills would develop thanks to Di Stefano's inspiration and support. Gento had a chequered start at Madrid and at the end of that first season was close to being dropped by Bernabéu. He survived thanks to Di Stefano, who argued forcefully that Gento was a winger with extraordinary pace but who needed to improve tactically – something which could only happen by playing alongside more experienced players like himself.

Undoubtedly Gento grew as a player thanks not just to Di Stefano but to the array of talent that Bernabéu built up around him at Real Madrid, with the Argentine's approval, during the 1950s. It was on Di Stefano's direct recommendation that Bernabéu signed José Hector Rial, the Argentine inside-left, who had also played in Colombia. Di Stefano wanted someone who could help him build up an attack from midfield with a series of quick one-two passes. But Rial also contributed to the team by connecting with Gento with his long passes. He helped improve the left-winger's timing and control while making full use of his speed to tear into defences. Gento had soon earned the nickname *El Supersónico*. Rial was joined at Real Madrid by other illustrious foreigners – Raymond Kopa of the French club Stade de Reims, Ferenc Puskas from Hungary, José Santamaria from Uruguay.

Bernabéu showed himself adept at constantly refuelling his team with talent that combined in a way that not only won matches but did so with hugely entertaining football. Yet not all his signings were equally successful. The Brazilian international Didi never gelled at Real Madrid partly because he never seemed quite up to the energy and speed of his team mates, and partly because of personal problems involving his wife, a journalist who claimed that Di Stefano was jealous of her husband and mistreated him with the unwitting racism of a blond Argentine towards a black South American.

Di Stefano later claimed that Didi simply didn't fight enough for the ball, and lost it too easily. 'The Bernabéu

stadium likes quality, but it also values effort, work, commitment – it wants a battle. It's a public that is used to winning,
and to win you have to fight.' In others words, Didi couldn't
hack it the Di Stefano way.

There was also some tension at first between Di Stefano
and Kopa, the 'Napoleon of football', in the early days
because both wanted to play towards the centre of the
forward line. When Kopa came to Real Madrid the number
9 shirt had already converted Di Stefano into a local hero
over three consecutive seasons. Neither he nor many of the
fans were prepared to let it go. 'The conflict was resolved,'
writes Julian García Candau in his biography of Bernabéu,
'by putting Kopa on the right wing, and when in 1958 Puskas
arrived, the president was able to bring together five world
stars in an attacking quintet the likes of which probably will
never be seen again.'

Puskas came to Real Madrid having already earned a
special place in history as a member of the 'Magic Magyars',
the Hungarian team that dominated European football in
the early 1950s before losing to Germany in the 1954 World
Cup final. It was these Hungarians who ruthlessly ended
England's invincible record with a 6–3 win at Wembley in
November 1953 and a 7–1 thrashing in May the following
year. Of Puskas, the England captain at the time Billy Wright
has commented: 'His was a name fit for any sporting hall of
fame, worthy of any and every superlative.'

In England the press had dubbed Puskas, the Hungarian
team's captain, the 'Galloping Major' because of his rank in
his country's army. As the journalist Brian Glanville recalled,
he was 'the star of stars, a squat little Budapest urchin-figure,
plastered hair parted down the middle, with superb control,

supreme strategy, and above all a left-footed shot which was unrivalled in the world, dangerous from a distance up to thirty-five yards.' In Real Madrid, where he arrived aged thirty-one after being dismissed as too old by some Italian clubs, he won enormous affection and respect for all these qualities as well as for the paunch that never left him in all his days in Spain.

One of the favourite Puskas tales often told by followers of the club involved *la barriguita* or little stomach as it was diplomatically referred to. One day Antonio Calderón, one of the club directors under Santiago Bernabéu, called in the then trainer Camiglia to inform him that the club had signed Puskas. 'Is that so? Well what are we going to do with that stomach of his?' asked Camiglia, making it clear that he was not best pleased. Calderón answered: 'That stomach is your responsibility to get rid of.' Hours later Puskas trained with the team for the first time. Then Calderón asked Di Stefano what he thought of his new team mate. Di Stefano replied, 'He controls the ball better with the left leg than I do with my hand.' No one raised questions about Puskas's *barriguita* ever again and he came to be known instead as *Cañoncito*, the little cannon.

Five times Puskas became the Spanish league's top scorer and his partnership with Di Stefano came to be seen as one of the greatest of all time. He went on playing at Real Madrid until the age of forty, two years more than Di Stefano, and when he retired he had established himself as one of the most prolific scorers in football history, 512 goals in 528 matches.

Of all the stars of that Golden Age, it was still Di Stefano who shone the brightest – without him there would have been stars but no firmament. His greatness lay in his ability to combine his individual skill with his talent for organization. He played the breadth of the field and from one end to the other with equal effectiveness, whether defending his own penalty area, organizing the midfield, or scoring from the edge of the six-yard box after taking the team on the offensive. Miguel Muñoz, his first captain at Real Madrid, once said that with Di Stefano on your side it felt like having two players in every position. Beyond the field Di Stefano was responsible for casting a whole club in his image. To Real Madrid fans he came to personify success on a global scale. He created a whole mythology around the club's invincibility, and consequently left a tough act for subsequent generations of Real Madrid players to follow. In one of the more revealing interviews he ever gave, Di Stefano, long retired, was asked by the former Real Madrid director Inocencio Arias what he thought defined the Real Madrid fan. 'It wants the team to fight . . . It wants it to win . . . but it wants it to win first and then to play.'

Because of him the Bernabéu became one of the most exacting stadiums in the world, where fans expected domination of the opponent, ritual humiliation and nothing less. Such arrogance had its flip-side in the creation of a culture of visceral adversity – the football equivalent of the two Spains, forever in conflict with each other, forever irreconcilable. Rivals created their own mythology around Real Madrid, a club that sold its soul to the devil during the Franco years and was damned for all time.

During the Di Stefano years my grandfather Gregorio died, and I was sent to school in England. I spent my childhood holidays in Spain, first in the Basque country, and then in

Catalonia. I went on to become a Barça fan for the same reason my grandfather stayed away from the Bernabéu – politics.

One month after Di Stefano made his debut as a Real Madrid player, Franco, dressed in a black uniform of the supreme *Jefe* (boss), marked the twentieth anniversary of the foundation of the Falange Española by José Antonio Primo de Rivera by addressing 125,000 blue-shirted Falangists in the new Real Madrid football stadium at Chamartín. The regimented choreography and nationalist speeches were designed to reassure the regime's right-wing supporters that Spain had not surrendered its sovereignty to the United States by allowing it to build its military bases. As every Spanish schoolchild had been taught from an early age, it was the US that had robbed the glorious Spanish Empire of its last colonies, among them Cuba where the loss had resulted in the establishment of the base at Guantánamo bay. Now the Americans had been given the green light to build their bases on mainland Spanish soil.

Franco defended the decision as part of his ongoing contribution to the crusade against communism. Fascist rhetoric would continue to echo through Spanish football for a few more years as Spanish newspapers like *Marca*, *Arriba* and *El Alcázar* blamed the poor performance of the Spanish national team during the 1950s on the arrival of too many foreign players and their 'alien' tactics which had diluted the manliness and courage of the Spanish race – the mythical *furia española*. An example was provided by General José Villalba, a senior official of the Spanish Sports Directorate, after Spain's 3–0 defeat by Portugal in June 1956. 'Today's match has been an authentic example of lost courage. The

surfeit of technique had made Spanish football effeminate,'
General Villalba declared.

Throughout the early and mid-1950s such rhetoric went
hand in hand with another left-over from the bleak post-Civil
War years: an economy which consciously attempted self-
sufficiency through heavy state intervention and protection-
ism. Spain remained isolated from the European mainstream,
restricting imports and foreign investment and with its only
significant export represented by an increasing number of
Spaniards who emigrated to northern Europe in search of
work, better wages and political freedom. Yet the apathy and
inertia that seemed to characterize those Spaniards who
supported the Franco regime did not extend to Spanish club
football which during the fifties developed its own dynamic.

Di Stefano's arrival in Real Madrid may have been followed within weeks by a pseudo-fascist rally but it also
coincided with a development involving the club that was to
have a much more fundamental impact on the future of
international football – the creation of a European club
championship. The idea of a competitive tournament that
would involve Europeans, north and south, west and east
across political barriers was prompted by the puncturing of
French national pride. In December 1954 the English league
champions Wolverhampton Wanderers beat the Hungarian
team Honved and Moscow Spartak in friendlies, a result
the *Daily Mail* jingoistically celebrated as a world conquest.
Gabriel Hanot, a former French international and then editor
of the sports daily *L'Équipe*, was furious. He accused the
English of being presumptuous and mentioned Milan and
Real Madrid as examples of teams that could aspire to greater
glory if given half a chance. What was urgently needed,

Hanot wrote, was a world club championship, or at least a European club championship, which was truly representative of international football at its best.

Hanot subsequently invited twenty leading clubs to discuss the project in a Paris hotel. Sixteen entered the first Champions' Cup tournament, which had the approval of FIFA and was administered by UEFA, European football's governing body, which had been created after the Second World War. Not all of them could lay claim to being technically champions but they shared a common enthusiasm for a competition that had the capacity to break into diplomatic ground as yet untrodden by governments and regimes in the Cold War era. Motivation was not simply ideological. Participants saw the opportunity of raising their international profile, and of making more money.

The reigning English league champions Chelsea chose to stay away, heeding the advice of a short-sighted and insular English Football Association. Their place was taken the following year by Manchester United whose boss Matt Busby was more than happy to grab the opportunity after watching the way the tournament galvanized the interest of the footballing public across the continent. In the words of Stephen F. Kelly, United's oral historian, 'nobody was going to tell Busby what he could do . . . It didn't take long for everyone to realize that here was a competition that combined all the romance of football with the finest of competition.'

In Spain it was FC Barcelona that showed recalcitrance. The Catalan sports newspaper *Mundo Deportivo*, the Catalan football federation and Miró Sans, the new president of FC Barcelona all argued, as Chelsea had done, that the tournament would put an excessive strain on the football calendar, putting too much pressure on players. By contrast Bernabéu saw it as a perfect vehicle for projecting the star-laden team he had begun to assemble, and for increasing the revenues of a club that had invested ambitiously in its new stadium and had advanced plans for a new training ground nearby.

The strategy had the blessing of the Franco regime with which Bernabéu had close links. 'This project pleases me enormously, just as it does my friend Santiago Bernabéu,' the president of the Spanish Football Federation Juan Touzon told *L'Équipe* in January 1955. That Real Madrid could be counted as politically sound when travelling beyond the Spanish border had been confirmed when the club had played in Venezuela in the Little World Cup of 1952. 'The behaviour of Real Madrid from directors through to players has been irreproachable in all aspects and they have left us with an unsurpassable impression of impeccable sporting good manners and patriotism,' proclaimed the official state bulletin when that friendly tournament was over. No such assurance could be given by FC Barcelona, a club whose loyalty to the regime was less clear-cut amid the simmering political undercurrent of Catalan nationalism that would periodically rise to the surface both at home and abroad during the Franco years. During one of Barcelona's matches in that summer of 1952, an exiled Catalan had created a major diplomatic incident by displaying the Catalan flag from the terraces before the start of a match. He was forced to remove it by the president of the club Marti Carreto, after the Spanish ambassador and former Falangist president of the Spanish Football Federation Manuel Valdes Larranga had issued a formal protest.

The incident was carefully censored from the Spanish media at the time, but it entered the collective memory of those pledged to maintaining Barça's cultural identity in the face of what was seen as Marti Carreto's cowardice – an impression that deepened later with his hopeless handling of the Di Stefano transfer saga.

What fuelled the resentment of Catalan nationalists was the way that Bernabéu's embrace of the European Cup mythologized Real Madrid as the only truly international Spanish football club capable of representing something bigger than themselves. In the season before the European Cup was dreamed up, FC Barcelona had won the Copa Latina with Kubala in Paris against the French champions Nice having earlier overwhelmed Juventus, until then considered by many experts as the best team in Europe. Thousands of Barça fans had celebrated in Paris and later in the Catalan capital in a show of solidarity. Before Bernabéu's Real Madrid had set out on their legendary conquest of five consecutive European cups, it was FC Barcelona that had reached out beyond the isolating borders of Franco's Spain.

It was nonetheless the European Champions Cup that quickly established itself as undoubtedly the most prized trophy in world club football, making reputations as easily as it has broken them, and creating an aura of romance and glamour about it that few other sporting tournaments have been able to equal. The legend of Real Madrid as the most successful sporting institution in the world is bound up with it because no other institution can claim to have won it so many times. From the outset the tournament seemed to spark enthusiasms across frontiers, marking new potential territory in political and diplomatic terms.

The 1955–56 season was marked by the inaugural European Cup, which was won by Real Madrid. Their progress to the final included a quarter-final encounter with communist Yugoslavia's Partizan of Belgrade, the first time any Spanish club had played against a football team from behind the Iron Curtain since the end of the Civil War. Both the first leg played in Madrid and the second played in the Yugoslav capital were brutal affairs fought in highly charged atmospheres, where the hostility of the home crowd towards the visitors seemed to respond not so much to a purely sporting rivalry but an enduring political bias orchestrated from above. Franco's Spain and Tito's Yugoslavia would remain mutually antagonistic throughout the Cold War years.

While there is in fact little evidence linking Real Madrid's subsequent successes to any major alteration in Franco's diplomatic standing in the world, there is no doubt that Real Madrid helped promote an image of Spanish success overseas, in effect converting itself, together with emigration, into Franco's most important export to the world. The contrast between Franco's diplomatic isolation and the new relationships which Real Madrid succeeded in building up beyond Spain's borders, both in competitive football and friendly exhibition matches, became apparent to the Spanish diplomatic service during the first European Cup tournament. On the eve of the final in Paris, the Spanish embassy hosted a reception which attracted an impressive guest list from the French sporting world as well as senior representatives from international bodies like FIFA and the International Olympic Committee. Telegrams from the Spanish ambassador to the ministry of foreign affairs in Madrid celebrated the success of his party and the subsequent media coverage praising Real Madrid's victory over the French champions Stade de Reims. The tributes to the Real Madrid players made clear the widely held opinion that they were deserving winners and that Di Stefano's team was opening up a new exciting era in the history of world football.

Yet days later the same Spanish ambassador found himself reporting to head office with gloomier news. Another invitation he had extended to senior members of the French government for a party celebrating Spain's national day – as proclaimed by Franco after the Civil War – had met with an unceremonious snub. Both the French prime minister and finance minister had sent letters of apology claiming alternative engagements. The minister of information had not even bothered to reply to the invitation. But worst of all, according to the mortified Spanish ambassador, was the attitude of the French ministry of foreign affairs. Rather than send the minister and at least one secretary of state as invited, the ministry had proposed sending a minor functionary. Such a gesture, the ambassador made clear, was adding insult to injury. His recommendation was that the Spanish government should reciprocate by sending no minister to the French embassy in Madrid on the occasion of France's national day.

The confidential report would probably still be languishing in the bowels of some secret government archive had it not been unearthed more than four decades later by Inocencio Arias. As a serving diplomat with many years of experience in the foreign service, Arias had privileged access to such documentation. I am grateful to him for drawing such material to my attention when I interviewed him for this book. The exchange of diplomatic telegrams certainly provides an illuminating backdrop to the words of Fernando

Maria de Castiella, who served as foreign minister under Franco. 'Real Madrid is a style of sportsmanship. It is the best embassy we have ever had.' With Real Madrid, the Franco regime felt it had friends in the world. Without it there could be no such certainties.

8. The Good Dictator

While his name may be forever carved in stone at the entrance to the Bernabéu – a stadium named after another legend – Di Stefano's days as a Real Madrid player effectively ended on the 27 May 1964, to paraphrase the poet T. S. Eliot, 'not with a bang but a whimper', for that is the way that the club has tended to deal with even its most prized heroes – until it's deemed fit to resurrect them. On that day Real Madrid crashed 3–1 to Internazionale in the final of the European Cup, a defeat that was widely seen as marking the end of an era during which the club had got used to considering itself not just the best in the country but the best in the world. Suddenly the superstars who had generated such enthusiasm across frontiers appeared mere mortals. The aura of invincibility gave way to a terrible sense of impending ordinariness, verging on mediocrity. As the Spanish sports writer Alfredo Relaño has put it, 'That Golden Age ended more or less with Di Stefano. They grew old, Di Stefano and all that luxury legion of imported players. They grew old, lost their hair, and grew fat . . .'

The decline had been gradual and susceptible to occasional revivals. Real Madrid had extended their unbeaten record in the European Cup to 1960, the 7–3 victory at Hampden Park, Glasgow, before 135,000 fans over the German team Eintracht Frankfurt forever remembered as one of the most exciting finals in the history of competitive football. Puskas scored four goals and Di Stefano a hat-trick.

But in the following season Real were beaten by FC Barcelona in the first round of the competition, a defeat the club's official historians would persist in blaming on unfair refereeing by the Englishman Reg Leafe and behind him an even less tangible conspiracy. This involved Mr Leafe acting as a paid-up member of a European football mafia – led by the English and no doubt Sir Matt Busby – determined to put an end to Real Madrid's hegemony. Such a theory, however ludicrous, managed to preserve Real's sense of dignity, assuaging for the humiliation it must have otherwise felt for the defeat at the feet of its arch domestic rival. That tournament was recalled differently of course by FC Barcelona as that of the Holy Grail nearly clinched, but lost in the end largely because of bad luck and the brilliance of Benfica's Eusébio.

In the following two seasons conspiracy theories were less forthcoming as Real Madrid themselves managed to be beaten by Benfica in the 1962 final, and then fell in the preliminary round of the eighth European Cup competition to the Belgian champions Anderlecht.

It was now that a bogey-man in the history of Spanish football struck his most devastating blow against Alfredo Di Stefano and his foreign legionnaires. The coach of the Inter team that took the European Cup from the Spanish champions was Helenio Herrera, a man with an extraordinary capacity for reinvention. Before moving to Italy for the first time, the Argentinian Herrera had pulled FC Barcelona out of the also-ran status of Spanish football, restoring their confidence and transforming them into a worthy challenger to the seemingly invincible Real Madrid.

In 1959–60, his first season with the Catalan club, Herrera

won the Spanish league championship and the Cup, the *Copa del Generalísimo*. FC Barcelona went on to lose their 1960 European Cup semi-final clash with Real Madrid. (The Catalans avenged that defeat by beating their Madrid rivals in the following season's competition.) That defeat cost Herrera his job at Barça, but he was still paraded up the Rambla by his adoring fans. Barça took handsome compensation after his departure by winning the 1960 European Fairs Cup. Herrera would always have fond memories of the FC Barcelona of the late 1950s, considering it one of the best group of players he had ever managed. Thirty years later, shortly before he died, he told my colleague Simon Kuper that he had played his 'tricky foreigners in attack' – Koscis, Villaverde, Czibor etc. – while basing his defence on 'my big Catalans' – Ramallets, Olivella, Rodri, García, Segarra, Gensana. 'To the Catalans,' Herrera told Kuper, 'I talked "Colours of Catalonia, play for your nation," and to the foreigners I talked money . . . I talked about their wives and kids. You have twenty-five players, you don't say the same things to everyone.' What were the differences between the nationalities? Kuper asked. ' "Hungarians are more reserved," he [Herrera] hunched his shoulders and screwed up his face in imitation. "So I mixed them, not Czibor and Kocsis alone in one room. I wanted them all to be the same, I wanted friendship. That is why we trained together, why we ate together . . ." '

Herrera's reputation as one of the world's most single-minded as well as innovative coaches was displayed by his decision to drop Kubala from the first team, the Hungarian who in the 1950s had become one of FC Barcelona's great idols. Herrera justified the move on loss of form. Kubala's defenders suggested envy of a potential rival. Herrera also forced out Pepe Samitier, the club's technical director who promptly moved to the management side at Real Madrid where he had once played, as he had done at FC Barcelona, before the Civil War.

There is no doubt that Franco himself considered Samitier not just a friend but a political ally as much at FC Barcelona as at Real Madrid. Franco exploited the friendship to counter the suggestion that he was by nature and principle biased against the football of Catalonia. On the few occasions Franco held a personal audience with the FC Barcelona board, he insisted that Samitier be present.

In Madrid Samitier was remembered, among others things, for harbouring an everlasting grudge against Helenio Herrera. It was Herrera who, as Alfredo Relano puts it, had become 'the baddy of the film . . . for many an innovator, for others a real anti-Christ of football'. It was Herrera who as coach of the Spanish national team first humiliated Di Stefano – a 'nationalized' Spaniard (that is, qualified by length of residence in Spain to play in that country's national team) – by picking him for the 1962 World Cup in Chile and then making sure he didn't play a game. Di Stefano pulled a muscle in his back just before leaving Spain for the Chilean capital Santiago. He blamed it on Herrera making him lose too much weight. Di Stefano was met in Chile by his father who had flown across the Andes from Buenos Aires. His dad had brought a 'magic' potion which he urged him to use. But the potion was unable to heal the conflict between Di Stefano and Herrera, two Argentines with similarly inflated egos.

Spain was drawn to play the world champions Brazil in the opening round. It was a game in which Didi had planned to take his revenge on Di Stefano for his mistreatment by Real Madrid – but Di Stefano was kept out of the team. Herrera used the *catenaccio*, the system he had first introduced at Inter. In it the sweeper stayed behind the defence, with the rest of the team marking man to man. To his critics such tactics were excessively defensive and stifled the game. In fact the Spanish team showed no lack of commitment or flair, stretching the champions, and losing 2–1 only after Brazil had taken the lead four minutes from the final whistle.

Nevertheless the defeat and subsequent elimination from the World Cup refuelled a national debate about the future of Spanish football, which resurrected some sinister prejudices from the past. Although Di Stefano had not played, three other 'nationalized' foreign players had been included in Spain's World Cup squad. They included Real Madrid's Hungarian import Puskas, who in the game against Brazil formed an attacking line-up with his club colleague Gento and three players from Atlético de Madrid. In addition one of the Spanish players, Luis Suárez, had moved with Herrera to Inter. The cosmopolitan nature of Herrera's line-up was sheer provocation to the extreme nationalists of Spanish politics. The state-controlled Spanish sports daily *Marca* led the charge, claiming that Spain had been eliminated from the World Cup for not being sufficiently Spanish. While conceding that foreign players like Di Stefano, Puskas and Kubala, and managers like Fernando Daucick, Ruben Fleitas and Helenio Herrera had added 'colour and excitement' and also helped Spanish teams like Real Madrid and FC Barcelona win European competitions, the newspaper argued that such foreign influence was blocking the development of home-grown talent. 'Even worse, the national team is now so full of foreigners and so conditioned by foreign tactics that it no longer plays like a team of real Spaniards, with passion, with aggression, with courage, with virility, and above all, with fury,' editorialized *Marca*.

Following the World Cup, FIFA tightened up the regulations governing the use of foreign players in national teams. In Spain it led to a ban on the further importation of foreign players until 1973. The Spanish football authorities continued to turn a blind eye to the entry of numerous South American players with documents claiming they were of Spanish parentage.

Nevertheless anti-foreign sentiments surfaced with a vengeance in 1964 when Spain met the Soviet Union in the final of the European Nations Cup, which by chance was played in the Bernabéu stadium. Four years earlier Franco had intervened personally to pull Spain out of the tournament when drawn against the Soviet Union in the quarter-finals. The prospect of one of the games being played in Moscow had drawn complaints from Civil War veterans within the regime that there were still anti-communist Spanish combatants detained in Russian concentration camps. Spanish police intelligence reports also predicted anti-Franco demonstrations by Spanish exiles. The subsequent withdrawal of the Spanish team, at a time when Real Madrid was at the peak of its glory and was helping to break Spain's sense of isolation, held the regime up to diplomatic ridicule as well as being unpopular with the growing mass of football fans.

By the time the two national teams next faced each other, in the 1964 final, the regime's sporting authorities had gone to considerable lengths to make amends to FIFA, securing the privilege of hosting the championship on home territory as a recognized member of the international football community. As for Franco he appears to have come round, with minimum persuasion, to the idea that the final against the Soviet Union, if won, could be of enormous propaganda value even if it was not quite what FIFA would have liked. José Solís Ruiz, secretary-general of the regime's political Movement, was strongly of the opinion that football could be used to divert an emerging post-war generation from any ideas of political dissidence.

'Less Latin, more football,' was the key to the future of Spanish education, Solís argued. Franco, still worried about the possibility that he might have to hand the trophy to the Russian captain, consulted his personal doctor Vicente Gil, a sports fanatic, who told him that Spain would win.

Few relished the encounter as much as Colonel José Villalonga, the anti-communist Civil War veteran who had succeeded Helenio Herrera as national coach. Villalonga claimed that in the two years since the World Cup in Chile he had built up – as he put it in a pre-match statement – 'a young, impassioned, aggressive, virile team based on typical Hispanic values'. When Franco entered the stadium for the match accompanied by his wife Doña Carmen, generals and other ministers, the cry of 'Franco! Franco! Franco!' spread across the 120,000 fans and was broadcast across fifteen nations. Spain won 2–1. Villalonga dedicated the win to Franco who in turn saw it as a logical culmination of his Civil War victory. 'The Spanish fury has returned at last,' the Spanish newspaper *Arriba* enthused. 'The victory has demonstrated to the world that the Spanish fury is invincible, when employed with passion, aggression, courage and virility.'

The previous autumn Di Stefano had captained a Rest of

the World team against England at Wembley on the centenary of the sport's foundation. The team included the trio who had been at the heart of Real Madrid's great side – Kopa, Gento and Puskas (who substituted Denis Law in the second half). Di Stefano was shocked by how the English players ate bacon and eggs for breakfast. Spanish players then, as they do now, eat soup, fish, and meat or pasta. (Di Stefano, half jokingly, claimed to have stuck to a diet of consommé and boiled ham.) The diversity of talent and technique, drawn from both sides of the Iron Curtain, never quite gelled and England won 2–1, a sign that English football was on the up. But the game had the symbolic value of a tribute to a fading star who many considered to have achieved the legendary status of the greatest all-round forward of his generation. Yet just seven months later the sense of warmth and respect that had enveloped Di Stefano with the international recognition of the Wembley game, had dissipated amid his acrimonious and undignified departure from Real Madrid.

After Real's fourth consecutive league championship win, Di Stefano led the team into its ninth European Cup campaign confident of clinching world football's most prestigious prize once again. In contrast to their premature departure from the tournament the previous season, Real Madrid seemed to have recovered some self-confidence, easily disposing of Glasgow Rangers in the first round, and next beating the Romanian champions Dynamo Bucharest, after carefully side-stepping a rather obvious plot by the communist authorities to destabilize the team.

The Real Madrid players had arrived in Bucharest to find a woman in each of their rooms, ready with free sex and whatever compromising secret photographs might ensue. 'The players got together and discussed the situation,' recalled Di Stefano later. '"We've come to play football, and after the game, whoever wants to go out somewhere, let him to do so. But before the game, let's stick to thinking about playing." They were beautiful girls, twenty-two- and twenty-three-year-olds. We didn't fall into the [honey] trap.' Real Madrid won the game, and some of the players couldn't wait to get back to their rooms. They were disappointed to find that the 'doves had flown'. According to Di Stefano, the oldest profession was not the only temptation the Real Madrid players had to contend with when on tour. Such was their paranoia that they used to drink coffee which they had brought with them from Spain just in case someone tried to spike their drinks before a game.

In the quarter-finals Real Madrid faced AC Milan, who had emerged as one of their most dangerous rivals for international supremacy during the late 1950s. The Italians had become European champions the previous season, inspired by their 'Golden Boy' Gianni Rivera and his cultured inside-forward play in partnership with José Altafini. But Real Madrid prevailed, beating them 4–1 in the Bernabéu, and winning on aggregate after the Italians won the second leg at the San Siro by 2–0.

After this tough test against the Italians, Real Madrid found their semi-final opponents a walk-over, beating Zurich 8–1 on aggregate. No one could quite understand how the Swiss had managed to get so far.

As the players prepared for the final against Internazionale in Vienna, the tension that had been simmering for a while in the Real Madrid dressing room bubbled over with Di

Stefano and the coach Miguel Muñoz disagreeing over tactics. Muñoz was focused on man-marking Giacinto Facchetti, the overlapping full-back. Di Stefano believed this left Real Madrid too flat at the back and dangerously exposed to a counter-attack through the midfield by Corso, the Inter left-winger. Corso could quickly switch inside and combine with the likes of Luis Suárez, the creative inside-forward Herrera had brought with him from FC Barcelona after considering him the 'legitimate heir' to Di Stefano as the greatest Spanish footballer. In his memoirs Di Stefano blamed Real Madrid's 3–1 defeat on the fact that he was proved right. 'We played the game minus one player, but Muñoz told me to go to hell and they threw me out of the club because I told him to go to hell.'

In fact Di Stefano's departure after the row with Muñoz was to take the form of a lingering torture rather than a sudden death, with Di Stefano embroiled in further internal rows and struggling to regain a sense of dignity after being dropped from the team and being told by Bernabéu that the club wanted him to stay but was not sure in what capacity. Di Stefano's final break with Bernabéu came when he went to see him at his home and the president of Real Madrid, dressed in his pyjamas, refused his appeal to be allowed to go on playing for the club.

Di Stefano felt humiliated and betrayed by a club for whom, as he put it, he had given so many years of blood, sweat and tears. Thanks to his arrival at Real Madrid in 1953, the club had been moved from the ordinary to the sublime. From winning only two league championships in thirty-two years, it had won eight in eleven years, in addition to a Spanish Cup, an Intercontinental Cup and five consecutive European Cups. He had played 510 games and scored 410 goals. If his departure suggested that no player is ever bigger than a club, Di Stefano left an enduring legacy as a man of huge skill and commanding personality – a point of reference for future generations of Real Madrid stars, not least David Beckham.

Although few could have imagined it at the time of his bust-up with Real Madrid, Di Stefano was destined to return years later as a coach, an inspiration for a new generation of young players determined to restore a sense of pride to a club that seemed to have lost its way and sense of identity in the interlude without him. He later was appointed honorary president of Real Madrid, its most distinguished living veteran, a position he held when Beckham went to Spain.

Among the accumulation of grievances that fuelled Di Stefano's sense of disillusion with his club when he was still a player was an incident that occurred later on the same evening that Real Madrid lost to Inter. The team had a planned post-match supper abruptly cancelled and the players found themselves being unceremoniously hustled onto a waiting bus by club officials. The bus was about to leave when Di Stefano asked for a short delay to allow the team doctor Julio Lopez Quilez to finish a telephone conversation with his wife. She was in Madrid and was about to have a baby. Di Stefano was told by a club official that the bus couldn't wait. Either the doctor cut off his wife or he'd get left behind. The player took this as a further sign that Real Madrid had somehow lost its nobility, its collective sense of dignity and respect, of 'one for all and all for one', the central ethos he believed had driven the team under his example through its glory years.

Forty years later I caught up with Dr Lopez Quilez. Our paths had crossed off and on since my early childhood days in Madrid largely on account of personal ties. He had once been a student of my late grandfather's and over the years had operated on various limbs within my extended Spanish family when not dealing with the sprains and injuries of football players. He had left the employment of Real Madrid in the early 1980s and carried on for a while with his private practice before retiring, while his son Fernando trained for a while in the club's youth team.

The Di Stefano era was in its later stages when Lopez Quilez was promoted from his post as medical assistant at one of Real Madrid's affiliate junior clubs to doctor/surgeon of the first team. His promotion coincided with the arrival of Miguel Muñoz as coach. 'Santamaria had a muscular injury and Muñoz asked me if I could fix it. I had him playing within two weeks,' Lopez Quilez told me late one autumn afternoon in his spacious Madrid apartment.

The Uruguayan-born José Santamaria had turned into one of Bernabéu's star foreign imports, a ruthless centre-back who helped close down the defensive gaps left occasionally by Di Stefano whenever the great man joined Puskas and Gento in attack. He formed part of a team whose sun set only gradually. 'I remember the European Cup tie when we beat Glasgow Rangers . . . Del Sol, Puskas, Gento, Di Stefano couldn't stop playing football, running, making magic. The Scots went wild, they couldn't stop clapping . . . Di Stefano was out of this world. He not only scored lots of goals but was also everywhere, making everyone play. If any of his team mates didn't he'd shout at them, insult them . . . The only other player I've seen with a presence like that on the field is Maradona, but he never defended like Di Stefano.'

So what was Di Stefano like as a person when he played for Real Madrid?

'There were times he could be not friendly at all . . . not like Puskas who was a delight at all times. He was *simpático*, cheerful, outgoing . . . whenever we were on tour and he bumped into fellow Hungarians who were living in misery, he'd help them out with some money.'

I had guessed that one of Di Stefano's less *simpático* moments – seen from the perspective of Muñoz and one or two club officials – must have been that night in Vienna. But then there are two sides to every story, and Di Stefano had claimed to have stuck up for the doctor's rights not just as an employee of the club but as a caring husband and father-to-be.

Lopez Quilez recalled only that by that evening he'd already realized that Di Stefano's days as a player were numbered, that the team he'd helped organize was breaking up. 'Gento went on playing well, but Del Sol had sold out to Agnelli's Juventus. As for Di Stefano, his age had caught up with him . . . he couldn't run as much as he once could, cover the same amount of ground . . . Muñoz spotted it first. I'd also seen his X-rays of his back. They weren't good.'

His home was scattered with mementoes from his time at the club – a ball signed by the team, some glassware from eastern Europe, newspaper cuttings of his son Fernando as a child, kicking a ball with the players. I noticed a portrait by the Spanish painter Lucas that had once belonged to my family. A valuable heirloom, as far as I know, it had been given to him in thanks for a successful operation he had done on my aunt's broken shoulder.

Lopez Quilez didn't like interviews. He had only agreed to speak to me out of respect for my grandfather, under whom he had studied medicine, and one of two men he said had had a big influence on his life and hugely admired. The other man was Santiago Bernabéu. Both men had long since died. The doctor said that Bernabéu was like my grandfather, a political liberal who respected everybody and was honest. I found that difficult to understand. My grandfather had been one of the founders of the Spanish Republic. Bernabéu had fought as a Franco soldier to destroy that same Spanish Republic. In the aftermath of the Civil War my grandfather had turned down the well-paid post of head of the new Institute of Medicine, Hygiene, and Health and Safety, a flagship project of Franco's ministry of labour. Bernabéu was the regime's candidate for the presidency of Real Madrid under Franco and accepted.

Nevertheless Lopez Quilez recalled a day when the president of Real Madrid had called him to ask if he could operate on the leg of one of the club's gardeners. The year was 1964. The gardener had a piece of shrapnel from a wound he'd received during the Civil War which was giving him trouble in his old age. 'Try and do what you can for him,' Bernabéu told Lopez Quilez. 'He was a communist during the Civil War but he's a good worker. Think of it as a work of charity.'

Real Madrid had also boosted its support base under Bernabéu thanks to a deliberate policy of keeping membership and entrance to the stadium relatively cheap compared to other clubs in Spain. Beyond the philanthropy there was no doubt that Real Madrid benefited hugely from the popularity of radio in the 1950s and the introduction of TV towards the end of that decade. Bernabéu was initially resistant to allowing live radio coverage and TV cameras in the stadium on the grounds that it would undermine gate receipts. In fact his club's popularity spread nationally and across social classes thanks to both mediums. In comparison to other clubs, Real Madrid was given more air time throughout the Franco regime when both radio and TV remained state-controlled, with coverage throughout the country overseen from the capital.

I asked Lopez Quilez if it was fair to equate Bernabéu with Francoism as claimed by Spanish football fans who did not support Real Madrid. 'He did Franco a lot of favours by making Spain better known around the world,' he said, including Spain's other 'countries' – those regions that had historically claimed autonomy from central government. 'Don Santiago had the gift of speech of angels. He wanted Spain to be united and unite Catalonia to Spain, integrate it, which is what *El Caudillo* [Franco] wanted . . . He didn't feel a particular antipathy towards the Catalans and he expected them to behave the same way towards the rest of Spain.' For Catalans read Basques, Gallegos, Valencianos or any other Spaniard who couldn't swallow the arrogance and presumption of Castile.

I suggested that FC Barcelona didn't quite fit into Bernabéu's scheme of things. After all was it not a club that claimed to identify itself with Catalonia first and foremost having suffered not a little on account of it? He again answered the question on Real Madrid's own terms. 'The reality is that Barcelona has always been jealous of Real Madrid and the success that it has had.'

As simple as that. Well, almost. At a later stage in our conversation Lopez Quilez recalled how fans from Madrid had flown with the team and found themselves cheering at matches together with Spaniards who had been forced to emigrate. There is in fact little evidence that Spanish refugees – those who out of ideological opposition to fascism had gone into exile – suddenly converted to Francoism, watching Real Madrid play. What is true is that Bernabéu used to take a recording of the Franco national anthem and the Francoist Spanish flag along with the team whenever they played abroad just in case either the host country or some of the fans sang the Republican anthem or waved the Republican flag, as occasionally happened.

Franco too would use Real Madrid officials not just as unofficial ambassadors, but propagandists. He'd debrief them on what life was like behind the Iron Curtain and what the mood of Spanish fans was. Lopez Quilez told me how the team would come back from its games against clubs from the Soviet bloc, full of horror stories about life in eastern Europe. 'There was a terrible sadness in those countries, hardly anything in the shops, the hotels smelt bad . . .' he recalled. You mean that for Spaniards who supported Real Madrid that made them feel that life was much better in Spain? I asked. 'Of course . . .' he answered without hesitation.

Our conversation seemed to move effortlessly between past and present. Lopez Quilez claimed that he no longer felt he had the energy to turn up at the Bernabéu. He preferred to watch cartoons with his grandchildren. His son, a former Real Madrid youth player, had recently returned from visiting the family home in Valencia, shocked at the hate local fans felt towards the *galácticos*. Lopez Quilez himself disliked the new wealth of the Madrid superstars which he felt was turning modern players into spoilt children. And yet when he watched players like Beckham he felt that in one respect humanity had evolved. From a purely scientific point of view, the game had become more demanding and footballers had become fitter and stronger. 'When I was a kid the team played with a goalkeeper, two defenders, three midfielders, and five forwards – the two defenders never moved out of their area, and the forwards never came back into their own halves. Di Stefano was very different, he ran all over the pitch ... Nowadays players like Beckham and Roberto Carlos do that, but they play more games and have developed the physique to deal with the pressures of the modern game.'

I wondered out loud what he felt about David Beckham four months into his first season at Real Madrid. 'Bernabéu may have had problems with his hairstyle and his earrings – he thought long hair and earrings were for women – but I think that as a footballer he would have played well alongside Di Stefano ... he goes for the ball, not like so many stars today who wait for the ball to come to them.'

But listening to the doctor responsible for keeping the players fit and healthy during one of the club's most successful periods, it was possible to identify the extent to which Real Madrid had done more than play sport in the Franco years. It had helped – unwittingly in the case of many of the players and some of the officials – reinforce a regime's sense of self-worth, justified its existence. To that extent the club was collaborationist.

And yet there is no compelling evidence that Real Madrid's own sporting success was due to the help it got from the regime, despite the black legend of corrupted referees and ministerial influence in the transfer of players. Real Madrid's own instinct for survival, its ability to pull itself up when doubt had set in, was perhaps no better personified during those years than by Ignacio Zoco, the tough defender born in Navarre brought into the team in 1962 when the glory of the foreign squad built up around Di Stefano appeared to have peaked. Zoco would go on playing for the club long after the big stars imported during the 1950s had left, forming part of the all-Spanish team that won the European Cup in 1966, and retiring from the game in 1974. Of the many players who passed through Santiago Bernabéu's hands, he was perhaps among the best loved by Real Madrid's longest living and most influential president.

Zoco and I met in the Veterans' Association bar of the Santiago Bernabéu stadium. It was a revered place within the club's premises for it was here the players shared their memories when not acting as a clearing house for the signed balls and shirts sought by autograph hunters, or suffering the periodical bouts of bad temper of its president, Alfredo Di Stefano. With its photographs of Di Stefano and collection of dedicatory plaques to Real Madrid's history from around the world, the veterans' room had the air of a shrine about it.

Zoco was more than happy to talk about the legend, that time when Real Madrid came to be seen by the Franco regime, and to see itself, as Spain's best export. The truth as conveyed by Zoco, not without a sense of humour, was that while the club may have generated envy at home, it was deservedly embraced internationally. 'We would usually be met by government dignitaries. They'd bring flowers for Di Stefano, Puskas, Gento. As for the rest of us – well, we carried the suitcases . . .'

To listen to Zoco was not only to be transported into Spanish football's past, but to be reminded about how Florentino Perez had drawn from it to recreate his modern version of celebrity, the Real Madrid of the *galácticos*, personified by Beckham, drawing ecstatic crowds and flowers from Seville to Toyko, with a fan base you could find in the streets of Kabul and Baghdad where young locals wore Beckham shirts when not throwing stones at American soldiers. One thing had changed – no player was a bag carrier. Everyone had become too well paid, too self-important for that.

Back in the 1950s and early 1960s when Real Madrid were establishing their global following, the team derived great pleasure, not just from winning but winning for the Spanish emigrants who used to come and see them. 'A lot of them had actually laid bets on us winning – at least that's what they told us when they came and saw us before the matches. The next day they'd go back to their places of work, with a sense of pride at being able to be part of something that was special. They could turn to the Germans, the French, the Swiss, the English, and say, hey, just look what football we can produce . . .'

It was not always flowers and patriotic fervour though. In Italy and North Africa the team was confronted with anti-Franco protests which Spanish exiles had helped organize. Zoco's arrival at Real Madrid had coincided with rising expectations of greater political freedom – something which Franco was reluctant to concede. Strikes and demonstrations were repressed. The brutal nature of the regime was brought into focus by the torture and execution in 1963 of Julian Grimau García, a senior official of the Spanish Communist

Party. Franco ignored appeals for clemency from around the world.

Zoco seemed slightly irritated to be asked about this. He considered it an irrelevance in sporting terms, a bit like Barça fans calling for their rights as Catalans. 'Oh yes, I remember there was a protest when we played against Juventus in Turin . . . it was the year they executed . . . what was his name? I can't remember . . . they said we were representing a country that was a dictatorship . . . Oh, yes, now I remember, he was called Grimau . . .'

Di Stefano described how the demonstrators wanted to hand him a letter of protest, but he'd referred them to Muñoz Lusarreta, a senior club official, 'who was hiding [inside the hotel] behind a column, trying not to get involved.' Di Stefano had always insisted that his role and that of the other players in Real Madrid was to play football, and not get involved in politics. 'After training, I go home,' Di Stefano used to say. That day in Turin the anti-Franco demonstrators were cleared by the Italian police or the 'army' as Di Stefano recalled them. Real Madrid were beaten by Juventus 0–1 although they later went through after a replay to the final, only to lose to Benfica.

Touching a subject carefully passed over in the official history of the club, I asked Zoco what he had felt when he heard people said he played for the Franco regime's team, that he was helping to export Francoism. 'I felt absolutely nothing at all. They [the protestors] said that Spain was the pits, that it was in ruins, that people couldn't live . . . Well, we lived very well and what's more we were proud of being Spanish,' he answered. So did that mean that people had a distorted view about the reality of Spain? I insisted. 'Look, what we liked was football, we lived for football, and we weren't going to get obsessed with politics . . . It wasn't that Real Madrid belonged to the regime, it was that we were the best team that the regime had, the best team in Spain.'

Zoco seemed happier about sharing his memories of Santiago Bernabéu. I asked him to begin by picking his favourite anecdote. 'I'd only been at the club about a fortnight when I bumped into him in one of the corridors of the stadium. In those days I stuck out because I was tall and thin and walked around with my head bowed, as if looking for something on the floor. He stopped me and said, "Hey, you country bumpkin . . . Do you think *Madrileños* are stupid? They don't leave pesetas lying around." The next day I understood what he was trying to say because the trainer took me to one side and said that from then onwards I had to start doing weights, to strengthen my back, and walk straight . . .' Those who respected Bernabéu saw him at best as an honest, straight-talking patriarch, at worst a benevolent autocrat. His detractors regarded him as a man of the regime pure and simple – Franco without his execution squads.

The official photograph of the Real Madrid team that won the 1966 European Cup shows the players – Zoco included and all of them Spanish – clean-shaven and short-haired, an image of total regimentation. The team was nonetheless nicknamed the *Ye-Yes* by Real Madrid fans a year after the Beatles played their first and only Spanish concert in the Madrid bullring. In a spoof photograph arranged by a Spanish journalist when they were on tour, the players agreed to pose with Beatles wigs. It was the nearest they got to rebellion.

Nevertheless there was an emerging post-Civil War generation of Spaniards that longed to break out of the social and political straitjacket imposed on their parents. Zoco conceded that Bernabéu found it difficult to come to terms with the sixties, with anything in fact that threatened his control of the club, and his traditionalist view of what Spain should be – united and upright.

'He didn't like long hair, beards, players who played with their shirt hanging out of their shorts or their socks halfway down their ankles . . . He liked to see a team play in its uniform. Whenever he came to see us in the dressing room, he'd know which of the players had had some fun the night before. He'd simply say quite firmly, an early bed is better. He wanted us all to keep on the straight and narrow,' Zoco recalled.

Bernabéu was not pleased when Pirri, one of his star players during the 1960s, became the first at Real Madrid to marry an actress. He saw the marriage as a potential threat to the discipline and cohesion he wanted to impose on the club. Zoco then married Maria Ortiz, the first player at the club to marry someone in the music business. But then Ortiz was neither a gypsy nor a diva – with her Spanish guitar, gentle serenades and fresh face she was rather less wild than the most traditional flamenco singer, 1960s Spain at its most contained.

'Bernabeu was delighted with my marriage. Mine was strictly a family-only wedding, with the religious ceremony in the Castle of Xavier, named after Saint Francis Xavier, the patron saint of Navarre. There were twenty-two guests . . . They said I had to invite someone from Real Madrid so I invited one of the directors . . . Maria met the president after we got married, when we were back in Madrid, and she got a bit of a shock. We were both walking in the training ground when she saw him. I told her, "Sorry, but we're going to have to say hello." So I went to him and presented my wife. The first thing Don Santiago Bernabéu said to my wife, whom he had never spoken to before, was: "Maria, the day Ignacio retires you'll have to leave him with me as a breeding bull." Maria was speechless.'

Listening to Zoco's personal memories, it was hard not to muse on how Victoria Beckham might have reacted had she been confronted in this way by a president of Real Madrid. After all it was as a singer that 'Posh' Spice had first marketed the slogan 'Girl Power' with which a generation of female fans could define themselves as equal if not superior to men. At Manchester United she had taken on one of British football's more unreconstructed male chauvinists, by refusing to be pushed aside by Ferguson in his obsession to control Beckham's life off the pitch as well as on it. But Florentino Perez belonged to a later generation of Spaniards who could no longer take women for granted, nor indeed allow morality to set awkward barriers between the private lives of the players and their relationship with the club. As long as they didn't impinge on his players' ability to deliver professionally, Perez turned a convenient blind eye to the private lives of his stars, not least that of Ronaldo who made a virtue of womanizing and scoring goals.

Bernabéu shared an equal passion for football and bull-fighting, equating the best players with the best matadors – those with courage and skill and with the ability to score good goals, like the perfect kill. Bulls, bullfighters, players, they all formed part of the same world, their images diffused in a common vocabulary of collective identification with what was perceived as the true spirit of Spain. Bernabéu never fathered children of his own but the players he adopted as if they were his own were all at Real Madrid. Why, I asked Zoco, was he Bernabéu's favourite son?

'I think he had a high regard for me as a player, of good stock, strong, Spanish . . .'

You mean the Spanish fury? I ventured.

'That's what I think, yes.'

Bernabéu's romantic sense of what set the Spanish race and Real Madrid at a superior level to the rest of the world – the spirit of *El Cid*, the *Conquistadores* and the great anti-communist crusade of the Civil War – began to be less prevalent after the club's 1966 European Cup win. Gento was the last survivor of the 1950s' 'famous five', and getting old. In the team of Spaniards who had gradually replaced the foreign stars, now that there was an extended ban across Spanish football on further imports, one player personified the excellence of the glory years – Amancio.

The young outside-right had been brought in from Deportivo La Coruña initially to replace Luis Del Sol, after he had deserted the cause for Juventus. Amancio became the spearhead of the post-Di Stefano reorganization of the team, playing first in midfield and then as a striker. But while Amancio proved himself a world-class player of outstanding technique and acceleration, he was unable to secure the European crown as its heir apparent. While Real's sixth European triumph set a record in world football which other football clubs would be unable to better in the twentieth century, it also marked the end of an era.

Since its inception in 1954 the European Cup had been dominated by the Latin countries – Spain, Portugal and Italy

– with Real Madrid easily the most impressive trophy hunter. Now the power base of European club football shifted from southern to northern Europe – to Britain, Holland and Germany. Milan would stage a Latin comeback, winning the trophy against Ajax in 1969. But from then on the change in trend was set. Real Madrid would not proclaim themselves European champions for another thirty-two years.

That the post-1966 period came to be considered by Real Madrid fans as *los años del desierto* – the wilderness years – does not quite equate with the club's continuing ability to clinch more league championships than any other Spanish team, and to maintain a significant presence in European competitions most seasons. Such a record would maintain the club's enduring self-belief as the best in Spain, if not the world. Nonetheless extraordinarily high standards were set by the reign of Di Stefano, who came to be regarded in the club's mythology as the product of divine intervention, and for many Spaniards the best player ever. For if nothing else the history of Real Madrid is of a club that came to have an extraordinary conviction that its greatness was pre-ordained.

The reality of course is that Real Madrid, like any other football club, was vulnerable not only to poor form but also to the circumstances and schemes over which it had no control – the emergence of better players and coaches elsewhere capable of producing a winning formula of their own. The changing landscape of European football was nowhere better exemplified than in the shifting fortunes of Real Madrid and that other club that has shared a similarly obsessive self-belief, Manchester United.

In the 1956–57 season Real Madrid stopped Manchester United's first foray into Europe dead in its tracks, easily beating them in the semi-finals. The victory was given pride of place in Real Madrid's official centenary history as the day when the English 'reds' were brought down to earth. With scarcely hidden relish the club's historian quotes Sir Matt Busby's pre-match assertion that he had a better team and would win. Whether the emerging generation of young United players – the legendary 'Busby babes' – would have gone on to steal the crown from the Di Stefano-led 'white machine' had they not been decimated by the 1958 Munich air crash will always be open to debate in nostalgic circles. But Manchester United reaped sweet revenge when the two clubs met competitively again a decade later – and this time it was Sir Matt's Spanish alter ego Santiago Bernabéu who was forced to eat his hat even if Real Madrid's official history suggests that his honour emerged untarnished. Manchester United won 4–3 on aggregate, going on to win the championship.

According to Real Madrid's official history book *One Hundred Years of Legend*, Manchester United's 1–0 first-leg victory at Old Trafford on 24 April 1968 was characterized by the excessively physical game of the English, the singular brilliance of Real Madrid, the anti-Spanish bias of the Russian referee and a solitary goal, of no particular worth, by George Best. The Irish 'pop' player off the pitch would come to represent all that Bernabéu abhorred, with his loose living and general indiscipline even if this was compensated by genius on the field. The return leg played in the Bernabéu on the day of San Isidro, patron saint of Madrid, was an equally frustrating affair for a Real Madrid team that clearly was incomparably superior to the opposition, according to Real Madrid's official history version: 'That "imperial" Real Madrid which could not surrender to adversity intimidated

Manchester. Three goals by Pirri, Gento and Amancio, combined with the unlucky own goal by Zoco, left the English team reeling . . .' But United, 'taking advantage of a couple of indecisions' to score twice in the second half, somehow managed 'an incomprehensible draw'.

As a postscript it quotes Pirri as saying, 'Manchester over the two games did not deserve to go through into the next round, but football is a game in which luck plays its tricks.' They say that history is written by those who win, but this was the version according to the losers.

Compare it with the memories of others – 'red voices' recorded by Manchester United's oral historian Stephen F. Kelly – like those of Cliff Butler, a lifelong fan and club statistician, who went to the Bernabéu on his first ever foreign trip with the team:

We'd won the first leg one-nil and nobody really gave us a chance. By half-time Real were winning three-one and it looked curtains for United. But in the dressing room Busby told them that they were really only a goal behind. We went out and scored two goals. Foulkes, the most unlikely scorer, got the winner and United were into the final. After the game the Real supporters turned nasty. They were throwing stones at us and wanting a fight. The Bernabéu was an awesome sight. It was all concrete, concrete tiers, concrete terraces and concrete seats. You didn't sit on a proper seat, you just sat on concrete. But it was a fantastic atmosphere when the Spanish chanted, it was just an incredible, amazing scene . . . the final [at Wembley against Benfica] was the answer to every United person's dream . . . the homecoming was unbelievable as well. Half a million people were in the streets, around Albert Square. United weren't as disliked in those days.

Every picture tells a story and one photograph taken at the end of the game at Old Trafford sums up all the tension generated by the encounter of two clubs that seemed destined – more so with the passing of years – to mirror each other in their global ambition. It shows Bobby Charlton turning to face Zoco with a steely glare as the Real Madrid defender, head bowed and protected by his team mates, walks off the pitch. It had clearly been a tough game, not least in the way it had pitted Charlton – a name already synonymous with what the English regarded as the highest tradition of sportsmanship and integrity – with Zoco, the uncompromising Navarrese bull who, so Bernabéu believed, exemplified the fighting spirit of the Spanish people.

Back in the 1950s Charlton had been so struck by the quality of Di Stefano and the 'white machine' that he had confessed to a measure of relief at being left out of the Manchester United team that was beaten in the 1957 semi-final. 'I thought, these people aren't human,' he reflected at the time. 'It's not the sort of game I've been taught.' This time he had played as a captain who felt among equals. The name Real Madrid had begun to lose its capacity to instil fear in their opponents, something which challenged their very sense of identity.

In the following two seasons Real Madrid were beaten in the quarter-finals of the European Cup by Rapid Vienna and by Standard Liège. Then they ended in sixth place in the 1969–70 Spanish league championship, which meant that for the first time ever they did not qualify for the European Cup competition. Having won the Spanish Cup, they played instead in the European Cup-Winners' Cup, only to be beaten in the final by Chelsea. After that, Bernabéu found himself with no choice but to swallow his pride and drop his refusal to participate in the Fairs Cup (since renamed the UEFA Cup). When FC Barcelona looked like dominating the tournament in the late 1950s, winning the first two, Bernabéu had dismissed the Fairs Cup as a lightweight village affair on which serious clubs like his from big capital cities did not waste their energies. 'It's a tournament played by small towns,' he'd sneer.

Real Madrid was knocked out from their first UEFA Cup by PSV Eindhoven in November 1972. They blamed the referee again, refusing to accept that a club as great as Real Madrid could lose in such a mediocre tournament. Bernabéu warned the fans that the club was going through one of the worst periods in their history. He also told them that he would continue as president until someone threw him out or Real Madrid was relegated to the third division. Neither ever seemed a real prospect during the Franco years. That Bernabéu survived for so many years with his own position unchallenged was a reflection of his enduring popularity even though there was no system in place that would have allowed an alternative candidate to be elected, had he come forward.

Subsequent presidents of Real Madrid forgot at their peril that they owed their existence to a popular mandate of the membership. Even more so because of the expectations that were generated, the Bernabéu crowd during Beckham's first season in Spain behaved like a Roman circus demanding instant gratification. When things went wrong Perez tried to protect himself by changing the team and sacking his coach and sports director.

Bernabéu shuffled his teams and his managers – and after

eleven years his governing junta – like Franco rearranged his cabinet. Gento was finally retired, the last cog of the old white machine. The fans grew increasingly frustrated at being left with a team that played without flair and seemed vulnerable, losing its dominance in Europe. In 1973 Bernabéu took advantage of the lifting of the ban on foreign players and bought in a German with long blond hair called Gunther Netzer. He would be followed by another German, Paul Breitner, who moved to Real Madrid after considering that his talent as a virtuoso defender and midfielder was being stifled at Bayern Munich. They both played well – too well according to some Real Madrid purists. As a result the club had a tendency to lose confidence in subsequent years against German teams.

Netzer's arrival showed that gone were the days when Bernabéu could have insisted on a haircut as part of his terms of engagement. As for Breitner, he not only looked like a hippy, like Netzer, he also made no effort to hide his left-wing political views. Other changes were on their way. Miguel Muñoz, the man who had thrown out Di Stefano before moulding a team of Spaniards capable of winning the European Cup, was forced to resign after serving the club for twenty-five years as a player and a manager, paving the way for the arrival of another non-Spaniard now as manager, the Yugoslav Miljan Miljanic. He was in charge of the team when Real Madrid in the 1975–76 season re-entered the European Cup, after an uncomfortable absence of two consecutive years. They got as far as the semi-finals where they lost 3–1 on aggregate to Bayern Munich.

In the first leg played in the Bernabéu stadium the teams were level with one goal each when the Austrian referee Linemayer turned down an appeal for a penalty for a foul on

Santillana. Within seconds a Real Madrid fan had jumped onto the pitch and punched the referee in the face. Much as the club would try and blame the incident on a madman, 'El Loco del Bernabéu', this individual act of thuggery came to symbolize the extent to which Real had lost their nobility on the European stage. Sanctioned with a heavy fine and an extended match ban by UEFA's disciplinary committee, Real Madrid no longer seemed quite the gentlemanly Spanish ambassadors they had once held themselves to be. In fact Real Madrid, like Spanish clubs in general, have always been extremely bad losers.

Nonetheless when Florentino Perez was elected president in 2000, he pledged to restore what he claimed was a core value that Real Madrid as a club should always aspire to in the spirit of Bernabéu and the early enthusiasts who had brought football to the Spanish capital – a certain nobility of conduct called *señorío*. While stricter controls were put on the access of the *Ultra Surs* to matches, including curbs on some of their more inflammatory and racist chants and banners, players and senior officials resisted being neutered; Beckham was among several Real Madrid players who were shown the red card during his first season, while even the *filósofo* Valdano lost his marbles against Sevilla when Zidane got his marching orders from the ref – in Real Madrid's view unfairly.

The 1960s may have been the wilderness years of Real Madrid but it was a decade when Spanish society reaped the harvest of an unprecedented economic boom, triggering all kinds of political and social pressures. In 1959 Franco, advised by a new team of technocrats, decided to ditch a policy based on state intervention and closed borders and open up the Spanish economy to imports of machinery and new technology. The economy grew on average 7 per cent a year throughout the decade. Spaniards who had been starved of choice in the aftermath of the Civil War began buying more cars, more telephones and more TVs as real income rose countrywide. The middle class grew in numbers. The economic boom was underpinned by the hard currency generated by tourism and from emigrant remittances.

The first arrival of foreign tourists had begun tentatively in the early 1950s on the island of Mallorca. In 1957 a London-based package tour operator flew the first charter planes to the Costa Brava and the Costa del Sol. In the following years cut-price mass tourism turned large chunks of Spain into what the jubilant advertisers of the travel industry called 'the world's leading host nation'. Between 1951 and 1961 the number of visitors increased from 1.2 million a year to 7.4 million, and by the beginning of the 1970s to nearly 35 million, a total larger than the entire Spanish population. 'Never before had there been such a mass migration of peoples to a single destination – and this to the most resolutely insular state in Europe,' wrote James Morris after a six-month tour of early sixties Spain in a Volkswagen van and armed with a Linguaphone course. Spanish youths looked on bemused as they were confronted by sexually liberated Scandinavian girls, long-haired Englishmen, and French philosophers clutching volumes of Sartre. Fashions and attitudes still restricted by the diehard veterans of the Civil War were flaunted all across Spain as recklessly as the hot African wind that blew in summer. As Morris put it, European capital was spilling over the Pyrenees and forcing the stubborn survivor of an earlier age to lower its barricades.

The movement faced resistance as symbolized in the grey-uniformed, leather-hatted Civil Guard issuing arrest orders to the topless bathers on the beach, and the dog-collared soutaned priest denouncing the creeping decadence from his pulpit. There were those too – not all of them Spaniards – who lamented the denigration of what they considered the essence of Spain with cheap flamenco and artless bullfighting, sold in bulk to coachloads of undiscerning tourists. Connoisseurs like Ernest Hemingway complained that Spanish bulls – less well-hung and with horns shaved lower than they used to be – were 'half bulls'. With his sexy French girlfriend and cheeky looks, *El Cordobés* embraced and was embraced by the new invaders, but older Spaniards grimaced at the sight of the pop matador frog-hopping round the bull, like a circus clown, dangerously diluting standards.

For the first generation of Spaniards born years after the Civil War had ended, it was difficult to grapple with the essence of Spain, so numerous were the paradoxes thrown up by the Franco regime. We were in the mid-sixties and still debating whether or not Spain should play the Soviet Union at football. The Russian goalkeeper Lev Yashin, the best in the world, was really the son of exiled Basques who had been brainwashed by the KGB, and Russian pensioners were turned into soap after they died – so Spanish school children were told in those days.

By contrast – or the other side of the same coin – it was the US who seemed to be helping revive the fortunes of post-war Spain, giving us their way of life in return for bases like so much manna from heaven. Overnight Coke bottles, California cafeterias and plastic came to be equated with the modernity that Spain had always lacked. But if the Americans had combined with the Spanish Directorate-General of Tourism to act, in Morris's words, 'as yeast to ferment the outlook of Spaniards', there were aspects of the old Spain that stubbornly dug in.

Franco's antagonistic attitude to the sporting encounters with the USSR illustrated the distance which separated him from the new emerging trends of Spanish society. While there were Spaniards anxious to have the same luxuries and freedoms as that shared elsewhere in the emerging European Economic Community, Franco continued to summon up the uncompromising spirit with which he had fought the Civil War and dealt with its losers. His political views lagged well behind the liberalization of the economy. Strikes, demonstrations and general demands for democratic freedoms which most of Western Europe had consolidated since the end of the Second World War, were repressed. Franco himself denied that his rule was dictatorial, and asserted that he governed through the popular will. He governed longer than any other head of state in Spanish history, never once allowing democratic elections. He relinquished power only on his deathbed, after an extended old age, debilitated by illness.

During his lifetime Franco liked sport. He was a keen partridge shooter and fisherman, and was a football fan from the late 1920s when he was a middle-ranking army officer. Once in power he used to fill in the football pools each week as a hobby. He'd sign with a pseudonym and is thought to have once won some money. Of all the Real Madrid players, Gento was Franco's favourite, maybe because Di Stefano was not Spanish-born and too much of a loose cannon. Franco and Gento shared the name Francisco. They also had a short stocky build in common. Franco was particularly impressed by the speed with which Gento ran with the ball and then stopped dead in his tracks. Franco saw a reflection of himself in the world of football, and nowhere more so than in Real Madrid, a club that claimed not only to fly the flag for Spain during his regime but who claimed to be greater than all the rest.

Real Madrid's games – particularly those played against foreign teams – got plenty of air time, and Franco would try not to miss any of them. Such was his interest in the team that on the occasions a game coincided with one of his partridge shoots, he'd take a transistor radio with him and listen from his post. The political links between Real Madrid and Franco were maintained by Raimundo Saporta, the club's head of public relations and close aide of Santiago Bernabéu, the president. Saporta regularly briefed Franco on the team's trips abroad and the mood among football fans. It was Saporta too who used his contacts with ministers occasionally to get help from the government, such as getting round the restrictions on importing foreign cars.

However, according to Zoco some players were kept on a tighter reign than others. 'In those days we all used to draw our pay through the same bank and our accounts were controlled by the club. In those days it was easy to buy nationally manufactured cars like a Seat or a Gordini but impossible to get a foreign one like a Fiat or a Simca or a Mercedes. I asked for a Fiat 1300 and Saporta told me, "Ignacio, you have not been in the club long enough to get a Fiat 1300." I'd been in the team for three years. It wasn't that I didn't want to spend the money. It was that they didn't want to let me have it.'

Saporta, who died in 1987, was part of a team of people with links to the banking and business community that Bernabéu built up around him to handle the club's financial affairs. He was asked once by Julian García Candau, Bernabéu's biographer, whether Real Madrid was the regime's team. Saporta replied: 'It's always been on the side of those who rule. It began being monarchist with King Alfonso XIII, then it was republican, and then *franquista*. If the Franco regime backed Real Madrid it was in recognition of the hard work it put in overseas.'

When Real Madrid won their first European Cup in 1956 Bernabéu declared, 'I believe that we have simply done our duty.' Thirteen years later he was more expansive: 'We are doing the nation a service. What we want is to keep people happy. People like football a lot and with football Spaniards can deal better with their everyday problems. We are living a moment of such misunderstanding and such horrible confusion that what people want is real calm. They don't want problems. Football is the source with which people can periodically forget about their problems.' Bernabéu was speaking in 1969 against a backdrop of mounting opposition to Franco by trade unionists, university students and the Basque separatist organization ETA. By this time state censorship was unable to contain the public exposure of some very dirty financial linen – the use of dummy companies and bogus credits to shore up a company that had been lauded as the archetypal entrepreneurial success of Spain's economic 'miracle'.

On top of the political repression and violation of human rights which characterized Francoism, the so-called Matesa affair came to symbolize the corrupt nature of the regime's economic development and the weak foundation on which rested the wealth of the new middle class and oligarchy that had made their millions during the so-called boom years of the 1960s. Money had been made by the new rich by currying favour with the regime, not convincing clients with products. This complacent class of businessman was poorly equipped to deal with the economic crisis of the 1970s.

Bernabéu's success predated the get-rich boom years of the 1960s. Indeed he seems to have found it difficult to come to terms with the social shake-up of that decade. He was at heart a traditionalist even if the Di Stefano epoch secured his legend as a visionary of global football. Even if he delegated the administration of the club, he saw his own role as running Real Madrid as a family and was helped in that by his wife Maria. She used to recite the rosary each morning for Bernabéu and his team. She would also give prayer cards of St Teresa and jerseys to the newborn children of the players. So far as her husband was concerned it was his players who were the children. 'A footballer is like a child. A child reading the Bible has the face of an old man; a thirty-year-old man playing with a football has the spirit of a child. I am absolutely certain that at the moment he hits that ball, the man has the nobility and conduct of a child,' Bernabéu told the writer Marino Gomez-Santos.

Despite the fact that the first Spaniards to kick a ball in Madrid were upper-class intellectuals, Bernabéu believed that to play really good football, like to be a really good bullfighter, and to know how to absorb the passion of the masses you had to come from lower down the social scale.

Bernabéu regularly visited the team during training sessions and sometimes before or after a match to encourage or commiserate, like a caring if domineering father. His enduring popularity stemmed from his apparent ability to remain uncorrupted by the power that his position gave him. Bernabéu was never accused of personally enriching himself on Real Madrid's account. He paid his players what he thought they deserved and no more, and kept a tight hold on their expenses – something which some of them found difficult to swallow amid the increasing conspicuous consumption that began to surround them.

'People don't understand modesty,' Bernabéu said in the mid-sixties, 'they don't understand humility, and they don't understand sacrifice. They do understand boldness, cynicism, audacity. Yes, they understand that easily. For God's sake, man! For the love of God! What about the ideal? Where is the ideal?'

Apart from football and bullfights, Bernabéu, like Franco, loved fishing. Those who visited his fishing boat for the first time were amazed how small and unassuming it was. As Zoco, his 'favourite son', recalled, 'Everyone expected it to be a gin-palace but it was a little shell, just big enough for a couple of people. It hardly had anything on board, not even an umbrella. If it rained you got wet.' The boat was called *La Saeta Rubia* in honour of Di Stefano, until the player quit the club. Bernabéu used to say that those who left the club never came back. But Di Stefano proved him wrong.

Of Bernabéu's successors it was Florentino Perez who most self-consciously projected the image of restoration. So the legend went, it was when Perez had first watched Di Stefano, Puskas and Kopa play as a young boy in the 1950s that the idea had begun to form in his head of forging a future team of superstars. Later, in his carefully selected interviews with the media he cultivated an aura of disarming normality. Those who interviewed him found themselves seduced by the fact that he hardly touched alcohol, considered fried egg and chips his favourite dish, and always seemed to wear the same dark suit and blue shirt (an unfortunate colour, blue, for those with memories of the days of the Falange). One British journalist went so far as to describe him as 'the most self-denying multi-millionaire alive . . . a far, far cry from Beckham'. And yet the exterior belied the ambition of an obsessively driven man, who was as ruthless in trying to recreate Real Madrid's past glory as he had been in building up his construction empire. To his critics, Perez's fatal flaw was a subtly concealed demagoguery that contrasted with Bernabéu's benign paternalism. Perez might have seemed a far cry from the glamour of Beckham, but he was responsible for bringing it to Madrid.

9. Changing Times

On 28 June 1979 Laurie Cunningham, one of the most gifted English footballers of his generation, made his first appearance as a Real Madrid player before a packed press conference. David Beckham was four years old, already captured on the family video kicking his first ball, wearing the new Manchester United kit his father had bought him for Christmas, telling anyone who would listen that it was for that club that he wanted to play when he grew up, his own arrival in the Spanish capital, a quarter of a century later, not even imagined.

Real Madrid's history of signing foreign players since the Second World War had not until Cunningham's arrival included Englishmen. This was partly a reflection of the lingering resentment fuelled by the Franco regime towards all things Anglo-Saxon, not least Gibraltar. It also sprang from a long-standing perception among Spaniards, despite the English roots of the game, that the best footballers were of Latin blood, or others originating to the east of the British Isles, among them Germans. Yet the £995,000 paid for Cunningham by Real Madrid was at that time the biggest transfer fee paid by the club. There was a belief that here was an Englishman who could make a difference in a club whose sense of self-belief had been dented by its inability to resurrect the glory days of Di Stefano.

Cunningham had been born to Jamaican immigrants in

London in 1956, three years after Di Stefano's arrival in Spain. He'd started his professional football career at Leyton Orient, but he'd been a relative unknown until after he signed for West Bromwich Albion, and was selected for the England Under-21s in 1977. Cunningham, together with Cyrille Regis and Brendan Batson – a legendary trio of black players – helped West Brom, or the Baggies as they were known by their fans, finish third in the English first division and so qualify for the UEFA Cup. The trio were nicknamed the 'Three Degrees' as a tribute to the black Motown singers who had played at the West Brom stadium. They were named thus by the club's manager Ron Atkinson, who himself was destined for a move to Spain as manager with Atlético de Madrid. (Ironically, Atkinson, a TV pundit, at the end of a Champions League broadcast in 2004, remarked that Marcel Desailly of Chelsea was a 'lazy nigger' when he thought his microphone had been turned off. ITV rapidly dispensed with his services.)

When Michael Owen substituted Darius Vassell in England's World Cup quarter-final match against Brazil in 2002, for the first time ever (albeit briefly) there were more black players representing the national team than white. It was something of a revolution in English social terms, the seeds of which were sown in the Midlands by the Three Degrees, twenty-five years earlier.

'They could have been yellow, purple, and have two heads [I would pick them for my team],' Atkinson told the BBC many years later. 'So long as they could play and they were good lads – and they were.' Cunningham gained his reputation as a talented midfielder with an ability to score goals. Atkinson described him as the finest British player since George Best.

Brought up in England at a time of growing discrimination against black and Irish immigrants, and playing during the 1970s against the background of race riots and the rise of the extreme-right National Front movement, Cunningham didn't have it easy. Yet far from intimidating Cunningham, such threats helped galvanize him into improving his performance. The Three Degrees became the role models for an emerging generation of black boys in England who wanted to play football and felt they had as much if not more to prove as their grandparents who had opted for passive support of the West Indies cricket team.

Cunningham was signed up by Real Madrid after a brilliant display in West Brom's third round UEFA Cup clash against Valencia. Immigration was not yet an issue in Spain. In fact Spain had remained ethnically almost unchanged for nearly five centuries since the expulsion of the Jews and the Muslims although the myth of the pure Spaniard ignored the surviving mixture of races within the majority of the population. Real Madrid had encouraged a culture of multiracial tolerance within football during the fifties when they brought in Didi, the Brazilian international, to play alongside other star players. If in one area Santiago Bernabéu was without dispute ahead of his time it was in recognizing long before most football club chiefs in Europe that multiculturalism was the future, in football at least. In 1969 Bernabéu had this to say as his contribution to a semi-official book on Real Madrid entitled *5,000 White Goals*: 'The avalanche that is coming from Africa and Asia,' he wrote, 'will in time translate into a huge sporting explosion and into a phenomenal footballing success.'

Didi's failure to succeed in the club stemmed mainly from disagreement with Di Stefano over tactics, a loss of form, and the antics of his journalist wife who reported among other things that her husband was among the few members of the team who didn't occasionally subsidize the Spanish press. But during his early days in the Spanish capital, Didi was much admired as the first player to perfect the 'dead leaf' free-kick, so that the ball curved up and down into the net, beating defensive walls and goalkeepers – something which other players, among them Beckham, would later develop. Di Stefano recognized Didi for his skills as a kicker and a passer but thought that he was too slow with the ball, and an insufficient fighter off it. He also told Didi once that he should give his wife 'a good kick in the ass' for what he claimed was her insidious inventions, not least her claim that Di Stefano treated Didi first and foremost as a black and only secondly as a player.

Cunningham began well at Real Madrid, scoring a goal on his debut, and contributing to the club's league and cup double in his first season. Of particular fond memory among the club historians and some of the older fans was Cunningham's performance near the end of the season in a league championship clash at the Nou Camp in which he was the inspiration behind a 2–0 win over FC Barcelona – a rare away victory in the history of rivalry between Spain's two biggest clubs. Cunningham helped set up the second goal, escaping from his marker, before dribbling down the left wing and putting over a perfect cross for Santamaria to volley past Artila, the Barça goalkeeper. His performance that day drew applause from the home crowd, a rare display of generosity of Barça fans towards a Real Madrid player, and a black one too. In later years Barça would receive Real's Roberto Carlos with monkey noises.

A match report by *Marca* described Cunningham as showing off his unique talent and being the most outstanding
player on the field that day. 'This has been one of the great
triumphant afternoons of the dark Englishman,' the sports
daily concluded.

While the press comment, using as it does a qualification
of skin colour in describing the player's nationality, does
suggest an unconscious racist attitude, there is little evidence
that Cunningham suffered anything like the racist intimidation
that some black players experienced in the 1970s and 1980s in
England while he was at Real Madrid, a club that was accustomed to having 'foreign' players and nationalized foreigners
years before the far more insular English clubs did.

I asked Vicente Del Bosque what it had been like to play
in the same team as Cunningham at Real Madrid. It was
when I'd gone to see Del Bosque in the summer of 2003
after his sacking as manager, and the arrival of Beckham. It
seemed an obvious thing to do, ask him – a Spaniard in body
and soul – about another Englishman, one whom he had
played with for three years, rather than one whom he had
been denied the opportunity of managing. Now, almost
twenty-five years on, Del Bosque remembered Cunningham
as if it were yesterday, generously. 'Cunningham was a great
kid. His problem was that despite being a physically strong
player with considerable skill he lacked consistency . . . He'd
play some brilliant games but then there would be others in
which one would hardly notice him. He fitted in really well
with the team, settled down well even though this was a
different culture . . . He felt happy here, and adapted himself
perfectly to the Spanish way of life and Real Madrid's . . .'
Del Bosque told me.

I asked him to define his best traits as a footballer. Again without hesitation, Del Bosque remembered him, as if they had just come away from a training session. 'He was fast with the ball, a good dribbler, with a goalscoring capacity. He was an athlete . . . He'll be remembered for taking corners with the outside of his foot . . . the fans liked the novelty but I'm not sure how efficient they were . . . one of them helped us beat Porto in the European Cup so I guess they did work sometimes.'

When Cunningham was signed up, Manolo Sanchis, who captained Real Madrid during the 1990s, was then in the club's youth team. Sanchis remembered the impact Cunningham had on the emerging generation of young players who valued style and imagination. 'Cunningham would stay behind after a training session and practise juggling the ball. He was a real magician, a juggler. He could spend up to thirty minutes moving the ball from one part of the body to the other without it ever hitting the ground. Me and the others would spy on him without him knowing we were there, and we'd watch, amazed by all his tricks,' he told me.

Others remember Cunningham at Real Madrid as a player who did not quite develop into the star that his previous track record, both at club and international levels, had promised, and therefore did not give the club its full money's worth. Despite his occasional flashes of brilliance and popularity within the team, he found it difficult to adapt always to the tactics devised by the Yugoslav coach Boskov, while his form suffered further as a result of a controversial foot injury.

Lopez Quilez, the long-serving club doctor, was not consulted after Cunningham had his big toe stamped on by a Betis player. Another doctor advised that the English winger was fit to play in Real Madrid's next game. As Lopez Quilez told me: 'The club thought there was nothing wrong with him, but he had an injury that needed treating. They ended up calling me after he'd played in that second match. I had to operate. The next day I sent him home . . . That night he was seen dancing in a night club with his foot in plaster so of course that toe didn't heal properly.'

It wasn't the doctors who were blamed by the club but Cunningham. His night out while injured was considered an act of indiscipline and the player was fined one million pesetas. Maybe as Lopez Quilez suggested, Cunningham enjoyed himself too much off the field in Madrid. '*Simpático* . . . he liked going out, having a good time. He could be a bit of a loafer. He liked his drink . . .' the doctor recalled.

If the collective memory of Cunningham is broadly a sympathetic one, it is because of the abrupt nature in which the player's football career was cut off just when he seemed to be entering a more positive phase in Spain. Cunningham played for three seasons at Real Madrid during which he played a total of sixty-six games and scored twenty goals, leaving the club in 1983. He then played for short spells, alternating mainly between English and Spanish clubs. He seems to have loved Spain and the adventure of living in a society that showed him respect as a player and a person. Tragically he was killed in a car crash on the outskirts of Madrid on 15 July 1989, just as he was making his way back in *La Liga* under contract with his latest club Rayo Vallecano.

When Laurie Cunningham began to play for Real Madrid, Spain as a nation was in the throes of the final stages of a complex and delicate political and social transformation from dictatorship to democracy. The death of Franco in November 1975 had unlocked an accelerated process of reform. Thirty-four years after the abdication of King Alfonso XIII, the Bourbon dynasty had been restored, skipping a generation, with the modernizing King Juan Carlos as the linchpin of political change. Franco had named Juan Carlos when he was still prince as his heir, to succeed him rather than his exiled father the liberal Don Juan, hoping that he had been sufficiently moulded in the old ways of the regime and would resist major change.

For a while Spain seemed poised between liberation and disintegration. While the death of Franco fuelled the activity of progressive forces who wished to advance towards democracy, the diehards of the old regime remained entrenched in extreme-right civilian political groupings, and sectors of the armed forces and the paramilitary Civil Guard. I was in Spain at the time filming a TV documentary. With its strikes, demonstrations, ongoing cases of torture, crackdowns by riot police, and murders of trade unionists by right-wing hit squads, Spain was a country struggling with the ghosts of the past, and yet history seemed on the side of those who wanted change. Football reflected it. One day we were filming in the Nou Camp during a match between Barça and Athletic Bilbao. The Catalan club was led out by Johan Cruyff, the Basque team by Iribar, who had joined the campaign against torture and for the release of political prisoners. The packed stadium was filled with fans waving Catalan and Basque flags, emblems which had been banned for so many years under Franco.

That Spain did not descend into widespread bloodshed was largely due to the skills of King Juan Carlos, the ministers he picked and the conduct of the democratic opposition parties. Within months of the coronation, and amid mounting popular pressure, Juan Carlos had forced out Carlos Arias Navarro, the last prime minister hand-picked by Franco, and replaced him with Adolfo Suárez, at forty-three years old the youngest member of the outgoing government.

The appointment at first stunned those calling for greater democracy. Suárez had loyally served the Franco regime in a number of posts, and everything except his youth seemed at variance with the new spirit of the times. But there was a method in the apparent madness which only subsequently would reveal itself. From the personal contacts he had with him both before and after Franco's death, Juan Carlos had come to trust Suárez as the man most likely to carry forward reform without splitting the country down the middle again. The king calculated that Suárez understood the intricacies of the Francoist power structure and was thus well qualified to understand when and how it could best be dismantled. Ironically those who initially most approved of Suárez's appointment – the hard-right Francoist civilians and military officers – were to be the ones destined to be less favoured.

Within a year of his appointment Suárez had legalized trade unions and political parties, including the Communist Party, and in 1977 presided over Spain's first democratic elections since 1936, which he won as head of the centrist UCD party. He was re-elected in March 1979.

By then Spaniards had a new constitution, arguably the most liberal in western Europe. It defined Spain as a parliamentary monarchy, scrapped the death penalty, fixed voting age at eighteen, and did away with the unqualified Francoist demand that Spain should be one, united and Catholic. There was to be no official state religion, and central government would devolve power to the regions, from then on reconstituted as autonomous 'communities' with the central government in Madrid retaining 'exclusive responsibility' for foreign affairs, external trade, defence and the administration of justice. The constitution was a necessary political compromise at the time but it left the door open for greater demands for autonomy, and even independence, by Spain's regions.

Such change did not come about without resistance. Within two years of Franco's death, a group of generals were rattling their sabres because of the legalization of the Communist Party and the root-and-branch shake-up of the military envisaged by the political reformers. On 17 November 1978 a military plot by police cadets and a small number of troops to overthrow the Suárez government while King Juan Carlos was on a visit to Mexico was discovered and defused. The plotters were dealt with leniently, allowing them to try again at a later stage.

The period of transition from dictatorship to democracy also revived another area of tension, with regions with a distinct language and culture led by the Catalans and Basques accelerating their demands for greater home rule. While such demands formed part of a wider trend within Europe, in Spain they translated into campaigns of particular intensity because of the memory of the repression used by Franco to impose his centralist regime. The political reforms, not least Spain's new constitution, far from defusing demands, merely raised expectations and accentuated divisions as the regions set up their new autonomous governments with powers still delineated and restricted by Madrid. These were the labour pains of Spain's nascent democracy. They reached a defining moment on 23 February 1981 when Colonel Antonio Tejero, one of those who had planned an earlier coup, and a group of paramilitary Civil Guards burst into Madrid's parliament building and took hostage at gunpoint Spain's democratically elected politicians.

The incident, caught live on TV, was broadcast to an astonished world. Within Spain a terrible sense of déjà vu descended on those who shared a memory of the military uprising that had signalled the outbreak of the Civil War. Thousands of Basques and Catalans fearing the worst hurriedly packed their bags and headed towards the frontier with France. King Juan Carlos, the captain-general of the armed forces, held firm and convinced a sufficient number of key army commanders not to support Tejero and his fellow plotters outside the parliament building. The attempted coup collapsed.

While historians still mull over the precise circumstances of what happened on the night of 23/24 February, the judgement made in its aftermath by my colleague Robert Graham, the *Financial Times* correspondent in Madrid at the time, remains persuasive. As he asserted, the most significant aspect of the *Tejerazo* – as the attempted coup was nicknamed – was not that it happened, but that it failed. As Graham puts it:

Spaniards may have been embarrassed by the banana republic image of a pistol-waving Tejero in parliament that flashed around the world, but the trauma of the coup also shocked them into realizing the benefits of the democratic system they were trying to build . . . Spain had changed profoundly during the long years of Franco's authoritarian rule. Those who wished to turn the clock back were a nostalgic minority.

Against this political backdrop, it is clear that Spanish football was not immune from the tension thrown up between the legacy of the past and the pressure for change. One incident, which was never reported by the media at the time but which was recorded subsequently in political memoirs, suggests the wind of change had begun to blow at the Santiago Bernabéu stadium around the time of Franco's demise. This involved the prime minister and future president of the transitional government Adolfo Suárez conversing with King Juan Carlos on intimate terms while watching Real Madrid play Zaragoza in a cup final. Suárez was at the time minister with responsibility for sport. Juan Carlos was still a prince but only weeks away from becoming the new head of state. Juan Carlos observed the octogenarian president of Real Madrid Santiago Bernabéu, and then the younger president of Zaragoza before turning to Suárez and saying: 'It's good to have young presidents!'

The youthful Suárez took this as a sure sign the future king was taking him into his confidence and marking him out in his future political role. But equally with hindsight it appeared to reflect a perception that Spain was moving ahead of Bernabéu, whose time at the helm of Real Madrid had been almost as long as Franco's at the head of his regime. Bernabéu, who had become president of Real Madrid in the aftermath of the Civil War, outlived Franco by nearly three years, his reputation as a visionary competing with his image as a benevolent dictator, ideologically more in tune with the Franco regime than with the democratic forces that emerged to challenge it. When he died in June 1978, Spain had already held its first post-Franco parliamentary elections. Bernabéu's long-serving vice-president Raimundo Saporta was determined to ensure an orderly transition in a way that maintained the structure and politics of the club generally unchanged. He immediately went about hand-picking the succession in consultation with other senior officials who had served under Bernabéu. Securing the signatures of a small minority of like-minded club members, Saporta oversaw the appointment of Luis de Carlos, the club treasurer and another long-standing Bernabéu ally as the new president.

De Carlos had narrowly escaped being shot by the anti-Franco militias during the Spanish Civil War. He had no love lost for the new left-wing political parties that were gaining renewed strength after Franco, and was anxious to keep Real Madrid well removed from the political currents that were moving the transition to full democracy. His own undemocratic election was the kind of continuity of the old Spain that Franco had hoped for and didn't get. As for Saporta, it was perhaps unfortunate that he saw himself in an analogous role to Admiral Carrero Blanco, Franco's closest collaborator for thirty-two years, who, had he not been assassinated by the Basque separatist group ETA in December 1973, would have in all likelihood tried to put a firm brake on the reforming tendencies of King Juan Carlos.

The steady-as-we-go attitude adopted by the close-knit group of Bernabéu collaborators was justified by Saporta and de Carlos as a contrast to the strategy adopted by FC Barcelona whose internal politics became radicalized during the final months of the Franco dictatorship and the first months of the reformist monarchy. FC Barcelona's identity as bastion of Catalan nationalism had long been at odds with Real Madrid's perceived alliance with the diehard centralism of the Franco regime. With Franco dead, FC Barcelona's differences with Real Madrid became more accentuated as an intense rivalry both on and off the field.

The unreconstructed Francoists at Real Madrid were horrified at the way directors of FC Barcelona had conspired to help the campaign for greater home rule within the context of a fully democratic Spain. FC Barcelona's Nou Camp stadium in October 1977 was chosen as the venue for the first major organized rally in support of Josep Tarradellas, the prime minister of the Catalan government during the Civil War. Tarradellas returned from exile after Franco's death to be the first president of the post-Franco Catalan regional government. In front of an ecstatic crowd of over 90,000 and with the stadium awash with the red and yellow stripes of the Catalan flag, the venerable Tarradellas recalled with pride the long way the football club had come since his early days as a fan. 'In those days we were few in number,' Tarradellas said, 'but we had the same faith as you have today. That was the Barça you have inherited, the Barça rooted in its Catalanism.'

The following May, a month before Bernabéu died, FC Barcelona held elections to decide on a new president. While Real Madrid remained controlled by essentially the same power structure that had dominated it since the aftermath of the Civil War, FC Barcelona now allowed its future to be decided by a ballot of its full membership which stood at just over 77,000. The ensuing campaign was a dirty one, both highly charged politically and personally. The favourite at the outset, advertising executive Victor Sagi, pulled out of the race after embarrassing allegations surfaced about his private life and business dealings. Another leading candidate Fernando Ariño promised a revolution from within, with more power to the membership. His campaign came to be identified with the PSUC, the Catalan Communist Party. This left construction magnate Josep Lluís Nuñez using the anticommunist card to appeal to the Catalan middle classes while attacking the small group of businessmen from the textile sector who had provided the majority of FC Barcelona presidents since the Civil War.

Despite being viewed by the Left as the construction arm of Francoism in Barcelona, Nuñez adeptly exploited the idea of himself as a modernizer using as his campaign motto, *'Romper con el porrón'* ('break with the wine jar'). Previously the running of FC Barcelona had been passed from one textile boss to another just as peasants pass their wine from one to the other. Nuñez thus told his electorate that he represented a break with tradition. Nuñez won with just over 39 per cent of the vote against Ariño's 36 per cent and 23.41 per cent for the third remaining candidate Nicolau Casaus. The turnout of 41 per cent of those eligible to vote suggested that the campaign had alienated many members. Even those who did vote emerged from it divided and restive.

And yet if there was one issue that united a majority of Barça fans it was their sense of identity with Catalan nationalism. The strength of it was made manifest in May 1979 when FC Barcelona beat Fortuna Düsseldorf 4–3 in the final of the European Cup-Winners' Cup in Basle. The victory was accompanied in the stadium by thousands of Catalan flags. The team's home-coming proved even more passionate, with more than a million people pouring onto the streets of Barcelona, in the biggest popular demonstration since Franco's death. Taradellas, as president of the new regional government, declared that the result had been a victory not just for the football club but for the whole of the Catalan people at a defining moment in Spanish history.

Those watching it all from the inner sanctum of Real Madrid saw dangerous ferment, as unsettling as Spain's own transition to democracy. They feared that throwing Real Madrid open to an electoral process would risk fuelling similar political passions and divide a membership which during Bernabéu's extended reign had forged its unity around a collective self-belief in the club's sporting greatness.

Yet de Carlos's strategy of opting for continuity rather than change, disengaging Real Madrid from the broader political process and refraining from any major internal reorganization, was relatively risk-proof as long as the club could continue to be successful. The club's record during the seven years of his presidency proved chequered by the high standards it had set itself historically. As Di Stefano famously remarked once, 'the word runner-up or sub-champion doesn't exist in the *Madridista* vocabulary.' Real Madrid won two successive league championships in the first two years, but then lost its hegemony in the remaining five, with four titles shared by Athletic Bilbao and Real Sociedad, and one going to FC Barcelona. In addition de Carlos's Real Madrid won two King's Cups and a League Cup. The major disappointment however was the club's continuing failure to regain its past glory in Europe. Even if Spanish diplomats were no longer as needy of Real Madrid to break Spain's isolation as they had been under Franco, success beyond Spain was important to a club whose sense of identity had been built around its own perceived international as well as national superiority.

It was in an atmosphere of huge expectation – partly

generated by de Carlos's own presidential pledge that the club would regain its European crown under his presidency – that 30,000 Real Madrid fans descended on Paris's Parc des Princes stadium on 27 May 1981 to face Liverpool in the final of the European Cup. Real Madrid had not won the competition since 1966. Many of the fans however remembered the last time the club had played in the French capital. It was ten years before that, on 13 May 1956, when the team led by Di Stefano won the first ever European Cup, their 4–3 victory over the French champions Stade de Reims ushering in an extended period of unrivalled excellence in Spanish and international football.

The hectic black-and-white newsreel film of that occasion would survive as a record of one of the great matches of football history personified by the gladiatorial encounter between an insatiable Di Stefano and another thoroughbred of the game Raymond Kopa, who would transfer from Reims to Madrid within the year. The scoreline reflected the attacking nature of the game, a fitting climax to a competition in which attack was the order of the day or night. The 29 games of that first European Cup chalked up a remarkable total of 127 goals – an average of 4.38 per match – with Real Madrid scoring 20 and Reims 18.

The 1981 final involved players of considerable stature on both sides. Liverpool, whose quality and consistency – thanks to the foundations laid down by Bill Shankly during the 1960s – allowed them to dominate English football during the 1970s and 1980s, included the world-class midfielder Graeme Souness, and other talented individuals such as Alan Hansen and Kenny Dalglish. Real Madrid fielded their own Englishman Cunningham and the German international Uli

Stielike alongside the Spanish star Carlos Santillana. The team also included some tough and committed players – in the eyes of the traditionalists good examples of the legendary 'Spanish fury' – led by Juanito, José Antonio Camacho and Vicente Del Bosque. The three had been brought into the team during the 1970s as promising replacements of those who had won the 1966 European Cup, their real quality as players tested by the lifting of Franco's ban on foreigners, among them Johan Cruyff.

The 1981 final proved something of an anticlimax, with each side apparently more concerned with defending itself from the other than developing a winning strategy of its own. It would be forever remembered by Real Madrid fans as the 'final of fear', such was the seeming lack of collective self-confidence or individual brilliance. Only the goal-keepers, Liverpool's Clemence and his young Real Madrid counterpart Rodriguez, showed flair worthy of their teams' reputations.

While Liverpool supporters celebrated their victory thanks to a goal by Alan Kennedy, Real Madrid fans made their way back across the border, silent and dejected. 'To have reached the final in those days was an achievement. It was a pity that we lost in the final but to have got that far was quite an achievement for the team we had then,' recalled Del Bosque years later when I interviewed him.

But second best had never been easily accepted by Real Madrid fans and there was a growing frustration with the team and the club as run by de Carlos. The sense that things could be better had filtered through the ranks to young players waiting to be promoted; this optimism chimed with the rising expectations among Spanish youth generally fuelled by the New Spain emerging after Franco. Sanchis was one of them, politically more open to change than his father, a Real Madrid veteran who had never concealed his right-wing views. 'There was a certain sense of disillusion at the time,' he recalled, 'a feeling of the need for something new. We had good players in our team but lacking the glamour of real stars . . . It was when we lost 0–1 against Liverpool that people began to demand change.'

And yet Real Madrid were not about to transfer to the Left politically. The radicalization of some of its fans was in part a rebellion against what was viewed as the cautious conservatism of much of its membership but it involved methods borrowed from the growing hooligan culture elsewhere in Europe, not least in England.

In the aftermath of the 1981 European Cup final the infamous *Ultra Surs* began to emerge as a distinct pressure group from within one of the biggest existing supporters' clubs, the *Peña de las Banderas* – the brotherhood of the flags. As a member of that supporters' club who was in Paris that day told me: 'There were some young Liverpool fans who'd turned up without tickets and assaulted some of the older Real Madrid supporters – several of them there as married couples – beating them up and taking their tickets. There was no one among the Spaniards that seemed prepared to react. Most of the Madrid supporters seemed too scared. But there were a few among the younger ones who saw what happened and decided to become as violent as the English, to imitate them . . .'

That autumn, angry fans invaded the pitch at Real Madrid's training ground forcing the manager Boskov to abandon a planned match between his team and the club's junior affiliate side Castilla. During the protest, Real Madrid players found themselves confronted with cries of 'mercenaries' and 'strikers'. In the aftermath of their European Cup defeat, Real Madrid players had been paid a promised bonus – regardless of the outcome – by de Carlos. They had later joined in a national strike with other Spanish players over the terms and conditions offered by the Spanish Football Federation. It seemed the reality of post-Franco politics had finally caught up with Real Madrid.

By then even those apologists within the club who had drawn a generous comparison between de Carlos and Adolfo Suárez, the mastermind of Spain's transition from dictatorship to democracy, were confronted by other developments over which they had no control. Suárez had himself resigned in January 1981 as a result of growing political disagreements within his party, and mounting criticism from the socialist-led opposition. Between the attempted coup and the next general election held in November 1982, Spain's nascent democracy swam in troubled waters. Gate receipts at the Bernabéu stadium declined as if *Madridistas* had matters more important than football to worry about.

Interest in Spanish football as a whole revived, however, thanks to the staging in Spain in June 1982 of the World Cup. The Bernabéu, along with other stadiums around the country, got a facelift. Real Madrid's own status as an institution close to the powers-that-be in the land was given a fillip with the naming of Raimundo Saporta, one of its long-surviving senior officials, as one of the main organizers of the tournament. The Spanish squad not only relied on star Real Madrid players like Juanito but was also coached by a remnant of its glory days, the naturalized Uruguayan José Santamaria. But the tournament turned into something of a poisoned chalice for Real Madrid, a club that during the Franco years had become synonymous with the Spanish nation, a point of reference and comparison with which to make judgements on the Spanish squad and Spanish football as a whole.

While the 1982 World Cup produced an exhilarating final at the Bernabéu, it was between Italy (3) and West Germany (1). The host nation could not progress beyond the second phase. Undoubtedly more acceptable politically than the previous World Cup held four years earlier under the auspices of Argentina's brutal military junta, the tournament did very little in positive terms for the image of the new democratic Spain, still less its footballers. When the draw was made in Madrid in January of that year, FIFA's president João Havelange praised the Spanish people – led by Saporta and others – for having accepted the challenge of organizing the event in the spirit of Don Quixote. It was an unfortunate analogy, as Spain's most famous literary figure made a habit of going after noble causes, not always with huge success. It turned into one of the worst organized World Cups in history with widespread complaints from visitors about ticket and hotel arrangements, and what was perceived as the biased refereeing in favour of Spain. One FIFA official, interviewed on TV, went as far as to suggest a conspiracy by admitting how important it was for the World Cup's finances that Spain should stay in the tournament.

To the hosts it seemed as if a long-standing point of friction in Spanish football had come home to roost. The advent of democracy had in recent years fuelled an acrimonious debate about the extent to which Real Madrid's success during the Franco years and beyond could be partly explained by biased referees. That no one had ever been able to produce any evidence that any referee had been financially corrupted or was politically motivated in favour of Real Madrid, and that the club itself could point to numerous matches in which dubious decisions had gone against it, mattered not one jot. Bent referees had become mythologized and accepted as fact throughout Spanish football. That the mythology survived Franco suggests that an explanation might have less to do with football as such than with an endemic national disease or another great paradox of the Spaniards as a people.

Just as Spaniards can be, in the words of the Irish Hispanist Ian Gibson, 'so anarchic that even anarchism strikes them as too organized', they have also imbued with literary value the *pícaro* (rogue or scoundrel) – he who tries to beat the system with his wits. And yet the referee could easily translate into the system as a petty official, or the biggest *pícaro* of them all, depending on whose side you were on when he blew the whistle.

Sporting Gijón fans staged one of the most enduring protests in a controversial league match at home against Real Madrid in 1979. It was in that match that in reply to a passionately disputed dismissal of one of the Sporting players, the crowd expressed their anger by chanting '*Así Así, Así gana el Madrid*' (roughly translated as 'that is how Real Madrid wins'). The chant would in subsequent years be revived by Real Madrid's rivals whenever a referee's action seemed to give the club an advantage. Cheekily Real Madrid fans, far from being silenced, occasionally chanted the slogan themselves, in response to a good move by one of their players or a brilliant goal. Within the collective memory of Real Madrid the suggestion that referees have always been on the club's side holds no water, particularly when fans remember not just the victories that were secured without their help but the defeats that came about because of them. An example is the unbending conviction that FC Barcelona beat Real Madrid in the final of the *Copa del Generalísimo* on 11 June 1968 in the Bernabéu because the referee was biased in favour of the Catalans.

In the 1982 World Cup Spanish club football rivalries were temporarily set aside, as the group games between national sides were spread out across the country. The Spanish squad began dismally in Valencia in their group, just managing to squeeze a draw with the tournament underdogs Honduras. They lost against Northern Ireland but managed to go into the second round thanks to an earlier 2–1 victory over Yugoslavia involving a disputed goal by the generally off-form Juanito. Playing in the Bernabéu in the second-phase matches, Spain drew with England but lost 2–1 to West Germany, with one goal the result of an appalling mistake by the Spanish goalkeeper Luis Arconada, forever remembered by Real Madrid fans whenever they encountered German clubs. Spain finished bottom of their group and were out of the World Cup. The sense of national humiliation was nowhere felt as much as in Madrid where the dream of the Spanish side lifting international sport's most prestigious trophy in the Bernabéu stadium evaporated as pathetically as Don Quixote defeated by his windmills.

The World Cup debacle sparked a national debate about the nature and future direction of Spanish football, nowhere more so than at Real Madrid, where the myth of the 'Spanish fury' – with macho toughness taking priority over any other consideration, not least decent passing and movement – had continued to be personified by some of the home-grown players. Twenty years on the stylized staccato play once identified as a foreign indulgence by some of the more uncompromising Spanish football traditionalists formed part of Real Madrid's universal approach to the game of which Beckham became part. Like other top clubs, Real Madrid benefited from the variety of national styles in its team. As Valdano told the *Observer* in an interview published in June 2004, 'Twenty years ago it was easy to say that Latin American football was about technique and talent, and European football was about organization, speed and fighting spirit. But with TV and player transfer, all these trends are coming together.' Or as Francisco Filho, Manchester United's Brazilian under-17 coach, put it slightly differently in the same article by Martin Jacques entitled 'Football's New World Order', as players play in different continents, there is a blurring of national styles. United, he said, were a 'Latin club with English characteristics', which passed, played with the ball, but also had the mentality to fight. It was such a fit that Perez was seeking to consolidate when be brought Beckham to Spain.

Back in the early 1980s, however, the sense that Real Madrid both on and off the pitch was losing its right to be respected, losing the vision and unrivalled superiority it had conveyed during the best periods of the Bernabéu years was in marked contrast with the new invigorated image that had taken hold at its rival FC Barcelona. During the dying years of the Franco regime, and its aftermath, the Catalan team spirit had been lifted by the skills of Johan Cruyff. Following the 1982 World Cup, they signed up another genius – Diego Maradona.

FC Barcelona had earlier that summer won the European Cup-Winners' Cup. Their 2–1 victory over Standard Liège before a 100,000 capacity crowd at the recently modernized Nou Camp (the preselected 'neutral' venue) contrasted with the frustration of narrowly losing the league championship to Real Sociedad, with Real Madrid trailing in third place. The victory, in the midst of a resurgent Catalan nationalism, drew euphoric multitudes to Barcelona's Rambla and San Jaume square. FC Barcelona's president Nuñez had been elected four years earlier on an election slogan that promised a 'triumphant Barça'. He had pledged to do so by transforming the Nou Camp into one of the great stadiums of the world and financing the purchase of some of the best players. Maradona like the rest of the Argentine squad had a lacklustre World Cup in Spain, distracted by his country's war against Britain over the Falklands. But FC Barcelona's talent scouts had done their homework and knew the huge potential that Maradona carried within him that had yet to be fully tapped. In Madrid the cautious men of football, and not a few conservative politicians, accused FC Barcelona of mindless extravagance when they paid $7.3m for the young South American. Maradona was twenty-one years old and had not played club football outside Argentina. Nuñez, however, spoke in a tone that brought back memories of the disarming self-confidence Real Madrid had experienced in the Santiago Bernabéu years, even if the concept behind it seemed to have much in common with the new mercantilism of Italy's football magnates. 'Maradona is going to revitalize football and thanks to him we're going to avoid a financial crisis. We deserve a monument to be built in our honour over this,' declared Nuñez unreservedly.

Maradona's ability to revitalize FC Barcelona during his first months at the club, the enthusiasm he instilled in his colleagues, and the palpable enjoyment shared by fans as they watched football played with talent and imagination, came as no surprise to his fellow countrymen for whom he was already fast becoming a legend. Few Argentines living in Spain were better placed to appreciate this than Alfredo Di Stefano. Seventeen years after his days as a player at Real Madrid were abruptly brought to a close, Di Stefano had returned to the club as coach – a legend in his own right but conceding that bringing Maradona with him was not in his gift.

After his falling out with Santiago Bernabéu, Di Stefano had ended his days as a player at Espanyol, before working as a coach in various Spanish and Argentine clubs, including Valencia, Boca Juniors and River Plate with whom he won league championships. Despite the bitterness he felt at the way Bernabéu had handled him in his final days at Real Madrid, Di Stefano had always harboured the dream of returning one day to the club that had given him the best years of his life. So he needed little persuasion when he was approached on the eve of the 1982 World Cup by de Carlos. The ageing Real Madrid president brought the legendary Di Stefano back into the fold as a calculated move aimed at securing another term at the helm.

Belatedly democracy had come knocking at the door of the Spanish 'White House', and de Carlos was forced to submit himself to a popular mandate involving a much greater participation of the membership than had hitherto been the case. On 10 October 1982, de Carlos – aged seventy-five – was re-elected with the votes of 10,750 members. His main challenger was a youthful if controversial business-man called Ramón Mendoza who had campaigned with a pledge to modernize the club, as Nuñez had done at FC Barcelona four years previously, and who obtained 7,500 votes.

Mendoza blamed his defeat on dubious tactics employed by a self-serving conservative clique within the club and their right-wing political allies. These had surfaced four years previously when his attempt to succeed Santiago Bernabéu had been partly stymied by a news magazine report that he had been employed as a Soviet spy by the KGB while trading with the Soviet Union during the latter years of the Franco regime. The report appears to have emanated from Spanish intelligence sources. The extent to which there was any substance behind the dirty-tricks campaign remains far from clear. While there was no evidence that Mendoza was involved in spying activities full-time, he did, according to sources consulted during the research of this book, fall into that category which during the Cold War years came to be known in western and eastern intelligence circles as an 'agent of influence'. Both British and US intelligence are thought to have suspected that Mendoza was considered by the KGB as an ally, not only for opening up new commercial links with Europe, but also as a potential source of information about political developments in Spain – not least its activities within NATO, which it had joined only in 1982. The fact that Mendoza was never arrested suggests either that the work he was doing for the KGB was too inconsequential to risk publicity over it at the time, or that he may have been offering similar services to the west, sharing information he had gleaned from his contacts with the Soviet political and business establishment. He may also have been simply too powerful to be touched.

Mendoza shared a drink with the legendary firebrand of Spanish Stalinism *La Pasionaria* while she was in exile in Moscow and helped publish the Spanish translation of the Soviet president Leonid Brezhnev's memoirs. He is also alleged to have financed the Spanish Communist Party. His biographer Juan Carlos Pasamontes points to Mendoza's less publicized contacts with a wide range of political interest groups – including loyal Francoists and supporters of the traditional conservative movement Opus Dei who had masterminded Spain's economic take-off during the Franco years – as evidence that here was a man whose only ambition was power and who sought to make money in a way that allowed him to go on enjoying life in a hedonistic way.

Mendoza described himself once as 'a political independent with a full belly'. Certainly this picture of a political operator, if not opportunist, who personified the enduring cronyism at the heart of Spanish business and politics, may be one explanation why Mendoza did eventually become president of Real Madrid, even if he never quite fulfilled his dream of enjoying the international high profile of his two great friends Silvio Berlusconi and Gianni Agnelli of Italy. He made lasting friendships with some of the Real Madrid players, among them Michel and Sanchis. Mendoza also openly courted the *Ultra Surs*, pandering to the whims of the extremist hooligan element among them by deliberately stirring up confrontations with FC Barcelona. On one occasion Mendoza accompanied a group of *Ultra Surs* at Barajas airport, greeting the arrival of the Real Madrid team from Barcelona, and happily joined in as they bellowed abusive chants against the Catalan people.

I asked Sanchis whether he had ever believed his president was a KGB agent. It was early 2004, over a decade since the fall of the Berlin Wall. Sanchis laughed at the suggestion. 'The *presi* a KGB spy? He was too much of a *cachondo* [he liked sex with women too much] and anyway he was an *Andaluz* [from the south of Spain where the local people have a reputation for enjoying wine, women and song above more serious political matters].' Whatever the truth, the media allegations about Mendoza were sufficient to raise question marks about his business dealings, and to make him equally suspect politically to the Franco diehards and traditionalists who lurked at all levels within the club – even if there was an emerging young generation of players and supporters for whom communist conspiracies belonged to a past they hoped had been buried with Franco.

Nineteen days after Mendoza's reformist ticket was defeated and de Carlos was re-elected as president of Real Madrid, on 30 October 1982, the Spanish Socialist Workers' Party (PSOE) was swept to power with a landslide majority, having campaigned on a simple slogan – *El Cambio* (change).

Led by a young charismatic lawyer from Seville called Felipe González, the party had galvanized the spirit of a new generation of Spaniards born after the Civil War and freed from the resentments of their parents. The average age of the PSOE's Executive Commission at the time was just over forty. González was still in his thirties. For the first time in post-war Europe a government was formed with the 'generation of '68' – those moulded by hippydom and student protest. Nevertheless González had deftly dropped the word Marxism from his party's election manifesto and expunged other doctrinaire policies from his electoral programme. He calculated correctly that an improvement in living standards during the 1960s and early 1970s had given the working class and an expanded middle class a vested interest in not rocking the boat too much.

While the party still referred to itself as the Socialist Workers' Party, it attracted votes across the class divide, presenting itself as social democratic, as moderate as any European centre party. As John Hooper, the *Guardian's* Madrid correspondent at the time, put it:

The PSOE didn't need to promise to change anything because its voters were already convinced that they were going to change everything. Just by being who they were – young men and women unencumbered by the intellectual baggage and ballast of a totalitarian past – they would be able to bring about a revolution in Spanish society when they applied to the nation's affairs attitudes regarded as normal in the rest of democratic Europe. Alfonso Guerra, Felipe González's lifelong friend who became his deputy Prime Minister, caught the spirit of the moment when he promised the Socialists would change Spain 'so that even its own mother wouldn't recognize it.' For a while it seemed as if they would.

During the PSOE's first term of office tough measures of economic adjustment to prepare Spain for entry into the EC in 1986 were implemented alongside an energetic programme of social reform principally in health and education. The more liberal legal environment surrounding divorce, abortion and sex in general which had emerged during the post-Franco transition, was consolidated. In the run-up to Spain's Expo trade fair and the Barcelona Olympics in 1992, vast sums were spent on improving the country's road, rail and air connections. Spain emerged from a recession and in a mood to celebrate, along with the rest of the developed world, the creation and enjoyment of wealth. 'What made Spain's eighties boom exceptional, and more entertaining than in many other countries,' notes Hooper wryly, 'was the degree to which serious money became associated with style, glamour, and ultimately, scandal.' Suddenly Spain whose historic poverty had led it to define the national essence in terms of the Quixotic values of dignity, austerity and sobriety, 'all of a sudden flung itself into the business of earning and spending money with, it seemed, scarcely a backward glance'.

Nowhere was the change more apparent than in the Spanish capital which thanks to its politicians and a new wave of artists managed to make the sombre architecture and landscape of old Castile seem to belong not just to another era, but another planet. Those in power displayed the consumption and sexual mores of ancient Romans with ministers and leading bankers competing for space in the glossy gossip magazines as they flaunted the lifestyle of the so-called 'beautiful people'. Much of their wealth was not so much earned as facilitated by government policies and contacts – the sell-off of family assets to foreign investors, speculation in stocks and shares and property. Elsewhere in the capital, the *movida madrileña* – roughly translated as the Madrid movement or scene – saw not just a proliferation of bars, discos and fashion shops, but a flourishing of creative talent that conveyed a sense of the frenzied energy of the time.

In May 1985, as the PSOE government was reaching the end of its first term, and soon to be re-elected for a second, Real Madrid adjusted itself to the changing times. Ramón Mendoza, the man whose challenge for the job had been voted down less than three years earlier, was appointed the new president of the club with the signed backing of a sector of the membership but without a vote being cast. His candidacy was uncontested. His past dealings with the Soviets no longer counted against him. Nor for that matter did the fact that he made his first lucrative business deal during the final years of the Franco regime trading coffee with Paraguay, for which Latin America's longest-serving dictator General Alfredo Stroessner had honoured him with the title of 'ambassador-at-large'.

Mendoza had cultivated the support of old and new, projecting himself as a businessman with the diplomatic skills and energy to reverse the fortunes of Real Madrid which had gone six years without winning the Spanish league, and lost its presence in Europe. Under Luis de Carlos the Santiago Bernabéu stadium had turned as grey in spirit as the concrete slabs that supported its structures. Fans either stayed away or turned up to express their frustration. The fact that Mendoza's hair was on the long side, that he openly flaunted his reputation as a serial womanizer, and liked to dress in flashy jackets without a tie, made him a most suitable and influential addition to the 'beautiful people' spawned by the PSOE government.

By the time that Mendoza took over the presidency, Alfredo Di Stefano had come and gone as coach after two seasons during which Real Madrid had finished runner-up in the league championship but failed to win any trophies – not a bad record but not good enough according to the high standards he himself had set as a player. This time Di Stefano's departure was handled with kid gloves: he was diplomatically told that his contract was not being renewed although the door would be left open for his return to the club sometime in the future. He himself blamed the absence of silverware on a lack of resources for buying foreign stars of the calibre of Diego Maradona at FC Barcelona. The fact that Di Stefano was forced to rely on developing the talent of Real Madrid's youth team meant that Mendoza inherited an emerging generation of new players that during the second half of the 1980s showed the flair and style the club supporters felt they had missed out on for much too long.

The resurgence of Real Madrid as a club worth watching was spearheaded by players such as Rafael Martin Sanchez, Manuel Sanchis, Miguel González 'Michel' and Emilio Butragueño. As Sanchis, a future captain of Real Madrid, explained when I interviewed him for this book: 'We were young guys from Madrid who shared a similar view on how football should be played – we wanted it to be bold and attacking – and we saw ourselves as reflecting what was happening in Spain more widely at the time, part of a generation that wanted change, that was prepared to take risks.'

The generation came to be remembered by the collective term *Quinta del Buitre*, literally translated as the 'vulture squad'. *Quinta* can mean a home, but among young Spanish people it used to be associated with a year of military conscription when friendships were forged with a common sense of purpose. *Buitre* is a vulture – and a diminutive for Butragueño, the most predatory of the four (and the biggest star). The bird, along with the military allusion, coined rather loosely by a Spanish journalist and forever absorbed into the club's nomenclature, does not quite explain the popular appeal that Butragueño generated in his heyday.

Off the pitch, of all the players he was perhaps the one who coped best with the increasing media frenzy that began to lay siege to the world of Spanish football in the 1980s. He was a natural charmer with the press and the fans, a trait he later claimed to have developed while working as a young boy in his parents' perfume shop. He had a long-term girl-friend who later became his wife, Sonia. 'At first I used to get followed all over the place by press men to see if they caught me with anybody, but then when they always saw me with the same girl I think they got bored,' he recalled when I interviewed him many years later.

Butragueño straddled tradition and modernity in a country still coming to terms with the meaning of freedom and where there was a lingering nostalgia for the days when life seemed more ordered, less selfish. As Sanchis put it to me, 'Emilio was not just a great player; he was the son that suddenly a whole lot of Spanish mothers wanted, the fiancé that a whole lot of Spanish girls wanted.'

Of Real Madrid's three myths, Butragueño had the discreet charm lacking in Raúl and Di Stefano. When Beckham came to Spain, he was Jorge Valdano's assistant (he later succeeded him as sports director), liaising with players and helping project an image of civilized intelligence to the world which contrasted with the fanaticism of the *Ultra Surs*. He described how much the world of football had changed since his days as a player, paying a sincere tribute to Beckham's survival as a reasonably balanced human being despite the huge pressure of his celebrity status: 'In my day there was just one state-controlled TV channel and less than half a dozen journalists permanently attached to the team. Nowadays there are numerous channels, hordes of journalists, many of them no longer interested in the game but in your private [life]. It's a high-pressure environment . . . Beckham manages it because he is like a major corporation, with his image handlers, security people, sponsorship deals . . . I used to do about one advertisement a year, in a good year – one time it was for a bank, another for a chocolate drink, nothing much beyond that. It was a different world. Beckham's marriage is different to mine – he and Victoria are celebrities . . . it's only to be expected that they generate such a following . . . but in the end it's what you do on the pitch that really matters. Beckham is not only a good player, he is a good person – he may be famous, but there is a certain nobility about him, and when you are with him he puts you in a good mood. I'd never met him before he came to Real Madrid. It's surprised me what a regular guy he is.'

Butragueño was given his opportunity in the first team when Di Stefano was still manager and had triumphed from then on. Both as a player and a coach Di Stefano always insisted that football was a twenty-four-hour profession, seven days a week, all the year round. You breathed and thought football. You followed a healthy diet, and slept well – but above all you put a lot of effort into your training. And yet what set Butragueño apart from the others were his special qualities not just as a person but as a player. Of the many tributes that have been made to him over the years few are as eloquent as his team mate Michel's. 'His talent lay in intuition, in the always intelligent spark of his play. He was not a football obsessive. His time was perfectly structured. The ball didn't surround him day and night. He found it quite easy disconnecting from the sound of football, he was untroubled by the media. He lived in freedom, without feeling any pressure . . . Perhaps there were people who would have liked to have seen him more involved in his profession, but Emilio was genuine and unique. He had his own personal vision of what football should be.'

He was as tolerant and intuitive on the pitch as off it. He seemed to personify the old maxim of yoga – which he assiduously practised – that 'the power within is always greater than the task ahead.' He was rarely booked even if he had the killer instincts of the striker. His talent lay in the speed with which he broke free from his markers and the seemingly effortless way he controlled the ball, often at a standstill, before tapping it into the net. It was one of these goals, against Cádiz one cold winter night at the Bernabéu in February 1987, that the writer in the sports daily *Marca* described as the 'goal of the century' and brought the Bernabéu to its feet. Butragueño didn't allow such accolades to delude him. He always insisted that Maradona was more deserving of the title, with his second goal against the English in Mexico, a year earlier.

No one, Butragueño made clear when I interviewed him for this book, could ever quite match Maradona at his peak, not Di Stefano, not Beckham, not anyone in Real Madrid or any other club for that matter. 'He personified genius, an inexhaustible creative capacity combined with technique to realize nearly everything he imagined . . . the only player I've seen capable of that,' he said.

Perhaps the greatest achievement of the *Quinta* under Butragueño's inspiration was that it connected on the field not only within itself but with other players of different personality and background but also of undoubted talent. Such was the case of the agile Mexican-born forward Hugo Sanchez who coined the phrase *Quinta de los Machos* just to remind the fans that the team was not just a bunch of intellectual luminaries that included the Argentine Jorge Valdano, later promoted to coach by Mendoza. Along with his team mate Juanito – a tough Spaniard of the old fury school – Sanchez relished provoking opposition defenders and goalkeepers as well as their fans – an attitude that won him the support of the club's hooligan element among the *Ultra Surs*, the same crowd which had occasionally accompanied Laurie Cunningham's moves with monkey sounds.

During the ten years Ramón Mendoza was president of Real Madrid (1985–95), the club won six league championships, two King's Cups, one UEFA Cup, three Spanish SuperCups and one Spanish League Cup. It was no mean achievement for an institution that values its silverware. Yet he was forced out because of the club's failure to win the European Cup and its mounting debts, blamed on his alleged financial mismanagement and dubious business dealings. The pressure on him became more intense when in 1992 FC Barcelona with Johan Cruyff as coach and his 'dream team' of Catalans and foreigners won the league and the European Cup – the first Spanish club to do so in the same season since Real Madrid in 1957 and 1958. Mendoza resigned, curiously, on 20 November 1995, the twentieth anniversary of Franco's death. Spanish politics was about to enter a new phase. The Spanish people had fallen out of love with the socialist government of Felipe González, its third term in office falling apart amidst mounting allegations of corruption and incompetence. The centre-right led by José María Aznar was about to take power.

Ramón Mendoza died on the 4 April 2001 while enjoying a massage on a Caribbean island. He was seventy-three years old and was holidaying with his latest lover, an attractive female lawyer forty-two years his junior. He was buried three days later in Madrid's Almudena cemetery, the final resting place of the capital's privileged and powerful, his coffin covered in the flags of Real Madrid and Spain. The many dignitaries and celebrities who personally gave their condolences to his family included King Juan Carlos. Somehow neither Real Madrid nor the Spain entering the twenty-first century could bring themselves to forget Mendoza or his times.

10. The Passion of Being Boss

Just before Christmas 2002 the Bernabéu stadium commemorated Real Madrid's centenary by hosting a friendly against a Rest of the World team, a fitting symbol for a club that had come to define its own identity in imperial terms. The tenor Placido Domingo, a Real Madrid fan, sang the club's new anthem – a stirring aria that reached out to a universal audience, urging it to participate in the spectacle of a 'stadium full of stars', with a club who saw its destiny inextricably associated with success. 'Madrid comes out to fight, Madrid comes out to win,' sang Domingo, in deference to the spirit of the Quixotic Spanish race so extolled in the original '*Hala Madrid*' song released in 1952. That more traditional anthem was a mixture of folklore and military march, a product of its age. Influenced by the triumphalist anti-communist ideology of the early Franco years for which the legendary Santiago Bernabéu had fought during the Spanish Civil War, it talked of the white (not red) flag flying, 'clean and white . . . club of noble descent and generous spirit, all nerve and heart and sinew . . .' But fifty years later Domingo was singing to a Spain, if not quite converted, certainly transformed, that felt part of the world, and a Real Madrid that fancied itself as a club worthy of support that defied tribal and national loyalties.

When the new hymn was first sung, Real Madrid's senior management appeased traditionalists by promising that it would be played only during the centenary year, but when the year was out the old anthem was not reinstated. Domingo's words – 'Let the universe know how Real Madrid plays' – was a message with a longer-term focus, on the global market place. As the club's head of marketing José Angel Sanchez put it to me, 'We wanted to modernize our message, turn it into a line of communication, beyond a region or a country, in a language that could be understood around the world.'

Over a period of twelve months any doubts that this was a centenary, not just of a mere football club but of a national institution which aspired to a global reach, had been laid to rest by enough printed material to replant parts of Castile several times over, and by various commemorative acts marking the 'one hundred years of legend', as the club's own huge official tome of history was entitled. In an official video marking the occasion, Florentino Perez – sombre-suited and with the self-assured air of a chairman addressing a mass audience of complacent shareholders – told his audience how proud he was to celebrate the centenary as president of Real Madrid. 'This is more than a sporting club . . . it is an emotion we all share.'

If nothing else it had taken Real Madrid one hundred years to reach such a degree of self-confidence that its president could commit what some of his Catalan friends would regard as sacrilege. He had plagiarized the motto that Real Madrid's historic rival FC Barcelona had virtually from its inception jealously guarded as the expression of its own cultural and political essence. As Spain entered the new millennium, no longer did Barça have a monopoly on considering itself '*mes que un club*' – more than a club.

Real Madrid had never been known for modesty. However, few accolades counted as much as the result of a worldwide poll conducted by FIFA in the run-up to its own centenary year to discover who was considered the best club of the twentieth century. With 42 per cent of the total votes, Real Madrid emerged as a clear winner, ahead of Manchester United and Bayern Munich, its accumulated silverware as of the 1999–2000 season evidence of its unrivalled status as a winner – eight European Cups, two UEFA Cups, two World Club Championships, twenty-eight league championships, seventeen Spanish Cups and SuperCups. In May 2002 Real Madrid added to its trophy list, winning its ninth European Cup, beating Bayer Leverkusen – in front of 52,000 ecstatic fans at Hampden Park, Glasgow, scene of that epic encounter with Eintracht Frankfurt forty-two years before.

Two years earlier, on 24 May 1998, Real Madrid beat Juventus in the final of the Champions League, lifting the European championship crown for the first time in thirty-two years. As a new century approached, the victory at the new Amsterdam Arena – before a capacity crowd of 47,500 and transmitted to millions of TV viewers worldwide – marked a convergence between the club's mythical past and the modern era of football, reinforcing the club's self-belief that its greatness had no end. As the author Manuel Vazquez Montalban once put it, 'Europe has always signified for Real Madrid and its fans either a distraction or an escape into the future. For these prisoners of the myth of Real Madrid – the winner of six European cups – the conquest of the seventh had become an indispensable condition for affirming an identity that has always revolved around domination.'

The sense of historic continuity was personified with the

lifting of the trophy by the team captain Manolo Sanchis, the last survivor of the *Quinta del Buitre*, whose father had helped Real Madrid win the 1966 European Cup. 'For me lifting that cup was the culmination of a footballing career. I knew after that that I could retire in peace, that there was nothing greater to achieve,' Sanchis later recalled.

The fact that Sanchis was just one of four Spaniards playing in a team largely made up of foreigners contrasted with the all-Spanish team of which his father had been part, but was consistent with much of the club's post-war history of drawing on the talent of foreign stars. More recently Real Madrid in common with other big clubs had wasted little time in taking full advantage of the historic European court ruling in favour of the Belgian player Jean Luc Bosman which liberalized the international transfer market, and catapulted Europe's major football clubs on an unprecedented spending spree during the 1990s.

'The victory in 1998 had a particular importance in the history of the club because it destroyed the lie that we were only capable of winning European championships in black and white, that we had lost our way in the era of global colour satellite TV. We had begun losing our confidence but with that victory we convinced ourselves that from then on we could be European champions every year,' Sanchis told me.

Elsewhere in Spain, notably in Catalonia, Barça fans who had been wearing Juventus shirts in the latter stages of the Champions League went into mourning. But in Madrid more than a million people gathered around one of the capital's most emblematic monuments – the fountain and Ventura Rodriguez statue of the Graeco-Roman goddess of fertility *Cibeles* (Cybele) – to celebrate that victory in Europe. It was one of the biggest outpourings of public emotion among Spaniards in the capital since the death of Franco.

The mood and sentiment of the crowd – aggressive, triumphalist, territorial – reminded those with memories of the occasional mass gatherings in the Plaza de Oriente in support of Franco when he was alive. Nevertheless the crowd also contained the new generation of Real Madrid fans, many of them adherents of the ruling Partido Popular, but not exclusively so. This was not the first time that Real Madrid fans had claimed the capital's central monument as their own: they had begun to do so in the early 1980s, but never in such numbers. The victorious Real Madrid players were transported from the airport through the city in open-roofed cars, three to a vehicle. They included two players who were destined for even greater days with the club – the Brazilian Roberto Carlos and the young Spaniard who had emerged as the natural successor to Butragueño, Raúl González, better knows as just plain Raúl and who was then reaching the peak of his form.

The foreigners included the Serbian Pedrag Mijatovic whose goal in the 66th minute – the one that secured victory over Juventus – entered the club's history books as a defining moment, even though the game continued to a nail-biting finish as the Italian club led by Zidane tried to equalize. Three minutes from the final whistle, Lorenzo Sanz, who had succeeded Mendoza as Real Madrid president, couldn't stand the tension any longer and left the directors' box, excusing himself on the grounds that he had to go to the bathroom. He spent the final moments huddled in a corner of an internal room of the stadium, clutching a live radio commentary to his ear.

'I just felt stricken by fear, with emotion – we were so close to winning and yet I knew that the whole illusion of victory could collapse in an instant. I couldn't deal with the tension of it all in front of all the VIPs so I just got out,' recalled Sanz.

The next day Sanz took up the rear of the triumphant cavalcade in a car alongside his commanders, the German coach Jupp Heynckes and Sanchis. The team captain was among those who climbed onto *Cibeles*. 'It seemed to me appropriate that we should be there at that statue which carries within it a great sense of victory of the city over Europe and the rest of the world. The happiness everyone felt was that of fulfilling a thirty-two-year-old wish.'

With Spanish flags flying, the celebrations served as a reminder of the extent to which supporters of the club considered themselves the standard-bearers of a defined and uncompromising sense of nationhood – a united Spain with Madrid as its heart and soul. Real Madrid's own self-projection as Spanish ambassador was underlined by the congratulatory message of King Juan Carlos, for ever imprinted in the official history of the 'royal' club. 'Today is a great day,' the Spanish monarch declared of the extended victory parade. 'It is a victory not just for Madrid, but for Spain.'

Among those equally delighted was José María Aznar, a Real Madrid fan, who two years earlier had led the centre-right Partido Popular to victory. The early to mid-1990s had seen the ruling socialist PSOE embroiled in financial scandals, its reputation further tarnished by the exposure of political dishonesty in its handling of the Basque country's demands for greater independence, in particular its cover-up of the use of semi-official death squads to assassinate ETA suspects.

Real Madrid's winning the Champions League two years into a government that had promised to restore Spain's credibility as EU partner and member of NATO, was good news for the new prime minister and the Madrid municipal and regional government controlled by his party. The waving of the Spanish flags in *Cibeles* – a symbol of natural abundance and perpetuity – dovetailed nicely with Aznar's own ambitious political agenda. His manifesto had pledged to boost Spain's economic growth and to wipe out terrorism by the Basque separatist group ETA by legitimate means, resisting any further concessions to regional governments that risked undermining the sacred unity of the nation.

Just as Aznar had his mind set on at least two terms in government, Sanz viewed the 1998 victory over Juventus as the beginning of a new golden era for the club in Europe where its international success would come to equal if not overtake the achievements of the Di Stefano years. In 1999 Real Madrid were knocked out by Dynamo Kiev in the quarter-finals of the Champions League, but the following year won Europe's blue-riband event once again, this time after surviving a memorable second-leg quarter-final clash with Manchester United at Old Trafford. It was a match Real Madrid and Manchester United fans would remember as one of the great nights of European football, as reflected in the final score of 2–3, with Raúl and Beckham – his transfer to Spain not even imagined yet by the player – grabbing three goals between them and sharing the honours as the men of the match.

That year was an all-Spanish final between Real Madrid and Valencia in the Saint-Denis stadium, Paris. It was played soon after Aznar's Partido Popular had been re-elected with an absolute majority. Both Madrid and Valencia had strongly supported the PP in the elections. From the perspective of the government it was a sporting event made in heaven, the projection of a triumphant Spain poised to take a more active part on the global stage.

After Real Madrid had been handed its latest trophy by Spain's Crown Prince Felipe, Raúl picked up a large Spanish flag and for a few seconds, in full view of a global TV audience, imitated a matador using his cape to fight a bull. The fact that Real Madrid had among its latest foreign contingent the Englishman Steve McManaman, and that on Valencia's side was the Basque (and a Spanish international) Gaizka Mendieta, mattered little when it came to the totemic image of a club that had always attempted to appropriate for itself the exclusive representation of a nation and its culture.

In his book on Spain's new Right published just before he died in 2003, Manolo Vazquez Montalban, a Galician turned Barça fan, draws an analogy between the politics of Aznar and Real Madrid, the latest example of the club's close relationship with the centres of power. It is a view that was strongly objected to when I put it to the man who coached Real Madrid to that victory in Saint-Denis in 2000, Vicente Del Bosque, when I interviewed him three years later.

'Raúl didn't pick that flag up against or in favour of anyone . . . perhaps in another period of history it may have had some significance, but not at the start of a new century. Raúl was representing Spain – there is nothing negative about that, even if, hell, the flag is everybody's to carry. And anyway, who picks up the flag or who doesn't isn't of much interest to me. What interests me is Real Madrid being champions of Europe, and that a team representing Spanish football should come out winning – the rest are mere gestures. Let everyone have the opinion they want,' Del Bosque told me.

Not for the first time nor the last would someone closely involved with Real Madrid deliberately attempt to defuse any political notions of the club while in doing so confirming the attitudes which its critics and rivals found most abhorrent. And yet Del Bosque seemed ultimately to recognize the right of every Spaniard to disagree which seemed a refreshing change from the Franco years.

Nonetheless Del Bosque owed his job as coach to Lorenzo Sanz, one of the more controversial figures in the history of Real Madrid, whose activities both before and during his presidency cast a shadow over the club and the politics surrounding it, dimming the glitter of the trophies achieved.

Sanz was born in 1943, the year Santiago Bernabéu, the most legendary of all Real Madrid's presidents, took office. While saved from the direct experience of the Spanish Civil War, Sanz belonged to a post-war generation that suffered its consequences while learning to exploit the opportunities it threw up. The son of a policeman, he was brought up as the eldest of ten children in working-class districts of Madrid – first in Chamberi and later Carabanchel – scraping his first pesetas together with a series of menial jobs very much identified with the old Spain. He sold drinking water out of a *botijo*, the traditional earthenware jug used by labourers and bullfighters. He also worked as a junior in a barber's shop.

One of his clients was Father José María Bulart, Franco's personal confessor who blessed the foundation stone of Real

Madrid's new stadium, later named after Bernabéu. Sanz went to the stadium for the first time as a young teenager in 1957 where he saw a Real Madrid team made up of the likes of Di Stefano, Gento, Kopa and Rial, win the European Cup final 2–0 against Fiorentina. 'Real Madrid have always been great. They were then on their way to becoming the best team in the world, and like it or not, a kind of religion for their fans,' he recalled many years later.

Sanz joined up as a member of the club relatively late in the day, in 1979, when he was in his mid-thirties and had some money to spend, thanks to working as a graphic designer and distributing commercial paper as Spain moved from a dictatorship to a democracy. He became rich during the socialist government of Felipe González, developing his interests in horseracing and his dealings in the property business. Of the property boom of the late 1980s, which individuals like Sanz took advantage of, there is a vivid description in John Hooper's portrait of contemporary Spain, *The New Spaniards*:

Those who had enough money to buy a house or flat in addition to their principal residence enhanced their families' fortunes as handsomely as many a sixteenth-century adventurer returning from the Indies. But just as the gold and silver of the Americas enriched a few in the short term and impoverished so many in the long term, so too the property boom of the late eighties did considerable damage to the fabric of Spanish society.

It was during the 1980s that Sanz drew closer to the centre of power at Real Madrid after helping finance the presidential campaign of Ramón Mendoza. As Mendoza later recalled in his memoirs, Sanz not only shared his interest in horseracing, he also knew how to obtain planning permission because of the contacts he had developed among local government officials. When Mendoza became president of Real Madrid in 1985, Sanz became vice-president, between them representing a club that within it contained many of the paradoxes of Spain itself, clinging as it did to aspects of its past while at the same time claiming to embrace the modern era.

Just as Mendoza played down claims that he had once worked for the KGB, Sanz came to dismiss as merely anecdotal the fact that during his graphic design days he had worked organizing advertising space at the official newspaper of *Fuerza Nueva*, the extreme-right movement and – according to some accounts – as a part-time bodyguard of its leader Blas Piñar. 'I did work for *Fuerza Nueva* but merely as an employee, as a professional that was responsible for advertising . . . The fact is they threw me out when I asked for too much money,' Sanz told me when I interviewed him for this book. He did not offer an explanation as to why he had chosen to work for such an outfit in the first place knowing its political connotations.

He was more expansive when I put to him allegations that during his time as vice-president and later as president he had encouraged the emergence of the *Ultra Surs*, during the 1980s, as a radical group of supporters prone to racist abuse and violence and one of the most self-publicizing and rampant hooligan elements in Spanish football. Former members of the group had told me how during the Mendoza and Sanz years, they had not only received tickets from the club but also been given their own room in the Bernabéu stadium where they could store their banners. I had also been told of the meetings some of them had had with first-team players during which they had photographs taken and autographs signed.

Sanz told me: 'The term *"ultra"* [extreme] has to be put in inverted commas . . . Inside the stadium the average supporter is very passive so one needs people that are more organized in their support without necessarily committing barbarities. The club will never admit that it supports them directly . . . but it backs them just as one backs other *peñas* [supporters' clubs] . . . I don't think one should get rid of them [the *Ultra Surs*], one needs to redirect them into being a non-violent group of support. . . Yes, the club has supported them with tickets, and yes there have been cases of players corresponding with *Ultra Surs*, giving them signed shirts, buying lottery tickets . . .'

Sanz insisted that throughout his time at the club he had cooperated in weekly meetings with government officials in order to minimize violent incidents. 'Sometimes we achieved this, other times we didn't,' he added. It seemed something of an understatement given the wealth of evidence pointing to the growth of the *Ultra Surs* during the 1980s and 1990s with its support base drawn from a mish-mash of political and social backgrounds. These included unemployed youths, middle-class Real Madrid fanatics, neo-Nazis and skinheads, united by a common attitude of generational rebellion and inherited prejudice against anyone outside the club. Their violence was a manifestation of feelings that had survived Spain's transition to democracy, with an added element of thuggery fuelled by the cynical contempt many shared for Spanish democracy.

As Fernando Carreño, a Spanish journalist who has investigated the darker side of Real Madrid as it showed itself during the Mendoza and Sanz presidencies, points out: 'The *Ultra Surs* are neo-fascist because although their space is theoretically open to anyone according to the basic requirement that he is a fervent Madrid supporter, in reality anyone who is not politically and socially to the right of Genghis Khan stands to have a bad time in their midst. When they attack they do it as a group and against victims who are smaller in number and with a variety of arms (chains, knives, baseball bats, knuckle dusters) . . . fans of other clubs, leftists, punks, anyone who they think may be homosexual . . . The attacks that in the immediate aftermath of Franco were carried out to the cries of "Christ the King" subsequently began to be carried out with the cry of *"Ultra Surs".'*

Of the many recorded incidents of *Ultra Sur* violence some are worth mentioning here for they show at the very least a lack of control by club officials. In September 1988, when Mendoza was president and Sanz in charge of the supporters' groups, a group of *Ultra Surs* violently disrupted the local fiestas in the Asturian town of Oviedo as they made their way by road to a match between Real Madrid and Sporting Gijón. Only a few days earlier Real Madrid as a club had been fined by UEFA on their account: a group of *Ultra Surs* had reacted to Real Madrid's defeat by Bayern Munich in a European Cup at the Bernabéu stadium by firing a flare at the referee and pelting the visitors' Belgian goalkeeper Jean Marie Pfaff with nails and other missiles.

During the Sanz presidency the official line from the club that it was dealing more effectively with hooligan violence was discredited before a worldwide TV audience tuning in to watch Real Madrid's Champions League semi-final at the

Bernabéu against Borussia Dortmund in the 1997–98 season. A group of *Ultra Surs* deliberately pulled down the wires holding the goalposts up, provoking the collapse of the posts which forced a long delay to the kick-off and another huge fine against the club.

I experienced at close quarters what it was like to visit the Bernabéu as a Barça supporter. The visitors arrived with their buses surrounded by police only to be made to walk the gauntlet of escalating abuse. Some of the police seemed to me to be smirking as the locals shouted phrases such as 'Catalan shits' and '*hijos de puta*' (sons of whores). I observed a certain complicity among the Barça fans, some of the more aggressive among them seemingly under the control of a club official. They were the *Boixos Nois* (Our Boys), an equally unsavoury mix which included supporters of Catalan independence and neo-fascists and which the then president of FC Barcelona Josep Lluís Nuñez tolerated just as Real Madrid under Mendoza and Sanz turned a convenient blind eye to the *Ultra Surs*. The animosity the rival hooligans developed against each other was fuelled by the uncompromising statements issued periodically by the presidents of their clubs against each other. Thus these little armies of bullies became the crude end of a long-running sporting rivalry which the nature of Spanish politics had always ensured ran close to the limit of what could be tolerated in a democratic society.

Just how close surfaced in Perez's first full year as president during the 2001–02 season when the Basque separatist organization ETA set off a bomb near the Bernabéu stadium before the Champions League semi-final clash between Real Madrid and FC Barcelona. The *Ultra Surs* went on a rampage, attacking police, journalists and anyone remotely suspected of not supporting the club. Such scenes contributed to undermining Real Madrid's image not just as a 'gentleman's club' as its older members liked to see it but as an institution worthy of worldwide respect, Spain's most cherished export. It forced Perez into adopting a strategy towards the *Ultra Surs* which tried, not entirely successfully, to maintain a balance between the passion they helped create in the Bernabéu and the need for it to be expressed in a way that did not damage the club's image. Supporters' groups including the *Ultra Surs* were offered tickets as long as they signed up to a non-violence pact. The club also offered them financial support to invest in replacement banners and placards for those banned as too provocative and abusive. While violence in the stadium was drastically reduced, confrontations outside the arena continued, including a pitched battle with Atlético de Madrid hooligans outside the Vicente Calderón stadium towards the end of Beckham's first season. A more radical policy was adopted by FC Barcelona's new president Joán Laporta who after being the subject of personal death threats imposed an all-out ban on the *Boixos Nois* being allowed into the Nou Camp. The result was a much reduced volume of sound in the famous stadium and rows of empty seats during several matches of the season.

Real Madrid belatedly came to terms with the transformation of football into a global sport during the 1990s largely because of an endemic administrative conservatism dating back to the Franco years. In 1994 an inside investigation by Spain's leading broadsheet newspaper *El País* painted a picture of a club still largely controlled by internal family networks, with staff that had worked there for years, grown old, and were professionally completely unprepared to meet the challenges of the new technological revolution. 'There are computers that have never worked, most of the staff can't speak any other language than Spanish ... recently, candidates for jobs that had fallen vacant at the club were shortlisted on the basis of their emotional attachment and their family ties to the club. Club officials are very resistant to any innovation,' an insider at the club told the newspaper.

Of all the officials few were as powerful as Manuel Fernandez Trigo, the manager in overall charge of administration since the mid-1970s. Trigo straddled not only the club's finance and legal departments, but also built up a lobby among the membership and the supporters' clubs to secure changes of policy in the management of the teams. Successive Real Madrid presidents were regularly told by Trigo that the club switchboard was inundated with calls from supporters complaining about a decision taken by the coach, whoever he happened to be at the time. The president would then contact the coach and suggest changes. One of Spain's top sports journalists Santiago Segurola called Trigo's meddling the 'syndrome of the telephone switchboard'.

It was only in 1998 that Trigo finally agreed to leave the club after being offered a great deal of money by Sanz, taking many of the club's secrets with him, not least his knowledge of a long-running trade in black-market tickets which had been handled for decades from within the club.

By then Sanz had been forced to turn to a group of external consultants to come up with a management shake-up plan that would ensure the club running on a more cost-effective and professional basis. Trigo's personal empire was transformed into new departments run by new executives covering areas such as human resources, marketing and IT. But Sanz's popularity was now declining – despised by the old guard for losing their power base, and distrusted by other Real Madrid supporters who blamed him for the club's mounting debt estimated at around £170m.

Sanz had inherited from Mendoza the negative financial consequences of a disastrously structured long-term TV and merchandising rights deal with a Spanish company, and the additional costs of a rebuilding programme at the Bernabéu. But he also participated in the post-Bosman transfer frenzy, spending millions on a plethora of international players. The boot of one of them was destined for privileged display at Real Madrid's museum for it belonged to Pedrag Mijatovic, whose goal in Amsterdam on 20 May 1998 would always be remembered as the spectacular achievement that ended a thirty-two-year drought in the European Cup.

Sanz also bought Roberto Carlos, whose reputation as one of the world's most versatile defenders would continue at Real Madrid into the new millennium. Others came and went, transient contributors to occasional moments of glory who failed to forge the real sense of collective and enduring identity that the generation of the *Quinta del Buitre* had managed in the 1980s – players like Clarence Seedorf, Davor Suker, Christian Panucci and Christian Karambeu. They were nicknamed the 'Ferrari boys' because their activity on the pitch never quite compensated for the spendthrift scandal-ridden lifestyles they conspicuously pursued off it. Faced with an avalanche of high-earning low-performing foreigners, many Real Madrid supporters invested their emotional baggage in Raúl, a *Madrileño* born and bred, who 'sweated' the white shirt and showed international star status and quality as a goalscorer – a worthy successor to Butragueño even if he lacked *El Buitre*'s warmth and skills as a communicator.

Of all Sanz's player signings few proved as controversial as that of Nicolas Anelka, bought for a handsome 5,000 million pesetas (£23m). It was his two goals against Bayern Munich in the Champions League semi-final that paved the way for Real Madrid's victory at Saint-Denis in 2000. But that was a rare contribution the Frenchman made during his tortuous time at Real Madrid. His failure to engage with other members of the team and to adapt to living in Spain drastically affected his form and gave Real Madrid supporters a general sense that Sanz had paid too much for the player, fuelling allegations of financial kick-backs that surrounded several transfer deals at the time.

As for coaches, Sanz managed to get through nine in five years – an unprecedented turnover which gave the impression of a president without a firm view of what kind of football he wanted to see played, still less of a long-term strategy capable of ensuring the financial stability that the club so desperately needed. The coaches – notably Fabio Capello, Jupp Heynckes and Guus Hiddink – all came with proven international track-records, and all left enveloped in a cloud of controversy, mainly produced by the tension of surviving one of the most pressurized jobs in sport under the shadow of a president whose judgement they did not trust but who nonetheless some of them found exploitable.

The Dutchman Guus Hiddink was approached by Sanz in the summer of 1998 after the former Real Madrid player José Antonio Camacho resigned as the club's coach following a row with Sanz's right-hand man Juan Onieva over team selection. Camacho had been in the job less than three weeks. Hiddink was exhausted after coaching Holland to the semi-finals of the World Cup, and felt he needed an extended break from football. When he got the call from Madrid, he consulted his old friend and fellow countryman Johan Cruyff. 'If they're offering the Madrid job, take it – it's a logical move. It doesn't matter if you don't get much time off. Just work, take the money, and then get out of there.' Hiddink was convinced he stood to make a clean £2.5m, even if he were to be sacked after two months.

During his first season at Real Madrid Hiddink gave his own detailed insight into life as a coach for a club that regarded itself the most successful in the history of football. In a conversation with Dutch journalist Hugo Borst for the football magazine *Hard Gras* Hiddink revealed:

Getting sacked here is like a game, it's not really a disgrace . . . It goes like this. The president invites you to his office and says, '*Mister*, I think it is better that you don't continue.' The atmosphere is good, very pleasant, very charming. The president gives you an *abrazo* [a hug] and adds, 'OK, drop by the Treasurer's office tomorrow.' So the next day you drop by the Treasurer's office and you collect a cheque and you go to the nearest bank and they hand you a suitcase of money, and boom it's all over. In Spain they kill you romantically.

Hiddink lasted a season, took his money and left.

Of the many widely publicized clashes between Sanz and his bench few were as colourful as that which pitted the property speculator against Hiddink's successor the tough no-nonsense Welshman John Toshack brought back for a second spell as a Real Madrid coach as the twentieth century drew to its close.

Amid laughable scenes of indiscipline among the players – Suker furious at being jokingly rebuked by Toshack for using his massive wages on a large English teddy bear for his high-profile Spanish girlfriend Ana Obregón, a punch-up during training between Ivan Campo and Seedorf – the Welshman not only accused Real Madrid of incompetence but added insult to injury by giving Spain's voracious sports press its best line in years: 'You'll see pigs flying over the Bernabéu before I take back what I said.' Days later Toshack was unceremoniously sacked, prompting an acrimonious legal action on grounds of unfair dismissal which he won, forcing the club to dig deeper into its depleted reserves to pay the compensation.

Years later, Sanz remained unrepentant. 'Toshack was a good coach, indeed the first time he came to Real Madrid, during Ramón Mendoza's time, the team broke a Spanish league goalscoring record,' he told the Spanish journalist Juan Carlos Pasamontes. 'But the truth is that he not only duped me, he was also a disaster. You'd agree something with him, and with the players, and he'd then do what the fuck he liked. It was impossible.'

Toshack's was replaced by Vicente Del Bosque, a non-controversial figure widely respected among Real Madrid supporters as a safe pair of hands because of his years of loyalty to the club. After retiring as a player, Del Bosque had trained the youth team before coming in on two previous occasions as a stop-gap first-team coach.

During Real Madrid's progress towards their eighth European Cup win in the 1999–2000 season, one match would in time be remembered as significant in more ways than one, not least in the sense that it began to define the future destiny of two of the greatest clubs in the history of football and of one player in particular.

The second leg of the Champions League quarter-final between Real Madrid and Manchester United played at Old Trafford in which the visitors won 3–2, after a goalless draw at the Bernabéu, produced one of the most thrilling European matches in the age of satellite TV. For Manchester United the defeat contrasted with their treble victory the previous season – League, FA Cup and European Cup – subsequently planting in the mind of some of its analysts the idea that the success of the Ferguson era might have peaked. It followed a decade during which Manchester United had managed to secure the kind of global projection that left Real Madrid under Mendoza, and then Sanz, well behind in terms of exploitation of TV and merchandising rights, and the general soundness of its economic management. Manchester United paid only for the players it could afford and felt could deliver while encouraging the emergence of home-grown talent.

In purely sporting terms the club had also come to dominate English football, emerging as the only serious contender for the European crown in competition with German, Italian and Spanish clubs. Prior to the quarter-final with Del Bosque's team, Manchester United's fans and the English press were confident of beating the Spanish champions. In the end Old Trafford found itself applauding the victors in a gesture of respect for the better team. Of that match David Beckham would later recall a piece of Real magic when, for the first fifteen minutes of the second half, 'everything they did seemed to come off and we couldn't get near them.' He remembered in particular the effortless tap-in goal by Raúl – the first of two in three minutes by the Spanish star – after Redondo, the Argentinian central midfielder, had skilfully manoeuvred past the United defender Henning Berg and crossed.

From the perspective of Real Madrid it was Beckham himself who seemed to be a cut above the rest in his team, with his commitment and vision on and off the ball. After all, you needed to score a goal after beating Roberto Carlos – as Beckham did that night – to earn some *Madridista* respect. Beckham's talent was not unknown to Del Bosque. The Real Madrid coach later told me that he had first been struck by Beckham's star quality a few years earlier, when he had begun to play for England, and had rated him among the best players in the world. 'What struck me then was his involvement with the team, his great touch, his good vision and creative play,' Del Bosque remembered.

That night Beckham at his magisterial best seemed unlikely ever to quit Old Trafford, let alone seek his fortune in Madrid. But the future is never easy to predict in Spanish football. That summer of 2000 politics played its role in ensuring that Sanz was replaced as president by Florentino Perez, the man fated within two years to translate an interest in an English player into a firm bid for Beckham once the English captain's long involvement with Manchester United deteriorated into a damaging conflict with club manager Alex Ferguson which could not be repaired.

The personal drama played out by Sanz towards the end of the 1998 European Cup final – a highly publicized and self-conscious attack of nerves as the final minutes ticked away – may have been the reactions of a genuine fan. But to his critics within the club they were symptomatic of a man with a deluded sense of his own importance, as was later shown by his high-profile involvement in his team's victory parade through Madrid, and his constant seeking of the media spotlight with his comments on players and the team's tactics. As things turned out, Sanz made a huge miscalculation in believing that his achievement in winning two European Cups, one World Club Championship and one league championship would be sufficient to win him his re-election in time for the club's centenary celebrations.

Undoubtedly Real Madrid's continuing image as a champion club struggling against financial collapse was not one that went down well with many of its voting members, nor for that matter with the club's allies in the ruling Partido Popular whose own re-election as a government had been based on its record of sound economic management directed from the Spanish capital by José María Aznar, the former tax inspector turned prime minister and a self-declared Real Madrid fan.

Sanz had taken steps to modernize a club which had in effect been stuck in the past for too long, but he was unable to convey a sense of having a serious long-term strategy that would help strengthen the club's self-image as the greatest in the world. When I spoke to him in the winter of 2003, Sanz was still struggling to come to terms with his defeat in what he refused to accept was a fairly conducted campaign. I met him in a smart office apartment he had retained round the corner from the Bernabéu stadium like a campaign headquarters that never gives up. On the walls were photographs reminding anyone who might have forgotten of two pastimes that had brought him notoriety – horseracing and football. The files of some of his property deals lay hidden only he knew where. Anonymous clients cruised the corridors. Sanz's mobile rang continually, turning our conversation into stops and starts. He told me that the number of his mobile was the date Real Madrid had won the European Cup again after thirty-two years.

In a rare extended interlude between his phone conversations, Sanz discoursed at length about the one subject that continued to haunt him: the realization that he had simply not carried the political clout of his main rival for the presidency of Real Madrid, Florentino Perez. During the days of Ramón Mendoza and the socialist government, Sanz had wielded his influence among national and local authorities to obtain numerous planning permissions for some of the club's building projects. But by his own admission he had struck a wall with the centre-right PP officials who from the mid-1990s through to 2004 dominated central government and the regional and municipal governments of Madrid when it came to drafting a plan for the redevelopment of the *Ciudad Deportiva*, the club's old training ground. His project was turned down, while Florentino Perez's was approved following his election victory.

'I think the Partido Popular government was interested in Real Madrid, to have a part in its future because it is the world's leading club . . . it supported the club with Florentino Perez more than any other previously elected government. But I wasn't part of the system. I was apolitical,' Sanz told me. 'Perhaps we just weren't good enough at selling our achievements,' he concluded.

*

Whatever one can say about Florentino Perez he was never an outsider. Born in 1947, Perez belonged to a generation of Spaniards able to build on the suffering and hard work of their parents without having to share in their deprivation and looking instead towards a better future. His father Eduardo ran a family perfumery business dating back to the nineteenth century which had survived the ravages of the Civil War; the scents and potions carried through from Roman times, and later from the Moorish kingdom deeply embedded in Spanish culture, whether in conflict or in peace. It was a business nevertheless, and Eduardo Perez instilled in his eldest son from an early age two guiding principles of conduct which he would carry within him into adulthood – austerity and hard work. In later years Eduardo, well into his eighties, would continue assiduously to visit the extended chain of shops he had come to own, preferring this to the leisurely early retirement to which he was entitled. One cannot begin to understand Florentino without reference to his father – he was driven not only to follow his example but to better it.

He did so against the background of an emerging institution that contributed to regenerating a sense of grandeur and ambition amid the hardship and isolationism of post-war Spain. The year Perez was born was also the year that Real Madrid inaugurated its new stadium, its bold concrete structures a symbol of urban and national renewal. His father, a passionate Real Madrid supporter, took him to the Bernabéu for the first time when he was four years old, and secured him a membership when he was thirteen. By then Perez had, as he later recalled, begun to 'understand the magic' that could be spun by a team made up of the best players in the world – foreigners and Spaniards – and the huge undertow of popular support they carried with them.

As a young man Perez studied civil engineering and carried out his military service, developing friendships that would later prove useful in public life. He also tried his hand at his first business venture. While travelling through Europe in search of a holiday job he came across a weekly entertainment guide in Paris, and decided to copy the concept for the city of Madrid. The Spanish *Leisure Guide* was published for the first time in 1975, the year of Franco's death. Spain was poised to experience a flowering of culture and entertainment. The timing for a magazine that told *Madrileños* where they could enjoy the fruits of freedom of a kind they had not experienced for over forty years could not have been better. 'It was a magazine that was very modest but it was very exciting to do something that one felt was bound to be successful, as it later became,' he recalled.

The end of the dictatorship not only opened up new business opportunities, but also provided additional avenues of political influence. Perez was offered and took a job in the new mayor of Madrid's office, as the head of a new department with responsibility for the capital's sanitation and environment. He then stood in the first post-Franco municipal elections and was elected as a Madrid councillor for the UCD, the new centrist party formed by Adolfo Suárez, the prime minister chosen by King Juan Carlos to steer Spain through the transition to democracy.

Perez spent a total of seven years working in the Madrid mayor's office under the UCD government before the socialist party of Felipe González was voted into power in 1982. The sorry state of the civil service during this transition period was exposed in a damning report published in 1980. It was the first officially tolerated critique, published as it was by the Ministry of Commerce. 'The Administration is a tangle of self-destructive vicious circles,' wrote its author Professor Alejandro Nieto. 'It is a lawless zone where the citizens are persecuted and where amid the ruins of public services a few civil servants and political parties successfully cultivate their own backyards with the fertilizer of corruption.' Nevertheless Perez emerged with his reputation for honesty and hard work intact, telling one journalist many years later that apart from Real Madrid he had never done anything 'with such love and enthusiasm' as in those early years as a member of the UCD.

As the author Juan Carlos Pasamontes writes in his biographical sketch of Perez for his book *La Casa Blanca*, 'The seven years Perez spent in the mayor's office in Madrid gave him more than enough time to gain some political nous, extend his circle of friends, and get to know better than anyone the intricate world of the civil service.'

Such was his accumulated range of friends already that Perez managed to survive the first internal crisis that befell the UCD, a contorted amalgam of diverse political groupings from social democrats and liberals on the Left to Christian Democrats on the enlightened Catholic Right with 'blue shirts' (former members of Franco's Movement) shifting alliances in an effort to hang on to power.

In April 1980 the UCD seemed in dramatic trouble after suffering some damaging electoral reverses in Andalusia, the Basque country, Catalonia and Galicia, and an upsurge in terrorist violence by ETA. The party was riddled with internal dissent and tales of plots against its leader, the prime minister Suárez. A macabre dance of vampires was how Spain's leading weekly *Cambio 16* described it. Among much bloodsucking a Perez ally, the former Madrid mayor José Luis Alvarez, was appointed minister of transport, tourism and communications. One of Alvarez's first decisions was to promote Perez from the mayor's office to the heart of central government as one of his ministry's most senior officials responsible for infrastructure. When Alvarez was moved in December 1981 to the ministry of agriculture, he took Perez with him, appointing him undersecretary of state.

Within a year the UCD had effectively disintegrated. In the election of 28 October 1982 the UCD obtained just over 6 per cent of the vote, its annihilation at the hands of the victorious socialist party the greatest electoral defeat suffered by a governing party in Europe since the Second World War. The Christian Democrats, however, had by then broken away and allied themselves with the Alianza Popular – a right-wing party headed by Manuel Fraga Iribarne, a former minister and ambassador to London, who projected himself as a stabilizing link between Francoism and democracy. AP, with strong backing from the employers' federation, emerged as the second most popular party. Also worthy of note, in understanding some of Perez's subsequent political man-oeuvrings, was the emergence of the centrist Catalan nation-alist party Convergencia I Unio (CiU) as the leading party in Catalonia, heading the regional government there from 1980 onwards, and polling more votes than the UCD nationally in 1982.

Perez emerged from the 1982 election somewhat shell-shocked. 'I knew that we were going to lose but not even in my worst dreams did I imagine that we would get such a beating,' he would later recall. Nevertheless within a year he had spotted an opportunity that was to form the foundation stone of his future business empire. He bought a bankrupt Catalan construction company Construcciones Padros from its banking administrators for one peseta (the equivalent of just half a penny) per share. The company had belonged to Banca Catalana, a banking group built up in the sixties by Jordi Pujol, the leader of the CiU. Banca Catalana and its associated companies were placed in administration in 1982 with losses of 138 billion pesetas.

During the Franco years and the transition to democracy, Banca Catalana had come to be considered by Catalans as 'more than a bank', much as FC Barcelona had become 'more than a football club'. All its internal memorandums were in the Catalan language and the bank went out of its way to support local culture and industry. Its patronage by CiU continued even after Pujol was obliged to sever direct links with the bank when he became head of the *Generalitat* (Catalan government) in 1979. For years after its collapse there remained a lingering suspicion in Catalonia that the banking group's difficulties were exaggerated as part of a campaign, orchestrated from Madrid, to destroy public confidence in the ability of Catalans to manage their own affairs.

Far from allowing himself to be caught up in such a conspiracy, Perez used the purchase of Construcciones Padros to extend his friendships and business ties in Catalonia, a region of legendary industriousness that in economic terms took full advantage of the greater political autonomy offered by Spain's new democracy during the 1980s. The construction business was a sector destined to reap benefits, not least from the social and cultural renaissance that

Barcelona experienced around its hosting of the Olympic Games in 1992.

'It was in Catalonia that Perez began his business strategy. He saw a very clear opportunity and took it. He also developed a respect for Catalan politicians. He believed they had a business acumen which other Spaniards could learn from,' Carlos Tusquets, a former treasurer of FC Barcelona and a leading Catalan banker, told me. In 1986 Perez became secretary-general of a short-lived centrist political grouping called the Democratic Reformist Party, which brought together some of the old UCD and Catalans from Pujol's CiU. The party had as one of its main figureheads Miquel Roca, a leading Catalan business lawyer who helped draw up Spain's liberal constitution after the death of Franco and became one of the country's most active elected politicians, championing the idea of an enlightened conservative grouping that would embrace nationalist parties. During the 1980s Perez came to believe that a Catalan president like Roca would be good for Spain, more serious and reliable perhaps than a socialist from Andalusia called Felipe González.

The Democratic Reformist Party failed to make any electoral inroads but Roca – a man of considerable influence in Catalonia – would remain a close political and business ally of Perez's as he built up his business empire through a series of acquisitions and mergers. Along the way Perez managed, in 1992, to avoid becoming embroiled in the 'Ollero case', one of the big financial scandals to hit the socialist government during its last tortured term in office. Juan Ollero was a senior official of the socialist regional government of Andalusia who negotiated road and motorway contracts. The president and finance director of Ocisa, a company in which

Perez had bought shares three years earlier, were fined and sent to prison after being found guilty of falsification of documents and bribery, as were Ollero and his brother Jorge. No blame was ever attached to Perez as there was no suggestion of financial impropriety but the case damaged the reputation of the construction sector and fuelled a creeping sense of corruption which eventually contributed to the socialists' electoral defeat in 1996. One year after the Ollero case surfaced, Ocisa was merged with Construcciones Padros in a new company OCP Construcciones with Perez at its head.

The Catalan politician Roca had this to say about his friend and associate Perez in a profile he wrote in December 2002 after the newspaper *El Mundo* – a close ally of the PP government – had named the new president of Real Madrid the 'Spaniard of the Year':

Florentino likes having friends and he is not one of those who keeps changing them according to convenience. He knows how to be loyal to his friends . . . it doesn't matter what party they belong to, or football club they support – not even his fanatical *Madridismo* has stopped him from accepting me as a friend, despite the fact that I am one of the better known *cules* or supporters of FC Barcelona . . . His territory is the negotiating table. It is there that he comes into his own, and is usually unbeatable. When he knows what he wants – and there are few times when he doesn't – he goes for it.

Undoubtedly it was Perez's extraordinary capacity to make friends across a wide spectrum of political life that allowed him never to be far from power as he developed his business interests, a natural predator always on the look-out for an entity that could be bought on the cheap. As a paid-up member of Real Madrid he also kept his ear closely attuned to the internal political manoeuvrings of the club. During the early 1990s the then president Ramón Mendoza – whose glory years had coincided with the popularity of the as yet untainted socialist government – started to lose his grip as internal factions began to plot his succession against the background of disappointing results on the field and mounting debt.

In a move he thought would strengthen his power base within the club Mendoza turned to Perez and offered him the vice-presidency. As Mendoza later wrote in his memoirs: 'I wanted to strengthen my ability to influence things by bringing in Florentino Perez, then president of OCP, one of the most solvent construction companies in the country, which builds most of the bridges that cross our roads and motorways. Drive around the country and you'd be hard pressed not to see a poster in a lay-by or service area with the OCP logo on it.'

Mendoza, however, was unable to reconcile his long-serving deputy Lorenzo Sanz to the idea of sharing the vice-presidency with Perez, not least because Sanz had already made up his mind to take over the leadership of the club once Mendoza quit. But Mendoza hung on and in 1995 sought re-election, leaving Sanz with no option but to back him on the calculation that his loyalty would in time be rewarded. Perez by then already carried sufficient weight both in the political and business worlds to make his first bid for the presidency of Real Madrid by challenging Mendoza. He lost by just 698 votes with about 30,000 club members participating in the election and amid allegations of fraud committed by the Mendoza camp which were never conclusively proven. Four years would elapse – with Sanz as president – before he threw his hat into the ring again. By then Perez's construction interests, renamed ACS, had grown into one of Europe's largest construction companies. It would soon dominate the sector in Spain by merging with Dragados, another big construction firm, together employing nearly 27,000 people and operating in more than fifty countries. He had gained a reputation – largely unquestioned – as one of the most successful businessmen in Spain, the personification of the thrusting global entrepreneurial spirit that the centre-right government of the Partido Popular had tried to monopolize as its very own political virtue once it was re-elected with an absolute majority in the year 2000.

Perez fought a slick campaign advised by some of the key strategists behind the ruling Partido Popular's electoral success. He named as his two vice-presidents Fernando Fernandez Tapias and Juan Abello, two of Spain's most influential businessmen, well-known power-brokers and fund-raisers. His supporters included members of the opposition socialist party and leading trade unionist supporters of Real Madrid he had cultivated over the years. He promised to free the club from the historic burden of its debt, to modernize its installations and management, and to build up a star-studded team capable of replicating the glory days of Di Stefano on the global stage of the twenty-first century. The membership looked at his record as a businessman and his network of political patronage and were impressed. Before the campaign was over, Perez delivered his trump card, pledging that if he won he would be in a position to sign up Luis Figo, the Portuguese star then playing at FC Barcelona.

Less than two weeks after being voted the new president of Real Madrid, Perez completed Figo's world record £37.4m transfer. Within a year he had bagged France's Zinedine Zidane for an even bigger £46m. In December 2001, as Real Madrid moved into its centenary year, Perez marked his first year and a half in office by granting a joint interview to David Owen, sports editor of the *Financial Times* and Thilo Schäfer, the Madrid correspondent of *FT Deutschland*. Perez, an avid *FT* reader, was faintly amused that the two journalists from one of the leading global business media groups declared themselves supporters of Bristol Rovers and Fortuna Düsseldorf respectively. It was as if he believed that the universe he was helping to create at Real Madrid made lesser teams without a global profile redundant. With Figo and Zidane playing alongside Raúl and Roberto Carlos, the club already boasted four players who would stroll into an imaginary World XI. The Bernabéu stadium was full every game. 'People enjoy the way the team plays,' Perez insisted.

If, as Owen noted, football was littered with examples of clubs which have brandished cheque-books only to end up with financial headaches, Perez seemed, in his view, 'to have worked even bigger miracles with Real Madrid's balance-sheet than its team sheet'. In May 2001 Perez claimed to have balanced the club's books through a complex property deal exploiting the valuable location of the club's old training ground the *Ciudad Deportiva* on the outskirts of Madrid. The deal involved the redevelopment of the land for commercial and public use including the construction of four office blocks destined to alter the skyline of the capital. After a great deal of lobbying by Perez, planning permission for the project was approved by a majority of votes of Madrid's elected councillors led by the Partido Popular and including representatives of the communist Izquierda Unida. Perez was not the first president in the history of Real Madrid to change the landscape of Spain's capital along and near the Castellana avenue, but his property deal was the most ambitious to involve the club since the building of the Bernabéu in 1947, and among the most controversial.

Socialist councillor Matilde Fernández lunched once and breakfasted twice with Perez during his campaign to get approval for the property deal. He failed to convince her and she voted against. Quite apart from her objection on environmental grounds, Fernández was not prepared to be seduced by what she perceived as Perez's power play, using his personal relations with politicians to pursue business objectives. Such mixing of politics with business was sympto-matic of immature democracies, she believed. Perez re-sponded by claiming that Fernández's problem was not with himself but with her own party – not exactly a bastion of political propriety when it held power during the 1980s and early 1990s. 'There are political rivals of hers in the socialist party who happen to be my friends and support the *Ciudad Deportiva* project, and I think she wants to take her revenge on them, at my expense,' Florentino Perez told *El País*.

But Fernández was not alone in questioning the transpar-ency of the project. In March 2004, prior to the Madrid bombings and the PP's general election defeat, it emerged that the European Commission was looking into a property deal reported to have netted Real Madrid 480 million euros.

The club's sale of large chunks of the old *Ciudad Deportiva* in 2001 had wiped out its debts and enabled it to buy world-class players like David Beckham and to start building a new training ground on the outskirts of Madrid near the airport. The first stone, with a commemorative urn containing shirts, boots and other club mementoes, was laid in May 2004 by Perez despite pending legal challenges over this and other developments linked to land owned or sold by the club. Those blessing the much publicized ceremony with their presence included Alfredo Di Stefano, Raúl and the PP leaders of the Madrid city and regional governments.

Perez made transparency a key theme of his election campaign in 2000 after the murky years of Mendoza and Sanz, promising to keep his business as a construction magnate separate from his presidency of Real Madrid. It is difficult to separate his election for his first term from the image he built up around himself as an honest, successful businessman, and his ability to make friends across the political and social divide. Once elected there is no doubt that being president of Real Madrid helped raise his profile even higher, increasing his global projection. 'I am the president of ACS which is a very important Spanish company,' he told the *Financial Times* in an interview in July 2003, 'but no one greets me because I am president of ACS. Everyone asks me for my autograph because I am president of Real Madrid.'

A few days before the interview, and much to Perez's chagrin as he was visiting London at the time, the *FT*'s widely respected 'Lex' column of financial analysis published a critical comment on the merger between ACS and Dragados, after ACS had begun by acquiring a dominant stake in Dragados from the Spanish bank Santander Central Hispano. Describing Spanish takeover rules as 'riddled with holes and Spanish boards still far from devoted to the interests of all their shareholders', the unsigned comment made clear its view that it regarded the terms of the transaction unfair. The problem lay not in ACS's tactics but in the laxity of Spanish takeover rules.

In fact the merger was the subject of one legal action by shareholders that was settled without publicity. The accepted Spanish practice which the columnist criticized was summarized thus: 'Pay cash for a stake big enough to exert de facto control over your target, but small enough to convince a complaisant regulator that you do not in fact possess this control; then merge your own company, complete with the debt incurred to buy your initial stake, into your target on far less favourable terms.' Some of the original shareholders in Dragados were not best pleased with ACS's tactics, but then, as the *FT* also pointed out, it was not an untested strategy and one against which professional investors could have no excuse for failing to take evasive action.

11. The Ballad of David Beckham Continued . . .

Whatever he may have done or had yet to achieve, on the night of 26 November 2003 David Beckham confirmed a special place for himself among the myths and legends of Real Madrid's history. In the 35th minute of Real Madrid's Championship League group match against Olympique Marseille, Beckham took one of his trademark free-kicks, bending it over the wall and into the net. It was his first for the Spanish team in a competitive European game, and the club's six hundredth goal in the European Cup – the one hundredth was scored by Alfredo Di Stefano.

But there was more to come in the second half after the French team had equalized. Beckham set up the second goal when he recovered a ball in defence, and passed it long and with knife-edge accuracy to Figo. The Portuguese international dribbled, and then passed diagonally to Raúl, who combined in a series of one-twos with Zidane before finding Ronaldo for the Brazilian to tap effortlessly home. The configuration of sublime individual skills across the length and breadth of the Velodrome was celebrated the next day by *Marca* with a graphic design of the move as a series of shooting stars – a galaxy designed by Florentino Perez not only to win, but to win with spectacular style.

There was general agreement among Spanish commentators: that Beckham was the man of the match showed Real Madrid to be a team that had begun to fall short of the expectations invested in it at the start of the season – an impression which had been building up since the team had been unceremoniously thrashed in a league match at Seville earlier in the month and then held to a 1–1 draw by Osasuna. Despite occasional touches of brilliance, the *galacticos* seemed to lack consistency.

Questions had intensified about Real Madrid's weakness at the back. With the exception of the talented goalkeeper Iker Casillas, the young defenders from the club's youth team struggled to prove themselves worthy successors to Fernando Hierro, Real Madrid's former captain who had left the club after an internal disciplinary row at the end of the previous season. Also missed was Claude Makelele, the experienced French international who had transferred to Chelsea in the summer. And yet it was the need to cover gaps in Real Madrid's first-team line-up that gradually transformed Beckham's role in midfield. He had to shoulder the burden not only of trying to maximize the potential of the star players, but also of covering up for the shortcomings of the others.

In the build-up to the Marseille game, Spanish media attention had been focused on the hopes generated by Zidane returning to the city of his childhood, for the first time in a Real Madrid shirt. But in the match's aftermath the editor of the sports newspaper *As* Alfredo Relaño was left meditating instead on the secret of Beckham's success as a player – his ability from an early age to meet whatever challenge was put before him, and to deliver. 'What a piece of Englishman,' editorialized Relaño in reference to the hard work Beckham put into helping create moves, and the equal tenacity with which he withstood some brutal tackling by the French team. It was one of Beckham's best performances since he electrified the Bernabéu with his first *La Liga* goal after just 126 seconds of the game against Real Betis, marshalling central midfield and combining his passes with an aggression that connected him with Real Madrid's demanding fans.

Beckham had also proved himself in other matches during the first half of the season as a player who had come to Spain to do more than simply sell shirts, as when towards the end of September he scored his second goal of the season from another free-kick, helping his side beat Málaga 3–1. *Marca* summed up a growing collective sentiment when one of its more critical columnists Julian Ruiz dedicated his column to the player under the title 'The law of David Beckham'. Ruiz claimed to feel humbled by the paradox in Beckham – one of the world's biggest celebrities who when it came to playing football was the 'true worker, the proletarian of the ball but with touches of genius which make him even greater'.

A few days after the Marseille game, on 1 December 2003, I was at the *Marca* offices, trying to gauge Beckham's feelings about playing football with Real Madrid and living in Spain. This was his first visit to a Spanish newspaper since arriving in the capital. *Marca* had come a long way since its early Francoist origins during the Civil War. It had kept in step with the wider political and social changes of the country over the years, through changes of ownership that maintained its unique status as the country's biggest-selling newspaper, an all-sports tabloid that boasted unique access to the power brokers of Spanish football – not least Real Madrid.

Since the start of the season I had followed Beckham and Real Madrid around Spain. I had not been surprised by the fact that moving to a new country had not made Beckham any more literate or expressive than he'd been as a Manchester United player; his comments to the press after training or after matches focused on the basics of the game amid many umms and errs. But the visit to *Marca* was not just another interview, it was a social and a political event, a gesture of engagement with Real Madrid and its fans.

Beckham was accompanied by two minders. One was Xavier García Coll, a former Real Madrid basketball player whose affable manner, experience in working in the club's marketing department and command of English had led to his appointment as the club's main liaison officer with its latest star purchase. The other was Terry Byrne, a former director of football at Watford and masseur with the England squad, a close friend of Beckham, who had arrived in Spain halfway through the season as a personal manager to help the player with his dealings with the media and advertisers. In 1998 it was Byme who ran out from the England bench and put a comforting arm round Beckham's shoulder after he was shown the red card in the World Cup match against Argentina. A year later it was Byrne who had once again offered much-needed moral support to both David and Victoria during the scare surrounding an alleged plot to kidnap their son Brooklyn.

But Byrne's previous experience of shouldering Beckham crises was destined to be dwarfed by the challenge of helping handle his friend's problems in Spain. Most people would find that keeping a handle on the life of a superstar like David Beckham might be more difficult than looking after all the players of a thirty-man football squad. Byrne arrived not speaking Spanish and was unfamiliar with life as lived by ordinary *Madrileños*, as well as the intricate politics of Real Madrid. In this sense, in the latter stages of Beckham's first season with Real Madrid, Byrne seemed poorly equipped to help control or contain the troubled waters in which his friend and client found himself immersed.

The murmurings earlier in the autumn in the British tabloid press, that Beckham's life in Spain was becoming complicated because of his wife Victoria's alleged refusal to spend more time in the country, had barely dented the player's popularity in Spain. Not only had sales of Real Madrid's all-white kit continued to do well with Beckham's number 23 a clear favourite, but the Bernabéu stadium remained packed for every game, and TV viewers turned in around the world to watch the club's games. Sky TV's promotion for the UK market of its *La Liga* coverage drew on an image of a white-shirted Beckham in a celebratory goalscoring twirl against the background of flamenco guitar music and castanets. In Spain Beckham was widely regarded by the club's fans as someone who 'sweated the shirt' on the field. But his popularity was sustained by the fact that Real Madrid were winning games – and that had as much to do with the contribution made by other players as Beckham.

Ronaldo could spend long periods of a match doing very little, then suddenly break from his marker, and with perfect control, power and acceleration cut through the opposing defence before scoring. The potency of Real Madrid's attack was reinforced by Figo with his extraordinary dribbling and crossing skills, and Roberto Carlos, a defender with a disarming ability to move with lightning speed onto the offensive. Then there was Zidane, who despite his heavy build was capable on a good day of producing elegant, visionary and seemingly effortless play of a magical quality. Of the team's main stars, only Raúl, the captain, saw his form dip early on in the season. He had lost some of his sharpness in front of goal and his character as a fighter for the ball, and his iconic status as the player who represented the spirit of the club seemed to diminish somewhat in Beckham's presence.

Real Madrid had cruised through the group stage of the Champions League and were riding high in the domestic championship, even if they were struggling a bit to overcome small clubs in the King's Cup. Of all the Real Madrid players, it was Beckham whose form seemed to be the most consistently good, and he had scored goals – two in the Champions League and three in *La Liga*.

At *Marca* a line of senior executives, editors, journalists and blushing PAs lined up to greet Beckham as he sauntered in, the general air of formality mixed with sheepish deference greeted with a smile by the player dressed in baseball cap, jeans and heavy knitted sweater. The entrance to the newspaper's offices was lined with photographs of every major player who had ever played in Spain, the pick of the best from world football, from Di Stefano to Maradona. Whether or not a star played for Real Madrid, all of Spain's big signings had paid a visit to *Marca* over the years, a necessary rite of passage for anyone who wanted to be taken seriously by a potential readership of over a million. To judge by his reception that day, Beckham had already served out his probation period with Real Madrid, and emerged a conquering hero.

Like an ambassador bearing gifts, *Marca*'s editor offered Beckham poster-sized blow-ups of the front pages he had dominated since his summer signing. There were quite a few of them, featuring photographs of Beckham scoring or celebrating goals, locked in embraces with the likes of Ronaldo,

Figo, Roberto Carlos, Raúl and Zidane. These images reflected Beckham's success at the highest level of world football.

A Spanish photographer who followed all Real Madrid games had told me how impressed he was with the way that Beckham always seemed to know the best pose to strike in front of the cameras when on the pitch. And yet there was little trace of narcissism as Beckham looked at the photographs with something of the air of a teenager caught photographed in her first bikini, restrained in his enthusiasm, almost embarrassed by the attention he was generating.

Beckham had been doing this for over ten years at least. 'Beckham's a class product of the Ferguson school: strutting confidence and flair on the pitch, charmingly bashful off it. A PR man's dream,' wrote Kate Buchanan in a profile in *FourFourTwo* magazine published in December 1996. And yet here we were in Madrid in December 2003 and Beckham seemed to those around him as fresh and with as much yet to prove as he had then. He gave the impression that he was genuinely still a little star-struck as a player. Since childhood, during his youth and in his early adult years, Beckham had told anyone who would listen that his dream had always been to play for Manchester United, the club he idolized, with the players he'd always admired. But once he had achieved that dream, another had come along, that of playing in a club that in footballing terms had achieved much more than Manchester United, with the biggest players in the world, national and international supremos, admired by a global audience. Real Madrid had offered Beckham a new role and a new meaning to his life as a player.

'Since I've come to Real Madrid I've been given the chance to play in the centre role and I've been playing some great football with a lot of great players around me,' he told us – not cockily, but as a matter of simple fact.

In his early days at the club Beckham had been given this new position not as a result of a predetermined strategy but by default – Figo had refused to relinquish his role on the right wing. Beckham insisted that he had always preferred playing in the middle, and it was the friendships he had struck up with the other Real Madrid players that had given him the confidence to play there. The words 'amazing', 'phenomenal' and 'great' had always been high in the Beckham vocabulary, so it was perhaps only to be expected that his favourite words should be applied to the firmament he had joined – Ronaldo 'phenomenal', Zidane 'phenomenal and amazing' and Raúl 'a great player and a great person'.

'I get on very well with Ronaldo and Roberto Carlos. They've really welcomed me. People have said from the moment I arrived in Spain that Raúl and I don't talk to each other but I don't know where those stories come from – I've always got on with Raúl as a person on and off the pitch and I think he is an amazing player.'

After the poster presentation Beckham signed some autographs before drawing a marker, with Terry Byrne's advice, as to what he was not prepared to do. He refused to pose with a *botijo*, the traditional earthenware jar from which old Spain used to drink its water or wine. He had also withheld his signature from an unauthorized DVD *Marca* had produced of Beckham's life as a player. Of all the footballers *Marca* had played host to in the past, few seemed so consciously in control of their image and its consumption.

During the interview Beckham fielded questions from various directions, but mostly from Hugo Brassey, a keen young trainee journalist whose background had given him the self-assurance to try and expose areas of ignorance in the world's most venerated sportsman. Educated at Eton, Brassey was an old school friend of Prince William who seemed unfazed by celebrity status. He was covering Beckham's year in Spain during his gap year at a British university.

After Beckham had praised his Real Madrid colleagues and expressed his satisfaction with his new life at Real Madrid, Brassey turned to the subject of Spanish culture. Beckham officially had been taking Spanish lessons. Unofficially he had picked up a few words and phrases from his team colleagues. No one in Spain had heard him utter more than a phrase, and a majority of Spaniards claimed to have seen him mouth it on national TV during a fracas with an opponent. '*Hijo de puta*,' he was clearly saying. So what kind of words had Beckham really learnt? Brassey asked.

Beckham laughed – something he often seemed to do to deflect attention from the insubstantial nature of his answer. 'I can't really say what I've learnt,' he answered. And the first swear word learnt? 'I can't remember.' You can't remember? He laughed again. 'No, I'm not going to say.'

Not much of a surprise there, I thought to myself. Nor in the fact, as he told Brassey, that the last book he'd read was not *Don Quixote* but his wife Victoria's autobiography, published two years earlier. But his smile rarely slipped; never once did he try and cut short the interview, or ask for sustenance. Only at one point did I feel the boy from Chingford struggling to restrain himself from telling the future King of England's toff friend where to get off. It was when Brassey asked him whether he knew who the president of FC Barcelona was.

Otherwise the 'full-on charm and modesty' which had struck Karen Buchanan as seemingly natural back in 1996, was still there – it had become part of Beckham, weathering as he had much more successfully than many others the pressures of fame and stardom which had multiplied several fold in the intervening seven years. His most revealing comment in an interview memorable only for its diplomacy and total lack of substance was that he had discovered a liking for Spanish cured ham, *jamón serrano*. Beckham claimed to like it as much as fish and chips. When Fabio Capello began his short stint as Real Madrid coach in 1996, he told his players that Spanish ham was unhealthy and ordered them to cut it from their diet. Only later did he come round to admiring its medicinal properties, becoming a net importer when he returned to Italy. Clearly times were changing in the world's most famous football club, as were the taste buds of one of the world's most famous players.

The *Marca* interview formed part of a calculated blitz of the Spanish media aimed at dispelling any doubts that the player was happy in his new adopted country, on and off the pitch. It came in a week when Beckham's visit to Buckingham Palace to collect his OBE provided an opportunity to establish the player in the collective Spanish mind as a cut above the average Englishman in more ways than one. Beckham was honoured by the Queen for his services as an ambassador for his country, not just as England captain but as a citizen whose behaviour as a devoted family man and mental sobriety – little booze and no drugs – had more than made up for his humiliating red card in the 1998 World Cup.

No matter that Beckham was being honoured as an

English patriot not a Spanish one, Spaniards were happy to see him as a striking contrast to the beer-swigging, loutish behaviour of the football hooligan, or the more unruly tourists that descended on the Costa del Sol, Mallorca and the Canaries every holiday season.

Earlier that year the seamier side of the English in Spain had surfaced with the arrest of an expatriate owner of a pub near Marbella, the prime suspect of an allegedly alcohol-induced assault and murder of at least one Spanish teenager. Now from their headquarters in the Spanish capital, sports newspapers like *Marca* and *As*, with a commanding readership among Real Madrid supporters, barely hesitated in renaming Beckham's OBE the *Cruz de Caballero* – the Cross of the Gentleman, an allusion to the mystical chivalrous values which the club had always identified as integral to its identity. The image combined perfectly with that of Beckham holding up his new Real Madrid shirt for the first time and uttering the one Spanish phrase he had learnt before all others – '*Hala Madrid*', the club's traditional rallying cry.

Behind the carefully stage-managed choreography of Beckham's photo-opportunities and media appearances, the player remained circumspect in his public utterances and selective in the more extended interviews he gave just as he had done at Manchester United. The reality of his season in Spain was already falling short of the idyll that the club, and his publicists, wanted us all to believe Beckham was living. On arriving in Spain he had said that all he wanted to do was play football, but David Beckham had long ago become more than just a footballer.

Writing in the *Observer* in the spring of 2002, Simon Kuper analysed why Real Madrid attracted Europe's finest. Kuper's premise seemed perfectly valid at the time – that at the start of a new century, great footballers had a choice between a limited number of European clubs. 'A few of the greats, such as David Beckham and Ryan Giggs at Manchester United or Oliver Kahn and Stefan Effenberg at Bayern Munich, have emotional and linguistic ties to one club in particular. For all the others, there is currently only one choice: Real Madrid.' The reason, Kuper argued, was partly an existentialist one – it had to do with place and people. Thus England was not just too rainy; it was also – when it came to London – expensive. Italian football was regimented and no longer as good as it once had been. Furthermore, 'footballers in Italy live under virtual house arrest, because when they go out people tend to behave as if they have just seen an apparition of the Virgin Mary.' As for Barcelona, 'great place, shame the club is such a mess'. So that left Madrid, a city where 'you can sit outside at night eating tapas, even if you are a footballer' and reflect that 'you are playing for the best club in football history.'

Within minutes of Beckham arriving in Spain for the formal signing, he, his wife and their elder son Brooklyn were under siege, at the first hotel picked by Real Madrid for them to stay overnight, the Tryp Fenix. Security broke down as photographers and camera crews gave chase. A *Marca* employee posed as an English tourist and got as far as the Beckhams' room. The intrusion of the couple's privacy, which the newspaper justified in the public interest, was in striking contrast to the paper's policy of not reporting on the private lives of other Real Madrid players like Ronaldo whose womanizing and other night-life exploits were notorious. Subsequently the Spanish sports press reverted to long-established practice, holding back from publishing some of the rumours about Beckham's private life which reached it from its sources inside Real Madrid before they surfaced in the British tabloid media.

It was with the intention of making the Beckhams' introduction to Spain more comfortable and settled that Real Madrid President Florentino Perez recommended the couple's move to the more sophisticated and exclusive Hotel Santo Mauro over the summer. The Santo Mauro was a converted palace which had belonged to one of Madrid's leading aristocratic families. It had been bought by AC, one of Spain's most enterprising hotel chains. AC were the initials of the company's founder and owner Antonio Catalan, a member of the generation of innovative post-war Spanish entrepreneurs, who treated the Real Madrid of Florentino Perez as a valued customer. 'Perez is one of the cleverest individuals in Spain, with clear ideas and a strong personality, who personifies the development of the Spanish business class, those who have created an enterprise starting from scratch – in other words self-made men,' Catalan told me.

Among the hotels Catalan owned around southern Europe when Beckham came to Spain, it was the Santo Mauro that prided itself most in its discretion and its ability to tailor its personal service to the individual client's needs. Its past guest list included Hollywood stars, rock stars, spies and Bill Gates. It was one of three AC hotels used by Real Madrid players in Spain. Figo had stayed there when he had first moved to the capital from Barcelona. So had Zidane after he was bought from Juventus.

The Beckhams had the use of several bedrooms to accommodate visits by family and friends. For much of their stay they were free to wander around the hotel's comfortable dining and sitting rooms or lounge in the gardens. They also had a lift which linked the underground garage directly to their quarters without having to go through reception. They often chose to do just that. 'It is a great pleasure to have the opportunity to have you in a hotel that always attempts to exceed your expectations . . . the comfort and the modern luxury, the quality of designs and materials . . . the daily attention to detail,' said a promotional pamphlet left in the Beckhams' bedroom. But no amount of PR could recreate the privacy and contentment of the mansion home the Beckhams owned in Staffordshire.

The Beckhams did not have the hotel to themselves and other guests who stayed there could not help but observe and listen when Victoria ventured into the restaurant or the garden with her children. Not long after the Beckhams had booked in, the hotel guest list included a team of senior British judges who, accompanied by their wives, stayed at the Santo Mauro while attending a joint conference with their Spanish counterparts on the future of the judiciary. It was a strange comedy of manners with the judges living under the same roof and finding it difficult not to take note of the comings and goings of one of the world's most famous celebrity couples in their midst. They were struck by Victoria's brashness and apparent difficulty in coming to terms with life in Madrid.

Hotel staff had to put up with Victoria insisting on having the gym cleared of other guests whenever she used it and on the hotel cook helping her maintain an occasional diet of well-boiled fish and pineapple. One of David's few complaints was that the hotel didn't have a TV system that allowed him to watch the Premier League. 'When Beckham was alone in the hotel, things were more relaxed than when Victoria was around . . . We had to look after her much more . . . I suppose it had to do with her being well known in England whereas in Spain everyone seemed interested only in him. They [Spaniards] didn't take much notice of her,' recalled Catalan.

Beckham was without Victoria in the hotel quite a lot in fact. She was away in London and New York preparing the release of her new album. Unlike her husband, she found it hard to engage with Spanish people. As her autobiography reflects, Victoria for all her globe-trotting as a celebrity was quintessentially provincial – English home counties – never quite at ease with foreign ways. Spaniards may have become more European in recent years, but they hadn't turned English. They found it difficult to understand her sense of humour, often produced by an inherent insensitivity to the world outside her own, which they took for aloofness if not downright rudeness. Examples included her widely reported statement that Madrid 'smelt of garlic' and her equally tongue-in-cheek pledge that she planned to throw one of the biggest New Year's Eve parties the capital had ever seen. In fact in the months following David's signing for Real Madrid, Victoria made few friends in Madrid. Despite an early appearance at a fashion evening sponsored by the Spanish version of *Marie Claire* magazine, and a much publicized visit to some of Madrid's most expensive clothes shops along the Calle Serrano, she seemed to lack the enthusiasm she showed on her shopping sprees in London, Milan and New York. For their part, Madrid's fashion editors did not rate her either in beauty or style in comparison with other local models who regularly filled the pages of their magazines.

The Madrid celebrity circuit was a mixed bunch of cultural posers, some of whom longed to seduce Beckham into their circle – preferably on his own. Bullfighters, hard-up aristocrats, second-rate Spanish actresses and singers of dubious credentials or quality had long monopolized the pages of Spain's *prensa rosa*, or glossy celebrity magazines, along with 'tell-all' celebrity TV programmes. There were also the intellectuals – writers, painters, and film makers – who populated the cultural pages of the Spanish broadsheets and weren't much interested in football. Neither world went overboard in opening its doors to the Beckhams. Among the celebrity encounters that drew the attention of the Spanish paparazzi was when the Beckhams set off from the Santo Mauro to have dinner with Isabel Preysler, former wife of Julio Iglesias, and her pop star son Enrique. According to Victoria, Beckham seemed rather taken with the jeans and T-shirt Enrique was wearing. The fact that Julio once played for Real Madrid as a goalkeeper did not seem to register that night.

Victoria did make an effort to turn up periodically at the Santiago Bernabéu when her husband was playing, but she missed his first game for Real Madrid. She had never pretended to be a huge football fan, nor had she ever wanted to be simply a footballer's wife. At Real Madrid the players' women seemed to fall roughly into two categories – dutiful housewives or publicity-seeking lovers. Figo and Raul had married models, neither of whom said very much in public but had long-established if discreet professional relationships with respectable Spanish fashion magazines. Zidane led the most discreet family life of all the players. Ronaldo and Roberto Carlos, both separated from their wives, made no secret of the fact that they liked to party. Ronaldo's ex-wife, the blonde, beautiful and charming Milene Domingues, stayed in Spain playing women's football and working as a sports commentator for the Madrid TV station TeleMadrid.

Victoria not only felt there was nothing professionally drawing her to Spain, she also had nothing in common with any of the Real Madrid players' wives – the way she looked, talked and acted. Her image was that of dedicated lover to Beckham and mother to his children but also very much a woman with firm views of her own, and not shy of expressing them. Perhaps it was hardly surprising, given the lingering male chauvinism that existed in Spanish football, that 'posh' was translated by Victoria's *Madrileño* detractors literally into the word '*pija*', a great deal more derogatory than the English when spoken in Spanish.

If Victoria failed to engage with Spain, it was not for want of trying on Real Madrid's behalf. Soon after Beckham had joined the club, Florentino Perez personally rang the headmaster of Runnymede College, a privately run English school in Madrid, which the Beckhams had shown an interest in, and made an offer he knew would be difficult to refuse. He told the headmaster that if he agreed to put Brooklyn Beckham at the head of the long waiting list that autumn term, Real Madrid would provide the school with sports kit and a football training ground. Brooklyn was duly registered. However, the promised delivery of Real Madrid merchandising and the construction of the school's first decent sports facility did not materialize because Victoria insisted that Brooklyn continue his schooling in the UK, a decision that some senior officials at Real Madrid believed did not bode well for the stability of the Beckham family life.

Finding a house in Madrid proved as complicated as finding a school. The fact that some of the capital's best houses were owned by survivors of the Spanish aristocracy, as they had been for much of the twentieth century, fuelled the inherent snobbism of some of their caste, as they haggled over terms and prices with Victoria who found Madrid property prices far higher than she had imagined. Unlike most *Madrileños* she could afford it, and they knew it. Eventually the Beckhams rented a spacious and secluded house belonging to a celebrity local TV journalist. Set in woodland and surrounded by a perimeter wall and security gates, it offered the couple better protection from unwelcome intruders.

Just over a month into David Beckham's first season with Real Madrid, the difficulties he and Victoria were finding in settling as a couple in Spain began to leak to the British tabloid press for the first time. The charge was led by the *Daily Mail* in its issue of 20 September 2003 with a full-page exposé detailing some of the tension which they said had been noticed inadvertently by fellow guests staying at the Santo Mauro a week earlier. 'Victoria was having what you can only call a hissy fit,' said one witness. 'She was waving her arms about insisting she couldn't have anything done in "this damn country".' Her alleged outbursts in the hotel had been reported to the newspaper.

There was a reference to the Beckhams' one-year-old son Romeo falling and cutting his head while out shopping with David's mother Sandra in the Corte Inglés, Madrid's

big department store. Although a minor accident, it had allegedly come to assume symbolic proportions with Victoria,
who had confided in a friend her belief that it could never
have happened in London – in other words, the instinctive
reaction of every English tourist in a foreign land.

The theme was picked up more sensationally the next day
by the *News of the World*, with the front-page headline 'Posh
& Becks in Marriage Crisis.' 'Friends' of the couple, the
newspaper reported, had said that 'Becks was fed up Posh is
not with him more as he makes his new life in Spain . . .
while Becks wows the fans at new club Real Madrid, Posh is
resisting moving to Spain to join him full time.' The *Daily
Express* reported that the couple had spent only '33 of the
last 83 days [in Madrid] together', while Sue Carroll writing
in the *Daily Mirror* claimed to share a popular anxiety about
Britain's most famous celebrity couple. 'Spain is full of *señor-
itas* happy to climb over the Duchess of Dolce & Gabbana
to get to Beckham . . . Victoria needs to get over herself.
More importantly she needs to get over there – permanently.
Before she scores the most spectacular own goal of the
season.'

The *Daily Mail* underlined the perception of Madrid as a
city of temptation when it reported that Beckham had stayed
out late three times in a week. One occasion had involved
attending the twenty-ninth birthday party given by Ronaldo,
Real Madrid's most hedonistic player. On another evening –
after the Beckhams had issued a statement denying that their
marriage was in any crisis – the Englishman and some of his
team mates went to a night club and stayed there into the
early hours of the morning. But predictably it was Ronaldo's
party that sent the Madrid rumour mill into a temporary spin.

The capital's TeleMadrid channel had fuelled the fires by running a programme comparing Victoria with one of Ronaldo's better-looking guests – Esther Canadas, the stunning twenty-six-year-old Spanish fashion model who had starred with Pierce Brosnan in *The Thomas Crown Affair* and had been romantically linked in the past to several celebrities. Canadas spoke English and at one point was spotted talking to Beckham. The programme hinted that she and David Beckham had struck up a relationship, a suggestion that sparked an angry denial by one of the couple's spokespeople and a rather more belated rebuttal by the model/actress.

There was certainly no shortage of Spanish women who seemed quite prepared to further their own celebrity status by having themselves linked by the media in some way with Beckham. They were to be found at the lower end of the *prensa rosa* and what had becoming an increasingly popular aspect of Spanish cultural life at the turn of a new century, the *TV rosa* – TV programmes based on a mix of nudity, swear words and general scandalous self-promotion by second-rate actresses and financially embarrassed public personalities. Few individuals straddled the *rosa* medium more aggressively than Nuria Bermudez, a twenty-three-year-old whose renown lay in her claim that she had slept with half the Real Madrid squad; now she vowed she would do the same with Beckham. It never got further than a publicity stunt. Nuria posed outside the Santo Mauro looking suitably predatory in photographs that were reportedly touted for £80,000.

A more serious allegation about Beckham in Spain involved Rebecca Loos, who was hired by the player's agency SFX when he came to Madrid. Loos, the daughter of Anglo-

Dutch parents, had been educated at Runnymede College in Madrid. She had a good command of languages and a young person's enthusiasm for Madrid's night life. She had first worked for SFX in London liaising with clients in the world of professional tennis. When she heard that David Beckham was moving to Madrid, she jumped at what she considered the job of a lifetime and approached SFX to be rehired in Spain.

'Rebecca was ambitious from an early age, a really determined girl who really wanted to go for it,' recalled one of her Madrid school colleagues. But her experience did not extend to delicate handling of Beckham's public image. On 18 September she was photographed having an intimate drink with him in one of a small group of Madrid night spots frequented by Real Madrid players. Victoria was reportedly livid when she saw the photograph and the accompanying tabloid story published ten days later describing the unnamed Rebecca initially simply as a 'mystery brunette'.

In separate interviews before the publication of the first compromising photograph of Beckham and Loos, the Beckhams complained of excessive media intrusion. They had done that for years but few tabloid offensives had been as sustained in suggesting that their marriage was under threat. That the Beckhams not only survived the initial tabloid onslaught in the autumn of 2003, but came back fighting, seemed to underline their resilience as a couple, as well as their ability to manipulate the media and spin stories when their image was under threat or needed positive promotion.

At the Santo Mauro the Beckhams' departures from the hotel individually or as a couple usually involved back-door escapes, decoys and accelerated dashes across Madrid, with the more relentless paparazzi giving chase. Yet it was not always like this. On one occasion the Beckhams drove out slowly and deliberately in their newly imported Aston Martin, sun-roof drawn back, smiles aplenty for the waiting media to snap away at their leisure – a perfectly controlled photo-op of the celebrity couple which no doubt did the sales of Aston Martin no harm either.

After the tabloids went on the attack over the pressures of living in Spain, a defiant Victoria demonstrated just how seriously she took media attention. The manner of her counter-offensive suggested she had lost none of the 'drive, commitment and perfectionist personality' identified by Andrew Morton as the keys to her success as a celebrity. She appeared at London's British Style Awards to pick up the Most Stylish Female prize. Victoria looked her best – extended hair tumbling over her bare back, the revealing crimson dress by Spain's Hanibal Laguna, pure designer *Carmen*, a teasing caricature of the Spanish femme fatale allegedly bent on seducing her husband, with a lot of style and more than a hint of Posh's trademark irreverent humour. 'David's not getting the award for being best-dressed but he's the best at undressing me . . . David I love you,' she told her audience after greeting it in Spanish. Later, just in case the message was not heard loud and clear, she told fashion journalists, 'I love this dress – I bought it in Madrid which has some fantastic designer shops. I just love being there. I really love it.'

This was not the impression she had given off earlier in the week in Madrid when she'd attended another fashion outing. The local press coverage of her appearance as guest of honour at the Spanish *Elle* magazine's style awards to pick up the International Woman prize underlined the difficulty *Madrileños* had in finding anything positive to say about her. *El Mundo* published an open letter entitled 'To Vicky who doesn't smile.' Describing her as the 'most badly behaved guest of the whole night', it said: 'You appeared late, you hardly spoke. Perhaps it was the smell of garlic – Spain is like that, I'm afraid . . . The only time you managed a smile was when you picked up your prize.' Other Spanish newspapers led by the conservative *ABC* criticized her surly mood.

The following week the Beckhams were together again in Madrid, on a widely leaked and perfectly choreographed outing designed to restore their image as a mutually loving and devoted couple. As related subsequently by the *Sun*, it began with a prolonged evening meal at the Ritz hotel's Goya restaurant, decorated with candles and orchids and serving some of the best food to be had in the Spanish capital. In a story headlined 'What a Cosy Couple', the Beckhams were portrayed as the perfectly romantic pair. 'They looked desperately in love. David had his arms around Victoria and she was leaning back into his chest. It was a beautiful scene,' ran the script. Readers were also given details of what the couple ate and drank. Medallions of veal, followed by roast lamb for David. Cold vegetable soup, lobster, and wild risotto for Victoria. It was all washed down with a bottle of Dom Perignon champagne.

The next day they were photographed sitting on a bench in the Plaza de Oriente, one of the capital's prettiest and most stately squares. It was there that *Madrileños* had once rallied in their thousands to hear Franco address them from the balcony of the royal palace. Nearby stood the Almudena cathedral, already chosen by the Spanish royal family for the wedding of Prince Felipe and Letizia Ortiz in May 2004. It is unlikely that the Beckhams had a conscious sense of Spanish history when they posed for the photographers. However, in this way the image of Britain's most famous celebrity couple was temporarily restored with the readership of Britain's biggest-selling tabloid.

The fact remained that Spaniards seemed rather less interested in the Beckhams as a couple than the British. If in Britain the Beckhams had fitted into a celebrity slot left vacant by the death of Princess Diana, their first weeks in Spain had coincided with the emergence of a Spanish royal story tailor-made for the production of reams of copy in the local media: the crown prince of Spain announced his engagement to an ambitious commoner, a TV presenter who seemed to personify the liberated Spanish woman. With her divorced background and lack of royal blood, Prince Felipe's bride-to-be Letizia Ortiz filled some of Madrid's more conservative aristocratic families with a sense of terrible foreboding. But the image that won through in the Spanish media was of a woman well suited to play her part as a member of a modern royal family in tune with its people. Moreover Letizia was attractive and fashion conscious. She knew how to look good in front of a camera and was well versed in the art of the interview. But most crucially she had the bulk of the Spanish media on her side thanks to the self-censorship about the royal family that was considered a necessary political trade-off. The royal family was seen as the guarantors of Spanish democracy, and whatever peccadilloes that lingered within it were considered best left unexposed. Only *El Mundo* broke the tacit pact between the media and the royal household by publishing a photograph of a painting which a partly nude Letizia had modelled for a Mexican artist, but the story did little damage to the collective popular enthusiasm about its latest royal wedding. Felipe and Letizia sold as a necessary good news story in the Spanish media, just as the king and queen did. It helped keep politics on an even keel, and boosted sales.

By contrast Victoria Beckham due to a mixture of design and circumstance could not be marketed in Spain as she continued to be in Britain and Japan. Neither her attempts to revive her pop career nor her interest in fashion were focused on Spain despite her token outings to fashion evenings and occasional appearances in Spanish magazines. That the most damaging story about David Beckham's alleged marital infidelity was pursued and first published in the *News of the World*, a paper that prior to the Real Madrid signing had enjoyed a working arrangement with the Beckhams – respectful coverage in return for exclusive interviews – suggested a possible loss of control not unconnected with the confusion surrounding the couple's representation.

The tabloids had gone on the offensive after Victoria had announced that she had appointed her agent Simon Fuller to help look after both her and her husband's image rights. Fuller had been instrumental in achieving the fame and fortune she had always craved, christening her 'Posh' when he became manager of the Spice Girls. The group never recovered from its decision to sack Fuller. With her own solo pop career faltering, Victoria had sought out Fuller again and he had agreed a reconciliation on the apparent understanding that this time he would represent the Beckhams as a couple.

The initial announcement that Fuller's management company '19' was taking over Victoria's representation took Tony Stephens of SFX, David Beckham's long-serving agent, by surprise. SFX's formal disengagement from David Beckham, after the player had decided to move into a business team with his wife, was only finally settled in December after protracted negotiations. It left SFX with a reported settlement of £2m and Beckham's career, including his endorsement deals, officially in the hands of his own company under the direction of Terry Byrne.

As Ellis Cashmore makes clear in his study of the Beckham phenomenon prior to the move to Spain, SFX's contribution to the player's global image since the mid- to late 1990s was considerable, perhaps even invaluable. Stephens helped position Beckham's image in the market 'precisely and strategically'. But the relationship flourished thanks to a number of factors that gelled during the 1990s, among them Manchester United's footballing success, its business strategy and the emergence of the Beckhams as a celebrity couple.

Stephens believed that it was the Beckham global image that he had helped promote which had driven Manchester United's multi-million-pound merchandising operation. But Beckham had signed a contract with Real Madrid that gave the club a half share of the player's image rights. There was clearly money still to be made in Asia and the US, but less certainty of Beckham maintaining his market value in Spain, where the player's future appeared to be rather more dependent on his and the club's success on the field than his celebrity status off it.

However much Florentino Perez wished to emulate Manchester United's business strategy, the fact remained that Real Madrid was not a PLC but a sporting institution, deeply embedded in the politics of Spain, and vulnerable to the volatility of its fans. Championship success, whether in Europe or in Spain, was not guaranteed, even if some Real Madrid fans and players, Beckham included, had come to believe that the *galácticos* were unbeatable. And while Spaniards cared rather more for David than Victoria, the strain on their marriage which the player's move to Spain helped provoke, was bound to threaten the ongoing viability of any marketing strategy based on the Beckhams as a couple.

Sensitivity to first suggestions in the British tabloid press that the Beckhams were no longer as perfectly compatible as had once been the case, led to them issuing a statement that 'we are extremely happy together as a family' and denying any suggestion that their marriage was on the rocks. At the same time the statement gave at least some credence to the uncomfortable realities that they were having to cope with, however strong their alleged marital bond.

Before 2003 was out Simon Fuller produced a TV documentary on the Beckhams in Spain in which Victoria was the dominant talking head. It showed her enthusiastically embracing promotional tours to the US and Asia while somewhat cynical about Spanish mores and culture as the couple went shopping in Madrid and moved from hotel to rented accommodation. Victoria also appeared on her friend Michael Parkinson's TV chat show. Unlike the cheekier Jonathan Ross who used his own TV interview with Victoria to mock her singing and apparent aspirations to be admired as an actress, 'Parky' was characteristically courteous, complicit even with his subject, putting to her the question she wanted to be asked in a way she could deal with. 'You're getting divorced, aren't you?' Parkinson asked in a tone that self-consciously resisted all seriousness.

'Apparently so! For someone who should be doom and gloom I'm very happy, which we are. I love David and the boys more than anything in the world. I think there are a lot of people who don't like that.'

The last time she had been interviewed by Parkinson, in September 2001, she had not appeared alone but with her husband. On that occasion Beckham is thought to have admitted nervously beforehand that he was worried that Parkinson might ask him questions with long words that he wouldn't understand. His subsequent performance drew mixed reviews. Perhaps because of the physical contrast between himself and another of Parkinson's guests – the burnt-out George Best – Beckham had one sports journalist describing him as 'very nice'. However, other viewers re-membered Beckham looking rather lost and holding onto his wife's hand throughout an interview in which he managed to say almost nothing of interest, seemingly only wishing to return as soon as possible to his natural domain – football – without fear of ridicule.

In his review of Beckham's autobiography for the *Observer*, Gordon Thomson drew a parallel between that TV appear-ance in September 2001 and the time of Beckham's arrival in Spain. Thomson noticed that Beckham was nervous and somewhat uneasy during the signing ceremony and his first press conference. Days later Beckham was the first of the Real Madrid players to turn up for a training session, but had hung back in the car park until Zidane and Ronaldo had turned up so that no one would think of him as a 'big-time Charlie'. 'Endearingly, Beckham seems to strive for anonymity, even if he has stopped believing that he might ever find it again,' wrote Thomson.

Few early *La Liga* encounters of the season courted as much public interest as Real Madrid's games in one week in December against first Atlético de Madrid at the Bernabéu and then FC Barcelona at the Nou Camp. That Beckham had chosen to do his first major round with the Spanish media in the run-up to both these vital matches showed, at the very least, that his advisers were well tuned to the industry and mythologies that drove the passions of Spanish fans.

Atlético had always claimed the allegiance of a part of the Spanish capital, even if it had never enjoyed the sustained links to political power or the international projection of Real, the club that had long ago arrogantly appropriated the shorthand of Madrid as their better-known title. Athletic Club de Madrid, as it was first known, was founded in 1903, a year after Real, its first teams drawn from a common pool of football enthusiasts in the capital, several of whom were Basque-born. Its first years were as an affiliate of Athletic de Bilbao with which it shared blue-and-white colours (later changed to red-and-white) and took the nickname '*colchoneros*' (the mattress men) because the striped colours were similar to the ticking used by a Basque company that specialized in mattresses. The club's attempts to forge an identity of its own in the shadow of Real were set back in the aftermath of the Spanish Civil War when on the verge of bankruptcy it was forced into a merger with the club run by the Spanish Air Force.

Renamed Atlético de Madrid, when Franco banned the use of foreign names by Spanish football clubs, it won four league championships during the forties and fifties – a record that some of its rivals put down to its links with the Spanish military even if many of its supporters came from the poor neighbourhoods of the capital. In later years Crown Prince Felipe became Atlético's President of Honour after his parents King Juan Carlos and Queen Sofia took him as a young boy to the club's Calderón stadium to watch a Madrid derby. Atlético in fact never benefited from the same organizational stability or patronage, political or royal, as Real, nor the same collection of silverware. But it had enjoyed enough triumphs over the years to sustain its rivalry in the capital. Real had always looked down on Atlético's inability to win a European Cup, its frustrated attempts at winning the league and cup double and periodic financial crises as confirmation of its more lowly status. At the same time a certain romanticism helped forge Atlético's collective ethos; faced with Real's triumphalism, the *colchonero* identity was defined as perseverance in the face of adversity, finding ways through with acts of faith. Atlético's was a curious tribal loyalty that had generally remained localized in the capital and passed down through generations, and which reflected, sometimes in microcosm, the idiosyncrasies of Spanish culture and society.

Few scandals in Spanish football were as widely publicized as that which embroiled Jesus Gil, the extrovert construction magnate and mayor of Marbella who became owner of Atlético in the late 1980s. Gil was prosecuted and convicted for fraud involved in financial transactions between his private businesses and the club. He dismissed the accusations as a conspiracy by envious political opponents and pursued a series of legal actions of his own, for libel, against those who had painted him as an uncompromising crook. Throughout the 1990s Gil counted on the support of Atlético fans who were grateful enough for the fleeting and unexpected triumphs he helped secure for them, even if his strategy of relentless hiring and firing of coaches generated more bad publicity outside the club than good. His death from a heart attack in May 2004 was hugely mourned by his club's fans.

After at last winning the league and cup double in 1996, Atlético saw its claim to being one of the Big Three of Spanish football challenged by the growing strength of clubs like Valencia and Deportivo La Coruña. But it was rarely out of the headlines, and did not lose its popularity. At the end of the century it found itself relegated to the second division, but the supporters stuck by the club, filling the stadium each home game and boosting season-ticket sales, their enthusiasm rekindled and eventually rewarded when Atlético was promoted back to the *Primera*, in time for the celebration of its centenary in 2003. 'The *colchoneros* remained faithful, like partners of a rock solid marriage, in sickness and in health, for richer for poorer . . . until death would part them,' wrote Carlos Levi, the club's official historian.

That the official history focuses on Gil's dedication to the club and his defiance of its critics and makes no mention of his political and financial shortcomings, shows the extent to which he had managed to continue to stamp his own personality on the club's identity. Despite the two years 'in hell', as the fans and the club's own promotional material referred to the time in the second division, Atlético had entered the 2003–04 season with a refuelled sense of optimism that it could get back into Europe. Its new coach Gregorio Manzano had a year earlier enhanced his track record as one of the most talented in Spain by winning the Spanish Cup while at Mallorca. The club also had an impressive assortment of players, two of whom in particular found themselves in the limelight as a historic rivalry between Madrid's two leading teams took on new life in the year that Beckham came to Spain.

The first, Fernando Torres, was one of the reasons why not all young *Madrileños* went weak at the knees at the sight of Real Madrid's latest *galáctico*. Eight years younger than Beckham, and as good looking, the Madrid-born Atlético striker was already well on his way to becoming something of a national icon, with the possibility of becoming one of the great players in the world. And he was much more than just a pretty face. '*El Niño*' ('the Kid'), as fans across the Spanish league affectionately called him, had emerged as one of the brightest of a new generation of Spanish players who had the skills, energy and projection to rival the superstar imports. His marketing pull was recognized by at least one multinational. The company that has contracts signed with the Spanish capital's two big clubs, dressed him as a gladiator and put him alongside Real Madrid players, all foreigners except for Raúl.

In the Spanish capital the excitement generated by Torres's play equalled that of an on-form Raúl and the best of the no-less legendary Emilio Butragueño, *El Buitre*, two players who had secured a local following partly because of their refusal to be bought out by any other club when they were reaching the peak of their careers. Torres also seemed to know something about loyalty having been one of the few members of the youth squad to have stuck it out at Atlético. In the promiscuous world of commercial football, where foreigners traded their skills like mercenaries, Torres seemed to belong to a seamless line of succession of Spanish players who maintained a sense of collective *Madrileño* pride in sweating and fighting for the colours they had worn through their passage into adulthood.

The encounter between two pop idols of the Spanish football scene, Torres and Beckham, was one theme that gave the Madrid derby an added frisson. The other was one that could not only be understood outside the context of Spanish football but which circumstances had dictated was now to be subjected to intense scrutiny on the playing fields of Spain. This was the renewed acquaintance between Beckham and Diego Simeone, an Englishman and an Argentine who together had unwittingly conspired to sustain the mythology of one of the stormiest football relationships in the history of the game.

The life of David Beckham, player and celebrity, could be divided into before and after the second minute of the second half of the 1998 World Cup second-round match between England and Argentina. It was at that precise moment in the Saint-Étienne stadium that Simeone clattered into Beckham's back and knocked him to the ground, before making as if to ruffle the Englishman's hair and giving it a tug. The prostrate Beckham reacted by swinging his right leg up at the Argentine, earning himself a red card. The aftermath, as they say, is history.

Beckham and Simeone next faced each other in Sapporo during the 2002 World Cup. This time Beckham shook hands with Simeone at half-time after using his right foot to score a penalty that secured England's victory over Argentina in the group-stage match. Thus was Beckham's restoration as a national hero confirmed just as it was clear, as David Dowding puts it in his history of Anglo-Argentine relations, that 'there was more than a little mileage left in a footballing feud which had already lasted half a century.' After that Simeone was transferred from Lazio to Atlético de Madrid, a club he had first played for during the early 1990s. The first derby of the *Primera Liga* in the 2003–04 season came weeks after Beckham had signed for Real Madrid. It meant that Simeone and Beckham faced each other at club level for the first time, in the Bernabéu.

The expectation generated around their encounter at one level defied rational analysis. Not only had Beckham played against Simeone since 1998 without incident, he had also, while at Manchester United, played with and befriended Juan Sebastian Verón, and had made it clear on countless occasions that he bore no grudge against any Argentine on or off the field. The very presence of Beckham and Simeone in opposing Spanish teams cut across national cultural boundaries and was a reminder of the globalization of football, as was the fact of the many foreigners – a lot of other Argentines among them – who played for Spanish clubs. And yet Beckham's presence in Spain meant the continuation by the popular media of a footballing feud that sprang from different cultural identities. As far as the Spaniards themselves were concerned, it sharpened the competitive edge of long-standing rivalries, fuelling what local fans described as the *morbo* or dark irrational obsessions of *La Liga*.

The British tabloids and Spanish sports media loved the 'Argie-bargy' that surfaced periodically during the season – the British because it rekindled a popular war, the Spanish because it showed Beckham had *cojones*. Indeed one of the more celebrated rows of the season involved Deportivo La Coruña's Lionel Scaloni accusing Beckham of 'touching his genitals' before offering to shake hands at the end of a Bernabéu clash, a few days before Christmas, which ended with the home team winning 2–1. Beckham's alleged gesture came after Scaloni had tangled with the England captain in the last minute, sparking a brawl involving several players. 'The referee told us to shake hands and, although Beckham offered his hand, it was a false offering. He made a gesture. He touched his genitals. Does that sound a nice gesture to you?' said a furious Scaloni after the match. Both Scaloni and Beckham were booked, but the two players continued to square up after the final whistle had been blown. As another of Deportivo's Argentine players Aldo Duscher showed solidarity with his fellow countryman, swearing at the Englishman in Spanish, Beckham cheekily smiled in their faces before turning his back and strutting away in the midst of a collective chorus of approval from the Real Madrid fans. It was the first time that Duscher and Beckham had met since the Champions League clash between Deportivo and Manchester United, the game in which Duscher broke Beckham's left foot, just weeks before the World Cup finals of 2002.

In the Madrid derby that December in 2003, it was the Brazilian Ronaldo who brought the Bernabéu to its feet, after taking on and beating not just one Argentine but two – first Simeone then Atlético's goalkeeper Burgos in the first fourteen seconds of the match. Real's victorious second goal was scored by Raúl from a pass by Beckham. It was one of those matches where the *galácticos* clicked with a harmonious display of individual skill, talent and execution. Only Torres showed real quality on the visiting side, frustrated by inadequate support and sheer bad luck in front of goal. As things turned out Simeone and Beckham rarely encountered each other on the ball. No matter. The media still singled out their 'duel' for special coverage, with *Marca* noting that Simeone's yellow card had restrained the Argentine's aggression, which probably gave Beckham the edge in this 'first round' between the two players. The expectation of *Madrileños* was of a conflict between symbols that had yet to draw blood.

A few days later Real Madrid travelled to the Nou Camp for the first of their two games of the season with FC Barcelona, a club that the politics of Spain had made its biggest rival. The phenomenon of this rivalry can only be understood in the context of Catalonia's perceived relationship with Castile, its aspirations as a regional power in an endless tug-of-war with the centralizing tendencies of Madrid, the potential of the city of Barcelona as one of the great capitals of the Mediterranean never fully realized. Real Madrid's identity was forged by triumphs, a sense of superiority that extended beyond Spain's borders. Catalonia existed as part of a Spain that had the Bernabéu as the diplomatic and operational headquarters of Spanish football. As for FC Barcelona, *Madridistas* had long maintained it was a club that used politics to divert attention from its own sporting failures, not least its inability to match Real's championship record at home and abroad. But for Barça the motivation came from a sense of persecution, an obsession with proving itself better than Real Madrid, whether by winning or simply by stopping Madrid from winning.

In the autumn of 2002 when Real Madrid had last travelled

to Barcelona, the presence of Luis Figo in white provoked such an uproar among the local fans that play was temporarily suspended. The missiles thrown at the Portuguese international every time he took a corner included a pig's head. Figo's transfer from FC Barcelona to Real Madrid after Florentino Perez had been elected president was viewed as the ultimate betrayal. The collective anger had a cathartic element about it. It helped transfer to the enemy the growing frustration Barça supporters felt with their president Joán Gaspart and manager Louis Van Gaal who they blamed for a deepening financial crisis and poor results. Both men were forced to resign before the season was over, paving the way for the election as president of Joán Laporta and the appointment of Frank Rijkaard as coach.

In the build-up to the FC Barcelona–Real Madrid match in December 2003, Laporta and Perez had adopted a publicly cordial attitude towards each other and held joint conferences against football violence. Both presidents had moved beyond the rhetoric and taken concrete measures to exclude violent fans from their respective stadiums. They shared the view that hooliganism was incompatible with their ambition to keep their stadiums filled with ordinary family members and to globalize the popularity of their respective clubs.

And yet an endemic tension and a whole industry of media coverage, TV rights and sponsorship still drove the rivalry between two football entities that considered themselves in cultural and sociological terms much more than simple clubs. Despite their public handshakes, Laporta and Perez were perceived by rival fans as opposing political figures. While Real Madrid fans looked at Laporta as a Catalan nationalist closely allied to the growing calls for greater autonomy, Perez was viewed by Barça fans as a man who, despite his business and political ties with Catalonia, was close to the ruling Partido Popular. Other divisions of a philosophical kind were rooted in history – a perception that Barça fans had of Real Madrid as a club that was simply driven by money and power but lacked a real soul.

The arrival of David Beckham in Spain had complicated this historic rivalry. Both clubs wanted him for the same reasons. They wanted him as a player and a celebrity. Beckham was the quintessential global icon who defied political allegiances and cultural identities. Having failed to get him, Laporta had settled for Ronaldinho, whose quality game and sheer delight in playing were destined to inspire a whole team and revive the Catalan club's fortunes. At the start of the season Real Madrid had contributed to the reputation it had among its Spanish rivals as the most arrogant club in the world when an unnamed member of Perez's inner circle – almost certainly a member of his marketing department – offered the following explanation for not signing the Brazilian: 'How ugly is Ronaldinho? There was no point in buying him, it wasn't worth it. He is so ugly that he'd sink you as a brand. Between Ronaldinho and Beckham, I'd go for Beckham a hundred times. Just look how handsome Beckham is, the class he has, the image. The whole of Asia has fallen in love with us because of Beckham.' During the latter stages of the season Barça fans came to believe that Ronaldinho was better than Beckham but as fate would have it Ronaldinho was unable to play in the Nou Camp that December through injury, leaving a mediocre FC Barcelona team vulnerable and exposed to whatever magic Perez's *galácticos* could conjure.

Twenty years had gone by since Real Madrid had last beaten Barça in a league match at the Nou Camp. That – along with the more recent memory of the two teams' last encounter in the stadium in April 2002 when the visitors had won in the semi-finals of the Champions League – provoked public interest in the match. Among the Madrid players, not just Figo but Ronaldo too had once played for the Catalan club and had something to prove – that stars like to play for the clubs that know how best to honour and respect their talent.

Beckham was stirred by his own memories of the Nou Camp. He had first come there as a young schoolboy, aged eleven. He had won a prize of a fortnight's training with FC Barcelona's youth team. Beckham would never forget his stay at the *Massia*, the college for the club's young hopefuls, next to the stadium. 'There were pennants and memorabilia on the walls, dating way back, alongside pictures of famous players from Barcelona's past. This was a place where legends were born.' The Nou Camp was also where Beckham had helped Manchester United to their victory over Bayern Munich in the 1999 Europen Cup final, before his relationship with Ferguson turned sour.

For me, it was a curious return to a stadium that I had grown to understand intimately from the perspective of its natural inhabitants when researching a book on the history of FC Barcelona. This time I came with the enemy, from the city of my birth to the city I had grown to love, in an effort more completely to understand one of world sport's greatest rivalries. I was in a party of some 150 Real Madrid supporters, boxed in by police high up in one of the upper tiers, surrounded by over 90,000 local fans. Unlike most of

European football, Spanish clubs have maintained their policy of strict segregation in the league championship by which only a small number of seats are allocated to the visiting club. To enter the Nou Camp as a Real Madrid fan thus marked you out as something of a fanatic.

Aznar was not with us – he only visited the Bernabéu stadium. But the outgoing Spanish prime minister had spent his last term in office defending the sacred unity of Spain, and provoking Basques and Catalans. Thus did the two sides of the political divide reflect and fuel each other's antagonism. Barça's renewed branding as the repository of local political and cultural identity under its new president Joán Laporta – as opposed to Real Madrid's renewed branding as Spain's major export under Florentino Perez – was underlined by the presence en masse in the presidential box of Catalan nationalist politicians, the singing of the Catalan national anthem '*Els Segadores*' and the waving of Catalan flags across the stadium.

Our little group of Madrid fans remained as defiant as Franco's soldiers in the siege of Toledo's Alcázar. They sang the Spanish national anthem and waved a solitary Spanish flag – the one with a bull and oversized testicles. '*España, España, España*' they chanted, before joining in at the end of the FC Barcelona song with the words, 'Barça, Barça, shit!' – not just shit, but the Spanish word for it, as diffuse as they could make it: '*Mieeeeeeeeeerda!*'

In the 37th minute David Beckham marked his first *gran clásico* in Spain with a perfect pass to Zinedine Zidane who in turn set up the first goal of the match – a thundering strike by Roberto Carlos which bounced off Barça's Dutch defender Michael Reiziger and beat the Portuguese goalkeeper Victor Valdes. The goal stunned a huge area of the Nou Camp into silence, except for where the name Roberto Carlos was sung cheekily to the tune of 'I love you baby' along with a familiar battle cry of victory – '*Reyes de Europa, somos los Reyes de Europa*' ('Kings of Europe, we are the Kings of Europe'). This small celebration was pointedly excluded from coverage by the local Catalan TV. But as one Real Madrid fan put it, 'Who cares? Here in the ghetto of the gods we are not only the best in the world but the closest to heaven.'

With Beckham constantly fighting for the ball and creating chances, it was left to Ronaldo in the 76th minute to drive home Real's second goal, enough to secure their long overdue victory at the Nou Camp. It was not the best performance by the *galácticos* but it was enough that Real Madrid's eternal rival had been beaten. It left Real fans with their sense of superiority intact. With Barça fans filtering out with heads bowed, some even tearful, one of the visitors phoned his father in Madrid and declared, 'I can report absolute silence in this city.' It was as if Barcelona had surrendered all over again to General Muñoz Grandes and a corporal called Santiago Bernabéu.

Later, as had become his habit whenever he played with Real Madrid, Beckham emerged from the changing room to be quoted and filmed by his waiting audience of local and foreign media. Clearly elated, he declared the match one of the biggest he had ever played in. 'The nice thing about coming back here was some of the memories . . . But I'm playing for a different team now. I'm with Real Madrid and beating Barcelona feels just as sweet.'

12. Bombing Madrid

When Beckham, aged twenty-eight, came to Spain in the summer of 2003, English fans who could not understand his abandonment of Manchester – one of Britain's most innovative towns with a football club to which Beckham had once pledged everlasting loyalty – may not have quite appreciated the nature of the country he was coming to or how much it had changed. Nor for that matter did the Beckhams.

Whatever Madrid was it was not as 'grey' as Di Stefano had described it in 1953, when the Argentine football star had arrived to play for Real Madrid, aged twenty-six. 'Of those years I remember being told by Bernabéu when I arrived that I wasn't allowed to buy a car because it wouldn't do to go round showing off. Bernabéu used to say that Real Madrid members were working people, humble people, and we had to show that we were of the same cause as the people and not provoke them,' Di Stefano recalled.

Madrid had long ceased to be a town characterized by its provinciality and austerity. It was now the capital of a modern European country proud of its cultural diversity and traditions but with frontiers clearly opened to a wider world. That the great majority of Spaniards remained divided as to what future they wanted, but argued about it publicly, and wrote about it rather than resorting to violence, was the fruit of a democratic system that for all its imperfections had helped heal some of the wounds of the Spanish Civil War.

At the start of the second millennium the president and leader of the centre-right Popular Party José María Aznar was re-elected for another four-year term with an absolute majority. The memory of the corruption of the last years of the socialist government during the late 1980s and early 1990s still weighed heavily on the electorate and contrasted with a marked economic improvement under the PP. The socialist vote had haemorrhaged through defections and abstentions.

By contrast Aznar's government entered the twenty-first century with a renewed sense of mission. Optimists pointed to a feeling that things were going well for Spain, or as Juan Pablo Fusi, the Oxford-educated historian, put it, 'We've lost the sense that Spanish history will always end up badly.'

PP activists talked about a second transition in Spain. The first had installed parliamentary democracy after Franco's death in 1975. The second was portrayed as a paradigmatic shift to a Spain economically strong enough and sufficiently self-assured politically to join in as a big player in international diplomacy, forming its own alliance with the US and Britain in Europe and elsewhere. The Spanish economy was growing faster than most others in the European Union, with Spain's GDP ranking eighth worldwide. The attacks on the US on 9/11 and the Bush administration's declaration of war on terrorism provided Aznar with the opportunity to project himself internationally by sending Spanish troops to Afghanistan and Iraq. At home he enhanced the powers of the police and the judiciary to deal with ETA and its supporters, outlawing the organization's political arm Herri Batasuna.

The New Spain's image as a country that clearly had more to deliver than just sun, ham, wine, flamenco and bullfighting was reflected in a special issue of the American magazine *Time*. 'Wherever you look – food, film, music, literature, business, architecture, sport – there's a Spaniard gesticulating,' it commented. In sport there was mention of the youngest winner of a Formula One Grand Prix, Fernando Alonso, the Basque mountaineer Juanito Oiazabal, the seventeen-year-old Davis Cup tennis player Rafael Nadal. When it came to football, there was José Antonio Reyes, the Andalusian striker transferred to Arsenal where the chant '*Olé!*' began to be heard in Highbury stadium. And last, but by no means least – one of the few football teams Americans had heard of, Real Madrid: 'With his own signings, who has turned Real Madrid into one of soccer's biggest global brand names? Businessman president Florentino Perez,' asserted the magazine. *Time* invited five high-profile Spaniards of differing professions and political affiliations to a lunchtime discussion about their country's strengths and weaknesses, hopes and fears. All agreed that Spain had something unique to offer the world, and was offering it with new gusto.

Spaniards around the world were certainly assuming an active profile as innovators in their field, with a youthful sense of renewal and inspiration that belied the fact that their country had one of Europe's lowest birth rates and a steadily ageing population. According to *Time*, what cut across those in their twenties and those in middle age was a feeling of a society with the wind in its sails, grasping with energy what the world had to offer. Spain was also living a peculiar historic moment, 'a country that is a mere generation from its emergence into democracy but can still connect with its past'.

With some 400 million Spanish speakers worldwide, there

were several examples of what *Time* headlined its cover story: 'Spain's New Conquistadores.' A British reader recalling a similarly enthusiastic celebration by a US magazine of the 'Kool Britannia' in the warm afterglow of Tony Blair's first election victory in 1997, may have been forgiven for being weary. But the *Time* reportage reflected the upbeat national mood in Spain conveyed by those who had voted for and benefited from the Aznar years. The spin was best summarized by the government minister Ana Palacio. 'Spain is a bottle of champagne that has been opened up, and now the whole force of the society that was compressed inside is flowing out,' she said.

There were the Spanish cooks laying claim to the effervescence and experimentation which the French had once monopolized, a subject to which the *New York Times* cookery expert had devoted pages in a special weekend issue. There was the growing popularity and critical acclaim of Spanish films, led by director Pedro Almodóvar, and the international recognition of Spanish actors like Antonio Banderas, Penelope Cruz and Javier Bardem. Impressive too was the stunning boldness of Spanish architects like Santiago Calatrava whose works extended from a new bridge across the Nervion river in Bilbao to an equally spectacular new transit station planned to run below Ground Zero in New York City. More imitative but no less successful as a Spanish export was the clothes chain Zara, with its capacity to respond to consumer demand among the young across several continents by quickly adapting and making available at a competitive price the latest fashion designs. Then there was the construction boom that had made the crane Spain's new national symbol – new houses, new office blocks, new subways, new motorways, new bridges, new stadiums, with Florentino Perez one of Spain's biggest builders.

When it came to the construction business, not everyone was happy though. Its unabated expansion continued despite an estimated 2.7 million empty dwellings in Spain. Those who bought new houses or apartments did so because of negative interest rates, risking increasing their indebtedness once – as always seemed likely – these rates rose above inflation. The apparent consumer boom contrasted with an increasing number of *Madrileños* who felt they were working longer, spending less time with their families, and finding they had trouble making ends meet.

From a more critical perspective, there was much in Aznar's second term of office that was unsettling. Aznar's presidential style became autocratic, undermining parliamentary accountability and damaging the professional reputation of the state-run media outlets which allowed themselves to be manipulated by the government. There developed a get-rich-quick society that was losing a sense of solidarity and the common good, and looked down on those who had failed to be successful. In Madrid the big urban sprawl of buildings and roads seemed relentless in its expansion despite the fact that 10 per cent of the population lived on less than 300 euros a month.

In November 2002 an oil tanker broke up off the northern coast of Spain, causing the country's worst ever ecological disaster. Green and left-wing activists mobilized as volunteers to help clean up the beaches. For several days the tanker was allowed to drift with the government unable to save the Galician fishing industry and local beaches from its pollution. Ministers agreed on a strategy belatedly. Some of them arrived at the scene late because they had been on a shooting party. Other government officials used the state-owned TV and radio to try and minimize the seriousness of the situation and to question the political motivation of many of the volunteers. Eventually the PP government paid local fishermen vast sums of money in compensation just in time to secure their votes in local elections. The handling of the crisis, contradicting as it did the government's image of efficiency and rectitude, did little to enhance Aznar's reputation.

The twenty-fifth anniversary of Spain's constitution, which had been drafted in 1978, reminded people how much had been achieved in the years since Franco's death and also how much had been left unresolved. In particular it revived a debate about the relationship between Madrid and the rest of Spain. Aznar's uncompromising refusal to concede further powers to the regions polarized opinion in the Basque country and Catalonia. Aznar argued that devolution following the death of Franco had gone far enough, and that any further concessions meant giving in to the terrorism of ETA. Basque and Catalan nationalists argued that the government was using terrorism as an excuse to negate political dialogue with elected regional politicians, and to maintain state control from Madrid. The gigantic flagpole and Spanish national colours which were erected by Aznar's government next to the statue of Christopher Columbus in central Madrid seemed to its critics emblematic of an absurd imperial pretention.

In its relations with the rest of the world, Aznar's government struck a strutting, often arrogant pose reminiscent of the days of Franco. In July 2002 he sent gunboats, submarines, attack helicopters and special forces to protect Spain's North African territories after twelve Moroccan soldiers landed on a tiny barren island which had been inhabited solely by goats for forty years. However, unlike Britain's brush with Argentina over the Falklands, neither side went to war. Spain's militarism under Aznar was largely reserved for an unquestioning alliance with the US. Aznar's part in the preparation for war in Iraq was recounted by the veteran American journalist Bob Woodward in his book *Plan of Attack*. 'Never feel alone at moments like that,' Aznar told Bush as the US president ordered the invasion of Iraq, according to the Woodward account. 'Every time that you sit down remember that we are with you. You can always see a moustache next to you.' Aznar's moustache was increasingly to become the butt of his opponents' jokes. Like his pursuit of sound public finances, and cigar smoking with Bush, Aznar seemed to regard his moustache as a sign of Spanish virility.

While his support for George Bush strengthened Aznar's personal friendship with Tony Blair, it did little to improve Spain's relations with the rest of the European Union. Moreover while Blair could point to the 'special relationship' between the UK and the US dating back to the Second World War, Aznar came to be seen inside his own country and within Europe at large as a self-important but a largely irrelevant transatlantic broker. Spaniards generally were unconvinced by Aznar's increasingly pro-US foreign policy – polls showed a clear majority against the presence of Spanish troops in Iraq as part of the US-led coalition.

Spaniards who felt that their democracy had found its roots thanks to a closer integration with Europe, also now feared that Aznar's refusal to agree to a constitutional treaty for the EU, after a dispute about voting rights, cast doubt on a long-term European commitment.

Born into a loyal Francoist family, and with an initial career as a tax collector, Aznar had always aroused the suspicions of the Left. In 1995 he had emerged, as if from the dead, from the ruins of his car after it had been hit by ETA. Aznar's survival of the assassination attempt imbued him with almost mythical qualities as a leader. To his supporters Aznar seemed to reflect the spirit of *El Cid*, the great Spanish lord who after being slain returned on his white mare and defeated the invading Muslims. But the longer that Aznar was in power, the more he seemed to symbolize the delusions of power – only his announcement that he would not stand for a third term helped undermine those who tried to equate him too closely with Franco.

Particularly controversial was his decision to offer his eldest daughter Ana a virtual state wedding in the Escorial. The monastery-palace was the residence of Spain's imperial monarch Philip II and was the burial place of a succession of kings, queens and princes. The last major state function to be held there had been the funeral of King Alfonso XIII. In his visceral book on the Aznar years, Manuel Vazquez Montalban had this to say about the wedding of Miss Aznar with Alejandro Agag, a political wheeler-dealer and entrepreneur, who famously was charged with showing Chelsea Clinton Madrid's night life before being appointed the government's main representative to the European parliament: 'The wedding brought together the liturgy of national Catholicism with the spirit of those who knew how to party but with the discipline and self-control that yuppyism introduced in the culture of the new right.'

Montalban, a one-time communist militant and passionate Barça fan until his death in 2003 (his essay was published post-humously), unsurprisingly had no love either for Aznarism or for the Real Madrid of the *galácticos* which he considered two sides of the same coin.

Other Spanish writers showed themselves more support-ive when tracing the parallels between the Spain of Aznar – its global ambition, its unbridled pursuit of the free market, its self-conscious linkage between the country's glorious past and the promising future of the new century – with the Real Madrid of Florentino Perez, football boss and construction magnate. Perez drew as his point of historical reference the Di Stefano glory years of the fifties. But his bold transfer policy, picking the best and most famous, projected itself as the spirit of an enterprise that aspired to stir the imagination of a global audience. A close ally of Aznar and admirer of Perez, the journalist and broadcaster Federico Jiménez Losantos commented thus in an essay on Real Madrid which was published in Spain's impeccably liberal magazine *La Ilustración Liberal* a few months after Beckham's arrival:

If the sign of our times, conventionally speaking, is globalization, perhaps no other enterprise represents it so successfully as Real Madrid. Let us not forget that this is a private organization that was formed through free association and is maintained voluntarily in a contract which is renewed each game, week or season, by hundreds of thousands, millions of people straddling four generations, and which has survived civil and world wars, mon-archies and republics, dictatorships and democracies, economic and social calataclysms, radical cultural mutations. Today it [Real Madrid] symbolizes success, prestige, popularity, physical beauty and money . . .

It's thus only logical that the enemies of the free market or simply of freedom . . . should spend more and more time fighting this phenomenon called Real Madrid, because in it they see one of the happiest symbols of the triumph of the individual, of the universal market, but one which is far more difficult to fight than McDonald's or Coca-Cola.

When he took over as president of Real Madrid in 2002, Florentino Perez inherited a club that was not short of trophies but short of cash. Real Madrid's weak financial situation reflected fundamentally a glaring imbalance between its spending on players and the underdeveloped exploitation of its image as one of the most successful clubs in the world. Over four seasons Florentino Perez focused on reducing debt by selling off high-value real estate in the face of intense controversy, and building up Real Madrid's marketing strategy around the purchase of a major new international star per year with the ability to draw in not just the loyalty of local fans but the purchasing power of customers across frontiers. The fact that Perez's transfer policy included shedding defenders to finance the purchase of goalscoring footballers reflected the businessman but showed his shortcomings as a football man which would in time return to haunt him.

Real Madrid developed its marketing apparatus in successive transfer deals over three years with Figo, Zidane and Ronaldo. Each of these players had achieved global stature as football stars. In 2001 Figo, after playing brilliantly at FC

Barcelona and for the Portugal national squad, had won FIFA's world player of the year award. Zidane had remained high on the pedestal to which he had been elevated when France won the 1998 World Cup. Ronaldo arrived at Real Madrid having recovered his form with the victorious Brazilian squad of the 2002 World Cup. While unable to replicate the consecutive European conquests achieved during the early Di Stefano years, Real Madrid was confirmed as a formidable force at home and abroad. With Figo it won the league championship, with Zidane the European Champions League and the World Club Championship, with Ronaldo the league again and the European Super Cup.

Beckham's transfer from Manchester United to Madrid was announced with masterly timing hours before he and Victoria flew to Japan on a promotional tour. At a stroke Beckham's red-shirted Japanese fans rushed to put on the white of his new club. By the autumn of 2003 Real Madrid's estimated annual budget of 293 million euros compared with FC Barcelona's budget of 170 million, more than four times bigger than its other league rivals Valencia and Deportivo. Marketing was built into Real Madrid's business strategy as the highest item of forecast revenue – an estimated 80 million euros compared to 70 million euros in TV contracts and 60 million euros in gate receipts. The modernization of the Bernabéu stadium, to make it a five-star UEFA ground suitable to stage a Champions League final in the future, included an expansion of the number of valuable corporate VIP seats with multinational companies based in Madrid more than happy to write off the costs as client entertainment.

In his examination of Beckham's evolution from ordinary player to global celebrity, first published in 2002, Ellis

Cashmore described how Manchester United provided Beckham with 'a platform, a stage and a theatre', allowing him to ripen into a brand of his own. He went on:

'Manchester United' resonates like a thunderclap in the collective imagination, as a club, a culture, a corporation, a business, an industry, a trademark – perhaps even, for some, a philosophy. Could any other club have showcased Beckham more effectively, more memorably? Probably not this side of Madrid. The names 'David Beckham' and 'Manchester United' have been twinned so often that it's almost unthinkable that Beckham could pull on the shirt of any other club. That we think in these terms has much to do with potency of the ManU brand.

The choreography that Florentino Perez subsequently designed and implemented confirmed Real Madrid as indeed the only other club in the world that in the summer of 2003 could make such effective use of the Beckham brand, both to its own and the player's advantage. The 8 million euros Real Madrid was paid to play four friendly matches on its first Asian tour with Beckham was simply the icing on a much bigger commercial cake – in the form of merchandising and sponsorship deals – of which Real Madrid assured themselves the biggest slice by ensuring that they received 50 per cent of the image rights of each of their star signings – Beckham included. Behind Real Madrid's signing of Beckham were the predatory business instincts which had seen Florentino Perez evolve from being the part owner of a Madrid leisure guide into the head of one of Spain's biggest construction companies.

As Real Madrid's head of marketing José Angel Sanchez

put it when I interviewed him in December 2003, six months after Beckham had signed for the club, 'Buying Beckham is like buying into a business. He brings with him a whole range of customers, not just because of his value as a footballer but also a celebrity, he is an icon of modern society . . . Real Madrid is not going to abandon its Spanish roots but right now it's a club with many followers around the world and that is a source of pride.'

Two years before Beckham arrived, Florentino Perez had coined a phrase which he claimed summarized the profile of the ideal Real Madrid team he was helping to create. It was a team of 'the Zidanes and the Pavóns'. Francisco Pavón was the name of a promising central defender, the most recently identified potential home-grown star of the future, who had come up through the youth ranks. Zidane personified the best money could buy. As Perez put it in an interview with *El País* at the time, 'If you want to take a risk, go for your youth players; if you are going to spend, go for those players whose quality is not in doubt.'

Perez argued that the combination of world stars and home-grown youngsters that guaranteed the roots of a very Spanish institution was consistent with the golden age of Real Madrid in the days of Di Stefano and Bernabéu. And yet his inflexible insistence on building a squad of expensive superstars and youth-teamers, while shedding players he considered 'middle-ranking' and too expensive, may have responded to the logic of a ruthless businessman but it contained a fatal flaw in football terms.

Beckham was already established as an industry in his own right, both producer and product. As Cashmore explained it, by the time he'd reached his last year at Manchester

United Beckham had 'effectively turned himself into a perfect commodity that can be bought and sold just like any other article of trade'. In Real Madrid he found a club big enough and commercially ambitious enough to exploit his image. Meanwhile Beckham maintained endorsement deals with companies like Pepsi, Vodafone, Police, M&S and Adidas that aimed to maintain the symbiosis identified by Cashmore, whereby endorser and product could feed off each other to the mutual benefit of player and product.

Nonetheless Beckham's year in Spain put to the test both the claim that the celebrity player was a portable brand, and Real Madrid's legendary status as the world's greatest club. It proved to be a story in two halves. The second half of the football season saw Real Madrid beaten in the final of the King's Cup by Zaragoza and then losing to Monaco on aggregate in the quarter-finals of the Champions League. Real Madrid also failed to secure the league championship which was won by Valencia. They lost four games in a row, and ended third behind FC Barcelona, a position the Catalan club celebrated as a major triumph given their disastrous start to the season which had seen them fall to twelfth place. The thousands of local fans that took to the streets of Valencia to celebrate the league title (later boosted by the club's win of the UEFA Cup) could not resist taking it out on the *galácticos* with the chant, 'No League! No Cup! No Champions League!' Just to rub salt into the *Madridista* wounds, Valencia captain David Abelda added: 'Money isn't everything, this is the league of humility' – a bit of an exaggeration but it did make a cheap football point that while money cannot necessarily buy you success, hard work, team organization and a dose of luck can.

Beckham was absent from the team that lined up in the second leg of the Monaco tie because he was suspended after picking up a yellow card in the first leg at the Bernabéu. Rather than accompany the team he had asked for and been granted by Perez compassionate leave of absence to try and put his personal life in some order. By then Perez and other senior staff at Real Madrid including coach Carlos Queiroz and Jorge Valdano were worried about the impact the separation from his family was having on Beckham's morale, seeing it as a possible explanation for the drop in his form. While his team mates were humiliated by Monaco, Beckham was in Switzerland with Victoria trying to save his marriage from the revelations that had broken in the British tabloid press about his alleged affair with Rebecca Loos.

The revelations threatened to damage Beckham's endorsement deals worth about £6.75m. Beckham had consciously developed an image as a self-styled doting family man, underlining it in his best-selling autobiography published on his departure from Manchester United. That his marital crisis surfaced at a time when Beckham's form dipped and Real Madrid as a team lost their dominance on the pitch surrounded his future in Spain with uncertainty.

When Real Madrid returned to Spain after losing to Monaco in the Champions League, fans staged a demonstration at the club's temporary training ground, holding up placards denouncing the players as good-for-nothing 'mercenaries'. One placard held up by a *Madridista* stated, 'For you money and whores; for us, indignation and repression.' Real Madrid were beaten by Mallorca in the Santiago Bernabéu, the weekend that Valencia secured the league championship by beating Sevilla, and in the final match of the season (lost against Real Sociedad) the deposed champions were whistled and booed. The desperate frustration of it all was personified by Beckham's sending-off in the embarrassing home defeat against bottom club Murcia after he had screamed *hijo de puta*, one of the few Spanish phrases he had learnt, at the linesman. It was Beckham's second sending-off of the season, the first being in January 2004 midway through Real Madrid's King's Cup quarter-final first leg victory over Valencia at the Bernabéu. In Spain being sent off by a referee was regarded as an honour by the player's fans. But Beckham's second dismissal of 2004 did not generate the support of *Madridistas* that the first one had, particularly when he took the opportunity of his suspension to turn out for Martin Keown's testimonial in London. Having been phoned by a furious Perez, Beckham played for just three minutes, then dashed back to Madrid.

Nevertheless it all seemed a long way from the effervescence surrounding Beckham's arrival in Madrid with his wife and children, and the prediction then from both the player and the club that the *galácticos* were on target to emerge as the Kings of Europe and of Spain in the 2003–04 season by winning the Champions League, *La Liga* and the King's Cup.

The massive coverage provided by the English tabloid media to Beckham's alleged infidelities and the crisis it stirred in his marriage was echoed in Spain's *prensa rosa*. But the mainstream media hardly mentioned the story, their sports journalists, like those of sports dailies like *Marca* and *As*, not even attempting to make any connection between the turmoil in Beckham's private life and his performance on the pitch. Spaniards on the whole had never factored in Victoria when they came to judging Beckham as a celebrity and a player.

They were in no particular hurry to do that now simply because Beckham was alleged to have done in his leisure time what other Real Madrid players had done before him. And yet Beckham was inseparable from the decline and fall of Real Madrid in the latter stages of the season. As Sid Lowe, the experienced Madrid-based English sports journalist, put it, 'As this season's *galáctico* the club's successes would forever be his. So too – and this was always the risk – its failures.' Lowe diligently followed Beckham through every training session and every game, while acting as his translator for a majority of the Spanish sports press that had no command of English. He declared *el año de Beckham* a failure as the season reached its close. 'Emotionally and physically shattered, Madrid have plunged into crisis,' he commented. In a profile of Beckham in *World Soccer* magazine, Lowe suggested that the team concept not the player was at fault: 'As Beckham looks around he sees tired bodies. More damningly, he sees players who, undermined by the divisiveness and incoherence of president Florentino Perez's "Zidanes and Pavóns" policy of youth-teamers and superstars, do not care as much as he does . . . He has a sense of responsibility and desire lacking at Madrid – one that has forced him into dirtier tasks, diminishing his creative importance.' Part of the problem Beckham faced in his first season, argued the insightful Lowe, was playing in the centre when defensive midfield was not his natural role. 'The battling Brit tag has returned to haunt him, almost becoming a self-parody,' he added.

Some Spanish journalists were less generous, suspecting still that the mass exodus of so many players at the start of the season would not have come about had Perez not decided to buy Beckham in the first place. Santiago Segurola, the hugely experienced sports writer at *El País*, told me he had no time for football players like Beckham who seemed to have become famous, their poor form on the pitch notwithstanding. At *Marca* my friend Ulises felt disappointed that after spending almost a year in Spain, Beckham had yet to learn conversational Spanish. And while he acknowledged that Beckham's industriousness continued to put some of his team mates to shame, he felt that for all his running around he had failed to inspire the team to greatness, failed to be the genuine playmaker he had always so wanted to become in midfield. *Marca* had dubbed Beckham *Forrest Gump*.

When Real Madrid lost 2–3 to Mallorca at the Bernabéu, their third successive home defeat, paving the way for Valencia's *La Liga* title win, Mallorca's coach Luis Aragones had this to say of Beckham at Real Madrid: 'He's finding it difficult in the middle. He passes acceptably and works hard, but he doesn't think quickly. In the centre of midfield it's very important to know where you are going to place the ball before it comes to you. He doesn't think in a hurry.'

By the end of that season in *La Liga* it was tempting to see Beckham ending up exactly where he had been before he went to Spain, having to prove himself as England captain in the European Championships in Portugal and likely to play on the right flank in the Premiership if and when he moved to Chelsea. And yet there was also a sense that his year in Spain was a defining period not just for the player as footballer and icon but also for Real Madrid, and Spain.

Florentino Perez sought re-election as Real Madrid president after admitting that his policy of 'Zidanes and

Pavóns' needed adjustment. Zidane, once the crown jewel of the *galáctico* project, admitted that he had lived through the worst days he had had since joining Real Madrid. He could not remember playing as badly as he did in the last games of the season. Some Spanish sports commentators blamed the coach Carlos Queiroz for not adequately rotating. Queiroz had been under pressure from Perez to make full use of his investment by playing his *galácticos* as often as possible, even if they were not entirely fit. The show had to go on. The global audience demanded nothing less. But Queiroz also seemed to lack sufficient trust in the quality of the home-grown youth. All too often he gave the impression of being a coach with his hands tied behind his back, unable to guarantee the success and domination the fans expected of the team despite its evident lack of depth. At the end of the season Queiroz followed the path of many coaches before him, paying the inevitable price of failure. Sir Alex Ferguson quickly snapped him up to return to Manchester United as his assistant manager for a second spell.

Real Madrid reached the end of Beckham's year in Spain, burnt-out, no longer able to instil respect, still less fear in their opponents. They had lost to teams that seemed to play with more joy and less arrogance, teams that showed quality and flair and determination, yet fell well short of Real Madrid's budget. The *galácticos* lost to Valencia, to Deportivo La Coruña, to Osasuna, and yes, they lost in the second half of the season to Barça, in the Bernabéu, with Ronaldinho contributing to a goal of sublime beauty.

The summer Perez had brought Beckham to Spain, he had also shipped out eleven players. They included Fernando Morientes who while on loan to Monaco helped them knock

Real Madrid out of the Champions League, and Claude Makelele, who played a part in Chelsea's run to the semi-finals of the competition, before also losing to the French club. By the end of the season Perez had this to say: 'We only had sixteen senior professionals and we played twice a week for most of the season. Maybe the team's mistake was to try to win all three competitions.' But the mistake was his too. As for Queiroz to excuse, as he did, the team's 'disappointing season' by pointing out that 'most clubs finish the season empty-handed', was to understate the nature of Real Madrid under Florentino Perez and the huge weight of history and expectation that the club carried on its shoulders.

Queiroz was sacked and replaced by José Antonio Camacho, a former player and one-time manager of the Spanish national team, whose tenure as coach of Real Madrid under Lorenzo Sanz had ended within days following a row. Camacho made as one of his conditions for returning to the club, a bigger squad of middle-level players than that which Perez had allowed the hapless Queiroz. As he prepared to captain England at Euro 2004 in Portugal, Beckham declared his intention of staying on in Real Madrid because he had still much to prove. Camacho liked fighters – he had been one himself, personifying the 'Spanish fury' when he had played for Real Madrid. He had also once called Vicente Del Bosque the 'best coach in the world'.

That Real Madrid's disappointing end to the season coincided with a period of dramatic political change may have been purely coincidental. However, such is the history of the club that one cannot separate Beckham's year at the Bernabéu from the wider context of the country's politics and history.

Six days before Real Madrid played in the King's Cup final
– the first of the season's trophies it had hoped to win –
terrorists blew up four commuter trains as they entered
Madrid's Atocha station, killing 192 people and injuring more
than 1,400 others. It was the worst terrorist outrage ever
suffered on Spanish soil, and the most shocking in Europe
since a bomb blew apart Pan-Am flight 103 over Lockerbie
in 1988. The previous evening I had experienced the euphoria
of the local fans as Real Madrid beat Bayern Munich at the
Bernabéu, qualifying for the quarter-finals of the Champions
League. In the immediate aftermath of the Atocha attack,
ordinary Spaniards showed an extraordinary degree of solidarity not just in terms of voluntary support for the victims
but in marching to express their disgust at the outrage. Many
of the wounded and dying were taken to the Gregorio
Maranon hospital, named after my grandfather, a one-time
footballer turned doctor and writer. In Madrid more than
three million people took to the streets in the biggest demonstration ever seen not just in the capital but the country at
large. Other demonstrations in sympathy with the victims
took place in towns and villages around Spain.

Walking as I did in the midst of the driving rain with that
multitude that evening along Madrid's Castellana avenue, the
city and the country I had been born in seemed to roll out
slowly from its past. I belonged to a generation which was
brought up with our parents' memory of barbarities committed on both sides during the Spanish Civil War, but which
reached maturity in a democracy achieved through reconciliation. My own experience growing up in Spain and starting
out as a young journalist was of the hatreds fuelled by the
Franco regime – the summary executions, the shooting of

demonstrators, the emergence of ETA as what then seemed a justified armed struggle on behalf of the repressed Basque people. I had become a Barça fan because I believed Real Madrid played for Franco. Then when Franco died a majority of Spaniards agreed to a future based on mutual respect and compromise, which brought peace as well as freedom. ETA was no longer seen as a liberation movement, but a bunch of cynical killers. To the voting majority of the New Spain, violence had lost its romanticism. I went on supporting Barça anyway because of history.

Months before the Atocha killings another large demonstration had taken place in Madrid against the Spanish government's decision to send troops to Iraq. Many of those who were marching again were doing so instinctively questioning the speed with which the Aznar government had blamed ETA for the Atocha bombings. In doing so Aznar had inflamed the political prejudice the Spanish Right had always felt against Basque nationalism. In the Basque country an off-duty policeman shot dead a local shopkeeper for refusing to put up a poster blaming ETA as ministers had done – an act that personified the crude intolerance of so much of Spanish history. National elections were due to take place four days after the bombings.

Despite the ruling Partido Popular's attempts to hold ETA responsible, questions were increasingly asked as to whether the terrorists were home-grown or from abroad. Slowly but surely the truth trickled out – the bombings of 11 March had been carried out not by ETA but by Islamic terrorists. Even before this was confirmed, as Spaniards prepared to vote, it was clear that whoever won the elections would inherit a very different country from the one which had existed only a few days earlier. Mariano Rajoy, the new leader of the Popular Party, exuded the confidence of an increasingly prosperous, economically successful and internationally assertive nation – the image created by his predecessor José María Aznar. The PP posters had a simple message appealing to indulgence and egotism – 'Vote PP, vote for more'.

And yet the bombings and their aftermath not only threw Spain into a state of shock, they also pricked the balloon of the PP's cocky confidence, and those who had shared in it. On Sunday 15 March Spanish voters elected the opposition Socialist Party led by José Luis Zapatero, a victory no one had predicted, not even the Socialists themselves. He was the first elected prime minister in his country's history to declare himself a Barça fan, a fact seized on by Catalans as a sign that perhaps history was at last looking on them favourably, even if the general secretary of the socialist trade union movement and Zapatero's first secretary for sport were both Real Madrid fans!

Sunday is a day for voting in Spain, as for church services – and football. Atocha station had always had a special resonance in the history of Real Madrid. It was there that the victorious team led by Real Madrid's legendary goalkeeper Zamora, *El Divino*, had arrived, to be greeted by ecstatic crowds on two occasions before the outbreak of the Spanish Civil War, clutching trophies. It was at Atocha that a twenty-six-year-old Alfredo Di Stefano and his young family arrived on an overnight train from Barcelona in 1953 to play later that day his first game for Real Madrid. More recently it was at Atocha that I had met up with David Beckham and his fellow *galácticos* before we all caught Spain's high-speed 'bullet' train to Seville for a *La Liga* game. The team, as had become customary, was surrounded by autograph hunters and excited young girls. They later lost the game. It was the night of the eclipse of the moon.

In their first home *La Liga* match after 11 March, Beckham and his team mates stood with their black armbands honouring the dead in silence, in a collectively subdued and still shell-shocked Bernabéu stadium. Not since the death of Franco had there been mourning like this. Later, when Real Madrid had ended the season without medals, there were some, like Gabriele Marcotti, who suggested that the club's admission of weakness was not just cathartic but also potentially dangerous. 'Once the authority is gone, it's difficult to recover,' wrote Marcotti.

But Real Madrid has had its low points and recoveries just as Spain, during its history, has often changed governments and even regimes. It is a club and a country with a lot yet to give. And both are bigger than Beckham.

Bibliography

Inocencio F. Arias, *Los tres mitos del Real Madrid* (Plaza & Janes, 2002)

Antonio Bahamonde, *El Real Madrid en la historia de España* (Taurus, 2002)

Phil Ball, *White Storm* (Mainstream, 2003)

David Beckham, *Beckham* (Hodder & Stoughton, 2000)

——, *My Side* (HarperCollins, 2003)

Victoria Beckham, *Learning to Fly* (Penguin, 2002)

Carlos Moreno Benito, *Una historia de fábula* (Soubriet, 2003)

Gerald Brenan, *The Face of Spain* (Penguin, 1987)

Julie Burchill, *Beckham* (Yellow Jersey Press, 2001)

Jimmy Burns, *Spain: A Literary Companion* (John Murray, 1994)

——, *Barça: A People's Passion* (Bloomsbury, 2000)

——, *Hand of God: The Life of Diego Maradona* (Bloomsbury, 2002)

Tom Burns, *The Use of Memory* (Sheed & Ward, 1993)

Francisco José Sanchez Canamero, *Vicente Del Bosque* (Globalia Ediciónes, 2003)

Julian García Candau, *Madrid–Barça* (El País Aguilar, 1996)

——, *Bernabéu, el Presidente* (Espasa, 2002)

Fernando Carreño, *La historia negra del Real Madrid* (Meran, 2003)

Ellis Cashmore, *Beckham* (Polity, 2003)

Michael Crick, *The Boss* (Simon & Schuster, 2003)

Bibliography

David Downing, *England v Argentina: World Cups and Other Small Wars* (Portrait, 2003)

Simon Freeman, *Own Goal* (Orion, 2000)

Toni Frieros, *Ronaldinho* (Sport, 2004)

Juan Pablo Fusi, *La España del siglo XX* (Marcial Pons, 2003)

Eduardo Galeano, *Football in Sun and Shadow* (Fourth Estate, 1997)

David Gilmour, *Cities of Spain* (John Murray, 1992)

Brian Glanville, *The Story of the World Cup* (Faber & Faber, 1997)

Mariño Gomez-Santos, *Santiago Bernabéu* (Saege, 1960)

——, *Vida de Gregorio Marañón* (Taurus, 1971)

José Miguel González, *El Fútbol de Michel* (Alhambra Marca, 2002)

Luis Miguel González, *Cien años de Leyenda* (Everest, 2002)

Robert Graham, *Spain: Change of a Nation* (Michael Joseph, 1984)

Che Guevara, *The Motorcycle Diaries* (Fourth Estate, 2003)

Ernest Hemingway, *Death in the Afternoon* (Jonathan Cape, 1950)

John Hooper, *The New Spaniards* (Penguin, 1995)

Roy Keane with Eamon Dunphy, *Keane* (Penguin, 2003)

Stephen F. Kelly (ed.), *The Pick of the Season* (Mainstream, 1997)

——, *Red Voices* (Headline, 2000)

Simon Kuper, *Football Against the Enemy* (Orion, 1994)

Carlos Levi, *Atlético de Madrid: Cien años de historia* (Silex, 2003)

Tom Burns Maranon, *Hispanomania* (Plaza & Janes, 2000)

Tom Burns Maranon & Josep Carles Clemente, *Juan Carlos I* (Cara Cruz, 2003)

Bibliography

Carmelo Martín, *Valdano, sueños de fútbol* (El País Aguilar, 1995)

Ramón Mendoza, *Dos pelotas y un balón* (El País Aguilar, 1996)

Manuel Vazquez Montalban, *Offside* (Serpent's Tail, 2001)

——, *Crónica sentimental de España* (Debolsillo, 2003)

——, *La Aznaridad* (Mondadori, 2003)

Andrew Morton, *Posh & Becks* (Michael O'Mara, 2003)

H. V. Morton, *A Stranger in Spain* (Methuen, 1983)

Juan Carlos Pasamontes, *Todos los jefes de la Casa Blanca* (Pearson Alhambra, 2003)

Raúl del Pozo, *A Bambi no le gustan los miércoles* (Esfera de Los Libros, 2003)

Paul Preston, *The Triumph of Democracy in Spain* (Methuen, 1986)

——, *Franco* (HarperCollins, 1993)

——, *Juan Carlos* (Plaza & Janes, 2003)

Keir Radnedge, *The Ultimate Encyclopedia of Soccer* (Hodder & Stoughton, 1996)

Alfredo Relaño, *Fútbol contado con sencillez* (Maeva, 2001)

Margarita Rivière, *Serrat y su época* (Plaza & Janes, 1998)

Antonio Salas, *Diario de un skin* (Temas de Hoy, 2003)

Duncan Shaw, *Fútbol y Franquismo* (Madrid, 1987)

Paul Simpson, *Gascoigne* (Virgin, 2001)

Alfredo Di Stefano, *Gracias, vieja* (Aguilar, 2000)

Hugh Thomas, *The Spanish Civil War* (Penguin, 1990)

Jason Tomas, *Soccer Czars* (Mainstream, 1996)

——, *Beckham and Ferguson* (Sutton, 2003)

Jorge Valdano, *El miedo escénico y otras hierbas* (Aguilar, 2002)

Jim White, *Always in the Running* (Mainstream, 1998)

Index

DB = David Beckham;   FCB = FC Barcelona;   RM = Real Madrid.

Abello, Juan 333
AC Milan 232
ACS (construction company) 333, 336–7
Aguirre, Gonzalo 161–2
Albornoz, Alvaro de 156
Alfonso XIII, King 141–2, 147
Alianza Popular (AP) 328
Alvarez, José Luis 328
Amancio 247
Anderlecht 225
Anelka, Nicolas 318
Annan, Kofi 67
Antic, Radomir 29
Archibald, Steve 40
Arconada, Luis 285
Argentina 201
    football in 197–8, 199, 200, 204
    versus England in World Cup 110–11
Arias, Inocencio 'Chencho' 63–70, 72–3, 222
Arino, Fernando 276–7, 277
Arsenal 108–9
Assis, Roberto 30, 51
Atkinson, Ron 264
Athletic Bilbao 135, 143, 176
Atlético de Madrid 39–40, 63, 366–70
Atocha station, Madrid 399, 401–2
Azaña, Manuel 147–8
Aznar, José María 306, 307, 323, 377, 380, 383, 384–7

Barça see FC Barcelona
Barcelona 373
    Franco visit 172–3
    RM football school 82–4
Barroso, Javier 183–4
Basques
    and Navarre 56
    terrorist groups 32, 400
Bassat, Luis 29, 30, 40
Batson, Brendan 264

Bayern Munich 115, 149–50, 253–4
Beckham, Brooklyn 114, 354
Beckham, David
    childhood 90–92, 93–5; visit to Nou Camp
        376
    and Argentine footballers 370–72, 373
    at Manchester United 95, 98–9, 102–3,
        108–9, 114, 390; attempted signing by
        FCB 27–8, 31, 32–3, 34, 40–41, 50–51;
        in matches against RM 120, 122, 321–2;
        and Sir Alex Ferguson 37–8, 99, 106,
        116–17, 118; transfer to RM 35–7, 38–9;
        leaving the club 33–4, 38
    on Cantona 101, 102
    celebrity status and image 45, 86–7, 107–8,
        113, 348, 365–6, 391–2, 393; Asian tour
        2–3, 50; autobiography 10–11; career
        management 363–4; Parkinson show
        interview 365; Sun interview 2003 10
    England player 103; 1998 World Cup
        109–10, 110–11; 2000 European
        Championships 117; 2001 World Cup
        qualifiers 118
    OBE 347, 348
    in Spain: arrival at RM 1–2, 3–5, 349; early
        appearances for RM 7–9; first goal for
        RM 11–12; first season at RM 14, 60, 150,
        338, 339–40, 343, 372, 394, 395; interview
        at Marca offices 341, 343–7; media
        coverage 13, 349–50, 352–3, 355–8,
        360–61, 394–6; private life 350–51,
        358–9; RM fans and 19; RM team mates
        and 12–13, 345; and RM/FCB rivalry
        375, 377–8; social life 353, 356–7
    and Victoria 6, 10–11; early relationship and
        engagement 103–7; marriage 115–16;
        pressures after 1998 World Cup 111–13;
        problems settling in Spain 355–6;
        possible marital difficulties 364, 393
    views on: Arias 67; Butragueño 297; Cruyff

Index

114; Del Bosque 123, 130–31, 322;
Grerardo Perez 55; Keegan 117; Lopez
Quilez 240; Valdano 43, 44
Beckham, Romeo 355–6
Beckham, Ted 90–91, 91–2
Beckham, Victoria 6, 86, 113
  career as pop artist 111
  early relationship and engagement to DB
    103–7
  pressures after 1998 World Cup 111–13
  memories of Italy 48
  birth of Brooklyn 114
  marriage 115–16
  Asian tour 2–3, 50
  and move to Spain 5, 6–7, 48–9, 351–3,
    354–5, 355–6, 359–61
  marriage difficulties denials 364–5
  and the media 359, 360, 362–3
Benfica 225
Bernabéu, Maria 260
Bernabéu, Santiago 125–6, 147, 148, 180,
  246–7
  birth 133
  during Spanish Civil War 156–7, 158
  interests outside football 261
  Lopez Quilez on 237, 238
  president of RM 52–3, 182, 210, 212,
    237–8, 252–3, 260–61; and Di Stefano
    196, 208, 209, 233; and European Cup
    219; football and politics 180, 181, 238,
    259; and multiculturalism 265; and new
    stadium 182, 184, 185; Zoco on 244,
    245–6, 247
  death 126, 133
Bernabéu stadium, Madrid 52, 183–5, 185,
  210, 241
Bermudez, Nuria 357
Best, George 249
Blair, Tony 109
Boixos Nois (Our Boys) 314, 315
Bolin, Luis 152
Brassey, Hugo 345–6
Brazil 227–8
Breitner, Paul 253
Brenan, Gerard 189, 191
Bugallal, Usera 147, 148
Bulart, Father José María 309–10
bullfighting 17–19, 256
Butler, Cliff 250
Butragueño, Emilio (*El Buitre*) 68–9, 69–70,
  295–8
Butt, Nicky 108
Byrne, Terry 341–2, 363

Caballero, Ernest Giménez 172
Calderón, Antonio 214
Camacho, José Antonio 280, 318–19, 398
Canadas, Esther 357
Cantona, Eric 100–2
Capello, Fabio 318, 347
Carlos, Roberto 317, 354
  DB and 345
  playing for RM 8, 121, 305, 342, 377
Carrero Blanco, Luis 31–2, 275
Carreto, Marti 206, 208, 209, 219–20
Casillas, Iker 121, 122, 150, 339
Castile and Castilians 125–6, 128
Catalan, Antonio 350
Catalonia and Catalans 129, 163, 172, 328,
  373
  Banca Catalana 329
  Cruyff and 31, 32
  and death of Franco 124
  FCB and Catalan nationalism 140, 219–20,
    275–6, 277–8, 377
Cela José, Camilo *The Hive* 188
Chamartín stadium, Madrid 142, 147, 148, 168,
  169, 170
  see also Bernabéu stadium
Champions League
  prior to 1993 *see* European Champions Cup
  1997 108
  1998 108, 303–4, 313–14
  1999 114, 115, 307
  2000 119–20, 307–8, 318, 320–1
  2002 303, 376
  2003 120–22
  2004 149, 338
Charlton, Bobby 251
Chelsea 218
Chingford, England 89
Clemente, Javier 8, 75
Coll, Xavier García 341
Colombia 204
Cruyff, Johan 26, 31, 32, 114
Cunningham, Laurie 263–4, 264–5, 266–9,
  279

de Carlos, Luis 275, 278, 282, 288–9
Del Bosque, Vicente 23, 127, 128, 129–30,
  131–3, 280
  coach at RM 22, 39–40, 130, 320
  on Cunningham 267–8
  on DB 123, 130–31, 322
  and RM and politics 133, 308–9
Del Sol, Luis 236, 247
Denstone, Gary 46

Index

Di Stefano, Alfredo 72–3, 196–7, 198, 203–4
  and Cantona 100
  and Che Guevara 202
  and Didi 266
  and FCB 205–6, 207–10
  football centenary match 230–31
  on football and politics 243
  playing in Argentina 197–8, 200–201, 204
  playing in Colombia 204, 205
  playing for Spain 227–8
  and RM 206–7, 208–9, 210–11; as coach
    234, 288, 294–5; as player 57–8, 211–12,
    213, 214–15, 224, 231, 232–4, 235, 236
Didi 212–13, 265–6
DND (Delegación Nacional de Deportes . . .)
  171, 176, 185
Domingo, Placido 301
Domingues, Milene 354
Duscher, Aldo 372

Edwards, Martin 97
Eintracht Frankfurt 224
El Juli (bullfighter) 17–18
England
  history of football 109, 136–7
  1950 World Cup 193–4
  playing Hungary in 1950s 213
  DB first playing for 103
  1998 World Cup 109–11
  2000 European Championships 117
  2001 World Cup qualifiers 117–18
  2002 World Cup 264
  football centenary match 231
Eriksson, Sven-Goran 117
ETA 56, 400
European Champions Cup 217–19, 220,
  247–8
  1956 221, 279
  1957 119, 248–9, 310
  1958 119
  early 1960s 119, 224–5
  1964 231–3
  1966 247
  1968 249–50
  1976 253
  1981 279, 279–80
  1993 onwards see Champions League
European Cup-Winners' Cup
  1971 251
  1979 277
  1982 287
European Fairs Cup 226, 252
European Nations Cup

1964 229–30
2000 117

Falange party 170–71, 183, 195
fans
  following players from club to club 44–5
  RM 17, 54, 55–6, 61–3, 281–2, 305; and
    DB 19; Di Stefano on 215; global
    following 242; in Navarre 56–60; and
    Nou Camp 376–7, 378; Ultra Surs 16–17,
    53–4, 254, 281, 290–91, 311–15
fascism 170
  and Spanish football 175–6, 195, 216–17
FC Barcelona (Barca) 73–4
  attempt to sign DB 27–8, 31, 34, 40–41,
    50–51
  and Catalan nationalism 140, 219–20,
    275–6, 277–8, 377
  and Copa Latina 220
  Cruyff at 26–7, 31, 32
  Di Stefano and 205–6, 207–10
  and European Cup 218–19, 225, 226, 299
  and European Cup-Winners' Cup 1982 287
  fans 314, 315
  Herrera and 225–7
  history 73–4; founded in 1900 135; in 1920s
    143; during Spanish Civil War 162, 163,
    169; after Civil War 172, 180, 181; 1950s
    196, 219; post-Franco 275–6; 1991–92
    season 299; 2002–03 season 29, 41
  players: foreign 28, 29, 51; Maradona 287–8;
    Recber 28; Ronaldinho 28, 30, 51, 375
  presidents: 1978 elections 276–7, see also
    individual presidents
  and RM 150–51, 177–9, 180, 181–2, 266,
    373–8
Felipe, Crown Prince 308, 361, 367
Ferguson, Sir Alex 22, 95–8, 99, 99–100, 108, 397
  and DB 37, 99, 106, 116–17, 118
Fernández, Matilde 335
Ferrer, Colonel José Vendrell 180
Figo, Luis 353, 388–9
  and DB 13
  joining RM 20, 334, 374
  Manchester United and 116–17
  playing for RM 8, 121, 338, 340
Flor, Ulises Sanchez 12, 13
football
  centenary match 230–1
  history in Spain 135–6, 169, 171, 172,
    175–7, 185, 192–5, 217–18, 282
  RM schools 82–5
Fortuna Düsseldorf 277

Index

Franco, General Francisco
  and Civil War 151, 152–3
  foreign policy 191, 216
  and Hitler's Germany 175
  and Marañón 187
  and Real Madrid 65, 133, 221, 239, 240,
    243–4, 257–8
  repressive regime 242–3, 257, 259–60
  and Samitier 227
  and Spanish football 130, 176, 229, 230
  and sport 257
  and Valley of the Fallen 182–3
  visit to Barcelona 172–3
  death 124–5, 126, 132, 270
Fuller, Simon 104, 362–3

Galdós, Benito Perez *Fortunata y Jacinta* 134–5
Gardel, Carlos 146
Gascoigne, Paul 93
Gaspart, Joán 25, 29, 127, 374
Gento, Paco (*El Supersonico*) 53, 211–12, 212,
    247, 253
  Franco and 257–8
Germany, England games against 117, 117–18
Giggs, Ryan 106, 115
Gil, Jesus 367–8
González, Felipe 291–2, 299
González, Miguel 'Michel' 295
Gonzalez, Raúl *see* Raúl (RM player)
Graille, Francis 30
Gran Familia (RM fan group) 52
Granado, Alberto 202
Greenbury, Sir Richard 101
Grimau García, Julian 242–3
Grondona, Julio 77
Guevara, Che (*El Che*) 201–3

Hanot, Gabriel 217–18
Harverson, Patrick 33, 34
Herrera, Helenio 225–7, 227–8
Heynckes, Jupp 306, 318
Hiddink, Guus 318, 319
Hierro, Fernando 22, 339
Hoddle, Glenn 103, 109
Hughes, Mark 97, 98
Hungary 213

Ibárurri, Dolores (*La Pasionaria*) 154
Iglesias, Enrique 353
Ince, Paul 97, 98
Inter Milan 224, 225, 233
Iribarne, Manuel Fraga 328
Irún, Spain 156–7, 157

Jimenez, José Manuel 57–8
Johnson, Arthur 137–9
Juan Carlos, King 149–50, 270, 270–71, 273,
    274
  and RM 8, 65, 306
Juanito 280, 299
Juventus 21

Kahn, Oliver 149
Keegan, Kevin 117
Kenyon, Peter 28, 33, 37, 39, 51
Kopa, Raymond 212, 213, 279
Kubala, Ladislao 196, 207, 226–7

Laporta, Joán
  attempt to sign DB for FCB 27–8, 31, 34,
    40–41
  campaign for presidency of FCB 25–6, 27,
    29–31, 40
  president of FCB 315, 374–5
Larranga, Manuel Valdes 219
Lastaraga, Eduardo 176
Laudrup, Michael 77
Leafe, Reg 225
Lineker, Gary 19
Liverpool 279–80
Loos, Rebecca 357–8
Lopez Quilez, Julio 234, 235, 268–9
  interview with 235–7, 238–40
Lowe, Sid 395

Madrid, Spain 66, 379
  late 19th century 134–5, 140
  during Civil War 154–6, 166, 168–9,
    169–70
  after Civil War 188–9, 190–91
    1980s 293
  2004 terrorist bombings 399, 400
Makaay, Roy 150
Makelele, Claude 8, 121, 339, 398
Mallorca, versus RM 8–9, 11
Manchester United 22, 96–7, 321
  1995–96 season 99
  1996–97 season 108
  1997–98 season 108–9
  1998–99 season 115
  1999–2000 season 117
  Beckham and 95, 98–9, 102–3, 108,
    114–15, 390; FCB attempt to
    buy 27, 31, 32–3, 34–5; leaving the
    club 33–4; transfer to RM 35–7,
    38–9
  Cantona at 100–102

Index

Manchester United – *contd.*
  and Champions League: 1999 114, 115; 2000
    119–20, 307, 321; 2003 120–22
  and European Cup 119, 218
  playing RM 118–19, 119–22, 248–51,
    321–2
  Sir Alex Ferguson and 95–6, 97–8, 116–17,
    118
  try to sign Ronaldinho 30, 51
Manolo (RM fan) 62–3
Manzano, Gregorio 368–9
Maradona, Diego 78, 87–8, 89, 95, 287–8, 298
Marañón, Gregorio 155, 187–8, 237, 399
Marca (sports newspaper) 157–9, 161, 176,
    340, 343
  DB visit and interview 343–4, 344–7
  on foreign players 228–9
Marquez, Ignacio 82, 84–5
Martínez, Raúl 59
Matthews, Stanley 194
Meléndez, General Adolfo 153, 155–6
Mendoza, Ramón 289–91
  president of RM 76–7, 294, 299, 332
  death 300
Menotti, Cesar 75
Mesa de Asta, Marquis of 178–9, 179
Mijatovic, Pedrag 305, 317
Miljanic, Miljan 126, 130, 253
Millonarios club, Colombia 204–5, 205, 206,
    208
Molowny, Luis 126, 181, 193
Morientes, Fernando 398
Morton, Andrew 105
Moscardo, General José 171, 172, 179, 209
Muguraza, Pedro 183, 184
Muñoz, Miguel 130, 233, 253
Mur, Angel 178

Navarre, Spain 56–60
Navarro, Carlos Arias 124, 271
Netzer, Gunther 253
Nike 29–30
Nou Camp stadium, Barcelona 287
  DB and 376
  RM fans at 376–7, 378
Nuñez, Josep Lluís 25–6, 277, 287

Ollero, Juan 330–31
Olympique Marseille 338
Onieva, Juan 318
Ordoñez, Fernando 66
Ortega, Lieutenant Colonel Antonio 168, 169
Ortiz, Letizia 361–2

Osasuna 56, 58, 60
Owen, Michael 111

Padros, Juan and Carlos 139–40, 141
Parages, Pedro 138
Parkinson, Michael 364–5
Partido Popular (PP) 306, 323, 380, 401
Pavón, Francisco 391
Pedralba, Antonio Santos 179–80
Peña Cinco Estrellas (Five Stars Group) 62
Peña de las Banderas (brotherhood of the flags)
    53, 281
peñas 56
  see also fans
Peralta, Spain 56–7
Perez, Eduardo 323
Perez, Florentino 261–2
  background 325–7, 327, 328–9, 330, 331–2
  president of RM 15–16, 41–3, 246, 254,
    302; and DB 5, 32, 35–7, 39, 43, 354; and
    fans 58–9, 315; international outlook 44;
    property deal 334–6; and rivalry with
    FCB 374–5; seeking re-election 396–7;
    transfer policy 19–24, 388–9, 391
  presidential campaigns 332–4, 336
Perez, Gerardo 52–3, 54–5
Perón, Juan and Evita 201
Peucelle, Carlos 200
Pollard, Diane 152
PP (Partido Popular) 306, 323, 380, 401
Prats, Matias 194
Premier League, English 97, 108–9
Preston North End, DB loaned to 98–9
Preysler, Isabel 353
Primo de Rivera, Jose Antonio 183, 216
Primo de Rivera, General Miguel 142,
    143
PSG (Paris St Germain) 29, 30
PSOE (Spanish Socialist Party) 291–4
Puerta del Sol, Madrid 66
Pujol, Jordi 50
Puskas, Ferenc 212, 213–14, 224, 228, 236

Queiroz, Carlos 22–3, 23–4, 127, 397, 398
Quincoces, Jacinto 171, 181
Quinta de Buitre (Vulture squad) 295–6, 298–9,
    304

Rajoy, Mariano 401
Raúl (RM fan) 62
Raúl (RM player) 13, 71–2, 77, 308, 317–18,
    342–3, 353
  DB and 345

Index

in RM matches 70–1, 119–200, 322, 338, 372
Real Betis 14
Real Madrid 387–8
anthems 301–2
Beckham and: at 2003 Champions League quarter-final 122–3; negotiations and transfer 1–2, 3–5, 35–7, 38–9, 47, 389, 390–91; early appearances 7–9; first goal 11–12; new teammates 12–13; first season 14, 338, 339–40, 343, 372, 373, 377–8, 393, 394, 395–6; new season 398
and Champions League: 1998 303–6, 313–14; 1999 307; 2000 119–20, 307–8, 318, 320–21; 2002 303, 376; 2003 120–22; 2004 149–50, 338, 392
coaches: in 1990s 318–20, see also individual coaches
and European Cup 219, 220; 1956 221, 279; 1957 119, 248–51, 310; 1960s 119, 224–5, 231–3, 247; 1969 & 1970 251; 1976 253–4; 1981 279–80
and European Cup-Winners' Cup 251
fans 17, 46, 54, 55–6, 61–3, 281–2, 305; at Nou Camp, Barcelona 376–7, 378; and DB 19; global following 242; Ultra Surs 16–17, 53–4, 254, 290–91, 311–15
and FCB 150–1 177–9, 180, 181–2, 266, 373–8
football school 82–5
history 74; early years 136, 137–9, 141, 142–3; 1930s 143–4, 144–5, 147, 150–51; Spanish Civil War 162–3, 167–9; post Civil War 170, 171–2; and Franco regime 133, 184–5, 219, 221–3, 239, 240, 243–4, 258–9; 1947–54 seasons 210, 211; post-1966 248, 251; in 1970s 126, 251–3, 278; in 1980s 278, 280–82, 285–6, 286, 294–6, 299; in 1990s 76, 299, 315–18, 324; centenary 2002 301, 302; 2002–03 season 21–2, 39–40; pre-season changes 22–3, 397–8; 2003–04 season 59, 60, 338–40, 342–3, 366, 372–3, 392–4, 395–7, 402; voted best club of 20th century 303
marketing and finances 44, 334–6, 388–9, 390–91
multiculturalism 130, 265
players 54, 55, 68–9, 263; attraction of RM for 349; women 353–4, see also individual players
playing Manchester United 118–19, 119–22, 248–51, 321–2
presidents see individual presidents

and referees 225, 252, 253–4, 283–5
and UEFA Cup 252
Valdano on 79–80
Real Sociedad 21
Recber, Rustu 28
Redondo, Fernando 77, 322
referees, RM and 225, 252, 253–4, 283–5
Regis, Cyrille 264
Regueiro, Luis 171
Reiziger, Michael 377
Reyes, José Antonio 59
RFEF (Spanish Football Federation) 169, 171
Rial, José Hector 212
Ridgeway Rovers 94
Rijkaard, Frank 374
Rio Tinto 135
River Plate club, Argentina 197–8, 206, 208
Rivera, Valero 161–2
Rivière, Margarita 190
Roberts, Mark 14–15
Robson, Bryan 92–3
Roca, Miquel 330
Ronaldinho 28–9, 30, 51, 375
Ronaldo 14, 354, 389
29th birthday party 356–7
DB and 345
joining RM 20
playing for RM 14, 121, 121–2, 338, 342, 372, 378
Rosell, Sandro 28, 29, 30, 34

Sagi, Victor 276
Salamanca, Spain 127–8
Salgado, Michel 150
Samaranch, Juan Antonio 177–8
Samitier, Pepe (El Sami) 144–6, 161–2, 205, 227
Samitier, Tina 145, 146
Sanchez, Hugo 299
Sanchez, José Angel 38, 44, 390–1
Sanchez, Rafael Martin 295
Sanchez Guerra, Rafael 148, 168
Sanchis, Manola 268, 281, 295, 304, 306
Santo Mauro Hotel, Madrid 350–52, 358
Santamaria, José 212, 235–6, 282
Santiago Bernabéu stadium, Madrid 52, 183–5, 185, 210, 241
Santillana, Carlos 280
Sanz, Lorenzo 309–11, 323–4, 332
president of RM 305–6, 316–17, 318, 319, 322–3, 323
and Ultra Surs 311–14

411

Index

Saporta, Raimundo 207, 208, 258, 259, 274–5, 282
Scaloni, Lionel 372
Schmeichel, Peter 115
schools, RM football 82–5
SFX sports agency 31, 358, 363
Sheringham, Teddy 115
Simeone, Diego 370–71, 373
Socialist Party 401
Solis Ruiz, Jose 230
Solskjaer, Ole Gunnar 115, 121
Soviet Union 229–30, 239, 256
Spain
    construction industry 333, 382–3
    Del Bosque on 132–3
    football: history of 135–6, 169, 171, 172, 185, 192–5, 216–17, 285–6; host 1982 World Cup 282–4, 285; national team 193–4, 195, 196, 216, 227–30, 285
    history 49, 134; Spanish empire 133; 1930s 151; Civil War 151–7, 159–67, 168–70; after Civil War 170–1, 172, 173–4, 188–90; and Hitler's Germany 174–5; 1950s 187, 188, 190–91, 191, 217; 1960s 254–7; post-Franco 269–74, 326–7; Socialist government 291–4; centre-right government 306–7, 308, 323, 324, 380, 383, 384–5; 2002 ecological disaster 383–4; 2004 terrorist bombings 399, 400; 2004 elections 400–401
    international relations 191–2, 221–2, 385–6
    modern New Spain image 380–83
    royal family 361–2
Spanish Cup
    1936 150–51
    1943 177–8
    1970 251
Spanish Socialist Workers' Party (PSOE) 291–4
Spice Girls 49, 111
Sporting Gijón 284
Stephens, Tony 31, 33, 34, 103, 363
Stielike, Uli 279–80
Suárez, Adolfo 271, 274, 282, 326
Suárez, Luis 228, 233
Sun newspaper, 2003 interview with DB 9–10
Sunyol, Josep 163, 164–5

Tapias, Fernando Fernandez 333
Tarradellas, Josep 276, 277
Tejero, Colonel Antonio 273
Tenerife, 1992 victory over RM 76

Teus, Eduardo 177
Torres, Fernando (*El Niño*) 369–70, 372–3
Toshack, John 319–20
tourism in Spain 255–6
Trias Fargas, Ramón 206, 209
Trigo, Manuel 316

UCD party 326, 327–8
UEFA 218
UEFA Cup 252
Ultra Surs (RM fan group) 16–17, 53–4, 254, 281, 290–91, 311–15
Unamuno, Miguel de 128
Underwood, Stuart 94

Valdano, Jorge 13, 22, 43–4, 74–81, 130
    and signing of DB 3, 36–7, 38–9
Valdes, Victor 378
Valencia 7, 307–8, 392
Valley of the Fallen, Spain 182–3
Van Gaal, Louis 29, 374
Van Nistelrooy, Ruud 121, 122
Veiga, José 116–17
Venables, Terry 95, 103
Verón, Juan Sebastian 121, 371
Villalonga, Colonel José 230

Watson, Dorothy 152
Watts, Joseph 94
Wenger, Arsène 108
World Cup
    1950 in Brazil 192–4
    1954 in Switzerland 213
    1962 in Chile 227–8
    1982 in Spain 282–3, 285
    1998 in France 109–11
    2001 qualifiers 117–18
    2002 in Japan 264

Yashin, Lev 256

Zamora, Ricardo (*El Divino*) 143–4, 150, 151, 159–62
Zamorano, Ivan 77
Zapatero, Jose Luis 401
Zarra, Thelma 192, 194
Zidane, Zinedine 14, 353–4, 389, 391, 397
    joining RM 20, 334
    playing for RM 14, 121, 150, 338, 342, 377
Zoco, Ignacio 241, 251
    interview with 241–2, 243–4, 245–7